PETER O'TOOLE

THE DEFINITIVE BIOGRAPHY

Robert Sellers is the author of the authorized biography of Oliver Reed, *What Fresh Lunacy is This?*, as well as the best-selling Hellraisers series and *Don't Let the Bastards Grind You Down*. He also wrote the definitive book on the genesis of the Bond franchise, *The Battle for Bond*, and the history of Handmade Films, *Very Naughty Boys*. He co-wrote *Little Ern*, the authorized biography of Ernie Wise, with James Hogg. Robert was also a regular contributor to *Empire*, *Total Film*, *Independent*, *SFX* and Cinema Retro and has contributed to a number of television documentaries, including Channel 4's *The 100 Best Family Films*.

ALSO BY ROBERT SELLERS

What Fresh Lunacy is This?
The Authorized Biography of Oliver Reed

Hellraisers: The Life and Inebriated Times
of Burton, Harris, O'Toole and Reed

The A–Z of Hellraisers: A Comprehensive Compendium
of Outrageous Insobriety

Hollywood Hellraisers

Don't Let the Bastards Grind You Down:
How One Generation of British Actors Changed the World

Very Naughty Boys: The Amazing True Story
of Handmade Films

PETER O'TOOLE

THE DEFINITIVE BIOGRAPHY

ROBERT SELLERS

PAN BOOKS

First published 2015 by Sidgwick & Jackson

First published in paperback 2016 by Pan Books
an imprint of Pan Macmillan
20 New Wharf Road, London N1 9RR
Associated companies throughout the world
www.panmacmillan.com

ISBN 978-1-4472-7888-7

CONTENTS

ACKNOWLEDGEMENTS

I would like to thank the many friends and colleagues of Peter O'Toole who agreed to share their memories.

Sheila Allen, David Andrews, Mark Linn-Baker, Keith Baxter, Frawley Becker (also excerpts from his book: *And the Stars Spoke Back*), Martin Bell, Philip Bond, Barbara Taylor Bradford, Ivar Brogger, Martyn Burke, Sally Burton, Michael Byrne, John Cairney, Barbara Carrera, Peter Cellier, Joe Chappelle, Petula Clark, Ray Cooney, Delia Corrie, Mary Coughlan, Michael Craig, Barry Cryer, Paul D'Alton, Michael Deeley, Pauline Devaney, Clive Donner, Donald Douglas, Patrick Dromgoole, Mark Eden, Susan Engel, Derek Fowlds, Billy Foyle, Christopher Fulford, William Gaskill, Jack Gold, Nonnie Griffin, Michael Gruskoff, Steve Guttenberg, Bryan Hands, Edward Hardwicke, Lisa Harrow, Elizabeth Harris, Rosemary Harris, Anthony Harvey, Arthur Hiller, Keith Hunt, Gemma Jones, Nicole Keniheart, Sara Kestelman, Terence Knapp, Nate Kohn, Phyllida Law, Brad Lewis, Kevin Loader, Peter Medak, Jane Merrow, Roger Michell, Royce Mills, Zia Mohyeddin, Bruce Montague, Michael Neilson, Lee Nelson, Richard Oliver, Tony Palmer, Basil Pao, Johnnie Planco, Amanda Plummer, Erik Preminger, Kevin Quarmby, Steve Railsback, Gary Raymond, Michael Redwood, Tony Rimmington, Malcolm Rogers, Richard Rush, Oliver Senton, Carolyn Seymour, Andrew Sinclair, Brian Trenchard-Smith, Bernardo Stella, Peter Strauss, Jeremy Thomas, Stephen Thorne, David Tringham, Joseph Wambaugh, Roger Young.

'All men dream, but not equally. Those who dream by night in the dusty recesses of their minds wake in the day to find that it was vanity: but the dreamers of the day are dangerous men, for they may act their dreams with open eyes, to make it possible.'

T. E. LAWRENCE (*Seven Pillars of Wisdom*)

'He was like Peter Pan, Captain Hook and Tinker Bell all in one.'

DIRECTOR ANTHONY HARVEY ON PETER O'TOOLE.

OPENING CREDITS

When I was a very young man, Peter O'Toole was a deity, he had the status of God. There was a different kind of celebrity then, than there is now. It was less defined by behaviour, by fist bumps and twerking as you leave the room. It was an international celebrity that included the greatest of artists, writers, philosophers, actors, royalty: Laurence Olivier, Kurt Vonnegut, Jackie Kennedy, Mick Jagger, Elizabeth Taylor, Princess Grace of Monaco, Jean-Paul Sartre, Simone de Beauvoir, Truman Capote. Squinting through the glare of this luminous world you could make out the dominant profile of Peter O'Toole. I was in awe of their world.

I remember asking my young bride, 'What do you have to accomplish in life in order to know these people, to have a cup of coffee with Peter O'Toole?' I'm telling you all this because I found out what. While we were making *The Stunt Man*, Peter and I became friends. We had coffee. And we talked a lot about the movies and about other things. I'm a pilot and Peter would go flying with me. I would give him the controls, and he loved to zoom down from the Santa Monica Mountains down into the city and out over Malibu. I'd occasionally meet his friends. I remember running into John Hurt in a coffee shop with Peter. It was the year Hurt won the BAFTA for Best Actor in *The Elephant Man*. Peter was teasing him mercilessly, guffawing loudly because John won the award for a picture where you never once saw his face. It was completely wrapped in a burlap sack. 'You won for the soundtrack.' John was happily sharing the joke.

On another occasion, I was having a meal with Peter and John Mills, who had won an Academy Award for his work in David Lean's film *Ryan's Daughter*. I was seeking advice from both of them as to whether the behaviour of Eli Cross as written in a certain scene in my film was too sinister. Mills gave me an example of David Lean's behaviour. They are shooting. Mills is in a boat, in the surf. The boat capsizes. Mills is seriously drowning. He screams for help. The crew rush out to save him as David Lean screams, 'Stop! You fucking idiots, don't cross the fucking beach! You'll make footprints in the sand! I'm shooting here!' Eli Cross seemed suddenly more benevolent to me.

After the movie, Peter was visiting the States and living with us temporarily. On the morning when he and I were going to the Oscar ceremony – Peter was up for Best Actor and me for directing and writing – Peter staggered sleepily out of the guest house to poolside, rose to his full height and stature, and proclaimed at the top of his lungs, 'Today, I am a movie star!' Truth is, he was a movie star every day, but never at the expense of sacrificing a speck of his perfection as an artist.

Richard Rush – 2014

PROLOGUE

In January 2003 the Academy of Motion Picture Arts and Sciences announced their decision to bestow upon Peter O'Toole their Lifetime Achievement Oscar. Far from chuffed about it, he told them to get lost. Here was an actor who over the course of his career had received seven nominations for Best Actor without a single win, a record he shared with Richard Burton. 'Can you believe it,' says his *Stunt Man* co-star Steve Railsback. 'He had all those nominations and not a single win! And some of the most brilliant performances we can ever see.'

They do say it's an honour just to be nominated. Well, for O'Toole it wasn't, not any more. 'It's a bore. I'm fed up. Second prize is no prize, thank you very much indeed.' And that's how he felt about this 'honorary Oscar' farrago. It sounded too much like a consolation prize and they could stick it. He didn't exactly put it like that, instead declaring in a note to the Academy that he was 'Still in the game and might win the lovely bugger outright.' And so he asked, 'Would the Academy please defer the honour until I am eighty?'

Somewhat affronted, the Academy's board of directors replied, 'We unanimously and enthusiastically voted you the honorary award because you've earned and deserved it.' The show's producer went further, branding O'Toole 'silly' for not attending the ceremony. Not half as silly as the Academy failing seven times to give the man a proper Oscar.

Some of those closest to O'Toole shared the Academy's disbelief – how could he turn it down, no one had refused an honorary Oscar before. Others got it completely, it was behaviour perfectly in keeping with his rebellious spirit. The Academy weren't giving up, though, and over the course of the next few weeks sent letters and made enquiries, until finally, perhaps fed up, delivered an ultimatum, that on such and such a date the offer would be withdrawn. 'So in the end he changed his mind, somewhat at the last minute,' says Johnnie Planco, who represented O'Toole in America. 'He had talked to a lot of people, those whose opinions he respected, and they'd said, are you crazy not to do this! So he agreed to attend the ceremony and flew his son Lorcan and his daughter Kate out there. It was a special night.'

Of course, having left it so late all the best hotels in Los Angeles were booked solid and he ended up staying at the Le Montrose, a popular hangout for musicians just off the Sunset Strip, but not the sort of establishment normally reserved for a star of O'Toole's standing.

The ceremony on 23 March was taking place under controversial circumstances. Just days earlier America had invaded Iraq and several actors had resigned from their roles as presenters citing safety concerns and respect for military families. Broadcaster ABC had even tried to postpone proceedings, but the show went on with thousands of anti-war protesters gathered outside the Kodak Theatre on Hollywood Boulevard. None of this seemed to affect O'Toole, who was taking everything in his stride. 'He had the whole of the Oscar people both at rehearsal and on the night in the palm of his hand,' confirms Planco. 'Because he was always so calm. He wasn't excited about, oh it's the Oscars! He remained composed and calm the whole evening.'

There was one tricky moment when he was led into the hospitality room and sauntered over to the bar to ask for a drink. 'We have lemon juice, apple juice, orange juice, or still or sparkling mineral water.' O'Toole looked at the barman as if he was speaking a foreign language. 'No, I want a drink.' The barman shook his head. The Oscars enforced a strict no-alcohol policy. O'Toole's face went ashen. 'All right, I'm fucking off.' Oscar officials managed to placate the star and a bottle of vodka was smuggled into the building.

To present the award the Academy had chosen Meryl Streep. The two actors hardly knew each other but their respect for one another's talent was obvious to see. O'Toole later let slip that as they stood backstage waiting to go on Meryl was desperate for a cigarette. 'I wanted a joint. In the end I just got the vodka going because she's a game girl. Likes a drop. The trick at those Oscar awards is to stay sober, because the evening goes on for-ev-er.'

After an amusing and celebratory speech by Meryl, followed by a montage of film clips, O'Toole walked onto the stage to a standing ovation from the cream of Hollywood. For now all the refusals and denials and recriminations were forgotten. Holding the Oscar in his hand he accepted the honour with grace and class. 'Always a bridesmaid, never a bride . . . my foot,' he started. 'I have my very own Oscar now to be with me till death us do part.' Mind you, he still had every intention of winning 'the lovely bugger outright'.

ONE

This book starts with a mystery. Just who was Peter O'Toole? Maybe even he didn't know, or wasn't telling. Previous biographies and the bulk of written material on the actor name his birth date as 2 August 1932, the place, Connemara, County Galway, in the Republic of Ireland. And that's the conundrum. I gave up counting the number of people I interviewed for this book who rolled their eyes when I brought up his nationality – 'He's not Irish,' they muttered, 'I always thought he was born in Leeds.'

In O'Toole's own memoir of his early days, *Loitering with Intent*, published in 1992, the matter of his birth is a rather fuzzy affair, as it names two separate dates and places, one in Ireland in June 1932, and another that August 'at an accident hospital in England'. His baptism was in England in November of the same year, he writes. How can one person be born twice? you might think. Or did his parents simply forget when the event took place, or merely mislaid his birth certificate, leading to all this confusion? So what is the truth? All it took was one phone call to Leeds City Council births, deaths and marriages to uncover O'Toole's birth certificate. The man who went through life proudly purporting to be an Irishman was in fact a Yorkshireman, born at the famous St James's University Hospital, or Jimmy's, in Leeds, 2 August 1932.

Does it really matter, though? Certainly to O'Toole it did not,

1

he loved the idea of being Irish (he owned an Irish passport), and once he'd made that identification he wanted it to be very much central to his life. A little phoney perhaps. 'He used his Irishness, like the good actor he was, to get attention,' claims his close friend Billy Foyle, 'but it was also deeply romantic. The truth is it doesn't really matter where you're born, O'Toole's father was Irish, which entitled him to full Irish citizenship. So fabricating some story that you're born in Ireland, that's a romance, just like wearing green socks, of varying shades, which he did every day of his life. So too a friend's memory that on occasions O'Toole would lay on the Irish accent with a trowel, he'd talk about 'filums'.

That O'Toole saw himself as more of an Irishman than an Englishman is irrefutable, it accounted for his passion, he liked to say, his intolerance of authority, his artistic inclinations, and of course his love of drinking. 'He insisted on being Irish,' says actor Michael Craig. 'I think it gave him licence to behave the way he did.' It was to an isolated cottage in Connemara that O'Toole would always retreat. It was his sanctuary. 'I go to Ireland for a refit, just like a car.'

Much of this love for Ireland is tied up with his father, unquestionably the single most influential person in O'Toole's life. Patrick was a real character and his son idolized him, swearing years later that he got his sense of style, showmanship, and sophistication from the man everyone called Captain. One can almost trace O'Toole's love of performing and theatricality from those days watching his bookmaker dad, dressed all dandy on a stool shouting the odds; the stool was his stage, the racetrack his theatre, the punters his audience. 'I thought as a boy, this is life lived in public! Life on display! It had an enormous effect on me.'

When he had money in his pocket Patrick drank and wasn't averse to picking a scrap with a policeman when sauced. He was also feckless, a real rascal. One day Patrick sat his son up on the mantelpiece. 'Jump, boy,' he urged. 'I'll catch you. Trust me.' When Peter jumped his father withdrew his arms leaving his son splattered on the hard stone floor. The lesson: 'Never trust any bastard.' One Christmas Eve, Patrick came home rather the worse for wear, with a tatty tree under his arm and assorted packages. An excited Peter, in his pyjamas, came running into the hallway asking if Father Christmas was on his way. Patrick chortled to himself, picked up a brown-paper bag and left the room. There was an almighty bang, a pause, then the reappearance of Patrick with the solemn message that Father Christmas had just shot himself.

Hailing from Irish stock, Patrick had served an apprenticeship as a metal plater and became a shipyard worker in Sunderland, where his mother ran a pair of second-hand furniture stores. On Saturday afternoons he was often to be found in the stands at Roker Park cheering on Sunderland AFC, a team he came to love and follow all his life. According to former broadcaster and friend Martin Bell, O'Toole once revealed that his father's ashes were buried under the goal posts at Roker Park, 'which is probably now a housing estate,' says Bell, 'because the team moved to the Stadium of Light.' Was O'Toole having Bell on, or is there some truth to this claim? Never much of a football fan, his sports were cricket and rugby. When pressed, O'Toole did reveal his love for Sunderland, but gave up supporting the team after the move to the new stadium in the late nineties. 'Everything they meant to me was when they were at Roker Park.'

Although the Captain was the apple of his mother's eye, his refusal to go into the family business caused ripples of bitterness but his independent and adventurous nature could not countenance so mundane a livelihood. It's why he jacked in his shipbuilding job too, going off instead to play football for a minor professional team. After that he became an itinerant bookie around the racecourses of Ireland and the north of England, an occupation that was illegal at the time. There are stories of him living for a while in Sunderland, on the fringes of the law, and being asked to leave the city by the police. 'I'm not from the working class,' O'Toole liked to say. 'I'm from the criminal class.'

It was on a racecourse that Patrick met Constance Ferguson, a young nurse. She was enjoying a picnic with friends when Patrick just happened to walk by, got chatting and offered to put a bet on for them. The horse in question came in third and he returned holding their winnings. Constance was seen by many as quite a catch, with wavy black hair that framed attractive and delicate features. Putting on the charm, Patrick left a collection of phone numbers scrawled on bits of paper where she might at certain times reach him and over the next few months they met up, fell in love and married. O'Toole always considered his parents mismatched, but as different as they were they got along and remained steadfastly attached to each other for almost fifty years. Even when their circumstances drastically reduced and money was tight, they never lost their pride and decency or good humour.

Born in Scotland, Constance was raised by a succession of relatives after the deaths of her parents. Despite this tragedy, O'Toole always remembered his mother as a truly 'joyful' person who did more than anyone else to foster a love for literature by reading poetry and stories out loud to him, Dickens, Buchan, Galsworthy and Burns, awakening the imagination that is so vital in any child. 'My mother was my literary conscience. Her knowledge of literature and language was tremendous. At five I was reciting Border ballads at the drop of a hat. She was my ear. Daddy was the persona.'

With work prospects bleak in his native Ireland, and now with a young child to support, a daughter called Patricia, Patrick moved permanently to England where, until his death in 1975, he lived a strange kind of self-imposed exile, never setting foot on Irish soil again. And yet he would never hear a bad word said against the place. The family settled into a small rented terraced house in the working-class area of Hunslet, Leeds, a slum of narrow back to back properties, 'rabbit hutches', O'Toole called them, with outside loos, cold-water taps and alleyways, all smelly and filthy black from factories, mills and chemical works spewing out their waste. It was said of the place that the crows flew backwards to keep the shit out of their eyes.

Hunslet had a large population of Irish expatriates, who jostled for space with other immigrants, resulting in the usual human intolerance. 'The sheenies [a disparaging term for Jews] hated the micks, the micks hated the wops, the wops hated the sheenies,' O'Toole related. 'When you're pressure-cooked into a Catholic slum upbringing, you don't forget it very easily.' And while it didn't mentally scar him, it did turn him into a socialist (though he ended up sending his son to Harrow). The slum clearances of the late 1940s began too late for O'Toole. When he paid the place a visit in the early seventies it had all gone, been completely erased; not a brick from his childhood lay standing.

Despite the harshness of the area, there was a keen sense of humour amongst the inhabitants and great communal pride. Life was simple. The milkman delivered from a large churn on a cart. If you weren't in, no problem, you just left a jug on the window-sill and it was full when you returned home. No one would think of stealing it. O'Toole found comfort in the closeness and kinship of his family. It was Constance who kept the household together. 'My little mum fair tore into troublesome tasks and made them seem glad duties.' For extra money she did cleaning jobs around the district.

There were warm memory-making weekend outings, like catching the tram to Roundhay Park, where the youngster spent hours in its enchanted woods or down by the lake, and excursions to the nearby market town of Otley to bathe in its outdoor swimming pool. He played football on Hunslet Moor and rugby in the streets with a loaf of bread instead of a ball. There were special trips with his dad to the Moo Cow Milk Bar, or 'Peter's pub', Patrick christened it, to drink thick flavoured milkshakes through a straw. Then it was off to the pictures to watch a programme of news reels, cartoons and one-reelers. Young Peter loved Donald Duck and Popeye, and the madcap antics of the Three Stooges. Watching *King Kong* for the first time had a profound effect as he found himself rooting for the huge hairy beasty against the nasty humans. For Peter the picture palace was a place of wonder and enchantment, and he never forgot the afternoon his dad took him to see a matinee performance of the Marx Brothers' *A Day at the Races* with what seemed like the entire horse-racing fraternity of Leeds.

One of his earliest memories was whizzing down hills on his bicycle one day with such wild abandon that after a while he'd no clue whatsoever where he was. In front of him was a half-painted lamp post – the worker had gone off for lunch, leaving his brushes and pots behind. Young Peter decided to finish the job himself and was found by a policeman, covered in green paint, and marched off to the nearest police station. 'I remember looking up at the desk, all white tile, white as a nun's hand, and then I remember seeing a big fucking nasty looking down at me.' Once back home he was dunked into the bath and smothered with turpentine and scrubbed as if he was a dirty pan. As punishment his bike was confiscated and he was told never again to wander off. Fat chance, the young O'Toole was always AWOL. 'Always where he shouldn't be, rarely where he should,' as his mother used to say.

Dressed in a dark suit, spats and his trademark billycock bowler hat, Patrick was a familiar face around the racecourses of Yorkshire. The Captain was unmistakable, with his hat tilted to one side, a cigarette perpetually stuck on his lips and his fingers wrapped round a pint of Guinness. On special occasions Peter was allowed to accompany him. He loved the excitement of the race track, the jockeys in their multi-coloured silks, the hubbub of the crowd, the parade of horses in the paddock and the book-ies all shouting the odds, white-gloved tic-tac men with their weird hand gestures. Sometimes Patrick miscalculated the odds and would need to scarper in a hurry. Grabbing little Peter's hand he'd urge, 'C'mon, son, let's be off!' and the two of them would slip through the shrubbery, not returning to the track for a few weeks.

It was a bizarre and haphazard lifestyle, with the whole family's income resting on success or failure at the racetrack. 'When he'd come home after a good day, the whole room would light up. It was fairyland,' O'Toole recalled. 'When he lost, it was black. In our house, it was either a wake or a wedding.'

For some inexplicable reason O'Toole was nicknamed 'Bub-bles' as a child: 'That cost me a lot of lumps.' He was very sweet and adorable looking, and rather tubby, 'with a mop of golden hair that I've tried to keep straight ever since'. But he was plagued by ill health. 'You mention it, I had it.' His eyes were a particular cause for concern and he underwent a series of trau-matic operations, eight on his left eye alone. The trouble persisted into adulthood; he was especially susceptible to bright light and had to wear special dark glasses. There is also evidence that his eyesight was further damaged during the shooting of *Lawrence of Arabia*. Actress Jane Merrow, while working with O'Toole on *The Lion in Winter*, remembers him telling her that David Lean insisted on some occasions that he stare directly into the sun. 'It is abusive behaviour in a way,' says Jane. 'It's misusing your actors to get the effect that you want.'

At the age of six O'Toole was raced by taxi to hospital with his mother. He'd complained all day of stomach ache but when suddenly the pain turned acute Constance thought something was very wrong. His appendix had burst leaving him with an infected abdomen and in the days before antibiotics the chances of survival for children weren't too hopeful. O'Toole underwent an emergency operation to remove the infection and was then swiftly moved to another hospital and placed in an isolation ward. When his parents and sister visited they weren't even allowed in the same room and had to make do with viewing him through a glass partition. Over the course of several months Peter recovered and was allowed back home, but he was weak, non-communicative and couldn't walk long distances. With encouragement he soon returned to his impish self. But it had been a traumatic experience for sure.

These medical misfortunes undeniably affected his schooling, and while he could read and write to a good standard by the age of four he was by inclination a poor pupil. School was ghastly and an institution to make one's escape from as soon as possible. About the only subject he enjoyed and was any good at was English composition. Being good Roman Catholics the O'Tooles entrusted their son to the care of Jesuit priests and 'flapping nuns with white, withered hands', in O'Toole's words. 'They'd never held a man, those hands.' He used to be scared stiff of them; 'their whole denial of womanhood, the black dresses, the shaving of the hair, it was all so horrible, so terrifying'. A penchant for rapping his knuckles with a ruler every time he attempted to write with his left hand instead of his right hardly helped the situation. Perhaps subconsciously, O'Toole always employed his right hand in times of violence, smashing it through glass, into concrete and people's faces. And it had the scars to prove it. As for his left hand, it was smoother than a baby's backside.

In art one day when he drew a picture of a horse and was asked by one of the nuns whether there was something else that might enhance the scene, the young O'Toole drew a huge dangling dick gushing piss into a foamy ferment. The nuns immediately tore the offending picture up and started to wildly hit him round the head.

The unfairness of being punished for merely expressing himself did not sit well with the young O'Toole. Nor did the religious discipline and doctrine, coming as he did from a household of gambling and drinking. He did, however, enjoy the theatricality of religion, the pomp and ceremony of its rituals, and successfully applied to be an altar boy. 'I loved every second of it. The mass was my first performance, it's as simple as that.' At this age he still believed in the concept of there being a god, of some benign divinity. When sweets were rationed during the war he sacrificed his toffees to a church charity.

By 1939 the omnipresence of God jostled for space inside the O'Toole psyche with an altogether less benevolent obsession. At the cinema one afternoon the cartoons had finished when on came the newsreels. There was a fat Italian, all done up with medals, who looked like one of the Three Stooges but he was getting pelters and ripe raspberries from the audience. 'Then along came Hitler and there were no raspberries and I was physically ill at the age of six, seeing this man.'

Adolf Hitler was the bogeyman of O'Toole's childhood, and his obsession with 'this profoundly strange mincing little dude from Linz' was never to leave him. His memories of the war never dimmed either, of trenches being dug and air-raid shelters springing up, and windows covered with crossed strips of tape to prevent injury from flying glass. At school the teachers warned that Hitler intended to send over poisonous gas and each child was given a gas mask in a plain cardboard box with a string carrying strap. One afternoon in the playground everybody was told to put on their gas masks as a teacher opened a canister and thick white smoke poured out. Either O'Toole hadn't put his mask on correctly or it had malfunctioned because the tear gas got into his eyes and mouth, producing vicious bouts of vomiting. In spite of the soothing attempts of his mother his eyes burned for days.

While Leeds didn't suffer as badly as other major cities, O'Toole remembered the ear-piercing sound of the sirens going off and running to the cellar with his family to hide and huddle together as the bombs rained down. One seemed to land nearby, exploding with such ferocity that Patrick instinctively threw himself over his son to protect him. In fact the bomb landed almost two miles away and next morning Peter and his sister Patricia went to investigate. It was the library and museum that had been hit and strewn around the street was the surreal image of burnt books and a charred stuffed giraffe.

After bombing raids it wasn't unusual for children to run and play amongst the craters, looking for shrapnel and other paraphernalia. Rummaging around one particular wasteland with his mates Peter came across a slim metallic object. 'Finders keepers,' he cried and picked it up proudly to carry it off back home. Outside a butcher's they sat a while to rest. One of the customers took one look at what they were holding, dropped his dinner to the pavement and hollered, 'Piss off, lads, it's a bomb.' Taking the thing at arm's length he placed it carefully in the middle of the road and with the help of the shop owner surrounded it with sandbags. The police were called and Peter walked home, minus his prize.

Another night he and his dad left the sanctuary of the cellar and opened the front door to watch the spectacle of searchlights in the sky and tracer bullets whirring about. Suddenly there was a white flash and an ear-shattering bang, followed by a heat blast so powerful that it actually lifted them off their feet. They were alive, if slightly singed: 'Completely awed, completely frightened.' Such incidents left their emotional mark, how could they not. 'It's one of the most incredible experiences in the world, being bombed,' he'd say. 'You play this mad, demented, passive role. I tell you, if you haven't been bombed, you haven't lived. Perhaps if more people had been bombed, they might be less generous in their supply of bombs.'

With the country in need of skilled labourers, Patrick applied for war work and landed a job repairing ships at a restricted naval base that kept him away from home all week. Every night without fail Constance would walk two hundred yards to the nearest phone booth to call her husband, often with Peter in tow. Not much of a journey, but this was the time of the blackout and mother and son would have to scramble around the streets in the pitch black, clinging to each other, sometimes stumbling and falling, shuffling along alleys, searching their way with their fingers. Sometimes they'd get lost in the dark and have to sense their way back home.

With no end in sight to the war and some schools closing, the eight-year-old Peter was evacuated to the Midlands and taken in by a kindly but dour couple. He remembers not feeling sad or apprehensive as he was loaded onto a train, a cardboard label stuck to his coat with a safety pin and his gas mask full of sandwiches. He went to the village school, adopted a new gang of friends, went scrumping in nearby orchards and played at Robin Hood in the woodlands. In one field they came across a well and saw buried deep down it a mysterious object the size and shape of a rugby ball. It was decided that O'Toole be lowered down to investigate. Hoping it wasn't another of those unexploded bombs, Peter gave it a good kick, only to realize he had disturbed a wasps' nest. A swarm of the bastards encircled him and began dive-bombing attacks. Scrambling out, he and his mates all ran for their lives.

Back in Leeds, Peter was met with the dreaded news that government men with bowlers and brollies were rounding up rogue children and sending them back to school. It didn't take long for O'Toole's collar to be felt and he was sent off to a school that was about as much fun as a penal colony. He played hooky as often as he could, and was sent to yet another school where he lasted precisely thirty minutes. It wasn't his fault, some bright spark set fire to one of the desks and the whole place had to be evacuated. Arrangements were made instead to allow him to attend the Catholic school that he had gone to as an infant. Here he was held in great reverence by the other pupils as he was 'popularly elected commander-in-chief of research into the dirty bits in the bible, possessor and generous distributor of dog-ends and whole cigarettes acquired from a wide acquaintance of adults, supplier of copies of *Picturegoer* whose covers provide inspiration for masturbators in the air raid shelters, considered a bit of a whizz at playground cricket, youngest member of the school swimming team and seldom out of the frame at high pissing'.

He was also quite handy with the bagpipes, having joined a local outfit of pipers and dancers called Lord Kilmorey's Own Hibernians. Indeed, O'Toole always claimed that the bravest thing he ever did in his life was walk through Hunslet at the age of eleven, 'when I was a Little Lord Fauntleroy in a kilt'.

For the majority of his years in education, religion was an overpowering part of O'Toole's life. It seeped into his soul, and for a while he flirted with the notion of the priesthood. There was a favourite Jesuit tutor who liberally sprinkled his speech with the word bloody and said that there was more faith in honest doubt than there was in reciting a thousand hollow Our Fathers. He also never forgot the time he caught one of the priests enjoying a crafty drag on a cigarette in church. Surely this was a sin, admonished O'Toole. Sharp as a button the priest replied that the bishop had personally told him that it was all right to smoke in church, just so long as he prayed at the same time.

As he approached adolescence O'Toole's faith reached crisis point. By the age of fifteen he no longer practised Catholicism and stopped believing altogether not long after, referring to himself as 'a retired Christian'. Under the harsh scrutiny of a teenager's view of the world the tenets of religion had come up wanting. It wasn't helped by tales of priests with wandering hands. 'It was abominable. I was lucky. I wasn't affected by it. The hard kids put a needle in their trousers so that when the priest went to touch them they got a nasty shock.'

In a 1960s interview with *Playboy* O'Toole criticized his religious upbringing and the Catholic Church in general. For weeks after he got angry letters from priests and nuns. 'They were shocked. I wrote back saying I was shocked – what were they doing reading *Playboy*.'

TWO

O'Toole left school with scarcely a backward glance. He'd no qualifications, as he had not sat a single exam, his one ambition was to flog second-hand Jaguars. He ended up instead working in a warehouse wrapping up parcels, learning the handy trick of breaking string without the aid of scissors. It was a friendly local priest who recognized potential in this wayward urchin and managed to persuade one of his parishioners, who happened to be the general manager of the *Yorkshire Evening News*, to take him on as a copyboy. O'Toole's mundane duties consisted of taking typed stories from desk to desk, making tea and buying horse meat for the chief photographer. In time he took on more responsibilities and graduated to apprentice press photographer. It was the beginning of a love affair with the art of photography that never waned. On his very last film, *Katherine of Alexandria*, O'Toole was often invited to look through the camera lens and on a few occasions director Michael Redwood even allowed the actor to come up with the composition of certain shots. 'His eye for photography was extraordinary.'

By the time he was sixteen, O'Toole had begun doing little bits of reporting on local cricket and football matches, along with the odd article and reviews of films and some theatrical productions. He remembered going to see Laurel and Hardy at Leeds' Empire Palace Theatre on behalf of the paper and going backstage to meet them. In a bid to improve his usage of the English language

14

he took to reading more and enrolled in night school, having reached the conclusion that education was a vastly important thing and since he hadn't got very much of it at school he'd better hurriedly acquire some. This rush for self-enlightenment earned him an affectionate nickname amongst his newspaper colleagues, 'the bard of the bog'.

As a junior reporter O'Toole regularly popped into the numerous city centre pubs, his lanky frame filled out with a heavy raincoat, cigarette nonchalantly positioned in the corner of his mouth, newspaper under his arm and a flat cap, props to up his age to the required eighteen. 'It didn't always work but it was well worth a try and, anyway, what could they do, shoot me?'

Every Saturday lunchtime reporters from the city's two main papers, the *Evening News* and the *Yorkshire Evening Post*, met up for a heavy drinking session. O'Toole always tagged along, usually in the company of a journalist he'd befriended on the *News*, a fellow Hunslet lad by the name of Willis Hall, the working-class son of an engineer's fitter. He had his eyes on a pretty lass, barely sixteen, who often showed up on these afternoons with a wild-looking individual with flaming red hair called Keith Waterhouse. Waterhouse had taken this young girl under his wing after she'd left the *Post*'s typing pool to become a junior reporter. Her name was Barbara Taylor. Waterhouse always dragged her along to these boozy sessions but insisted she always leave after two pints for fear she might turn into one of the lads. That didn't stop O'Toole fancying his chances, as Barbara recalls. 'Peter always used to ask me out. "Do you want to go ta pictures?" he'd say in his broad Leeds accent. I was a bit shy and I'd say, "No, no, thank you very much." Or Keith would tell him, "She can't, Peter, she's too young." '

According to Barbara, O'Toole was very much a fixture among that drinking crowd and despite his unwanted chat-up lines was pleasant company, genial and good fun, but hardly boyfriend material. 'He had lanky hair and spots and looked waif-like, rather like a starving poet in a garret. There was nothing that made him stand out, no charisma at all. He was very ordinary was Peter back then. He was just another lad.'

Then one Saturday lunchtime Barbara noticed that O'Toole wasn't there. When he failed to show up the following week she asked Waterhouse what had happened and was told that having turned eighteen he'd gone off to do National Service. Barbara wouldn't see O'Toole again for another ten years and when she did got one of the shocks of her life.

Not fancying the army very much, O'Toole had opted for the Royal Navy to see out his military obligations to the nation, gamely bullshitting that he came from a long line of Irish salty sea dogs. 'I preferred the sea and I vomited over every square inch of it.' His first port of call was Victory Barracks, Portsmouth, arriving with a ragtag assortment of other recruits. After a fearsome encounter with the barber and collecting an ill-fitting uniform, next on the agenda was an intelligence test. Before him was a collection of wooden pegs, some round and some square, which the naval bigwigs wanted fitted into the relevant holes. O'Toole spent ten minutes doing the exact opposite. Other officers were called into the room to watch this farce, wondering if they had a nut on their hands. The only one smiling was O'Toole.

Next came a series of questions to ascertain whether the recruit was officer material. Asked, 'How would you lift a heavy barrel over a thirty-foot wall using only two ten-foot lengths of rope?' O'Toole replied: 'I'd call the chief petty officer and say to him, "Get that barrel over the wall!" '

Following six weeks of basic training and a signalling course, O'Toole was posted to HMS *Montclare*, a submarine depot ship on patrol around the North Atlantic and the Baltic. For the most part though it was anchored in Rothesay harbour on the Isle of Bute, where on his days off O'Toole commandeered a dinghy to take some of the local girls on picnics around the loch.

It didn't take him long to start kicking against the pricks, insisting on calling the deck the floor, portholes were windows, and as for funnels, well they were chimneys. Fibbing to the ship's doctor about a hereditary in-growing toenail he became the only member of the crew not to have to wear regulation boots. Having got away with that one, O'Toole next acquired an imaginary curvature of the spine and was allowed to sleep in a camp bed rather than the conventional hammock.

It did look as if the navy and O'Toole were an ill-matched pair. 'I would stand alone on deck at night talking to seagulls for hours.' When he was arrested for taking extra rations of rum, his reason was it was a cold day. Most of his thoughts turned to fixing some grand scheme to get out. 'What was I doing marching to the left and marching to the right? What was I doing darning socks? It was a bloody nightmare. Once, I drank about eighteen bottles of wine, took a lot of aspirins and a drug that was supposed to turn me grey, but it didn't work.'

Hating the system was one thing, as for his fellow sailors O'Toole had nothing but respect. Many had fought in the war, knocked out German destroyers, been torpedoed in the Battle of the Atlantic, watched their comrades machine-gunned in the water. These were tough men, real men and O'Toole grew up pretty quickly in their company.

As a signaller, one of O'Toole's duties was to decipher weather forecasts sent in code by a Wren ashore. Like most of what happened in the navy, O'Toole couldn't fathom this at all and saw the ninety minutes it took sometimes to carry out the decoding a complete waste of time. Why not simply telephone the woman and get her to read it out in plain English, which is what ended up happening. When the ruse was discovered, however, the Wren was dismissed and O'Toole was thrown in the brig. Even worse was the occasion HMS *Montclare* sailed to Stockholm where it received a hero's welcome as the first British warship to enter the harbour since the Second World War. Various admirals were required to walk ashore to greet the Swedish king, but when a fog descended the fleet got lost and couldn't find the correct place to dock. As the story goes, a group that included O'Toole was hurriedly sent out in a boat with a walkie-talkie to locate the exact position of the king. O'Toole accidentally dropped the radio into the sea. He was thrown in the brig, again.

A few days later they docked in Copenhagen. Besides patronizing the local breweries, O'Toole played in a naval rugby team against a bunch of thugs from the Swedish police force. Falling gallantly upon the ball, he was kicked full on the chin, slicing his tongue almost in half. He was rushed to hospital where doctors closed the wound with clamps, which left him with a slight lisp that was only eradicated at RADA by the endless reciting of the tongue twister 'Two ghosts sat on posts and drank toasts to their hosts'.

There is a bizarre end to this story. It may or may not be true, but it has gone down in the O'Toole legend. Once discharged from hospital he caught a train to get back to his ship before it sailed. He was on it for half an hour before discovering it was going the wrong way, and he eventually arrived at the harbour just in time to see the fleet on its way back to Scotland. O'Toole later swore he hired a funfair boat and paddled out until it came alongside the supply ship and they threw a rope ladder down to him.

Life in the navy wasn't all bad, really, he enjoyed the male camaraderie, played the drums in the ship's band and had time to read the complete works of Shakespeare. But there were long periods of isolation, and a lot of time to think. One morning he was halted on the deck by the captain, who asked what he wanted to do when his National Service was up.

'Well, I'm trying to be a journalist.'

'Is that going to be your life?' asked the captain.

'I think so, sir.'

'You don't sound convinced. Have you any unanswered calls inside you that you don't understand or can't qualify?'

'Yes, I do. I quite fancy myself either as a poet or an actor.'

'Well, if you don't at least give it a try, you'll regret it for the rest of your life.'

When it was all over O'Toole described his National Service as 'a total waste for everybody, particularly His Majesty'. As a grand gesture, and to purge the navy out of his system before resuming civilian life, O'Toole took his uniform and threw it in the Thames. But he was never to forget that conversation with the captain.

Back in Leeds, O'Toole returned to his job at the newspaper, 'where it soon became clear to those who knew me that I would not be staying there for long'. He had reached a crossroads in his life. His early ambition of becoming an editor of some fancy rag like *Picture Post* or *Life* had faded, superseded by a notion that rather than being a chronicler of events, 'I wanted to be the event.'

As a young man O'Toole had scribbled an oath into his notebook, words that must have found some resonance with him. In 1952 an American politician called Dean Alfange wrote a statement entitled 'My Creed', which was published in the *Reader's Digest*: 'I will not be a common man because it is my right to be an uncommon man. I will stir the smooth sands of monotony. I seek opportunity, not security. I want to take the calculated risk; to dream and to build, to fail and to succeed. I prefer the challenges of life to the guaranteed existence, the thrill of fulfilment to the stale calm of utopias.' Looking back at this period from the comfortable position of his seventies, O'Toole ruminated that there seemed to have been an inevitability, call it fate if you will, to every step that he was taking. 'But that had not been the case when I was falteringly taking them.' Something was driving him on.

It was around this time that O'Toole made the acquaintance of a man that was also determined not to travel along life's common pathway. A colleague of his boss at the *Evening News* was having difficulty with his son, a gifted and intelligent boy but a little wayward and rebellious. In fact, in manner and attitude he could very well have been O'Toole's twin. It was decided that the two of them really ought to meet up to see if they shared any common ground. It turned out that in Patrick Oliver, O'Toole was in the company 'of a delinquent fellow spirit', and a friendship was formed that lasted until Oliver's death in 2009. No one, O'Toole insisted, outside his own immediate family, had a greater or more timely influence on him.

Described by his new friend as 'two yards and more of long bones and wild un-weeded hair', Patrick Oliver was a budding painter who sporadically attended Leeds College of Art. O'Toole liked his work, his figures and portraits; Oliver had yet to make the transition to the bold, intense landscapes that prompted Barbara Hepworth to call him one of the finest painters of his generation. He'd also return to Leeds College of Art as an inspirational teacher between 1964 and 1993 where one of his pupils, Damien Hirst, recalled how his critiques made him laugh and changed the way that he looked at art for ever.

Soon after their first encounter the two young men began to patronize an arts centre; there were pottery and painting classes for Oliver, while O'Toole was leaning towards being a playwright. He'd written a few short plays already, some so bad he'd thrown them in the fireplace in disgust. He loved the arts centre, its bohemian ambience spoke to him much more than the hurly-burly world of the *Yorkshire Evening News*, where he was appearing less and less now. He felt a little guilty about his absences, the paper had done its best for him and here he was letting it down. It wouldn't be long before he quit altogether.

In Christmas 1952 the arts centre staged its annual panto-mime. O'Toole volunteered his services and had a ball playing Idle Jack. A few weeks later, the producer of a semi-professional drama group that put on productions at the centre asked if he could have a quiet word. By a quirk of fate the leading man of their next production, Turgenev's *Fathers and Sons*, had fallen down a flight of stairs and broken his leg; O'Toole never did forget the unfortunate man's name – Gordon Luck. This producer, Ben Awad, a Turk by birth but raised in Yorkshire, had caught his performance in the panto and thought he displayed considerable promise. Did he fancy taking over? O'Toole thought the man had flipped, the panto had just been a bit of fun and the only time he'd ever seriously acted, discounting the obligatory school play. 'Why don't you give it a crack?' Considering the offer, O'Toole reached the conclusion that he didn't really have anything to lose. While the idea of acting or some career in the theatre had played across his mind from time to time he'd never given it much weight. Now here he was, learning lines and shaping a proper performance for the first time. Rehearsals at first were strained: 'I had been awkward, self-conscious and desperately unsure of myself.' Awad noticed this and was able to calm O'Toole and in time build up his self-confidence.

The production lasted two weeks and O'Toole enjoyed it enormously; the excitement backstage before curtain-up, the thrill of the performance, the buzz of a live audience, it was a heady brew. Edith Evans once said of acting, 'You catch it, like influenza.' Well, O'Toole was a willing victim. He began to see more plays and to study books on drama. He was already a huge fan of George Bernard Shaw, having since aged sixteen 'read aloud to myself every wise and comical, choice and cracking syllable of the plays'. He also took private lessons from a dowager former actress. The next step was to write off to local repertory companies for work, but he was repeatedly turned down for lack of experience.

Having given up journalism, O'Toole worked for a time as a steeplejack and demolition man. 'Blowing things up and knocking things down with a bloody great hammer. Nobody gave a flying shit for health and safety in those days. It was glorious.' Saving some of his wages, O'Toole planned a trip to London. Patrick Oliver and he hitchhiked their way to Birmingham and then Stratford-upon-Avon, where they kipped in the bus station. In the morning they walked to the Shakespeare Memorial Theatre to buy a pair of tickets to see Michael Redgrave play King Lear. Before curtain-up they took in a tour of the town, visiting Shakespeare's house and Ann Hathaway's cottage. Alone, O'Toole took a stroll along the river that snakes past that grand old theatre, watched as people fed the swans and occasionally glanced up at the shifting figures in the windows of the dressing rooms, wishing one day he might be one of them.

After the performance the pair downed a few pints in the famous Dirty Duck pub, followed by a rather rapid search for a convenient bed for the night. It turned out to be a bale of hay in a farmer's field, but as they comfortably nestled themselves O'Toole made the stark discovery that the hay was merely a soft covering for a very large heap of manure. 'Did you ever find yourself in the dark up to your shoulders in hot shit?' O'Toole was able to say years later with some authority.

After cleaning up as best they could in the biting cold river next morning, O'Toole and Oliver took breakfast at a roadside cafe, making a bolt for it without paying when the waitress wasn't looking. A few years later when he was the toast of Stratford, O'Toole made a point of hunting down that very cafe, this time leaving a generous tip.

Cadging a lift in the back of an open-top lorry, keeping several empty beer barrels company, the boys jumped out at Euston station and made their way to the YMCA in Tottenham Court Road. Cutting through Gower Street, about halfway down O'Toole stopped in his tracks. There in front of him was the most famous and accomplished drama school in the world, the Royal Academy of Dramatic Art or RADA. 'That's your shop, isn't it, Pete?' said Oliver. The nondescript stone entrance wasn't nearly as imposing as he'd thought it might be for such an august institution, so he decided there and then to case the joint, as it were. This in spite of the fact that the windswept journey down had done little to erode the odour of fertilizer.

Trudging round the entrance hall, looking a bit lost, O'Toole was approached by a scholarly gentleman who asked whether he was a student. 'Indeed not,' said O'Toole. 'But I fully intend to be one.'

The man introduced himself as Sir Kenneth Barnes, who had run the academy since 1909. With impeccable timing, O'Toole had arrived on the very week the auditions were being held for the new term; alas the candidates for these highly sought after places had already been carefully selected. O'Toole wondered whether the rules might be bent ever so slightly, just this once. Barnes looked at his watch. It was 2 p.m. 'Be at my office at four forty-five this afternoon.'

With a hearty thank you O'Toole raced out into the street where Oliver was leaning against the entrance, smoking. 'Some interesting customers coming in and going out of this shop,' he said. 'Did you get your shitty foot in the door?'

At the hostel O'Toole took a quick shower, shaved and arrived on the dot at RADA. Barnes welcomed the eager youngster into his office and explained that he'd be required to perform two speeches before a panel of judges. 'Choose something from that,' he said, passing over a sheet of typed paper. 'The other speech you can select yourself. The audition is set for two days' time.'

O'Toole's nerves ran riot, forty-eight hours wasn't a very long time to decide one's future. Scanning the list, his heart sang when he saw Professor Higgins from Shaw's *Pygmalion*, a speech he already knew by heart. Things suddenly didn't look so bad. For his other piece O'Toole went with 'O, what a rogue and peasant slave am I', from *Hamlet*.

Before the audition O'Toole and Oliver took a quick tour round the West End and Soho. What happened next Oliver enjoyed recounting many times and is remembered by his son Richard. 'Peter decided upon a whim to climb up onto Eros in Piccadilly, strike an archer's pose identical to that of the statue and release a timely and comical fart. Unfortunately, relaxation of the sphincter resulted in the expulsion of more than merely gaseous matter. Trousers were rendered, in the short term, unwearable. This is why Dad spent several hours in a cubicle in a public lavatory (or was it the YMCA?), after he had loaned Peter *his* trousers to attend the RADA audition.'

With his new trousers, O'Toole presented his two speeches as best he could, then was told to wait outside. After several agonizing minutes the panel was pleased to offer him a place at the academy. Further good news followed: he was to be awarded a scholarship and a grant of £5 a week. 'So there it was. My life had completely changed.'

THREE

It was 1953 and O'Toole's very first morning at RADA saw him standing in the foyer doing his best to listen to instructions about where to hang his donkey jacket, what forms to fill in, all that stuff, while a constant parade of women went up and down the staircase, a beautiful Indian girl in a sari, a blonde bombshell in tight slacks; his eyes were on stalks.

In his first lesson O'Toole watched as the students rehearsed a scene from *As You Like It*. There was one particular chap he couldn't keep his eyes off who 'buzzed with a confident energy'. His name was Albert Finney, the Salford-born son of a bookie. O'Toole ended up in the same class as Finney right through till the end of the course and they acted in numerous productions together. It wasn't just Finney that radiated talent, that year's intake was the most remarkable RADA had ever known: Alan Bates, Peter Bowles, Roy Kinnear, Ronald Fraser, James Villiers, John Stride, Julian Glover, Richard Briers and Frank Finlay, every one of them going on to enjoy substantial careers. 'Though we weren't reckoned for much at the time,' recalled O'Toole. 'We were all considered dotty.'

Inevitably there was keen competition amongst everyone; excellent training for the harsh realities of the theatrical profession. 'It was because we all knew we had potential,' said Peter Bowles. 'Finney, O'Toole and Bates were all swaggering around.

They threw down the gauntlet. They said, "There, that's my Macbeth – beat that!" '

O'Toole though had an uneasy, difficult first year finding his feet. It was all very disciplined, a bit stifling and lacking emotion and freedom. 'RADA was a fairly conservative and traditional school,' remembers fellow student Bryan Hands. 'But it did provide a good basic grounding in theatre techniques.' The school's criteria reflected very much the personality and vision of Kenneth Barnes, an attitude entrenched in a kind of theatre that had already disappeared, typified by grand-standing actor-manager types of the nineteenth century like Henry Irving. 'That was the sort of theatre Kenneth Barnes represented and believed in,' says ex-student Keith Baxter. 'But even we knew that that had gone. And we also knew that what we were being schooled in was not right.' According to another RADA alumna of the time, Sheila Allen, Barnes wasn't progressive in any way, 'But I think he knew talent when he saw it.'

Barnes had populated RADA with a large number of teachers who came from a sort of cobweb-strewn twilight world, theatrical equivalents of Miss Havisham. There was Ernest Milton, a Shakespearean actor very definitely of the old school. Finney recalled seeing Milton once huffing and puffing after a departing train yelling at the top of his voice, 'Stop! Stop! You're killing a genius!' And there was Nell Carter, whose claim to fame was that she had been Nerissa to Dame Irene Vanbrugh's Portia before the First World War. Even the German fencing teacher had a duelling scar!

Most of the students held their tongue. Female students were especially timid in those days, just out of school and too afraid to say boo to a goose. It was different with the boys, many, like O'Toole, had already done their National Service and were mature beyond their years and not intimidated by the teachers at all. O'Toole could at times display sheer contempt for them, screeching during rehearsals, 'My god, what the hell does he know? If he were any good he wouldn't be teaching here, would he?' There was a wildness in him, inherent, God-given, that simply would not be subsumed. 'He'd never take direction,' remembered Roy Kinnear. 'That's the confidence of youth. Peter would tell the director how he was going to do a scene and then do it.'

During a diction lesson, where students performed a speech and then were submitted to a critique, O'Toole arrived with absolutely nothing prepared. 'That's all right,' said the teacher, handing him a book. 'Read something out of that.' O'Toole started. 'No, no,' said the teacher. 'Do it again.' O'Toole sighed audibly before beginning once more. Just a few lines in he was interrupted again. 'No, no, no!' O'Toole threw the book at him and stormed out, not returning to the class for a week. He later apologized. 'Even then Peter did not suffer fools gladly,' says Malcolm Rogers, who witnessed the altercation. 'Peter didn't have a great deal of respect for that teacher, he was quite old and wasn't very good. It was a flash of temperament and not what most students would do.'

Voice production and the teaching of 'standard' English, or Received Pronunciation, were important at RADA. Teachers could be quite scathing with those who had a regional accent. Some students did rebel against the need to eradicate the regional tone in their voice, others like O'Toole were more philosophical, leaving RADA with their northern vowels totally flattened out and condemned to the dustbin. Looking back today, Keith Baxter also sees the value of those diction classes. 'I was from Wales. One of my teachers told me that I sounded as though my mother dug for coal with her fingernails. It wasn't that we wanted to talk posh, that's not it, we didn't want to talk like the Royal Family, we just wanted when we got into the theatre to talk like Olivier, or Ralph Richardson or Gielgud, actors who spoke beautifully, we all wanted to do that. Not to mimic them, that was easy and we all did it, but what dazzled us was the power of their voices and we all got a sense of the craft that goes into an actor's speech.'

Students were actively encouraged to attend as many theatre performances as possible. That winter of 1953 Richard Burton, back from his first foray in Hollywood, reigned supreme at the Old Vic. Tickets were like gold dust with the twenty-eight-year-old hailed as the new Olivier. A group of RADA students, O'Toole amongst their number, decided to see *King John*, with Burton playing Philip the Bastard. Taking it in turns to queue for cheap tickets they sat up in the gods, crackling with anticipation.

The curtain that evening fell to applause like thunder and O'Toole stepped outside into a cold, windy Waterloo Road almost traumatized by what he'd seen. 'When Richard Burton strutted his Bastard on to the stage, he fetched with him a virility and poetry which neither before nor since have I seen matched in any playhouse.' Conveniently located nearby was a pub and O'Toole's group made haste inside. He was halfway through his pint when Burton and other cast members bounded in, calling out for refreshment. O'Toole watched the Welsh wizard 'lift his pint with an ease and sure-handedness that told of diligent practice'. It was a strange sensation to sit so close to actors who had entertained him so grandly, there was laughter, good humour, it delighted him, yes, 'but though I can see and hear all this, I cannot yet touch it'. They were professionals, O'Toole was still very much the apprentice. At one point O'Toole distinctly recalled Burton catching sight of his own gaze and staring back with a grin, 'as big as it was friendly. He raised his glass to me, to my friends, we raised our glasses to him, and then with the grin still on him he ambled away.'

That same season O'Toole saw Strindberg's *The Father* and was captivated by the veteran actor Wilfrid Lawson. Not long after, travelling in the tube and swotting up on some text, O'Toole realized he was sat opposite the great man, who was glaring at him. 'Not in public, my boy. Not in public.' It was the beginning of a great friendship that lasted till the old man's death in 1966. Lawson became something of a mentor to O'Toole, he was his kind of actor, brazen, slightly daft and not giving a fuck for convention. He was also an alcoholic but amazingly remained in work. There were antics galore with Lawson. During one theatrical run he took strongly against a particular actress. In one performance she was starting her big speech when the audience was diverted by a large puddle of liquid seeping onto the stage. Lawson was behind the prop door taking a piss.

O'Toole lived in a succession of dingy bedsits and friends' sofas during his two years at RADA, even for a time on a barge that came perilously close to disaster one night during a party after too many revellers came aboard: 'We had to man the pump at the stern and wank the bastard in dread of her sinking.' This kind of haphazard existence led to regular greetings of, 'Hello, Peter, which hedge did you sleep under last night?' as he bounded through the academy's door. One night after seeing the musical *Guys and Dolls* in the West End and endeavouring to walk home with a bottle of whisky for company he spent the night under the stars on the old bandstand in Green Park.

Money was difficult too, especially in that first year, and O'Toole was forced to look for work. Most of his colleagues seemed to have their own suit, which got them hired as shop assistants; with no such finery O'Toole had to settle for a job on a building site working the cement mixer. He also washed dishes at Lyons' Corner House restaurant in the West End for ten shillings and a free meal. His fellow washer-upper was an equally young and broke showbiz hopeful, Danny La Rue. During the holidays he'd go back up to Leeds, where he often found part-time work as a postman.

O'Toole's confidence as a performer had now grown to such an extent that he often displayed impatience and contempt when given small roles in productions. It was an attitude that earned a stern rebuke one day when his teacher Hugh Miller yelled at him in front of the whole class, 'O'Toole, there are no small *parts*, there are only small *actors*.' It was an important lesson, that even the smallest role can make a telling contribution, can steal the show if played with imagination and bravura. It also endeared him greatly to Miller, who became one of the few teachers at RADA he ever had any time for. A great raconteur, Miller had worked on Broadway and knew his stuff and would become a huge influence. 'He was the one who turned the key that unlocked and set free whatever abilities as an actor were held inside me.' As would another teacher, Clifford Turner, one of the foremost authorities on voice production, who like Miller had a big personality and wasn't afraid to inject a bit of fun into proceedings.

There was much respect, too, for Ernest Milton, who directed O'Toole in a student production of *Twelfth Night*. 'Tristram Jellinek was in it who was a great friend of Peter's,' recalls Malcolm Rogers. 'And Peter had sent Tristram off for his cane, "I must have my cane!" and Ernest Milton roared, "I'll not have you fetching and carrying for Peter O'Toole!" '

The bigger stage roles did begin to come O'Toole's way that second year. One in particular stands out for Keith Baxter: Catherine's brother Prince Potemkin, in George Bernard Shaw's *Great Catherine*. 'It was a real knockabout part,' says Baxter. 'And Peter was falling over, doing prat falls, the whole works.' Baxter had gone that night with Roy Kinnear and afterwards they trudged back to the flat they shared in Battersea, a distance of some miles. In those days the tubes stopped early and there were no late-night buses, and with taxis a financial no-no, hard-up students had no choice but to walk. 'So we'd been pounding the pavement hard for two hours almost in complete silence,' recalls Baxter. 'And then we crossed Battersea Bridge and there was a roadside cafe for late-night lorry drivers and so we sat and had a cup of tea. We really hadn't talked much, then Roy looked at me and said, "He's fucking incredible isn't he." And I said, "Yes." There was something about Peter that was absolutely irresistible, overwhelming. As an actor he was just something beyond any of us, any of us.'

O'Toole didn't run around with any particular crowd at RADA, though he'd a nose for finding the best parties and the pubs that sold the cheapest beer. Already his penchant for the bottle was the subject of much gossip. 'The main thing I remember about Peter is that he seemed to have a very romantic attitude to alcohol,' reports fellow student Pauline Devaney. 'Peter always used to say that he wanted to be dead from drink by the time he was thirty, which always seemed to me a curious ambition.'

Certainly odd things seemed to happen to O'Toole and O'Toole alone. On his way to a RADA production he was a passenger in a car that hit a ten-ton lorry on the A1. He was taken to hospital, his leg bursting with pain, but discharged himself after being kept waiting for an X-ray. He caught a train down to London where a sympathetic doctor pumped him full of enough painkillers to give a performance. The next day the X-ray proved that he had a broken leg. Elizabeth Rees-Williams shared many classes with O'Toole and can't recall an occasion when she saw him without a plaster or a bandage somewhere on his person. 'And a bloody bandage, because he'd been in some scrape or other. Even in those days there was a frisson about him.'

O'Toole's final year at RADA was all change for the academy, when Sir Kenneth Barnes, approaching his eighties, was pensioned off; not before time most would say, as he was in serious decline and quite deaf. 'Really to impress Sir Kenneth when you acted you had to shout it,' admits Malcolm Rogers. 'Subtlety didn't really come into it.' His successor was John Fernald, who'd had a long career in the theatre as a director, and with him came an air of efficiency and vitality and more forward thinking. Fernald really intended to mix things up and was instrumental, for example, in organizing a student production of Bertolt Brecht's *Caucasian Chalk Circle*, the first time this play had been performed anywhere in Britain, with O'Toole in a principal role. Among the chorus was a first-year student by the name of Glenda Jackson.

O'Toole's reputation at RADA was by now well established, along with his wild ways and eccentric behaviour; he once took an ironing board onto the pavement outside the academy's doors and did his shirts. The actress Lisa Harrow was told one story of the time O'Toole, Bates and Finney all appeared in a play together. 'And apparently O'Toole came on stage as someone bringing in these glasses of wine, and he'd peed in all the glasses.'

Delia Corrie had just begun her first year at RADA but already had heard all about O'Toole. 'He cut a dashing figure when he used to sweep into the canteen making all us silly young actresses adore him! There was no doubt that he was going to make an impression to not only lowly RADA students but in the outside world.'

Pauline Devaney, however, found O'Toole strangely aloof and insular. 'Peter was not into getting on with people. Normally if you're in a very confined space, as we were for both rehearsals and performance, you get on with each other, but I have no recollection of him ever being particularly friendly.' Conversely Elizabeth Rees-Williams remembers O'Toole as 'an embracer'. Someone with enormous charisma who was larger than life. 'There was so much excitement when he was around, anything could happen and you never knew if it was going to be good or bad or whatever.'

By the end of Fernald's first term, Elizabeth was gone, unceremoniously booted out. Feeling sorry for herself, she agreed to take part in a small fringe-theatre production, where she made the acquaintance of a young actor studying at another drama school, LAMDA. The physical attraction between them was undeniable and they began dating. His name was Richard Harris. It's Elizabeth's recollection that not long after their relationship started she introduced Richard to O'Toole in a pub, thus beginning an extraordinary friendship. The connection between the two men was instant. 'Richard recognized in Peter that spark and that quest for life and appetite for life, because they really wanted to enjoy life and live it to the full. And I think they both did.'

O'Toole enjoyed telling one story of Harris the drama student living in a distressing bedsit in Earls Court. After one mighty bender they returned to this hovel rat-arsed and starving hungry. A desperate search for food uncovered nothing but a solitary pork chop in the fridge; ancient it was, clearly it had been there a long time. They smelt it, looked at it, and thought better of it, so threw it out of a window and went to bed. Came the morning they left the squat and under the window from which they'd thrown this pork chop there was a dead dog.

There is also the tale of when the pair drove down to Brighton for the weekend to catch the pre-London try-out of Paul Scofield's *Hamlet* at the Theatre Royal. Arriving outside one of the resort's grander hotels they booked the presidential suite and proceeded to go nuts on room service. After the second day, Harris came to his senses. 'We've got to leave now, Peter, how much money have you got?' Nothing, as it turned out. Harris was likewise skint. It was pouring with rain, storms; the beaches were windswept and dangerous. Harris had a brainwave. 'Take your clothes off, Peter, all of them.' Rolled up into a tight ball, the garments were turfed out of the window into a little side street. 'Come on, let's pretend we're going for a swim.' Covering their modesty with towels they casually walked through the lobby towards the main doors. The manageress, a stern-faced woman, looked up from her work. 'Where are you going?'

Harris smiled. 'We're going for a swim.'

The woman looked incredulous. 'A swim, in this! The waves are ten feet tall out there, the currents . . . '

'Yes, we're going for a swim,' countered Harris. 'We're Irish, we're tough. We can handle it.'

Once out of sight they snuck up the street, quickly changed and made a bolt for it. In the late 1960s Harris was on a one-man concert tour and arrived to play a gig in Brighton. Not just that but his promoter had booked him into that very same hotel. 'I recognized the lobby. Oh my god. I signed my name and it was the same woman behind the desk. I hurriedly finished and made my way to the lift when, "Oh, Mr Harris." I said, "Yes." "We thought you and Mr O'Toole drowned." '

One of the advantages for RADA students was the end of year public show, which theatre managers, agents and critics were invited to attend. It was a terrific chance to be noticed, maybe even get a job. In it O'Toole performed a piece from Pirandello's *The Rules of the Game*. Strange as it may seem, although O'Toole and Finney were the undisputed stars of RADA (as Elizabeth explains, 'When Peter or Albie were doing anything, you'd all go and watch') they were not expected to win the gold medal, the prize given to the year's best student. Everyone expected it to be John Stride, who was seen very much as the golden boy. There was a gasp when at the end of the show the prize went instead to Bryan Pringle.

According to theatre director William Gaskill, the names of O'Toole and Finney were reverberating around the theatre world long before they graduated. 'People already knew who they were before they'd gone into the profession. People in the theatre knew how good they were.' It was no surprise to Malcolm Rogers that it was these two who came out of the starting gate first. 'They were the two, I felt mentally, who'd got it together, they knew where they were going. They had a sense of direction.' Indeed, they had already been hired by two of the country's most prestigious repertory theatres: Finney was heading to Birmingham rep, while O'Toole had come to the notice of the Bristol Old Vic's general manager, Nat Brenner, who sensed something special. 'He was absolutely riveting. I was smitten.'

FOUR

O'Toole left RADA, aged twenty-three, with a little blue book that every student was given upon graduation, *The RADA Keepsake and Counsellor*. It gave indispensable advice for the rocky road that lay ahead, gems like: 'It doesn't matter if you don't get the job as long as the shoes you were wearing at the audition were clean.' Goodness knows what O'Toole did with the thing, chucked it into the nearest bin most likely.

Walking up the steps of the Bristol Old Vic for the very first time was to O'Toole the high spot of his life. 'It always will be.' Here was a theatre that had seen such eminences as Kean, Kemble and Irving ply their trade, and in recent years, under the formidable stewardship of artistic director John Moody and Nat Brenner, evolved into one of the most important repertory companies in the country. 'There was so much energy pouring out from that stage from a strong company at that time,' says actor John Cairney. 'It was a proud thing to belong to the Old Vic at Bristol because it managed to combine the best of the old, yet contain all the surging talent of the new.' Just a year prior to O'Toole's arrival it had staged the first production outside America of Arthur Miller's seminal play *The Crucible*, after no producer in the West End would mount it.

Edward Hardwicke, a young actor who had already established himself at Bristol for something like a year, and would later achieve huge success as Dr Watson to Jeremy Brett's Sherlock

Holmes in the Granada television series, never forgot the morning Nat Brenner approached him to ask, 'We've got this young actor coming soon. Would you mind if he shares your dressing room?' They instantly hit it off.

Most provincial theatres enjoyed a healthy relationship with the local newspaper, and newcomers to the Bristol Old Vic were often announced in the entertainment pages, sometimes with a little biographical profile, especially if there was something colourful about them. Hardwicke has good reason to remember O'Toole's particular entry. 'It said that he was related to a Victorian actor called J. L. Toole who played the Fool to Henry Irving's King Lear, and I was terribly impressed by this. Then years later we were chatting and I'd recently been to the Garrick Club and in the lobby somewhere was a bust of J. L. Toole and I asked Peter, "Did you ever follow up your connection with J. L. Toole?" And he said, "It was bollocks, dear boy, pure bollocks." '

So why had he done it? After admitting his deception, O'Toole offered Hardwicke this fascinating and revealing explanation. 'Peter said that when he first auditioned at RADA he was standing in the foyer and there used to be a sergeant who looked after the front door and there were students coming down the stairs and the sergeant said to Peter, "You see that guy there, his father is a famous actor, Sir Cedric Hardwicke." And it was me! And Peter said, "I remember looking at you, Edward, and you had a bow tie on and suede boots, you looked frightfully confident, so the next day I went to look to see if I could find an O'Toole in the acting profession, there wasn't one but there was a J. L. Toole." So he turned himself into a relation.'

The Theatre Royal, home of the Bristol Old Vic company, was an extraordinary theatre. Situated on King Street, close to the centre of the city, it proudly boasts of being the oldest continually working playhouse in Britain, retaining much of its original Georgian splendour. Pretty quickly O'Toole was put to work.

His first role was a couple of lines playing a cab driver in a production of Thornton Wilder's *The Matchmaker*, which opened in September 1955. He shared the stage with a fellow newcomer, Glasgow-born John Cairney, who remembers O'Toole carrying around with him a big whip, 'which I'm glad to say he never used on me.'

In a production of Chekhov's *Uncle Vanya*, starring Eric Porter, O'Toole had even fewer lines, just one in fact as a Georgian peasant who announces at one point, 'Dr Astrov, the horses have arrived.' Not much to make an impact with. Faced with this problem, O'Toole decided that the peasant he was playing was in fact the young Stalin. For hours he worked diligently on the make-up from old photographs of the Russian dictator and affected a slight limp. Come opening night, on he walked, 'smouldering with resentment for the aristocracy. I could hear a hush come over the audience.' A glaring O'Toole pronounced, 'Dr Horsey, the Astrovs have arrived.' He knew he'd cocked it up, it was written all over his face for days. Phyllida Law was a young actress at Bristol and remembers being quite taken by the actor's public show of remorse. 'He was so depressed, saying how awfully bad he'd been, which I thought was enchanting.'

One of the grand old dames of Bristol Old Vic, who'd been there for years and liked to think of herself as something of a barometer of talent, was less forgiving, recalls Hardwicke. 'She invited Peter and me out to lunch, which was quite a thrill, and Peter went off to the loo and she leaned over to ask me, "Is he a good friend?" I said, "Yes, we get on very well." She said, "Well, do try and persuade him to give it up." '

While O'Toole, even at this early stage, was, in Hardwicke's estimation, 'an extraordinary personality', he had a long way to go yet. 'This may sound odd, but in those early days at Bristol Peter was just another actor. It's only when you look back and you think, I suppose the seeds of what he turned into were there, you don't necessarily at the time recognize any of that, he's just another mate in a company of actors.'

John Cairney remembers O'Toole as 'a whirling windmill of passion and enthusiasm. I can still see Peter and me wrestling on the Green Room floor of the Theatre Royal, during some kind of young-blood quarrel – why, I cannot remember. He was constantly going round and round, seemingly unsure of which way the wind was blowing. But there was no denying the innate power that was there, though it had yet to be applied fully to the talent. But, he was all go – and he went.'

One of the highlights of the year at the Bristol Old Vic was the annual pantomime. Nat Brenner was a great visionary, who saw theatre as an instrument for social good and social improvement and happily put on music hall and panto alongside Shakespeare and Chekhov. O'Toole's first taste of the Bristol panto was *Dick Whittington*. John Cairney was in the cast, coping as best he could with O'Toole's 'long gangling legs and arms and wild eyes'. Halfway through the performance both corpsed, neither could remember the next line, nor could they hear what the prompter was calling out because of the laughter from the audience. 'So we both marched into the prompt corner and lifted the girl out on the high stool and put her centre stage and made her point to the place in the script. Then, to further laughter, we carried her off again and resumed the action. As a result of this, we were both on the carpet before John Moody, the director of the company, and threatened with instant dismissal. But fortunately for theatre, especially in Mr O'Toole's case, he changed his mind the next day. The incident was all part of our mutual excess.'

Following his first panto experience, O'Toole played in his first Shakespeare, a production of *King Lear*, with Eric Porter in the title role. O'Toole would later class Porter as one of the two best Lears he ever saw, the other being Donald Wolfit. Porter was the star of the Bristol Old Vic, 'and very much the father of the company', says Susan Engel, a pupil at the nearby Bristol Old Vic theatre school. And there is little doubt that O'Toole watched and learnt a great deal from him, later citing the actor as a huge influence and 'a real catalyst for me. He released a lot of my own energies because of his great looseness and power.' Dazzling on stage, Porter could be enormously generous off it, treating his fellow actors to grand dinners at some of Bristol's most expensive restaurants. But after his success there Porter was sadly not to have the career that his talent deserved. His memorable performance as Soames in the BBC's 1967 television adaptation of *The Forsyte Saga* should have led to greater things, but it didn't. 'He couldn't cope with his own sexuality,' says Susan. 'It was so awful for gay men in those days. I don't know how some of them managed to survive; and many didn't. You went to prison if you were caught. I think he suffered terribly. He was tortured.'

For the rest of 1956, O'Toole appeared in small roles in a number of productions including *Volpone* by Ben Jonson, *Major Barbara* by George Bernard Shaw, *The Recruiting Officer* by George Farquhar, *The Rivals* by Richard Brinsley Sheridan, *Ondine* by Jean Giraudoux, *The Empty Chair* by Peter Ustinov and *The Skin of our Teeth* by Thornton Wilder. There was also a production of *Othello* that featured a truly memorable opening night, as told by O'Toole during a mid-nineties appearance on *The Tonight Show* with Jay Leno. Amongst the cast was an old actor by the name of Robert Atkins, who in the thirties and forties had essayed all the great Shakespearean roles, and taught at RADA during O'Toole's spell there. The two had got on well and on the day of the first read-through Atkins approached O'Toole and asked, 'What are you playing, old son?'

'I'm playing Lodovico, sir.' A minor part.

'Lodovico,' said Atkins. There was a pause. 'Oh, the clown who forgets the letter.'

O'Toole hadn't the first clue what the old thespian was on

about so did a quick scan of the text and sure enough there was a scene in which Lodovico arrives at Othello's palace to deliver an important letter from the Doge (Atkins must have misremembered it).

To achieve a sense of perspective, the set designer had constructed an intricate series of arches that formed the palace entrance, the last of which was a mere five foot high. 'You don't mind ducking under it as you make your entrance, do you?' the designer had kindly asked O'Toole. Not at all. The opening night arrived. O'Toole was ready in the wings, dressed in a long green velvet cloak. The trumpets sounded, his cue to arrive bearing the all-important letter. Ducking under the first arch he felt jammed. 'My cloak had got wrapped round both sides of the arch. I didn't know this, I just thought what it needed was a hefty heave.' And that's what he gave it, only to watch in stunned silence as the arches toppled over like dominoes. The poor actress playing Desdemona looked distraught wondering how on earth she was going to make her own entrance and Joseph O'Connor's dark make-up as Othello was running into his eyes. And there stood O'Toole, alone amidst the rubble, his hand rummaging inside his cloak – he'd forgotten the letter.

Parts like Lodovico were typical of those O'Toole was being asked to play during this season; largely inconsequential. 'That's because they were always worried he wasn't going to turn up,' reveals Edward Hardwicke. 'I can remember being in the dressing room at one point and he hadn't showed yet and a taxi was sent up to his digs and he was still fast asleep with a smashed alarm clock lying about the floor. Peter was a bit of an enfant terrible.'

Episodes like this were not uncommon. Sheila Allen, an actress who had recently joined the company from rep in Birmingham, recalls that the incidents of O'Toole turning up late for rehearsals or not turning up at all were perpetual. 'He'd go to bed plastered and not hear the alarm go off or maybe he hadn't set it, and he'd be full of courtesy and apology on arrival. Peter was adorable, but impossible.'

After most performances O'Toole retired to the Royal Navy Volunteer, a public house just across the road from the theatre, often staying for late-night drinking sessions. When he wasn't in the pub O'Toole was busy brewing his own whisky. 'We made gallons of it. We had a distillery. The only trouble was we couldn't find anything to store it in. So we got some of those big carboys they keep acid in and filled them with the stuff. Judging by the taste of the whisky, we left some of the acid in.'

The Royal Navy Volunteer was a favourite haunt in Bristol, but he'd a tendency to ferret out some of the city's less salubrious bars, downing his pint of Guinness amidst a clientele of drunks and miscreants. As Nat Brenner observed, 'He cultivated the friendship of people who were plainly psychopathic.' When O'Toole turned up at the stage door one afternoon wearing a face of cuts and bruises Brenner asked, 'Why do you do this to yourself? Why do you court this kind of trouble?' O'Toole didn't need to think about his answer for too long. 'I need it. I need to feed on it in order to inform myself about these people.' Brenner got used to receiving calls at all hours from the local Casualty department reporting that a Mr O'Toole had been admitted and had readily arrived at the conclusion that here was 'a young man with a sense of self destruction'.

He was beginning to forge a reputation; sometimes the police would pick him up out of the gutter and drive him home. Susan Engel claims that a rule came into force at the beginning of one of the terms at the Bristol Old Vic theatre school stating that no girl be allowed to walk unaccompanied in King Street. 'All the other actors were little tiny mice in comparison to Peter. They were ordinary blokes, Peter was a bit outrageous, in fact he was major outrageous. So one had already heard of O'Toole by the sheer fact that we were forbidden to go to King Street because there was an outrageous actor down there. He got himself well known in the town quite quickly.' Of course, the female students all went charging down there for the very reason they were ordered not to.

In spite of this growing reputation for wildness his obvious talents were not overlooked by the theatre's hierarchy, especially Nat Brenner. 'Nat was a big guru for Peter,' says Susan Engel. Supportive and approachable, Brenner was a quiet, reserved and precise man, and a master of a myriad of classic styles, Chekhov, Restoration, Elizabethan, and taught his students and actors a healthy respect for the text, a lesson O'Toole never forgot. With Brenner as his champion, O'Toole began steadily to gain more prominent roles during 1957. He played Alfred Doolittle in a production of Shaw's *Pygmalion* in March before essaying *the* role of the moment – Jimmy Porter in John Osborne's groundbreaking *Look Back in Anger*. Phyllida Law appeared opposite him as Helena. 'I had to biff him one, didn't I, had to smack him round the chops and he took it on the chin, so he did.' Osborne travelled up for a performance and later declared O'Toole the best Porter he ever saw. 'I would think that was the case,' says Phyllida. 'Peter was Jimmy Porter really, in many ways.'

In May, O'Toole appeared as Lysander in a sparkling production of *A Midsummer Night's Dream*. It typified the sort of grand productions Bristol put on, with large casts and beautiful set design and costumes. Phyllida had been cast as Titania and her fiancé Eric Thompson was playing Puck. Midway through the run the pair married. 'Peter came,' recalls Phyllida. 'And in the evening performance, by which we must have all been nearly dead, he threw rice all over the stage and there were fairies skidding all over the joint.'

An even bigger success was an old-fashioned musical entitled *Oh! My Papa*, which saw O'Toole burst into song and play

opposite an equally combustible performer in Rachel Roberts.
Needless to say the pair of them got on famously. In July it transferred to London's Garrick Theatre. As the curtain fell on the
opening night boos rang out around the auditorium and the show
never recovered. To drown the memory of his calamitous West
End debut O'Toole knocked back several measures of hard liquor
and was arrested at three in the morning for harassing a building
in Holborn. He spent the night in the cells and in the morning
explained to the court, 'I felt like singing and began to woo an
insurance building.' The next morning his spirits were somewhat lifted by the critics' reception of his performance. 'While
the play itself got hammered Peter was picked out,' recalls Phyllida. 'He was very good in it.'

It led to O'Toole's first real bit of national exposure, when he
and Finney (then appearing in Ben Jonson's *The Alchemist* at
Birmingham) shared the cover of the theatre magazine *Encore*.
'What have these young actors in common?' its leading critic
asked. 'Above all, the magic touch of personal magnetism. Love
them or leave them, you can't ignore them.'

O'Toole awoke pissed, not the first clue where the hell he was,
only that he'd scribbled down on a piece of paper that he was
required to show up to rehearsals in an Irish club somewhere
in Islington for a television play. Quickly he grabbed whatever
clothes were lying around on the floor and left the flat in a
bedraggled state, 'and somehow found wherever this bizarre
place was where we were rehearsing.'

He was already two days late.

The play was *The Pier*, James Forsyth's social drama about a
gang of teddy boys, and Kenneth Griffith, a lanky, neurotic type
of actor who had appeared in several films, was inexplicably playing the leader. As rehearsals passed into the third day Griffith
could still see only eight members of his gang when there should

have been nine. 'Where's this other chap, then?' As if on cue O'Toole arrived, barging through a pair of swing doors. 'And there was what appeared to be a tall young tramp,' Griffith recalled of the occasion. 'He looked down at us and said, "Sorry I'm late, darlings." Then his eyes fixed on me, he came thundering down the stairs, picked me up, kissed me (we'd never met) said: "I think you're bloody marvellous," put me down, and retreated to a corner.'

Griffith was perturbed, this was after all just a bit-part player and they shared only the one scene together. When Griffith suggested they do a quick run through of it: 'Bang! He gave a performance which was devastating,' Griffith remembered. 'I knew immediately that this was the most formidable competition I'd ever come across. I felt as if I had just met the young Edmund Kean. I had no doubt whatsoever.'

The Pier was broadcast that October on the ITV network, by which time O'Toole was back at Bristol where he was about to make his greatest impact yet, beginning with an extraordinary production of Samuel Beckett's *Waiting for Godot*. Susan Engel didn't miss a single performance. 'I saw it for three weeks every night. Peter was cast as Vladimir and was just a mercurial, riveting presence. And his voice, his rasping voice, and his intonation, I can still remember his inflections and I've seen it perhaps ten times since, different productions, with wonderful actors, and none of them came close to the performance Peter gave. He kind of spoilt it for any of the other actors.'

Another Bristol theatre student who saw O'Toole's Vladimir was Patrick Stewart, then just seventeen years old: 'And O'Toole has been my benchmark for stage charisma ever since – just the intensity of his presence. I came out of that production shaking with excitement, even though I was at times puzzled and scared by the play. I said to myself, "One day I'm going to do that part."' It took something like fifty years to finally fulfil that promise to himself.

Then came the panto, *Ali Baba and the Forty Thieves*. Eric Porter had left the company so O'Toole was given the responsibility of playing the Dame and practically took charge of the entire production. 'I can't remember who wrote the script for *Ali Baba*,' says Susan Engel. 'Not that we kept to it at all, O'Toole kind of invented the whole thing.' Susan was now able to observe O'Toole at close quarters since she'd taken over the role of the Dame's sister after one of the actresses was forced to pull out. It was an experience she has never forgotten. Susan remembers O'Toole telling her that he'd based his whole Dame routine on Max Miller. 'He absolutely worshipped those old music hall comics, and Max Miller's timing was O'Toole's bible.' On stage O'Toole would suddenly, and frighteningly, grab hold of Susan's arm: 'Wait for it, wait for it,' he'd command. 'And you'd have to wait for the laugh. He was dictatorial, but for the reason of getting it right, getting the laughs. And every night he would improvise.'

Susan fell prey to this on one occasion when she was exchanging silly dialogue with O'Toole downstage. 'I suddenly thought, that's a bit weird because as I was talking to him Peter was getting smaller and smaller. I couldn't believe it! I'd never been on stage hardly before, I was as green as a gooseberry, let alone on stage watching somebody go down a trap door.' As soon as Susan had begun her dialogue O'Toole cued the stagehands to release the trap door and down he went.

Susan ran to her dressing room almost in tears. Peter Jeffrey, who was playing the King, popped his head round to offer some sympathy, laced with a bit of free advice. 'It's all right, darling,' he said. 'It was terribly, terribly funny. Now here's what you do, I've thought it over, because he'll do it again tomorrow, keep that same expression on your face because it was just divine, pretend you don't know what's happening, be really upset, then give it a beat, look out front and say, "Poor Nellie, she never did learn to keep her trap shut," 'and you'll get a laugh.' Susan practised it diligently all the next day and when O'Toole began descending she gave the line and the audience roared with laughter. 'After the show Peter came up to me and said, "What did you say when I was under the stage?" And he didn't do it again. He wouldn't be trumped.'

No cast member escaped his mischievousness. In one scene, O'Toole's Dame and Susan wandered along a row of shops, all painted flats that came down on wires, until they arrived and entered a hat shop, and there followed a silly scene about choosing hats. A young actress had a walk-on part as the hat-shop girl with barely three lines. 'And Peter couldn't stand this girl,' recalls Susan. 'And she couldn't cope with his improvisation, she'd try to say her lines but never got a chance.' One night they came on, and the unfortunate young woman was waiting behind the flat. O'Toole walked up and turned the shop sign around from 'open' to 'closed', turned to the audience and said, 'Oh, it's closed, never mind,' signalled his mates for the flat to be hauled back up, took Susan's hand and they walked off. The poor girl never got on the stage. 'Peter, that's not very fair,' Susan would try and say. O'Toole's response was, 'To every man his little cross and mine is that girl.'

On the night Susan's Jewish mother came to see *Ali Baba*, O'Toole played his whole Dame in a Yiddish accent, which bewildered most of the audience but delighted Susan's mother: 'He'd done it all for her.' To be fair this was panto and great panto is largely improvised. 'It's got to entertain the audience,' says Susan. 'And Peter was very funny.' But O'Toole's general attitude was severely wanting during this period, as Phyllida Law confirms. 'He was so badly behaved at Bristol. I used to get very puritan about it and look disapprovingly at him and be fed up because he would alter our rehearsal time because he would have been in London having a lovely time and coming home on the train and he would fib about it majestically; we all knew what he'd been up to.' For her troubles Phyllida earned the unflattering nickname of 'Virgin Vinegar', which O'Toole delighted in calling her.

A guest director at Bristol called Warren Jenkins thought O'Toole's behaviour so disgraceful he complained to Brenner about it. 'A young actor like he ought to be sacked – or horse whipped.' But nothing was ever done, which didn't surprise Phyllida in the least. 'This was when Peter was doing awfully well at Bristol, and he had a bit of power. The authorities were pretty pathetic with him. The director of the theatre John Moody was fairly innocuous and would have known by that time that Peter was important and would have given him free rein. And Peter knew it, he wasn't daft. He was gold dust, he was Bristol's star and he was spoilt.'

It wasn't just O'Toole's wildness that meant he was late so much, he suffered from acute insomnia. To remedy the situation Brenner went to the extreme lengths of hiring the city's rat-catcher to forcibly remove him from bed if he'd overslept. Mostly, though, it was self-inflicted. He could sniff out a party like a veteran bloodhound. 'Often you'd follow O'Toole because we knew that's where the action would be,' says Sheila Allen. 'He was a roaring boy; life was for living. And he would never go to bed before three in the morning.' One Bristol student, walking to the university early one morning, recalled coming across a distraught O'Toole sitting in a doorway looking at a hole in his sock and crying.

While he might dodge the odd rehearsal, O'Toole never missed a single performance, that was sacrosanct, and he wasn't afraid to get stuck in either. During *Ali Baba* he never complained in the least about having to sell ice creams in the interval.

One evening, still dressed as the Dame, he sold an ice cream to the Bristol-born Hollywood star Cary Grant.

Sheila Allen got to know O'Toole quite well during this period, and in spite of the lead roles now heading his way never detected any fierce ambition; a little vanity perhaps as she observed he used to put shoe polish on his hair to make it darker. 'I don't know that he really cared about the ambition, I just think he loved acting. I don't think he had a sculptured ambition of any kind. There was no scheming, but he would know what he thought was available in the script that he had in front of him and he'd go for it. He had an ambition just to be very, very good, O'Toole just thought that was mandatory.'

Often Sheila would join the gang of regulars that hung around O'Toole in the pubs of Bristol. These nights had a tendency to grow boisterous but whatever sin or misdemeanour O'Toole committed, the sheer power of his personality forced people to excuse him. What fascinated Sheila the most was a side to his nature that perhaps a less discerning eye might miss. 'There was a quiet side to him, which was totally hidden and you only noticed it if you were hanging around and you could see this inner attention going on, when he wasn't doing something cranky. He hid it like mad. And he could sometimes get stroppy and when he was stroppy he was impossible, you couldn't break through.'

At the time Sheila was living with a young BBC television producer called Patrick Dromgoole, who was part of O'Toole's drinking gang, the Bristol set that also included up-and-coming playwrights Charles Wood and Peter Nichols, John Boorman, then at the BBC, and a junior reporter by the name of Tom Stoppard. 'Because Peter was always getting thrown out of wherever he was staying, I said he could move in with us for a while,' recalls Dromgoole. As a flatmate O'Toole was difficult to get out of bed and almost religiously against doing any daily chores. There were also numerous boozing sessions and rows; O'Toole was a great one for having arguments but nearly always never gave a damn and had forgotten about them after a few days.

One disagreement between the pair almost resulted in O'Toole's early demise. They were sharing a bottle of whisky while drunkenly making their way back to the flat along the ill-lit streets of Bristol. O'Toole had recently received some bad news about a relationship, and his mood was not helped by Dromgoole at one point yelling at him, 'You're just a drunken twit. You and I have no idea how she feels or thinks or anything about it.' That did it. 'Peter looked at me and turned his back and ran off very fast, contemptuously dismissing my attitude and my presence. He was a fast runner when he chose to be, even when drunk, and he vanished round a few corners.'

Dromgoole followed and found him sitting on the pavement leaning back against a set of poorly constructed railings, his long spindly legs drawn up in front of him so that his kneecaps were under his chin. 'Come on, get up,' said Dromgoole. 'We've got to get home and go to bed.' There was no response whatsoever. Tired and bored, Dromgoole got hold of one of O'Toole's legs and pulled it straight, resulting in his whole body curving round and falling some twelve feet through a gap in the railings onto a filthy roadway. 'I was terrified,' says Dromgoole. 'I shouted, "Dear God, Peter, are you all right?" I ran down to where he had fallen and he was lying deadly still there and I felt his head and my hand came away greasy and very wet. I really was shit scared now and started yelling, "Help. Help. Someone fetch an ambulance." '

At that moment Dromgoole sensed a stirring next to him, then a voice. 'What are you making that fucking noise about.' It was O'Toole.

'I thought you'd hurt yourself.'

'Don't be silly,' he said, clambering to his feet and dusting himself down.

Off they trotted back to the flat, with Dromgoole watching

O'Toole fairly carefully the whole time. Only later did he realise it wasn't blood he'd felt, it was machine oil. Once home Dromgoole made sure O'Toole was tucked up before climbing into bed with Sheila, where he immediately fell asleep. 'In the middle of the night I woke up to find Peter was in the room with us leaning over the bed looking at me with grave suspicions and saying, "My head hurts. Why does my head hurt?" I told him I didn't know and that perhaps he had a headache. He went back to bed. I never did tell him that story from my point of view and I don't think he ever knew exactly what happened that night.'

Following a convincing turn as John Tanner in George Bernard Shaw's *Man and Superman*, O'Toole was lauded as perhaps the Bristol Old Vic's greatest acting find. 'He was a very striking actor,' affirms Dromgoole. 'You couldn't take your eyes off him on stage. Real stars all have a slightly dangerous quality about them and Peter had an unpredictability that bordered on menace.'

When Bristol declared its intention to stage a production of *Hamlet* no one was surprised to learn that O'Toole had been designated with the task of playing the Prince of Denmark. But on opening night, 23 April 1958, he suffered 'a humbling and humiliating' case of stage fright just as he was about to walk on. He felt as if every ounce of energy and crumb of confidence had been sucked out of him and that he'd blown his big chance when the curtain came down. The critics disagreed, his performance was hailed as a triumph. For Sheila Allen, after all those missed rehearsals and adolescent misbehaviour, it was the moment of truth. 'I sat in the back of the stalls for the opening night of his *Hamlet* thinking, well, here goes, let's see, and I could swear that ectoplasm was coming out of him on that very first night; it was just extraordinary.' Tom Stoppard caught as many performances as he could, if he was working he'd try to get a fellow reporter to cover for him so he might at least catch the end. 'It was everything it was supposed to be. It was exciting and mysterious and eloquent.'

O'Toole had deliberately steered clear of the usual Shakespearean delivery and presented a very different kind of Hamlet, a more common Hamlet, a Hamlet of the streets rather than some omnipotent luvvie. Shakespeare was a man of the theatre, not a deity, said O'Toole, and his characters should be presented as real people. 'You can smell their breath. They piss against the wall. That's the way I play Shakespeare.' This new presentation was not lost on audiences or critics. *The Times*' positive review of the production began with the headline: 'An Angry Young Hamlet'.

O'Toole's tenure at Bristol was drawing to a close and one of his final appearances there saw him reunited with Richard Harris. Since leaving LAMDA, 'Mickser', as O'Toole fondly called him, had found employment with Joan Littlewood's theatre company in London's East End, but the pay was risible and he was always looking for extra jobs. Bristol took Harris on for a short spell and he acted alongside O'Toole that May in *The Pier*, the play O'Toole had already done on television. Appearing this time as the gang leader, O'Toole's performance was so realistic that walking home one night down King Street he was set upon and roughed up by a gang of local thugs.

Many nights were spent in the bars and pubs of Bristol. 'Golden days,' Harris called them. 'We kept each other up half the time, we never slept. It was days of chat and yarn-spinning and great, legendary boozing.' Elizabeth was there, sharing digs with Richard, and remembers the chaos they caused. 'Nobody knew how to deal with them. These two together, it was madcap. They made directors shake.'

Harris gloried in telling one particular story. There was a fifteen-minute portion of the play when neither he nor O'Toole were required on stage, time they spent every night across the road downing pints; conscientiously keeping an eye on their watches. 'One night we got so engrossed in telling stories that we forgot we were on stage. The next minute the door burst open and the stage manager came rushing in. "Harris, O'Toole, for God's sake, you're on!" We dropped our drink quickly down our throat and rushed across the street. I had to make my entrance just before O'Toole, as I hit the stage door, over the tannoy I heard my cue, I thought, I'll never make it. I dashed on, tripped over a wire, slid right across the stage, right down to the foot-lights and hung over onto the lap of these Bristolian old women. And this woman looked at me in shock and said out loud, "Good God, Harris is drunk!" And I looked at her and said, "Madam, if you think I'm drunk wait until O'Toole makes his entrance." '

FIVE

After three years at Bristol, O'Toole had decided it was time to move on. He came to London and with nowhere to stay, and virtually potless was put up by Kenneth Griffith at his mews flat in Belgravia. Together they went off on a mini-grand tour of Italy, finding themselves in a hotel on Lake Como. One night O'Toole received a telegram that distressed him so much that he dashed out into the night and leapt on a wall overhanging the lake. 'Griffith!' he yelled. 'It's got to end!' and flung himself into the water. The first thing that flashed through Griffith's mind was – 'My God, I can't swim!' Unknown to either of them, Lake Como at that particular point was only two feet deep.

Later that summer of 1958 O'Toole was recruited to join a touring production of a comedy entitled *The Holiday*, hoping for a West End engagement. It broke down in the provinces, but not before O'Toole had become intrigued by his leading lady, a twenty-five-year-old Welsh actress by the name of Siân Phillips. The daughter of a retired policeman, Siân had graduated from RADA in 1957 with the Bancroft Gold Medal, the academy's highest accolade. She was seen very much as an actress to watch and had already begun to receive job offers from film studios, major theatre companies and television. Siân, in turn, admitted to being 'dazzled' by O'Toole; he made her laugh, sometimes out loud and during performances, much to the annoyance of the company manager. They began to date, secretly as Siân was already married, if separated from her husband, a university lecturer she ill-advisedly wed while still a drama student. According to actor Michael Byrne, however, the two young lovers had encountered each other before. 'Siân once told me that when she was a student at Cardiff University a bunch of them would go across to the Bristol Old Vic and they always thought, who is this lovely old man who is playing all these old character parts, who must have been a beautiful actor at some point. And of course it was Peter playing all these old men.'

The pair categorized themselves fairly early on as soul-mates, their likes and dislikes chimed perfectly. All except alcohol, that is, Siân didn't touch the stuff. The first thing O'Toole did to the poor girl was initiate her into the dark arts of boozing. During the tour he'd inflicted whisky and beer upon her. Where before alcohol played little part in Siân's life, now it seemed to revolve around it. Evenings were spent invariably in a pub where Siân would sit sipping the black nectar, taking it down as a child might medicine, while O'Toole quaffed away like a man possessed. It was a strange life that she felt peculiarly drawn to and it wasn't long before she was sharing his room at Kenneth Griffith's mews house.

There were early warning signs, however, of what was to come, such as the occasion O'Toole threw her clothes out of the window, claiming she wore too much black and violet. 'You look as though you're in mourning for your sex life,' he announced suddenly, and out it all went, practically the whole of Siân's wardrobe strewn across the wet cobbles outside. When a bewildered Siân queried what on earth she was going to wear now, O'Toole's solution was that she should wear his clothes. They became the only couple in town with a shared wardrobe of cotton trousers, lumberjack shirts and fisherman's sweaters.

Peter introduced Siân to Richard Harris and Elizabeth, who had recently married. Elizabeth liked Siân enormously, but could see that she had her hands full with O'Toole. 'Siân was doing her best to quieten him down – she didn't stand a chance!' Occasionally they'd all go out as a foursome, most memorably to a big dinner dance at the Festival Hall organized by the London Welsh Society, of which Elizabeth's father, Lord Ogmore, was President. 'Of course, Richard and Peter took great exception to all these Welsh being together,' recalls Elizabeth. 'And they started interrupting the speeches with cries of, "What about the Irish, then?" and chasing and jumping in-between the tables, basically screwing up the whole event. I was mortified. My poor parents.' After threats from delegates that they would resign from the society unless the pair were ejected, Harris and O'Toole were asked to leave. 'They did burn the candle at both ends and in the middle. And enjoyed every minute of it,' says Elizabeth. 'They were just like wild, naughty characters, but they weren't vicious. The side effects would be accidental, and half the time they wouldn't remember them. And when they were told about their exploits they'd be very contrite, but then the next day they'd go off and do exactly the same thing.'

Other laddish japes included the time they were competing for the affections of the same woman; as was often the case. 'Peter and Richard were incredibly good looking,' says Elizabeth. 'With enormous energy, enormous charisma and enormous sex appeal. God help all the women that they ever met.' On this particular night of drinking they had said their farewells, only to bump into each other later outside this girl's block of flats. There was no answer when they knocked, so O'Toole scrambled up the drainpipe, knocked on the window and gained entry. Looking back he saw Harris still trying to navigate his way up. 'He must not have had my experience with drainpipes, growing up in Limerick.' About two storeys up the pipe broke away from the wall, leaving Harris dangling in midair. O'Toole helpfully summoned the authorities. 'When they'd got him down, I shouted from the window, "Officers, arrest that drunken Irishman. He was trying to break into our home!" '

What spurred on people like O'Toole and Harris to these ridiculous exploits, fuelled almost exclusively by drink? Even O'Toole himself confessed he didn't really know what he got out of it. 'What does anyone get out of being drunk? It's an anaesthetic. It diminishes the pain.' For much of his life O'Toole was plagued by stomach ulcers and these occasional bouts of intestinal pain were both alleviated and aggravated by drinking. And there was the insomnia. He'd always been a night person anyway and detested having to get up for early morning film calls. 'The man who invented mornings was no Christian. I prefer to go straight into the afternoon.' Again drink came in handy there, too, having discovered that a bottle of cognac or fine burgundy would send him off to sleep nicely.

There was something deeper too, a reaction against the times they were living in. It was more than ten years since the end of the war, but England was still in the grip of harsh austerity measures. Despite economic miracles in Germany and Japan, the government were still advising everyone to tighten their belts. Bollocks, hailed O'Toole. 'We didn't want any of that. We wanted the roaring twenties, please. There were some of us who saw it as our duty to be truants from the system. The drinking was liberation from the fear and the restrictions of the post-war years. The frivolity and the fun had gone. Booze was a way of recapturing it. We certainly had a bloody good time.'

O'Toole liked to quote the often repeated line that if you can remember the sixties, you weren't really there. 'Well, we were doing that in the fifties.' Much of their free time did appear to revolve around pub opening hours, and there were parties galore. They even took their merriment on the Underground, taking over a train carriage on the Circle Line where it was warm and there were seats, and with battery operated gramophones playing

45s round they'd go till the system shut down. 'We'd get off at Sloane Square, pop out to the pub, get some more booze and get back on again. Great fun! And the Sixties were only a continuation to that.'

One of O'Toole's earliest admirers at Bristol was the theatre impresario Oscar Lewenstein, who along with the actor-director George Devine ran the English Stage Company at the Royal Court, which had premiered Osborne's *Look Back in Anger*. Several times Lewenstein had caught O'Toole in performance at Bristol and believed the young actor to be achieving similar things to Albert Finney. 'They were the two foremost actors of their generation, and the best examples of the new non-university breed of actors that the new times and plays were demanding.'

A play had recently come into Lewenstein's possession by a young writer called Willis Hall, one of O'Toole's old comrades on the *Yorkshire Evening News*. Based on Hall's own military experiences, *The Disciplines of War* dealt with a small band of British soldiers on patrol in the Malayan jungle during the Japanese advance of early 1942. It was Hall's own statement against the stiff-upper-lip heroics then proliferating in British war films. There were no mock-heroics here, only the dank sweaty odour of real conscripted men's experiences of fear, danger and death.

O'Toole was given the play to read with the prospect of him playing one of the main leads, Private Bamforth, the classic 'barrack-room lawyer', up to every dodge and skive in the book. He loved the play and wrote to Lewenstein saying whoever played Bamforth would become a star, 'and please let it be me.'

It was scheduled to open at the start of 1959 at the Royal Court, and Devine and Lewenstein chose as their director Lindsay Anderson, whose first act was to ditch the original title in favour of *The Long and the Short and the Tall*. He then began to cast the play with a brilliant eye, choosing earthy, working-class actors as the soldiers: Edward Judd, Alfred Lynch and two old RADA colleagues of O'Toole in Bryan Pringle and Ronald Fraser. To play the platoon's tough sergeant Patrick McGoohan was first choice but when he turned the part down Robert Shaw was hired. As for Bamforth, O'Toole was left disappointed when he was beaten to the role by Albert Finney.

On the second day of rehearsals Finney arrived looking rather the worse for wear. A clearly concerned Anderson was hastily reassured that it was nothing more than the result of a late night. 'I'd been at a party and got through a bottle of Pernod,' said Finney. 'Mostly uncontaminated by water.'

The next day Finney's pallor was if anything even worse. The excuse this time was an overindulgence of vermouth but Anderson wasn't convinced and urged the actor to see a doctor. It turned out to be an acute case of appendicitis and Finney was rushed into hospital. When it became clear that Finney needed a great deal of time to recuperate, the search for his replacement began. The obvious first port of call was O'Toole, but he didn't much fancy the idea of substituting for Albie. Ultimately he saw sense and accepted the part.

Playing the wireless operator was David Andrews, the youngest member of the company. Within hours he had been adopted by O'Toole and taken under his wing. 'After that first rehearsal I found myself in Kenneth Griffith's flat, where Peter was staying, and we sat in the front room drinking and singing all night, and we'd hardly met. Peter was a great singer and taught me a couple of folk songs. He was a lovely guy and incredibly charismatic, he had the most wonderful, sparkling, piercing blue eyes. That's one of the things that made me attach myself so closely to people like Peter, they were magnetic people, you couldn't resist them.'

Disappointed at losing Finney, Anderson consoled himself with the fact that at least O'Toole ticked all the right boxes; he was working class, had a chip on his shoulder and didn't hail from the Home Counties. Anderson believed northerners lacked 'the curse of middle class inhibitions'. The two of them should have got along famously then, except it turned into a war of attrition from day one. Anderson considered O'Toole 'too much of a star performer', while O'Toole thought 'Lindsay's idea of the working class was perfumed shit'. The relationship never healed. 'Peter hated Lindsay,' confirms Andrews. 'Thought he was rubbish. He used to pick up bits of script and pretend to wipe his arse with them.'

The Long and the Short and the Tall opened in January 1959 and played to near capacity audiences. Very quickly O'Toole, Shaw and Ronnie Fraser fell into a pattern of drinking in a nearby pub prior to curtain-up. Sometimes with only minutes to spare they'd stampede back into the theatre, rub dirt over their faces and change into a khaki uniform looking as if they'd spent an hour in make-up to achieve the desired bedraggled jungle look. Anderson was almost driven bonkers. 'I'm furious!' he'd yell at them. 'I've never known anything quite so monstrously unprofessional,' while the expert hired to make the actors look like real soldiers suffered a nervous collapse and left.

However, for Bruce Montague, a young RADA student, who had recently done his National Service in Malaya during the emergency, the play was wholly authentic. Willis Hall gave the occasional lecture at RADA and invited Montague and a dozen other students to see his play and introduce them to some of the cast in the bar before the performance, including O'Toole, 'who, in those days, displayed a large nose, wild hair and a fondness of Guinness', recalls Montague. When the curtain came up the young student was mesmerized. 'The sweat patches on their jungle greens were just right: the performances spot on. Peter, commanding the Japanese prisoner to put his "flingers on bonce", remains with me to this day.'

Certainly David Andrews has never forgotten those months he

spent with O'Toole, nor the special thrill of appearing in what was a significant theatrical event. 'I hero-worshipped Peter. He was breathtaking to act with, so instinctively and intuitively intelligent, also clever and cunning and wily. To see him and the rest of the cast playing the same roles night after night and always making it sound as if it were just happening for the first time, that they were under this appalling pressure in the jungle, it came over so clearly, it resonated so well.'

As Bamforth, O'Toole had plenty of showy speeches, during which Andrews was usually seated at his radio set. During one such speech, Andrews worked out a bit of business that involved darning a sock. 'My confidence growing, I perfected a moment when the thread being drawn through the darn was pulled out just a tiny bit too far and my eyes followed the liberated end as it jumped into the air. This got something of a titter so I kept it in the following night. During a dramatic pause in his speech, Peter sauntered across to me and with bright blue laser-like eyes pierced me with his angry look and under his breath said – "If you do that medieval business again I'll sew your fucking bollocks together, you little bastard!" ' When the curtain came down Andrews went to O'Toole's dressing room, with some trepidation, to remonstrate with him for not saving his comments until the interval. 'He beamed at me in an avuncular way and said, "Come on, son, you're a wonderful actor, don't fuck things up for yourself before you've even started." He poured out two whiskies and we sat and chatted like old pals. But I never dared do that business again!'

It didn't take long for word of O'Toole and Co.'s antics to spread around theatre land. One Saturday evening, after the show had been running for a couple of weeks, stage hand Michael Seymour was alone in the auditorium clearing things up when through a door on the prompt side of the stage a man emerged. 'I say, where can I find the boys?' Seymour directed him to the dressing rooms. 'He thanked me, saying, "Oh, my name's Noël Coward." I later saw him in happy conversation with them all in the local pub.'

The critics, too, took notice. Kenneth Tynan especially singled out O'Toole for praise: 'I sensed a technical authority that may, given discipline and purpose, presage greatness.' Tynan was also astute enough to sense that the play was performed 'in what, for the London theatre, is a new style of acting'. Not just a new style of acting, but by an entirely new breed of actor. The cast of *Long and the Short*, together with people like Finney and Harris, were lauded as the embodiment of a new, gritty realism in film, theatre and television. With hindsight, it's easier to see that O'Toole was much more of an old-school successor to the likes of Irving, Olivier and Richardson. But what heavily linked him with these other actors was a propensity to raise hell. 'They were so self-destructive, that group of actors,' says David Tringham, who worked as an assistant director on *Lawrence of Arabia*. 'They all wanted to be Robert Mitchum.'

Working class and proud of it, it's probably too simplistic to say that their drinking and revelling was a two-finger salute to the middle-class acting establishment, although it's fair to say that for some of this generation acting wasn't a true vocation, merely a way to make money. 'We didn't want to be the best actors in the world,' said Harris. 'We didn't want to be the best King Lear. What a boring ambition.' Instead they wanted to experience everything that life had to offer and have as good a time as they could. 'We weren't pause and think,' claims Elizabeth Harris. 'We were doers – go out and do it!' Yes, these actors were talented, supremely so in some cases, and took what they did seriously, but they were also totally fearless and the noise they made was their way of saying, 'We've arrived, ignore us at your peril.' 'It wasn't that they broke the rules,' says Elizabeth. 'They didn't accept them.'

At the time Robert Shaw was the established big-cheese actor, he'd had his own TV series and made a few movies, which gave him the right to occupy the only dressing room with its own toilet. O'Toole had to make do with a big sink. One night he was merrily pissing when he heard an unmistakable voice at the door. 'Hello, my name is Katharine Hepburn.' Swiftly popping his old feller away, O'Toole invited the Hollywood icon inside. The actress happened to be in London working with Elizabeth Taylor and Montgomery Clift on the film *Suddenly, Last Summer*, and the next day discussed O'Toole with its producer, Sam Spiegel. Clift had a tendency to drink himself into a stupor or disappear altogether, so Spiegel was scouring London for an actor to come in and take over if the need arose. O'Toole was sent for and arrived at Shepperton Studios for a screen test. Hustled into make-up and dressed in a white coat, he was taken to the set of a doctor's office. Holding up an X-ray, O'Toole couldn't stop himself and cracked: 'Mrs Spiegel, your son will never play the violin again.' When Spiegel watched the rushes the next day O'Toole's playful prank did not find favour; indeed it nearly came back to haunt the actor a little over a year later.

Regardless of how poorly the audition went, Hepburn continued to sing O'Toole's praises both in London and back in Hollywood. For years he would bump into people who'd say, 'Katie Hepburn told me all about you.' Another early champion was the formidable Dame Edith Evans, best known for her definitive portrayal of Lady Bracknell in *The Importance of Being Earnest*. Actor Oliver Senton recalls a story his father used to tell of when he was President of the Oxford Union Dramatic Society in the late fifties. Quite often the Society managed to lure top theatrical names to give lectures or readings and on this particular evening Dame Edith had agreed to give up her time to read some poetry. 'When my father collected Dame Edith as she arrived from the railway station, lying unconscious on the floor of the cab was this long, thin man that she was carrying about as her protégé, which was O'Toole.'

Following its successful run at the Royal Court, *The Long and the Short and the Tall* transferred in April 1959 to the West End and the New Theatre (now the Noël Coward Theatre), conveniently located next door to the Salisbury pub on St Martin's Lane. The Salisbury remained the prominent watering hole for the cast. For years it had been a beacon for those in the arts to relax and drink, thanks to its location bang in the middle of London's theatre-land. Back in the early fifties John Osborne referred to it as 'The Rialto for loud-mouthed actors and lounging fairies'.

The cast drank there practically every night, slipping out of the back of the theatre after the show, across an alleyway and straight into the side entrance. Some partook of the brew before performances, O'Toole notably, which did no favours to his under-study, who'd stew in suspense backstage wondering if he'd return from the pub or goodness knows where else in time. The under-study in question was Michael Caine and his agonies lasted three months. One evening his nightmare became reality when O'Toole failed to show up with barely minutes to go.

'Michael began to get extremely agitated,' recalls David Andrews, who witnessed the whole episode. 'And eventually the stage director came into the dressing room and said, "You'll have to get the uniform on." And I can remember, Michael was trem-bling putting this stuff on and we were all thinking, Christ, is he going to cope with this. And then we heard the click on the tannoy as the microphone was switched on for the front of house announcement and thought, Christ, it's act one. So there we all were, waiting in the wings for the curtain to go up and suddenly the stage door burst open and O'Toole rushed in and they grabbed him and put him in his outfit in record time. And there was Mike, sweat pouring off his face.'

What had happened was O'Toole had been at a wedding somewhere in Hampshire and presumably got smashed and when he looked at his watch it was getting very late in the day. 'Christ, how am I going to get back to London?' Luckily the father of the bride was a wealthy man and raced him over to Blackbushe, a small private airport nearby. 'And this guy chartered a Viscount, which is a four-engine passenger plane, and got Peter onto it and flew him to Heathrow,' says Andrews. 'I don't know how true that story is, but it's the one Peter told.'

On another occasion O'Toole ran in just in time screaming, 'Don't go on, Michael!' as he bounded into his dressing room, shirt and trousers cast asunder. 'He was changed within seconds,' recalled his old drinking pal from Leeds and now a Fleet Street reporter, Keith Waterhouse. 'And, pausing only to throw up violently out of the upstage window of the set – which the audience thought was part of the action – gave a flawless performance.' Andrews always had his doubts that some of these near misses were not contrived, since O'Toole never actually missed a single performance. His inebriated state on occasion though did have repercussions, such as the time Bamforth was required to lie down on a wooden bench and O'Toole fell sound asleep and had to be given a sharp boot in order to wake up and deliver his next line.

Besides his job as understudy, Caine's other functions were to fetch booze, find out where the best parties were and acquire girls. 'I'd have made a wonderful pimp,' he later joked. One memorable Saturday night after the show O'Toole invited him to a restaurant in Leicester Square before going on to a party. 'This for a start was a surprise,' Caine recalled. 'Because I had never seen Peter actually eat anything. I thought he was one of those people who could get protein from alcohol.' Ordering a plate of egg and chips was the last thing Caine remembered until waking up next to O'Toole, both fully clothed, in a strange bed in an even stranger flat. Sunlight was pouring through the window. It turned out they were in Hampstead, and it was 5pm on the Monday; somehow they'd managed to miss an entire Sunday! Racing to the theatre, they arrived to see the stage manager waiting for them. The owner of the restaurant had been in and henceforth the pair of them were banned from his establishment for life. Caine was just about to ask what they'd done when O'Toole whispered, 'Never ask what you did. It's better not to know.' Caine bowed to O'Toole's greater experience in such matters but made a point of never going out on the booze with him again.

Other evenings O'Toole might spend walking around Covent Garden. Sometimes if he was in the mood he'd scale the wall of Lloyd's Bank. The first time he took Siân on one of these nocturnal jaunts she thought it the behaviour of someone not properly equipped with the requisite set of marbles. But after a few nights the actress came to accept this as unremarkable, as far as O'Toole was concerned. Indeed, this kind of architectural mountaineering wasn't a one-off. There is a tale of when O'Toole heard that his old RADA chum Frank Finlay was in town and a guest at the local YMCA. It was early morning when he arrived only to find the entrance locked. Undeterred O'Toole climbed his way four storeys up, and with bottle in hand manoeuvred his way along the narrow ledge to Finlay's room hammering on the glass like a mad thing. 'Open up, open up!'

When *The Long and the Short* finished its West End run to go on a national tour, O'Toole left the company. His part was taken by Caine, who later identified his success in the role as 'my first step towards becoming a star'. David Andrews also bowed out, replaced by an intensely shy young man by the name of Terence Stamp, making his professional debut. Stamp never saw the original production but often walked past the theatre gazing at the photographs of O'Toole and Shaw on the hoardings outside.

One night in the Salisbury he witnessed O'Toole holding court, before an irate stage assistant burst in, 'Mr O'Toole, please, it's time. We're waiting to start, sir.' After more pleading the desperate assistant grabbed O'Toole by the lapels and literally dragged him out. Stamp was impressed, was it endorphins that kicked in when O'Toole walked on stage, 'Because an icy soberness becalmed him until the interval, when he was once again legless. I thought I could be pretty flash myself until I saw this fella.'

Despite huge personal success as Bamforth, neither O'Toole nor Caine appeared in the film version of the play. Former head of Ealing studios Michael Balcon had secured the rights and desperately wanted O'Toole, failing that Finney. His American backers had different ideas and insisted on a 'name' that would play in the US market, settling on Laurence Harvey. During the West End run the cast knew a film was in the pipeline and one night Bob Shaw sidled over to O'Toole on stage and whispered, 'Row A, seat 12, he'll be playing your part in the movie.' O'Toole looked out over the footlights to see Harvey. Three nights later, O'Toole took great pleasure in whispering to Shaw, 'Row G, seat 9, he'll be playing your part in the movie.' It was Richard Todd.

SIX

It was never in O'Toole's scheme of things to be a film star, he was quite content at this time simply to become the best actor he could be. While at RADA he'd done a few walk-on bits on television and performed some stunt work on films shot at Elstree Studios, falling off the odd horse and hurling himself with abandon through windows. He enjoyed it, in spite of the resultant bruising, and would perform under various pseudonyms such as Walter Plings, Charlie Staircase and Arnold Hearthrug. There was also a small role in the adventure series *The Scarlet Pimpernel*, set during the French revolution. Playing a soldier, O'Toole was required to chase after a coach on horseback. 'I swallowed a fly, lost a wig and said: "You are to make the acquaintance of Madame Guillotine." End of part.' Still, it constituted his first spoken lines on television when the episode aired in March 1956.

Much more substantial were his roles in three episodes of the US/UK anthology series *Rendezvous*, all filmed in 1959 at Elstree but not transmitted in Britain until 1961. Of special note was the episode 'London–New York', where he appears opposite the distinguished actress Patricia Neal. In a gripping tale they play passengers seated next to each other on a long-delayed flight out of a fog-bound London airport that runs into trouble.

Thanks to his success as Bamforth, O'Toole was beginning to come to the attention of movie makers, notably the renowned director Joseph Losey, who thought he had tremendous talent.

'He also had the arrogance that goes with it when you are young.' Losey was setting up a film entitled *Blind Date*, a psychological thriller, and wanted O'Toole to play the police inspector, essentially the second lead alongside German actor Hardy Kruger. Despite a nasty head cold O'Toole impressed at the interview but the financial muscle behind the picture refused to accept him, he wasn't a 'name'. Losey had to look elsewhere, eventually casting Stanley Baker.

When it finally arrived, O'Toole's film debut came about purely by accident. Walt Disney were bringing Robert Louis Stevenson's classic novel *Kidnapped* to the screen in glorious Technicolor. Peter Finch had been chosen to play the Scottish hero Alan Breck and work was underway at Pinewood Studios. In one scene Breck indulges in a bagpipe contest with a fearsome Highlander. 'There's only one actor I know who can play the part and the fucking bagpipes,' said Finch and O'Toole was hired.

The part itself wasn't of any interest but the fee of £175 for a couple of days' work certainly was, and when it came time to view the rushes of his scene with Finch, O'Toole thought to himself, I can do this. 'It never occurred to me I'd be mediocre.' He'd behaved like a star from the get go. As Kenneth Griffith alleged, becoming a star isn't entirely down to being a great actor, 'It's how you handle those bastards.' During a Michael Parkinson chat-show in the 1970s Griffith was bluntly asked why he had never become a star, despite appearing in a string of films from *Lucky Jim* to *I'm Alright Jack*. By means of a reply he told an anecdote about O'Toole's very first day on *Kidnapped*. The movie company had rung that morning demanding to know why the actor was not at the studio. 'I told a lie. I said, this is a very large house, I'll see if I can find him – and I popped my head round his door. He was fast asleep, and I said, "O'Toole, you are forty-five minutes late," and he said, "Has my car come?" "No?"

I replied. "No car, no me." And he went back to sleep. From that day to this, there has been a Rolls waiting for him. That's why I'm not a star. I'd have been there on the dot.'

By the time he came to star in *Kidnapped*, Peter Finch had already carved out a fearsome reputation as a drinker of some note. It's no surprise then that he and O'Toole became drinking partners and firm friends until Finch's untimely death in 1977 at the age of sixty. Without doubt the best O'Toole/Finch story, which O'Toole used to tell with glee, involves the time Finchie was living in Dublin. He and O'Toole were on the lash one night and as they struggled back to Finch's pad in the early hours came upon a tiny hole in the wall bar and decided to drop in for a final snifter. After a couple of drinks the landlord said, 'Boys, you've had enough. You're having no more.' This is not what O'Toole and Finch wanted to hear. 'Oh no, no, no, we're having much more.' The landlord was adamant. 'You're out.' So they bought the pub. Out came their chequebooks and two cheques were duly signed. Come the morning the full horror of what they'd done came into sharp focus and they immediately called their bank to cancel the cheques only to find they'd not been cashed. Racing to the scene of the crime, there was the landlord holding both cheques, which O'Toole and Finch had the pleasure of tearing up. 'You two boys have got to behave yourselves,' he admonished. After that, the bar became a favourite haunt for both of them and when a year later the landlord died O'Toole and Finch were invited to the funeral. Arriving at the cemetery they gathered round the open grave with the other sobbing mourners until a woman gently tapped O'Toole on the shoulder to tell him they were at the wrong grave.

Joseph Losey remained convinced enough of O'Toole's potential to recommend him to Nicholas Ray, then casting a new film, *The Savage Innocents*. O'Toole was eager to work with the director of *Rebel Without a Cause*, but the whole experience ended up something of a personal disaster. The plot revolves around an Eskimo, played by Anthony Quinn, who runs foul of the law and is captured by a Canadian trooper, O'Toole. The camera unit had achieved some spectacular exterior footage in the Arctic zones of Canada and Greenland but the majority of filming took place on sets at Pinewood, where the snow was several tons of salt mix. Two polar bears brought in from Dublin Zoo to lend authenticity were deemed not white enough against the salt so had to be covered head to toe in peroxide, which drove them crazy.

With O'Toole's growing reputation for drinking and staying up all night the film company put in place contingency plans. At the time he and Siân were renting a fourth-floor flat in Bryanston Street, just behind Marble Arch. 'As second assistant I was delegated to go in the limo and wake him up and make sure he came out on time,' recalls David Tringham. Often Quinn would be in the same car and the two actors built up a rapport of sorts, but Tringham was witness to an important moment between them on set. 'There was a scene set in a storm, with the wind machine blasting snowflakes everywhere, and Quinn was a master of upstaging and Peter was still quite naive and physically not strong. When Ray shouted action they started to struggle and instead of being saved by the Mountie as planned it was Quinn who saved the Mountie, he upstaged Peter and Peter couldn't handle it because he didn't know how to. It was Quinn's force of personality. Peter learnt a valuable lesson from it because when I worked with him on *Lawrence of Arabia* he was much more confident.'

O'Toole's relationship with the maverick Ray was awkward at times, with the American failing to appreciate his sense of the absurd. With a script that was being rewritten every day, they were stuck with the problem of how the men were going to make a sledge to escape the snowy wastes. O'Toole helpfully suggested the Eskimo eat his character and make a sledge out of his bones and skin. 'We want a happy ending,' said Ray. 'Couldn't he whistle?' offered O'Toole.

They did become friendly enough for O'Toole to take Ray that summer of 1959 to Stratford to see a production of *Coriolanus* starring Laurence Olivier. While Ray thought Olivier 'unbelievable', the sheer force of his presence actually damaged the play; when he was off stage, 'It lost colour and became uninteresting.' Except for one young actor that Ray found fascinating. 'Who is that?' he asked. 'Next to me,' O'Toole answered, 'he is the best young actor in England.' It was Albert Finney.

The Savage Innocents ended badly for O'Toole when Ray decided that the Irish accent he'd used for the character was too strong and dubbed him with the appalling mid-Atlantic drawl of another actor. Incensed, O'Toole demanded his name be taken off the picture, since it was no longer the performance he had given. 'I don't want anything to do with it,' he bitterly complained to the press. 'As far as I'm concerned the whole thing is a shambles.'

One man determined that O'Toole would not suffer such professional discourtesy again was an American film producer by the name of Jules Buck. The son of a cigar-store owner on Broadway, Buck served as cameraman for the US Army Signal Corps during the Second World War, notably on the John Huston directed documentary *The Battle Of San Pietro* (1945). After the war, Huston encouraged Buck's Hollywood career, where he was assistant producer on the film noir classic *The Killers* (1946), which Huston co-wrote, and serving the same function on the Huston directed thriller *We Were Strangers* (1949). After producing several more films, including *Love Nest* (1951), featuring one of Marilyn Monroe's earliest appearances, Buck moved his young family to Europe, discouraged by the oppressive atmosphere sweeping Hollywood following Senator Joe McCarthy's Communist witch-hunt. He was the whole of his life a liberal idealist, but also a savvy operator when it came to business.

In London, Buck attended a performance of *The Long and the Short and the Tall* and immediately recognized the potential of O'Toole. He signed him up to an exclusive contract; henceforth if a film or theatre producer wanted to acquire the services of O'Toole they had to deal with Buck. Michael Deeley, an eager young filmmaker who later produced the iconic movies *The Italian Job*, *The Deer Hunter* and *Blade Runner*, worked for Buck in the early sixties and believes the partnership with O'Toole, which was to last almost twenty years, was a perfect match. 'Jules was very charming and knew how to get what he wanted. And I think he also knew how to handle Peter, he knew how to treat him. And there was great affection between them.'

Quickly Buck began to organize O'Toole's life, both private and professional, such as his tax affairs, which he had treated with a nonchalance bordering on contempt for years. It was a similar situation with his car, for which he had no licence. According to Siân, O'Toole had learned to drive on holiday in the Swiss Alps, though his manic driving style did tend to shred the nerves. He once fell asleep while driving on a motorway and woke up to find himself careering down the grass of the central reservation. 'There was nothing for it but to put my feet up on the dashboard and wait for the crash.' One friend who accepted a lift off O'Toole swore afterwards that she would never do so again. During the journey he ignored a keep left sign on the grounds that it was 'silly' and narrowly avoided driving down a flight of steps. 'He should never drive anything! He's lovely, but I thought we were going to die on that journey.'

Finally in the winter of 1959 he agreed with Buck that perhaps a driving licence might be in order. A professional instructor was hired and on the morning of the first lesson O'Toole was brimming with confidence, if a little hung over. Requested to execute a three-point turn, O'Toole took an unerringly long time over it, eventually connecting violently with a pillar. The shaken instructor requested to be driven back to the start and for O'Toole to withdraw from the vehicle. He then said a very firm goodbye and walked off. The solution was simple, O'Toole spent thirty shillings on an Irish driving licence, which was perfectly legal in the UK, and carried on regardless.

On the professional front, Buck set to steer O'Toole's career in the right direction and searching for a suitable film project landed upon a book by John Brophy set in the early 1900s entitled *The Day they Robbed the Bank of England*, about a group of Irish rebels who set out to plan the perfect robbery. O'Toole would be ideal casting for the leader of the gang, but the role didn't interest him. Instead he wanted to play their chief antagonist, an English Guards officer. Buck raised the cash for the film, but did feel that O'Toole needed a little outside help if he was going to make it in the movies. 'Do you just want to become a successful actor or do you want to be an international star,' he asked his client one day. 'Jules, I want in,' O'Toole answered. 'Right,' said Buck. 'You'd better have a nose job.'

The O'Toole nose was far from ugly or misshapen, it was just slightly bulbous on the end, but it gave his face character. What Buck was suggesting was just a trim, nothing dramatic, more of a clean-up operation. When his theatre friends heard what had happened there was a sense that he had sold out. 'It was a great nose, very sardonic,' recalls Phyllida Law. 'When he grinned it moved on his face, which is why they had it bobbed, of course, it would cause terrible shadows on a film set.' At Bristol, Phyllida can't recall O'Toole ever being self-conscious about it. 'I'm sure he wasn't. I can't imagine him being self-conscious about anything. No, it was a great nose, a wonderful nose, I was outraged when I heard he had it bobbed.' David Andrews was equally aghast when he saw it. 'Peter's nose was massive but it was beautifully proportioned, you could never say his nose was big, it was beautiful and I think they ruined it when they turned it into a horrible Hollywood snub.'

When it opened *The Day they Robbed the Bank of England* went virtually unnoticed, though the influential critic Dilys Powell wrote in the *Sunday Times* that O'Toole 'looks like being a gift to the British cinema as well as the theatre'. More importantly, the film provided a valuable lesson when he went to watch himself in rushes one day. 'I was horrified and for days afterwards I was posing and strutting about. It made me feel self-conscious, which is death for an actor.' From that day onwards O'Toole vowed never to see his rushes again.

While O'Toole was working steadily, Siân was spending most of her days alone in the Bryanston flat watching her career being ignored as Jules Buck talked of a future framed around O'Toole. Sometimes she wouldn't see him for days, a situation she reluctantly grew accustomed to. He was never going to be a straightforward nine to five guy, that she knew ('If you don't like me – leave me,' he'd say), but often he'd simply arrive drunk at 4am and expect her to make breakfast. O'Toole was so incredibly charismatic and fascinating and wonderful to be with that it made up for the long days and nights of depression and loneliness. His pursuit of pleasure and joy of living were irresistible. Quite often Siân didn't know what the hell he was going to do next. Once he showed up in a new sports car yelling, 'Get your passport, we're off.' He wanted to show her Venice, but it was cold and wet. After a few days they wanted sun and headed south towards Rome, except they took a wrong turn and ended up in Yugoslavia. It was the beginning of a grand mystery tour around Europe that took in Germany, Austria, Switzerland and Holland. For Siân each day was a challenge and a hilarious adventure, with O'Toole the perfect travelling companion, who seemed to draw people to him wherever they went, people who had no idea who he was.

When talk turned to marriage, Siân was warned by her friends and even acquaintances of O'Toole that her own burgeoning career would suffer, that he would be overbearing and suffocating. Kenneth Griffith held grave doubts, indeed told Siân to her face not to marry O'Toole. 'Understand, he is a genius, but he is not normal.' She ignored them all, preferring to choose love over fear, happiness over caution.

The proposal when it came was typically unorthodox, O'Toole grabbing Siân in the kitchen and stating, 'Have my children.' What could the poor girl do except agree. Thanks to Jules Buck, Siân managed to get a divorce, not an easy thing to do in those days, and in December 1959 she and O'Toole flew to Dublin for a low-key ceremony in the city's solitary registry office; actress Marie Kean acted as best man. Neither of their parents were present but both families expressed delight with the union. Following the ceremony the small party caught the evening performance at the famous Abbey Theatre and then went on a pub crawl, amassing well-wishers and friends along the way.

SEVEN

When twenty-nine-year-old Peter Hall was handed the reins at the Shakespeare Memorial Theatre in Stratford, one of the most prestigious repertory companies in the country, late in 1959, he was hailed as the new shining light of the theatre world. His first season was shaping up very nicely, with Paul Scofield agreeing to play two of Shakespeare's great roles: Shylock and Petruchio. Contracts were drawn up and duly signed. A couple of months before rehearsals were due to begin Scofield suddenly changed his mind and withdrew. Minus his leading man, Hall began a desperate search for a replacement.

The name of Peter O'Toole was already a familiar one to Hall, having seen him burn up the stage at Bristol as Hamlet. 'Peter as a young man had extraordinary animalism and wit, a kind of extraordinary anarchy in his spirit on the stage. He was one of the best Hamlets I've ever seen for that reason; he was dangerous, really dangerous.' What at first glance looked like a wild gamble, Hall decided to offer O'Toole Scofield's entire line of parts. At twenty-seven this would make him the youngest ever leading man at Stratford.

Before his hectic Shakespearean duties, Siân took O'Toole to Wales for a short break, and to introduce him to her relatives. He was an instant smash. The Phillips clan had scarcely seen anyone like him and many of the men folk stayed up all night sharing jars with him and shooting the breeze. But even a country cottage O'Toole could turn into a disaster area. One night he suddenly decided to do the cooking himself, although Siân had never seen him actually do anything in a kitchen before. He declared French toast a particular O'Toole speciality; minutes later the stove exploded into flames.

Arriving in Stratford the couple rented a picturesque Edwardian house called Mount Pleasant (immediately christened 'Mount Unpleasant' by O'Toole), not far from Ann Hathaway's cottage. Here O'Toole began preparations for his first major role, Shylock in *The Merchant of Venice*, poring over books on Jewish law and traditions, and reading the whole of the Old Testament. Actor Donald Douglas recalls that it was obvious from the beginning that O'Toole already had an aura of stardom about him. 'Not in a grand way, but full of charisma and confidence.' For Hall, the first thing he noticed was that the great O'Toole conk he'd seen at Bristol, which would have come in handy for Shylock, was no more, replaced 'by a delicate, almost retroussé nose.' When asked what on earth he had done, O'Toole replied, 'I'm going to be a film star.'

Mid-way through rehearsals for *Merchant*, Siân gave birth to a daughter, christened Kate, in honour of Katharine Hepburn. Barred from the birth, O'Toole turned up outside the maternity ward with several other drunken actors to serenade the new arrival, but Siân was hardly in the mood to receive such musical joy and couldn't wait for them to leave.

When O'Toole's parents came down to 'wet' the baby's head, father and son got customarily slaughtered. With everyone else upstairs in bed O'Toole junior lay spread-eagled on the floor, 'Not asleep, but crucified.' Patrick tried lifting his flagging son to his feet, but to no avail. Instead he opened another bottle and joined him on the floor. That's where the pair were found the following afternoon.

Hall's inaugural Stratford season had begun with a modest

production of *The Two Gentlemen of Verona* at the beginning of April 1960. But the real fireworks were due to begin not long later with O'Toole's Shylock. Would Hall's gamble pay off? As the first night drew near O'Toole began to feel the pressure, fully aware of its importance, that the critics could make or break him. One morning the nerves got so bad he stayed cooped up in bed rather than attend rehearsals. When the theatre rang asking after his wellbeing he refused to take the call. On the morning of the opening night, 12 April, O'Toole was not on speaking terms with anyone, staying wrapped up in bed, insulated from the outside world until late in the afternoon when he emerged all energy and fireballs, running round the house, downing endless cups of tea, looking at his watch and generally hurrying everyone else along. Siân would later describe him that day as deliberately perching himself on the edge of a cliff, only at the last minute deciding to pull back.

Of course the performance was a triumph; standing ovations and untold curtain calls. Siân sat in that vast auditorium with tears welling up, it was the moment she realized whatever hell or madness this sod might drag her through, here was a talent worth protecting and nurturing. Rushing back home, she began to organize the after-show party but of O'Toole there was no sign. He duly turned up hours later when all the guests had gone having wandered around fields for hours in the dark searching for that 'haystack' of dung that had been his bed years before. In his mind he had perhaps turned it into a symbol for a past that after tonight's triumph would soon be out of reach.

O'Toole's performance met with near universal praise. Bernard Levin called it 'a radiant masterpiece', and Mervyn Jones in the *Tribune* wrote: 'Peter O'Toole gives a performance as Shylock that will stand as a great chapter in theatre history.' This was not the grotesque and crude cliché Jew of previous interpretations. For fellow cast member Donald Douglas it was a thrilling new interpretation. 'He brought tremendous naturalism to the role. When he said to Tubal, "Ah, thou sticks a dagger in me!" It was as if he'd said, "Don't rub it in!" In a low key, over the shoulder way.' For audiences used to seeing older Shylocks, this was a young, vibrant and lusty Shylock. Dangerous and magnetic, too. O'Toole entranced audiences, drawing their eye even when only sitting and sharpening his knife on the sole of his shoe. Certainly Hall was fully vindicated in his choice, calling O'Toole 'mesmeric' in the role. 'On opening night it was clear a new star had arrived.'

One young actor lucky enough to see the production was Derek Fowlds, later a popular actor on British television (*Yes Minister*, *Heartbeat*), and he's never forgotten it. 'O'Toole's is still the best Shylock I ever saw. I thought it was the most electric performance I'd ever seen. He was a very dangerous actor, very exciting to watch.'

In those days most of the company were heavy drinkers and smokers; actors would store a bottle of beer away for the interval, no one raised an eyebrow, it was the done thing. Stephen Thorne, who had been at Stratford for three years, recalls watching O'Toole arrive in the wings with a cigarette in one hand and half a bottle of whisky in the other. He'd take a swig of the whisky and then put the bottle and the spent cigarette butt into the fire bucket before coming on. 'On several occasions he would walk on having taken his last drag of the cigarette and turn up stage and blow the smoke into the face of the nearest actor as he passed. And you'd think, this is extraordinary behaviour, but then he would give this amazing performance.' Sometimes, as the whole company waited onstage for his final entrance, O'Toole would lift up his robe to reveal a pair of red underpants. 'He'd quickly drop the robe again as he strode on,' reports Donald Douglas. 'I reckon it probably gave him an extra bit of adrenalin!'

O'Toole used to get up to all sorts in the wings. One of his best pranks was at Bristol and his victim was a young actress called Wendy Williams. At one point in the play Wendy had to wistfully look off into the wings where O'Toole was ready to come on, only the lighting was such that all she could see was his silhouette. One night she was looking off when O'Toole methodically and quite deliberately began to undo his flies and produce a hefty and erect phallus. Wendy watched with mounting incredulity as he proceeded to snip the top off with a pair of scissors and pop it in his mouth, at which point she fainted. There was pandemonium as people rushed to see what was wrong. Coming round, she pointed in the direction of the wings – 'Peter! Peter!'

O'Toole pleaded ignorance. 'What's up with Wendy?'

'She's fainted,' said one of the actors. 'What were you doing?'

O'Toole smiled. 'I was eating a banana.'

While drinking was tolerated backstage, the real boozing came after the performance and usually in the nearby Black Swan pub, otherwise known as the Dirty Duck. There O'Toole would regularly down a yard of ale, that's two and a half pints. 'That was his party trick,' says Thorne. Returning to Stratford late in the sixties he attempted to repeat the feat, without success. 'Either I wasn't that parched or my stomach had shrunk.'

The Black Swan had a special dispensation to stay open late for the actors and so it became everyone's regular. After closing time the doors would be locked and the drinking carried on until two or three in the morning, when people left to continue boozing round somebody's house, usually at the prompting of O'Toole. 'For the younger and impressionable members of the company, myself included, it was rather like seagulls following the plough,' recalls Thorne. 'Drinking after hours in the Duck and going to parties, you knew you were safe if O'Toole was there, because you knew there was someone who took care of anything that came up. He was a natural leader, without being obvious, he just was.'

Take for example the party Thorne held at the cottage he was renting. In the early hours of the morning there was a furious banging on the front door. O'Toole was nearest and opened it to reveal an old man hammering away with the handle of a sickle. 'Oh my God, who is this, Father Time.' The man didn't see the joke, he was demanding that everybody shut up because he couldn't sleep. O'Toole suggested the silly sod close his windows and slammed the door shut and the party carried on. Half an hour later there was another knock at the back door this time, it was two policemen demanding to see whoever it was who had the altercation with the old man. O'Toole was sent for and led by the coppers into the backyard. 'Ten minutes later somebody peered through the curtains to see how they were getting on,' says Thorne. 'And Peter had a bottle of Scotch and three glasses and the policemen were sitting down drinking and laughing with him. And then off they went quietly home and that was that.'

It was at Stratford where O'Toole's reputation as a hell-raiser was sealed and he earned the title of 'the wild man of Stratford'. At one after-show party he held court on stage sitting on a throne, sustained by two pedal bins on either side of him, one full of beer, the other of hard liquor into which he would alternately scoop a pint mug. Ex-RADA chum Roy Kinnear once watched O'Toole down a bottle of whisky without pausing for breath. It was behaviour like this that made people flock to the town in the hope of seeing this outrageous bunch of actors in the flesh. At one point, according to Stephen Thorne, O'Toole was told by Peter Hall that he was a bad influence on the company. 'That didn't go down very well with Peter, I can tell you.'

Not everyone in the company was so taken by its new star. Denholm Elliott, himself a boozer, was so nervous around the bombastic O'Toole that he could hardly bear to be in the same room. 'I get awfully nervous with the kind of actor who looks as though he might be about to hit you, even though he never does.' On-stage there was little respite, with Elliott finding O'Toole 'very, very difficult' to perform with. 'He acts at you and it becomes a sort of battle. He is just completely overpowering.'

It is interesting to note at this juncture how the O'Toole 'personality', for he was above everything else a personality, did seem to grate with some people. While a good deal of his colleagues seem to have found him a charismatic actor, to others he was a narcissistic and ruthless prima donna. There is a sense here that O'Toole was already becoming affected by power and success, which only served to accentuate the two extremes of his persona.

Another actor who found O'Toole, shall we say, a little intimidating, was a young Ian Holm. 'Probably because he was so melodramatically different, so alien to me. He had an independent manner, confidence, star quality and an air of ruined glory.' Holm recalled Peter Hall confiding in him that he thought O'Toole had the 'sparks of genius', even though he was a loose cannon when it came to authority. 'There was something unconsciously gladiatorial and threatening about him,' said Holm. 'I developed into a company man and chipped in, whereas O'Toole never seemed as if he could take direction, just telling the director how he was going to do a scene, and then doing it. He was an enigma wrapped in charisma and sprinkled with booze.' Holm theorized that while the booze encouraged O'Toole's gift, it also in the end dissolved his talent, 'helping to create the louche, genially insolent shaman that he became. In many ways he was an actor from the nineteenth century; strangely ridiculous, often riveting, and unpredictably raw.'

Other actors, though, felt instinctively drawn to O'Toole, such as Dublin-born Jack MacGowran, a former member of the Abbey Theatre. MacGowran liked his liquor every bit as much as O'Toole and often exhibited the most bizarre behaviour. 'I remember one evening,' says Stephen Thorne, 'MacGowran having to be carried across a bridge by Peter because he was fearful there were trolls underneath and he wouldn't cross back into Stratford unless he was carried.'

By this stage O'Toole's drinking had become reckless. Playing Shylock one night, during the intense court scene, O'Toole spied a packet of fags close to the front of the stage. 'I was wondering what they were doing there, my cue came and I was off, "Now we have expressed our darker purpose . . ." It was the wrong play. I'd gone into *King Lear*.'

A frazzled brain was one thing, but Siân genuinely feared for his survival beyond the season. She might wake and find him asleep downstairs intoxicated in an armchair, having obviously driven back home from the pub or the theatre drunk. There were rows, sometimes lasting hours. After one heated argument Siân discovered O'Toole walking precariously on the roof of the house. Surely this couldn't continue if Siân was to keep her sanity. Pretty quickly in their relationship Siân had identified a dark side in O'Toole's psyche, one that enjoyed leaving chaos in his wake. He was someone who expected the household to run to his volatile whim and Siân came to understand that 'clever women never nagged. Clever women dodged the flying crockery and went away to where they could get some peaceful sleep and never in the morning referred to the excesses of the night before.'

It was difficult sometimes. When drunk, O'Toole could be savage in the things he said, and Siân learnt quickly not to take personally the hurtful diatribes aimed in her direction whenever her husband was under the influence. He also developed an unreasonable objection to her previous sex life; the sheer temerity of having had lovers before they'd even met. O'Toole would think nothing of raising the subject, sometimes in the company of others, resulting in her public humiliation.

At one point she could take it no longer and left. O'Toole's old

RADA colleague Gary Raymond was staying with them in Stratford at the time. 'They had this almighty row and her parents came to pick her up from Wales. Peter was distraught, really quite distraught. He was potty about Siân, he really was.' She returned after a few days.

Professionally O'Toole was proving to be the hit of the season, with people queuing up all night for tickets to see him. In his *Daily Express* column Peter Evans posed the question: 'Is this the next Olivier?' It would have been quite natural for O'Toole to have gone off on some raving ego trip, but Stephen Thorne saw no real noticeable change in him. 'I think Peter Hall was a bit nonplussed by it all, though, in that he rather thought that the spotlight would be on him as the new leading light of Stratford, and O'Toole came along and swept the whole thing out of his grasp.'

The BBC even sent an interviewer down to profile this rising star, though it was immediately clear the fellow hadn't done much research. 'Well, what have you done?'

'Eh,' said a startled O'Toole.

'Let's see,' he scanned his rough notes. 'There was that army thing. Come on, come on, what else have you done?'

O'Toole had had enough of this. 'Well, I played the Dame in *Puss in Boots* once.'

The BBC man's face turned sour. 'Look, we don't have to do this interview, you know.'

'In that case, I suggest you fuck off.'

O'Toole's second leading role of the season was Petruchio in *The Taming of the Shrew*. Hall had cast fifty-two-year-old Dame Peggy Ashcroft opposite him as Kate, much to the actress's discomfort – she felt she was far too old. Her misgivings soon evaporated when they played a few scenes together and sparks flew. O'Toole warmed immediately to Peggy upon discovering a shared passion for cricket. One great Peggy story has her appearing in a matinee when England were playing at Lord's: the stage manager whispered from the wings, 'All out for a hundred and twenty,' and she blasted out, 'Oh fuck!' in the middle of her lines.

Rehearsals, however, did not go well when O'Toole clashed with director John Barton. He went on to have a distinguished career in the theatre, but was then a junior don from Cambridge who Hall had invited to join him at the Memorial Theatre. While Barton had some excellent ideas, it was his overly academic approach, the intellectualizing of everything, that O'Toole took umbrage with. 'Peter became difficult,' remembers Stephen Thorne. 'Not taking direction or suggestions. And then I think Dame Peggy realized that unless something was done the production was going to collapse in a great heap. In the end Jack MacGowran went to see Peter Hall and said, "If John Barton doesn't go, we do." ' Reluctantly Hall had to take over the final stages of rehearsal.

The production was another huge success when it opened that June. O'Toole's on-stage chemistry with Peggy was positively electric, helped greatly by the fact she had developed real romantic feelings for him. Susan Engel came to see her old Bristol colleague and heard the gossip about Peggy. 'She was in love with him, she worshipped him and she adored him. And she loved acting with him because he was so superb as Petruchio. He had the audience in the palm of his hand. It was dazzling.'

It was a flamboyant performance, no doubt. 'Full of hell raiser energy and chutzpah,' recalls Donald Douglas. In the wedding scene O'Toole arrived cheerfully playing the bagpipes. London theatre critic Felix Barker declared O'Toole a major actor in the making, 'An actor with so much personal magnetism that he seems to be centre stage even when he is half hidden in the wings.' Stephen Thorne can attest to that, there was something almost supernatural about O'Toole. 'He had this sort of force field round him. On the stage you could almost feel the vibrations coming from him. It was quite extraordinary because it was almost touchable.'

It didn't take long for O'Toole's name to begin to spread further than the environs of Stratford and the closeted theatrical world. Eddie Fisher, the husband of Elizabeth Taylor, came backstage one night with a tantalizing offer to play opposite his wife as Count Vronsky in a planned film version of Tolstoy's *Anna Karenina*. O'Toole liked to say that he sped down to London to see Liz in her suite at the Dorchester, 'took forty quid off her in blackjack and said I'd be delighted'. In the end the project never materialized.

It wasn't just his name that was being spoken about, but the boozing, too. A reporter for the *Evening Standard* newspaper argued that while O'Toole was predicted to become one of the country's greatest actors, one needed to add the proviso – if he doesn't destroy himself first. O'Toole was having none of it. 'I get drunk and disorderly and all that, but I don't really think it's true that there is any danger of me destroying myself.' Yes, he admitted to a bit of hell-raising. 'How often do I get drunk and smash up the furniture! Oh, not more than three or four times a day.' Asked what he got from being drunk, he replied: 'A bloody hangover and grim looks from the missus.'

By July, however, O'Toole's drinking had finally caught up with him and he began to suffer horrendous hangovers and severe stomach pains. Worried, he saw a specialist who told him to stop drinking, or at least rein it in significantly. For the next few weeks he made a great show of drinking nothing but milk.

On stage, too, things were unravelling when he was cast in the relatively minor role of the deformed slave Thersites in *Troilus and Cressida*. O'Toole did not enjoy the experience. 'I don't think he was particularly happy with Thersites,' recalls Donald Douglas. 'Which surprised everyone, as it seemed like a perfect opportunity to give a totally different performance, away from the swagger of Petruchio and the tragedy of Shylock.' In the end he didn't quite know what to do with the character, and perhaps Hall didn't know what to do with O'Toole in it, but he looked extraordinary in his make-up, with his flesh covered in pustules and scabs. The critics certainly sensed the actor's unease, using words such as 'disappointing', 'miscast' and 'ranting' to describe his performance. O'Toole conceded the failure was all his own making. 'I couldn't make the words flesh.' Perhaps he was only truly happy now when leading from the front.

Overall the season had been a huge success, and not just on the stage. In previous years at the Memorial Theatre there had been a highly visible hierarchy, you had the star actors at the top, a sort of middle rank and then everyone else, the bit-part players and the spear carriers. The O'Toole season was really the first breaking of that privileged order. 'In the old days you didn't really instigate conversations with the stars,' recalls Stephen Thorne. 'It was almost like being at public school, calling the top stars sir until you were told otherwise. The top billing and the lower orders were also paid at separate times, and after the first night there was a party for the stars while the rest of the company went to the wardrobe party. And it was O'Toole and Peggy Ashcroft who stopped all that, who said bollocks to that, we're going to the wardrobe party with everybody else. And so those star parties fell into abeyance. It was the beginning of the actual ensemble, of we're all in it together.'

Shortly before the season closed Peter Hall addressed the entire company, revealing his bold plan to turn Stratford's six-month Shakespeare festival into a year-long operation built around a permanent company, with a base in London that also handled contemporary work from home and abroad. To achieve this goal Hall needed Arts Council subsidies and stars to make sure the inaugural productions were a success. Within days both

O'Toole and Peggy Ashcroft had committed themselves to the creation of what was soon to become officially known as the Royal Shakespeare Company. However, an American tycoon and the Croydon-born son of Quakers were about to throw a major spanner into the works.

EIGHT

T. E. Lawrence wanted nothing to do with the movies. When it was mooted in the 1930s that the renowned producer Alexander Korda was preparing a film of his life, Lawrence made it known that he had no wish at all to be 'celluloided'. This British scholar and soldier who mobilized the Arab revolt against the Turkish occupying army in the First World War and wrote about his exploits in his book *The Seven Pillars of Wisdom* had for years been trying to find anonymity from a world that had dubbed him Lawrence of Arabia and turned him into a national figure. When in 1935 this remarkable man died as a result of a motorcycle accident, aged just forty-six, Korda pressed ahead with the project and Laurence Olivier, Robert Donat and Leslie Howard all tested for the role. Eventually Korda lost interest and after several other abortive attempts to bring Lawrence's famed exploits to the screen it emerged in 1955 that Terence Rattigan had written a screenplay to be directed by Anthony Asquith. With financial backing from the Rank Organization, the man chosen to play Lawrence was Dirk Bogarde, then Britain's top box-office attraction. For the next year Bogarde immersed himself in the life of Lawrence, but while Asquith was in Iraq scouting locations Rank unexpectedly pulled the plug. No reason was ever given. At least Rattigan managed to make some use of his screenplay, reworking it into a stage play, *Ross*, that featured Alec Guinness as

Lawrence. Bogarde, however, took the film's cancellation badly, declaring it to be 'my bitterest disappointment'.

At much the same time David Lean had been out in India trying to set up a film about Gandhi, but budgetary concerns and logistical problems proved insurmountable and he turned his attention instead to Lawrence, a childhood idol. After the huge success of 1957's *The Bridge on the River Kwai*, Lean and his producer Sam Spiegel were hot property and in February 1960 they purchased the screen rights to *Seven Pillars of Wisdom*.

Spiegel wanted Marlon Brando to play Lawrence, having worked well with the temperamental star on the classic *On the Waterfront*. Lean wasn't so sure, anxious about his ego and that the film might turn into 'Brando of Arabia'. In any case, Brando turned the job down. For a while Richard Burton and Anthony Perkins were considered, and every week Lean was pestered by phone calls from Montgomery Clift begging to play Lawrence. Lean, however, had come to an important decision. In life Lawrence was very much an enigma, even to himself, so it made sense to cast an unknown actor rather than an internationally recognized star. The man chosen was Albert Finney, who had just completed his first lead role in a film, *Saturday Night and Sunday Morning*, playing working-class antihero Arthur Seaton.

Finney's screen test for *Lawrence of Arabia* at the MGM studios in Borehamwood in August 1960 must rank as the most elaborate in movie history. Lasting a total of twenty minutes, it took four days to shoot at a cost of thousands of pounds, with its elaborate sets and costumes. Both Lean and Spiegel expressed delight at the result and Finney was formally offered the part, only to ultimately turn it down when he learnt he would have to sign a multi-picture contract with Spiegel that would see him tied down to the American producer for years.

Left with no lead actor, Lean took drastic action. 'I started to spend all of my days in the cinema watching as many films as possible. I was going from one cinema to the other, everywhere in London.' *The Day they Robbed the Bank of England* just happened to be playing and Lean caught an afternoon performance. He had never seen nor heard of the young actor playing a Guards officer but he had an interesting face and could clearly act. There was something else, too, that indefinable quality that actors, however good they may be, either have or haven't got – screen presence. Could he be Lawrence? Lean was convinced of it. Wasting no time, he put in a call to Spiegel. 'Sam, I've got him.'

'What's his name?'

'Peter O'Toole.'

There was a slight pause. Then, 'He's no good.'

'What do you mean, he's no good.'

'I tell you he's no good. I just know it.'

O'Toole was still playing Shylock in repertory at Stratford when Lean contacted him to set up a meeting in London. He arrived in the full beard he'd grown for the part and scraggy hair dyed black. With his hawk-like features Lean scrutinized the figure in front of him before finally speaking. 'Peter, what do you look like underneath all that stuff?'

'I'm quite fair-haired, really.'

Lean appeared only slightly convinced. 'Well, I saw you in a film called *The Day they Robbed the Bank of England* and I thought you didn't put a foot wrong. And I really want you to do Lawrence.'

'Who's the producer?' asked O'Toole.

'Sam Spiegel.'

'Not a chance.'

Lean smiled and reassured O'Toole that everything was going to be fine, that he was going to fight hard for him. And that's exactly what Lean did, persistently badgering Spiegel. 'Look, Sam, what do you want to do, we haven't got Finney, we haven't

got anybody! I think Peter will be wonderful. I want to test him.'
Spiegel still cast something of a gloomy figure but Lean got his
way and O'Toole was auditioned on 7 November 1960. Instead
of the four days that Finney got, O'Toole was tested over the
course of a single day, reciting lines from *Seven Pillars of Wisdom*
and repeating bits of dialogue Lean threw at him from behind
the camera. After it was over Lean turned to Spiegel in buoyant
mood. 'Look, Sam, look at it, come on!' But the tycoon still remained unconvinced and suggested a couple of new candidates.
'I've forgotten who they were,' said Lean years later. 'But hopeless, hopeless, hopeless. In the end he finally had to agree.' It was
only much later that Lean discovered Spiegel's reluctance to cast
O'Toole was due to his earlier encounter with the actor. 'Sam
thought I was a tearaway. He thought I lived up a tree. He didn't
want to have to go looking for me every day with a net.'

When O'Toole was finally offered the role by Spiegel, he
couldn't resist one last joke, asking, 'Is it a speaking part?'

So that's Lean's story of how O'Toole came to be Lawrence,
but there is another tale suggesting that it was largely down to
the persuasive powers of Jules Buck. And there is a witness,
Michael Deeley. At the time Deeley worked for the MCA agency
in London and was in the office during the casting of *Lawrence*.
'When Jules heard that Finney's people were sticking on the
issue of options he went to see Spiegel, who he had worked with
in Hollywood, and said, "I think my boy will be better, and he'll
give you the options." And so O'Toole signed the contract that
Finney had refused.'

Whatever the truth, O'Toole's fee was a grand £12,500 (something like £125,000 in today's money) and to celebrate he waltzed
into the Salisbury and slammed £150 on the bar. For the rest of
the day the drinks were on him. There is also a story of O'Toole
being rushed over to New York to be paraded in front of the
big shots at Columbia, the studio bankrolling the picture. 'When

I look at you,' one of the suits said, 'I see six million dollars.' 'How'd you like a punch up the throat?' O'Toole replied. It wasn't his scene at all. 'It made me feel like a prize bull.'

In the midst of all this celebrating, O'Toole knew deep down that he couldn't possibly play Lawrence and shouldn't have accepted it. The reason was simple, he had already made an agreement with Peter Hall to lead the Royal Shakespeare Company's inaugural season in London at the Aldwych, reprising his Stratford successes of Shylock and Petruchio, as well as taking on an exciting fresh challenge. Hall had managed the coup of securing the rights to Jean Anouilh's new historical play *Becket*, a huge hit in France, over the heads of every West End impresario. O'Toole would play Henry II opposite his old Bristol colleague Eric Porter in the title role. Hall never forgot the day O'Toole walked into his office to announce that he'd been offered *Lawrence of Arabia* and simply had to do it.

That Hall wasn't entirely happy with the situation is an understatement, he was depending on O'Toole and refused to release him from his contract. Spiegel, one of the wiliest operators in Hollywood, advised O'Toole to 'walk and let them sue you'. It was enough to make Hall think twice, he couldn't risk the financial implications of a probably lengthy court case. 'So Peter nearly wrecked the start of the RSC,' Hall later claimed. 'He was one of the staunchest people to commit to the Company and suddenly he was gone.' Theatre director William Gaskill recalls Peter Hall telling him that after it was all over and O'Toole had got what he wanted he had the nerve to say: 'Still friends?' Or words to that effect. 'Peter Hall was absolutely furious,' says Gaskill. 'Because it altered the whole nature of the RSC. If Peter had been leading the company it would have been a different company. That incident characterized the RSC ever after, I think, because when you have an actor of remarkable talent, it always makes a difference, it gives colour and accent to the whole work. And if you have

Eric Porter and Patrick Wymark, you settle for something different, something less exciting, perhaps more manageable, perhaps finally better, I don't know, but you lose the sheer excitement of the actor on stage.'

Not surprisingly Hall and O'Toole would never work together again, and although O'Toole always harboured a slice of guilt over the course of action he took there remained inside him an enmity towards the theatrical knight. As late as 2005 during the shooting of *Venus* O'Toole still spoke of Hall in disparaging terms and one day on the set when someone brought in Hall's autobiography he tore it in two like a strong man at the fair.

With the role of Lawrence safely in his pocket, O'Toole settled down to celebrate the festive season with Siân, presenting her on Christmas morning with a brand-new Morris Minor, a huge ribbon neatly wrapped round the bonnet. Thrilled by the gift, if apprehensive of the prospect of more terror-stricken journeys, Siân hardly had time to take it for a spin round the block when O'Toole commandeered the vehicle for a sentimental journey up to Bristol to bid the city farewell before leaving for Jordan. That night Siân received a phone call from the police explaining that O'Toole had been arrested and was currently keeping one of the cells warm. Pissed, O'Toole had rammed the back of a squad car. Siân never did see her Morris Minor again; it went to that great scrap heap in the sky of cars O'Toole had wrecked.

O'Toole's arrival in Jordan, four months prior to the start of filming in May, was accompanied by a massive hangover. It would be his last for quite a considerable time. As the film's technical adviser, Spiegel had hired the British diplomat Anthony Nutting, who had a peerless reputation in the Middle East and had successfully negotiated with King Hussein the use of Jordan as the film's main location, along with the participation of its army. Nutting had another important function, to keep O'Toole off the bottle, and having seen him arrive in Jordan looking more than a little bit the worse for wear decided that a stern lecture was in order. 'Look, if you don't stay sober you're going to leave Jordan on your arse. You're the only actor we've got for Lawrence, and if you get bundled home, that's the end of the film, and that's probably the end of you. So you'd better behave yourself.'

O'Toole came to admire Nutting enormously and tried his best not to let him down. As his guide to the history of Jordan and the ways of the desert, Nutting arranged for the actor to stay for a time with the Bedouin and travel across the desert with a camel patrol, sleeping rough under the stars, just as Lawrence had done. O'Toole soaked it all up. Where another actor might have cracked having to exist in the desert for three months before even a foot of celluloid was exposed, 'Peter sniffed a battle and responded to it', according to Beverley Cross, the English playwright Lean had hired as 'continuity writer'. Cross had carried out his own research into Lawrence, 'But Peter must have read every single word written by and about Lawrence – twice.' There was also the Jordanian heat to contend with, so hot that it physically hurt. 'But within a month I adjusted,' said O'Toole.

One of the principal reasons for O'Toole's early arrival was to give him plenty of time to master riding a camel, although he heard it from someone that no one in fact can ride a camel, that it was impossible. 'All that you can do is to find a beast whose discomfort you can tolerate.' His teacher was a sergeant from the Jordanian army and at first the lessons played havoc with O'Toole's 'delicate Irish arse'. Becoming more proficient the two of them would ride out into the sand dunes for hours.

O'Toole was out somewhere riding his camel when Zia Mohyeddin arrived on location. Mohyeddin, a Pakistan-born actor trained at RADA, had been cast as Tafas, Lawrence's guide who is famously killed at the well, and as such was also required to be proficient in a camel saddle. Late in the afternoon, Mohyeddin was sitting in his tent brooding about the forthcoming ordeal when O'Toole walked in with a welcoming smile. 'O, that I were a glove upon that hand that I might touch that cheek,' he boomed. It was a wonderful welcoming gesture and tribute to Mohyeddin, who had recently played Romeo at Stratford under the direction of Peter Hall.

The next day Mohyeddin was invited to O'Toole's well-furnished tent to go through their lines. 'Around mid-day I suggested that it was time for a cold beer. Peter looked at his trainer as if to say, What are we to do? The trainer said he would see if he could organize something. He returned after a while bringing me a tankard full of cold lager. "Go ahead," Peter said. "What about you?" I asked. He stroked his chin thoughtfully before saying, "I don't think I feel like it." I was taken aback. I had heard many tales about his drinking capacity. It was rumoured in the Buxton club that he could out-drink anyone. I felt a bit guilty sipping the liquid offered to me.' Throughout his stay on the film Mohyeddin never once saw O'Toole partake of any alcohol. 'His trainer, who stayed with him like a bodyguard, had apparently been instructed to see to it that he kept to his vow to remain on the wagon.'

After a week of camel riding all Mohyeddin had learned was how to trot. 'Peter was already claiming that he was about to acquire the knack of galloping. We were told not to use our reins and try to feel being one with the camel. We had to ride two hours in the morning and two in the late afternoon.'

It seemed to Mohyeddin that when O'Toole wasn't preoccupied with his camel training, he was deep in preparation about how he was going to play Lawrence. At O'Toole's insistence Hugh Miller, one of his favourite teachers from RADA, had been brought out to Jordan as the film's dialogue coach; his primary function to assist O'Toole with his speech. Miller was courteous enough to allow Mohyeddin to be present when he conducted his initial sessions with O'Toole. 'Peter read out his lines and Miller interrupted him only when he felt that Peter was not inflecting the right word. I was sitting next to Hugh Miller at dinner one evening, Peter wasn't around, and I asked him if Peter's speech was far removed from that of T. E. Lawrence. "Mmm . . . No," he said. "I wouldn't say that, but Peter tends to flatten his vowels now and then, and we are trying to sort that out." Peter worked assiduously with his coach. After dinner, other people either played cards or exchanged anecdotes or discussed their ailments, but Peter would sit with Miller in his tent and be engrossed in the script. It was evident that he was more than determined to spend every ounce of his energy in building up Lawrence.'

The film unit had set up base at a dilapidated army barracks in the Jordanian city of Aqaba, at the north-eastern tip of the Red Sea. A barbed-wire fence separated Aqaba from Eilat, the Israeli seaside resort. 'You could see plump ladies swimming or sunbathing on the sand,' recalls Mohyeddin. 'Peter would sometimes scan the scene through his field glasses. If he ever spotted a "tasty chick", as he put it, he would lend his glasses to me to share the view.'

While there were a few air-conditioned Nissen huts, the majority of the unit lived in two-man canvas tents with a partition and a fly-screen door. The wooden floor was reinforced by bits of balsa wood stuck around the edges to stop the scorpions getting in at night. Tony Rimmington, the assistant art director, recalls that the man sharing his tent caught yellow jaundice and had to be flown back to England. The heat was so draining that you had to take salt tablets every day. 'I collapsed once simply because I hadn't taken my salt tablet,' recalls Rimmington. 'It was rough.' But as Lean observed, 'Physical discomfort is the price of authenticity.' Lean, however, did insist on shipping over his air-conditioned Rolls-Royce.

As the start of filming approached, some of the cast began to assemble in Jordan. The integral role of Sherif Ali had first been offered to Horst Buchholz, one of the stars of *The Magnificent Seven*. When prior work commitments ruled him out, Lean chose Alain Delon. Again conflicting schedules got in the way. His replacement was another French actor, Maurice Ronet, but when he arrived in Aqaba it was very quickly apparent that he spoke with a very heavy accent. 'David Lean was a bit perturbed about it,' remembers Mohyeddin. 'He asked me and Peter to spend some time with him in the evenings. "See if you can straighten out his speech a bit," he said. Scripts in hand, we used to go over his lines. Ronet tried, and he tried hard, but could not manage to "straighten out his speech".'

After a few days O'Toole got bored and when asked by Lean how Ronet was getting on said, 'Ask Zia, he has been conducting most of the lessons. I think he's a bit poncey.' By this time another young actor had arrived. His name was Omar Sharif. A big star in his native Egypt, he'd been brought in to play a comparatively small role. David Tringham, the film's second assistant director, remembers the impact Sharif made when he arrived at the Aqaba camp. 'All the Arab workers knew him and were following him, it was amazing to see, he just strode along with real regal bearing like, I'm a star.'

Tringham stood and watched as Lean made Ronet and Sharif run through a scene together. 'Maurice did one page of dialogue and David said, "Umm, that's good," looking very intense, with those jumbo ears like an African elephant. "Umm, now, let's just change it a minute. Omar, you do the lines and Maurice, you just stand there, umm, yes, mmm." And afterwards I think David whispered to one of his assistants, we've got our Ali. So they paid off Maurice Ronet.'

O'Toole was introduced to his new co-star probably later that same day and the first thing that struck him was that nobody in the world could possibly be called Omar Sharif. 'Your name must be Fred.' Henceforth Sharif was known as Cairo Fred.

For a short while Siân visited the location. Prior to her arrival Mohyeddin had enjoyed hours of sitting with O'Toole in his tent 'chatting' about life and literature and learning and actors and the London Theatre. 'He was fond of holding forth. Chatting is not the right word. He held forth. I was mostly a silent listener. I would offer an opinion now and then, but he remained much too absorbed in whatever he was saying ever to register it.'

After Siân's arrival the scene changed, Mohyeddin's long chats with O'Toole became less frequent. Instead Siân would invite him to join them over lunch or dinner. 'She was a remarkably self-possessed lady,' recalls Mohyeddin, 'who made sure never to give the impression that she was on location to keep an eye on Peter. She had a stately presence and a calm demeanour. It was interesting to note that Peter, who spoke and behaved like an upper-middle-class chap, turned into a devil may care, flamboyant Irishman in her presence. Whether it was an act he put on for me, or whether he wanted to send up the sophisticated etiquette of Siân, I don't know. Siân was an actress of no mean standing, but whenever there was talk of a play or a performance, she would offer her opinion guardedly as though she was unsure that what she was saying would meet with Peter's approval.'

One evening they all walked along the beach after dinner. The sea was calm and the moon shone heavily on the bobbing waves. Inspired by the moment, Siân began to recite the famous Dylan Thomas poem 'Do not go gentle into that good night'. Mohyeddin recalls she spoke the lines beautifully, but then stopped. 'You do it, Peter,' she pleaded. 'You do it so much better . . . go on, darling.' O'Toole's version was pure Irish blarney. 'I was in fits,' says Mohyeddin. 'Siân laughed as much as was befitting. She seemed to want to live up to his expectations at every moment. To be honest, there was something slightly odd about their relationship. It was too well stage-managed. I wasn't too surprised when I learned, some years later, that they had parted.'

Principal photography on *Lawrence of Arabia* began on 15 May 1961 in a remote region of the desert called Jebel el Tubeiq. On that very first day Lean walked purposefully over to where O'Toole was standing and declared, 'Pete, this is the beginning of a great adventure.' Those words proved something of an understatement.

Mohyeddin has never forgotten that opening day of shooting. When Lean cried action for the very first time he and O'Toole had to ride their camels towards a mark and then stop. 'Peter takes a gulp from his canteen and then offers it to me. I don't take it. He insists that I do and I say something like, I am a Bedouin, I don't need it. "Cut," shouts Lean. He was obviously not satisfied. "Let's do it again," he said tersely. There were seventeen if not nineteen takes. Peter was sweating and so was I. After the first two or three takes Lean didn't give us any specific directions. "Let's try it once more," he would say. And we went on until we heard him say, "All right, chaps, that's a wrap." '

When it was time for Mohyeddin to say goodbye to Lean after he had finished his work on the picture, the actor found him quite relaxed. His face was less stern, now. 'I think you'll like your work when you see it on the screen,' he said with his winsome smile.

'May I ask you something?' said Mohyeddin. Lean nodded. 'What was it that I was doing wrong on the first day of the shoot? Please tell me now.'

'Oh,' Lean chuckled. 'It was a bit of a joke. I wanted Peter to realize that filming is going to be a bitch of a nightmare. I just wanted to knock the wind out of his sails.'

The impression of Peter O'Toole that Zia took back to

London with him was that of a man totally absorbed in himself, an extremely self-centred person. 'Later on I changed my view. Peter was ambitious, more ambitious than any other actor I had ever come across. His was the kind of ambition that brooks no obstacles. He wanted to pluck the stars and put them in his pocket. He wanted to own the world and that is not a bad thing for a young actor to desire.'

The logistics of shooting in isolated places like Jebel el Tubeiq, 250 miles from Aqaba, were incredible, with temperatures often touching 120 degrees; film stock had to be kept in refrigerated trucks to stop it from wilting. One of the toughest things to deal with for the largely British crew was the feeling of total isolation. There was also the clash of cultures. Everywhere they went an Arab escort was provided, armed with rifles or Bren guns. 'Everybody was armed out there,' says Tony Rimmington. 'Even the bloke digging up the road was carrying a Webley pistol. Unbelievable.'

One of the most famous scenes shot at Jebel el Tubeiq is when Lawrence goes back to rescue one of his men stranded in the desert, played by the Indian actor I. S. Johar. Both actors were required to ride a single camel but appeared to be having great difficulty remaining mounted. It transpired they'd been smoking hashish and were stoned out of their minds. Shooting had to be abandoned for the day.

The Lawrence unit were attempting stuff no film unit had attempted before. 'And you never questioned that you could do it, or what was needed and what had to be done,' says David Tringham. 'You just did it.' Much of that blind faith was due to the inspirational presence of David Lean, although as a director he could be a real bastard in getting what he wanted, someone who tested people to the nth degree, gave them hell. Lean was particularly hard on O'Toole, pushing him almost to the limits of endurance, though his confidence in him was unshakable. 'David was very intense with Peter,' confirms Tringham. 'But I never saw Peter argue with him once.' It was tough and there were moments when O'Toole came close to breaking down, but his admiration for Lean was unqualified. Here was someone he could learn from and he did, coming away from the experience knowing more about filmmaking than a lot of directors. 'I graduated in Lean, took my BA in Lean.' It meant that in his career O'Toole could look at something and immediately discern whether or not it met the standards that he was used to and he wanted. The critical eye that he cast upon everything on film came from Lean.

The two men, however, never worked together again, although there were several opportunities to do so. A real shame since creatively they worked extremely well together, and a great loss to cinema since they did make a superb team. Take the scene where Lawrence is first given his Arab robes. Lean shot it several ways but it wasn't working, something was missing. In the end he took O'Toole to one side and said, 'What do you think a young man would do alone in the desert if he'd just been handed these beautiful robes?' He then pointed out towards the desert. O'Toole's eyes followed. 'There's your theatre, Peter. Do what you like.'

Suddenly the scene came to life with O'Toole's idea that the egoist Lawrence would immediately want to see what he looked like. With no mirror to hand O'Toole improvised by pulling out a ceremonial dagger from its scabbard, holding it at an angle and peering at his reflection. 'Clever boy,' Lean muttered to himself.

The crew drove to these desolate places in Land Rovers and Austin Gipsies every morning. Eventually Lean got so far into the desert an old Dakota was chartered to fly everyone in and out, landing on a salt flat because there was no runway. 'There used to be much merriment among the English crew during these flights,' recalls Rimmington. 'Jokes about making wills and the like.' There was one near calamitous incident Rimmington got to hear about when Anthony Quinn arrived to play the great

Arab tribal leader Auda Abu Tayi. 'They flew him in this old Dakota from Amman airport to the desert site, which was a spot in the middle of nowhere, the pilot had to find it. As he was coming in to land the other passenger, this English doctor who had been in Malaya during the war, recognized the warning horns go in the cockpit – beep – beep – beep – in other words, the pilot hadn't put the undercarriage down and he belly landed, all in the bloody sand. Quinn got out of there shaking like a leaf, "I'm never flying in that bloody plane again!" '

Stars of Quinn's stature would often just pop in, play their part and then drift off again, it was O'Toole that remained a permanent fixture. When Alec Guinness arrived to play Prince Feisal, he came away highly impressed by O'Toole, writing in his diary: 'He has great wayward charm and is marvellously good as Lawrence. He's dreamy good to act with and has great personal charm and gaiety.' Some time later, when the film crew were working in Spain, Guinness' admiration had cooled dramatically due to O'Toole's excessive alcohol intake. Notably there was the occasion they were invited to dinner by a Spanish grandee. 'O'Toole got drunk, quarrelled with his host and threw a glass of champagne in his face. Peter could have been killed – shot, or strangled. And I'm beginning to think it's a pity he wasn't.'

As the weeks of shooting passed into months the strain began to show. Some members of the crew literally couldn't take it any more and left for home. There were fears O'Toole himself would crack, go AWOL. At one point he begged Siân to come out again and raise his spirits: 'Here, you have to be a little mad to stay sane,' he told her. At the camp in Aqaba there was very little to occupy oneself with. 'It was like being in the army,' Omar Sharif recalled. 'We sat in the bar and got pissed every night. There was nothing else to do.' The beer marquee was very popular and used to be packed every night; there was a dart board, table tennis and the odd air-rifle competition. All the booze was provided by Spiegel. But the air conditioning never worked so it was always as hot as hell. One of the riggers marched through the tent one night completely naked except for a pair of boots, past the astonished glances of a couple of production secretaries and Phyllis Dalton, the costume designer.

O'Toole was one of the beer-tent regulars and Rimmington never forgot one particular evening when the actor walked in, clearly well gone, and punched the solid wood upright support of the marquee, punched it with his bare fist. Then walked out again. 'His knuckles were in a terrible mess the next day. God, he was in a real state.' There were also practical jokes he played, some more appreciated than others. One night he collapsed the tents of the crew as they lay sleeping. 'After a day's hard work in 120 degrees of heat, that wasn't funny,' said second unit cameraman Peter Newbrook.

To keep from going completely crackers O'Toole and Sharif would occasionally fly by private plane for a few days off in Beirut, to enjoy the flesh pots of what was then the sin city of the east. 'We misbehaved ourselves appallingly!' he later verified. They visited nightclubs and gambled. 'We once did about nine months' wages in one night,' confirmed O'Toole. To keep awake, because they didn't want to waste time sleeping, they took Dexedrine. Looking for female companionship, they ended up in one place only to be left wondering why the women there were so unresponsive. They were in a nunnery.

As filming progressed, Sam Spiegel, who resided on his yacht off the coast of Aqaba and rarely ventured inland, became increasingly fed up over the time Lean was taking, fearing he'd never leave the blasted desert or finish the picture. It's true Lean had become despotic, paranoid and a perfection fetishist. On one occasion he found a perfect spot of desert only to return the next morning to find somebody had strayed across it leaving very distinctive footprints. 'I want to find out who that is,' Lean raged. 'I want a shoe inspection!' The culprit was never found.

After firing off several cables ordering Lean to speed the pace, which only served to antagonize him more, Spiegel took the dramatic decision to shut down production in Jordan at the end of September, after 117 days of filming, and relocate after a break of two months to the more manageable Spain. Production designer John Box recalled that Lean 'had to be dragged screaming from his caravan'.

O'Toole felt very differently. It meant a return to Britain for a long recuperation and he began by immediately checking into hospital for a refit and recharge. Once out he went on the ultimate bender. 'After six months in the desert, I should think so.' Inevitably he got into trouble whilst visiting friends in Bristol. When police stopped his erratic drive down a street at four in the morning, O'Toole stepped out of the vehicle to confess. 'OK, Skip. Let's go to the station. I'm drunk.' Spiegel was far from pleased. 'You're not supposed to get up to that kind of caper on a film like this!' The outcome was a £75 fine and a driving ban.

NINE

Filming on *Lawrence of Arabia* resumed on 18 December 1961 in Spain, primarily Seville, where many of the interiors were shot in and around authentic Moorish buildings. There was also location work done at Almeria, on the Mediterranean coast, which O'Toole dubbed 'Pontefract with scorpions'.

The biggest sequence shot in Almeria was the attack on Aqaba. Lean hadn't been able to recreate the famous battle on the real site since wherever he placed the camera the vista was occupied by oil-storage tanks, so John Box replicated the town in the south-east of Spain. The approach was daunting, a mile and a half of shale, all downhill. Lean had insisted no doubles, O'Toole and Sharif were to lead the charge themselves, which involved several hundred camels and horses. The rehearsal was, in O'Toole's word, 'chaos'. Come the morning of the real thing O'Toole popped into Sharif's tent to see him sat up and playing with his worry beads, a painful expression on his face. 'What are you doing?'

'Peter, I've been working out the odds.'

'What odds?'

'Whether the camel will fall over or I will fall off the camel,' said Sharif.

'And what have you decided?'

'There's more chance of me falling off the camel than there is of the camel falling over.'

'I see,' said O'Toole. 'And what do you intend to do?'

'I'm going to tie myself to the camel.'

'Well, I'm going to get drunk.'

Sharif smiled. 'Oh, I'm going to get drunk, too.'

Everyone was nervous and apprehensive as Lean made his final preparations. Then a series of rockets fired into the air began the stampede. All hell broke loose. Somehow O'Toole managed to remain on his mount and made it through the 'fake' Aqaba and out the other side, where his camel, along with the others, came to rest at the water's edge. Still in one piece, apart from a broken thumb, O'Toole scanned the other riders for Sharif. There he was, still tied to his camel, but now hanging under its bulbous belly.

Having bonded during their trips to Beirut together, O'Toole and Sharif were now firm friends. David Tringham remembers them both having a music hall song and dance act that they used to perform at parties. 'It was quite funny.' They'd also get up to other tricks.

In Almeria a French film producer called Raoul Levy, who made *And God Created Woman* with Brigitte Bardot, came down to the Hotel Alfonso XIII, where the actors were staying. 'He had this fabulous looking Mexican girl with him and Peter really fancied her,' recalls Tringham. 'If you want her, she's yours,' said Levy matter-of-factly. 'I'll fix it. She's got to go back to Mexico first, but she'll be back soon.'

'OK, OK,' said O'Toole excitedly. 'I'd love to see her again.'

By this point Sharif was feeling somewhat left out. 'What about me?'

'She can bring a friend, can't you, Lucia,' said Levy. The girl nodded.

Two weeks went by and the girls were due to arrive, remembers

Tringham. 'Peter was rubbing his hands with excitement. So, these two women turn up. Lucia still looked fabulous, but the girl with her was a really sorry sight and she was carrying a small sewing machine. Omar said, "Who's that?" Lucia said, "This is the friend for you, Omar." And he went, "Oh please!" Major disappointment.'

O'Toole had also become extremely pally with Jack Hawkins, who'd arrived in Spain to play General Allenby; drinking late into the night with him. And there was plenty of larking about, too. In the scene where Allenby grills Lawrence on his mistreatment in prison in Deraa, O'Toole, annoyed at the amount of takes Lean was making them do, blurted out, 'I was fucked by some Turks.' Without skipping a beat Hawkins replied, 'What a pity.' Lean was furious. In fact he took a dim view altogether of their friendship and actually asked Hawkins to keep his distance from O'Toole, since Allenby was supposed to be a father figure to Lawrence, aloof. Hawkins thought Lean was talking bollocks. 'The fact that we used to have some rousing sessions together in no way impinged on our work; maybe it even improved our performances.'

In Spain, Spiegel was a much more visible presence around the set. At one point O'Toole was summoned to see the producer on his yacht, and was given an almighty bollocking. Whether this was meant to spur him on in the final stages of filming he never discovered. 'I left feeling dreadful. Just as ever, destruction was Sam's game. I couldn't bear that man.' Pissed off, he looked for a bar to drown his sorrows and found one already propped up by John Box, who'd got the same rough treatment. After consuming several bottles the pair decided to have their revenge and climbed up the yacht's anchor chain, crept into Spiegel's private quarters and stole all his prize cigars.

The crew had left Spain around the end of June 1962. It had been a fun shoot: Siân had again visited, as did O'Toole's parents; he'd taken his dad to see a bullfight. But the picture was far from finished. Lean was desperate for more desert footage and persuaded Spiegel to let him film for a short period in Morocco. King Hassan II kindly arranged for the use of the Royal Moroccan Cavalry and the Camel Corps and a hundred nomads from the Sahara desert to serve as part of Lawrence's army. During one charge an effects gun loaded with small pellets went off too soon, hitting O'Toole in the eye, temporarily blinding him. Unable to control his camel he was thrown in front of several hundred charging Bedouins on horseback. Luckily the camel stood guard over the prone actor, as they are trained to do, shielding him from serious injury and probably saving his life. O'Toole was flown to hospital for treatment and was back on the camel the next day.

Base camp was in a fly-blown town called Ouarzazate, with the production office situated in a building that was once occupied by the French Foreign Legion. It was so inhospitable that legionnaires were still being sent down there as punishment. The heat was tremendous and once again there were casualties amongst the crew. Most alarmingly, a Moroccan army officer acting as an adviser cracked and took to shooting his rifle out of his tent at night. 'Anything he saw, he shot at,' recalled production assistant Norman Spencer. 'So he had to be taken away.'

Whilst in Morocco, O'Toole, Sharif and Hawkins were invited to the British Consulate for dinner. Arriving, they were asked if they wanted something. 'I'd love a Martini,' said Hawkins.

'I'm sorry, sir, but alcohol is forbidden.'

Hawkins looked dumbfounded. 'This is the British Consulate, we're not really in Morocco, are we, we're in Britain.'

'I'm afraid not, sir.'

'Well,' said Hawkins, 'how do you go about getting alcohol, because we're not going to make it through this.'

The answer was a prescription that categorized them as alcoholics. 'I'll call this doctor who facilitates these things.'

'See if he'll come right away,' said Hawkins. 'This is an emergency!'

The doctor arrived and promptly wrote them out a prescription. Armed with this valuable piece of paper they left for the nearest pharmacy and were handed a bottle each in a brown-paper bag. 'It was some kind of pure alcohol,' reports Johnnie Planco. 'They went outside into the street and drank the lot and they were out for like three days. The way Peter told me the story, that was the most he ever drank.'

Convinced that if he let him, Lean would happily stay in that sand paradise, cranking his camera over and over, never stopping, Spiegel announced a December opening for the film in London and New York, meaning Lean had just four months to edit his spectacular. 'I must say it was a master stroke on Sam's part, fixing the premiere dates before we were even through,' said O'Toole. 'Sam knew we were going on too long; David and I had begun to forget we were making a film. After two years it had become a way of life. So Sam nailed us with the dates – and that was that.'

Filming came to an end on 18 August. The final scene was O'Toole sat in an army jeep with RADA classmate Bryan Pringle driving, his feet in a bucket of ice because it was so hot. 'And David just shot it and shot it and shot it. He was amazingly reluctant to let go.'

O'Toole felt very differently, he didn't much care if he ever saw another blasted sand dune in his life. That evening he got very drunk at a grand celebration party at a hotel in Casablanca. Waltzing in through the big swing doors into a large packed lobby he screamed at the top of his voice: 'The fucking picture's finished!'

Well, not quite. Back in England, Lean filmed Lawrence's fatal motorcycle crash. The bike was mounted on a trailer that was attached to the camera car by a towing bar and a length of rope as backup. During one take the bar snapped and O'Toole would have careered off into the road at great speed if not for the rope, which luckily held firm. Clambering into the back of the camera car, O'Toole breathed a huge sigh of relief and wondered if it wasn't just Lawrence, 'up there, teasing'.

Principal photography was finally completed on 21 September outside St Paul's Cathedral, where Lean shot the exteriors for Lawrence's memorial service, bringing to an end perhaps the longest shooting schedule for any single film in cinema history – May 1961 to September 1962; a total of 313 days.

It had been an extraordinary adventure for O'Toole, as Lean had promised it would be. Costly, too, in purely physical terms. As well as his various camel misfortunes O'Toole lost two stones in weight, received third-degree burns, sprained both ankles, tore ligaments in both his hip and thigh, dislocated his spine, cracked an ankle bone, tore his groin, sprained his neck and received concussion twice. Thankful to be back with Siân and Kate, O'Toole readmitted himself into hospital for several days in a bid to restore his health, quite unable to comprehend the enormity of what he had just been through. It all now seemed like a distant memory, a different lifetime.

Still Lean, who was working round the clock with his editing team, couldn't let O'Toole go. A call went out, he was needed for one more day. The famous appearance of Omar Sharif, arriving astride a camel from out of a mirage as if by magic, had been one of the earliest things in the can. Running it through again Lean was unhappy with some of O'Toole's close-ups. On 6 October the actor was hauled into Shepperton Studios, put in an army costume, covered in sweat and sand and stood up against a blue sheet to resemble the burning Arab sky. When the brief shot was spliced into the existing footage O'Toole was amazed. 'I was twenty-seven in the first shot and then eight seconds later, there was another close-up of me when I was thirty years old! Eight goddamn seconds! And two years of my life had gone from me! The difference was astounding. I'd lost the bloom of youth. We're in a strange situation, film actors. We can watch the process of decomposition in the flesh.'

As he sat and waited for *Lawrence* to open, O'Toole and Siân moved into a home of their own, a vast and glorious four-storey Georgian mansion at 98 Heath Street, Hampstead, called Guyon House. After the exertions of the last two years it was exactly what O'Toole needed, a little bit of stability, an anchor in his life, and a fine and dandy place to raise a family. Kate was now two but already a cause for concern, having inherited her father's poor eyesight. 'Daddy, Daddy! I broke my eyes!' she announced one day. 'Don't cry, Kate, don't cry, we'll get you a new pair.' These turned out to be thick NHS glasses.

Financially the purchase of Guyon House had wiped O'Toole out. 'I haven't got a penny,' he told a reporter. 'The difference is that I'm now luxuriously broke.' Plans for the future had been put in place, however. With Buck he formed his own independent production company, called Keep Films: 'As in I keep what I earn and don't give it to anyone else,' O'Toole explained. Stars have always wanted to become their own producer and with Buck, O'Toole had someone who could provide the money and the expertise he didn't have. Right from the start, however, it was made very clear that the centrepiece of the enterprise was O'Toole and that there was no place for Siân, save for her role as loving wife and mother. She had continued to act in theatre and television plays, building a reputation as a fine actress, but was dismayed to hear Buck say that it was OK for her to continue her career just so long as it didn't interfere with her husband's. The hope was that once *Lawrence* had established O'Toole as a star, some of the time and energy of the accountants, lawyers and secretaries Buck had assembled for Keep Films might be diverted ever so slightly in her direction. O'Toole would insist on it, wouldn't he, after all, hadn't he told friends before their wedding that in his opinion Siân was the best young actress in Britain?

As a couple their profile was already beginning to rise, as invitations to high-society gatherings and showbiz events testified. At one elegant dinner given in Belgravia they watched Rudolf Nureyev dance on table tops and drink brandy from a bottle. Soon he was very drunk and very sick. O'Toole, no stranger to such conditions, took immediate charge, seizing his legs and bumping him down the thickly carpeted stairs, 'Come on, mush,' much to the consternation of guests who complained, 'Be careful with him, take care of his feet.' 'To hell with his fucking feet,' roared O'Toole as he bundled the Russian into a waiting cab.

The week before *Lawrence* was due to open, Spiegel hosted a press reception for the film at the Jordanian embassy in London. Invites were sent out all over Fleet Street. When one landed on the desk of Keith Waterhouse he immediately phoned Barbara Taylor Bradford to see if she was going. Like Waterhouse, Barbara had left behind the sweaty news offices of Leeds to work in the fleshpots of Fleet Street and had landed a job on the *London Evening News*. She was very much looking forward to attending, with the express intention of meeting Omar Sharif. 'Of course, who strolls in halfway through, this gorgeous, blue-eyed Hollywood-polished movie star called Peter O'Toole.'

Waterhouse looked at Barbara and Barbara looked at Waterhouse. 'Don't you dare tell him it's me,' she said. 'Barbara, luv, he'll recognize you.' Anyway, he did come over to say hello. 'And he had been polished,' recalls Barbara. 'It was a gloss that you can only get when a lot of money has been spent. His dirty blond hair had become *very* blond and sleek and brushed back, and the eyes even seemed bluer. He looked positively drop-dead gorgeous.' For Barbara though the most astonishing change was the voice. 'It had become mellifluous and without a hint of the North. That night was a revelation because I remember thinking, gosh, he's going to be a very big star.'

Lawrence of Arabia opened on 10 December 1962 with a glittering Royal Premiere at the Odeon, Leicester Square, with the Queen and Prince Philip in attendance. There is a story that Richard Harris was being driven through the West End that night and happened to pass the cinema, at which point he looked at his watch and said, 'In fifteen minutes O'Toole's era of anonymity will be over.'

Afterwards Spiegel threw a lavish midnight party for five hundred guests at the Grosvenor House Hotel on Park Lane. There was Noël Coward, who had loved the film, unable to resist the opportunity to congratulate O'Toole on his performance. 'You were very good, Peter,' he said. O'Toole smiled back, it had been an evening of congratulations. 'Yes, very fine indeed,' Noël continued. 'And far, far more attractive than Lawrence could ever have been. If Lawrence had looked like you, Peter, there would have been many more than twelve Turks queuing up for the buggering session.'

The critics raved. Alexander Walker in the *Evening Standard* summed it up best when he called *Lawrence of Arabia* 'an epic with intellect behind it'. As for O'Toole, most agreed he had given a performance of which few other actors would have been capable. 'He had to interpret one of the most complex characters ever under some of the worst acting conditions ever,' said John Box. 'And what he achieved is incredible.'

By the end of the week O'Toole was in New York for the American premiere, followed by a trip out to Los Angeles for the film's West Coast opening. Almost overnight he had been propelled into the major league of stardom. 'I woke up one morning to find I was famous,' he reported. 'I bought a white Rolls-Royce and drove down Sunset Boulevard wearing dark specs and a white suit, waving like the Queen Mum. Nobody took any fucking notice, but I thoroughly enjoyed it.'

Predictably, he hit the bars, where he was to encounter his first American Martini. 'I'm a whisky drinker like every good Irishman, and I thought I was drinking lemonade. It was a memorable experience.' Most of his nights out were spent in the company of actor Jason Robards, then married to Lauren Bacall. One night they arrived back particularly wasted and couldn't get in the front door so were forced to climb through a window. In the lobby they saw Lauren Bacall descending the stairs with those huge curlers women used to put in their hair. O'Toole took one look at her and howled, 'Yikes, it's a chicken hawk!' Miss Bacall grew so exasperated by their antics that she barred O'Toole from her house.

One night O'Toole and Sharif saw the controversial stand-up Lenny Bruce do his act at a small club near Sunset Boulevard. Afterwards Bruce invited the boys back to his apartment, only for the place to be raided by the drug squad. Bruce was charged with possession and along with O'Toole and Sharif hustled into the back of a police van and thrown in a cell.

Sharif used his one phone call to contact Spiegel, who arrived at the police station with a gang of lawyers and disappeared into a room with several officers. After a lengthy gap they emerged and O'Toole and Sharif were told they could go. O'Toole refused to budge, he wasn't leaving without Bruce. More discussions followed. Finally all three were released. 'The story never hit the papers,' revealed Sharif. 'But it must have cost Sam an arm and a leg.'

There was another police incident involving Bruce and O'Toole, which only came to light when the officer in question wrote about it in a *Los Angeles Times* article a few days after the actor's passing. Joseph Wambaugh, later a successful crime novelist (*The Choirboys*, *The Onion Field*), was in 1962 working the vice detail. One night his small team was keeping tabs on an address known for prostitution and illicit sale of alcohol when they stopped a taxi that had picked up two 'customers'. Within seconds the occupants shot out of the door, leaving behind a bag of marijuana and uppers on the back seat. Wambaugh immediately recognized Bruce, but the other passenger was a complete mystery. 'He was a tall, fair-haired young man with an upmarket Brit accent and was volubly denying any knowledge of how the bag could have gotten onto the taxi seat.'

When told that since neither claimed ownership they'd both be charged, O'Toole cried – 'Wait!' Walking over to the sergeant he asked for the man's name. It was Irish. Seizing on this good fortune O'Toole declared his own Irish heritage and told of how he was in Los Angeles promoting a movie that was going to make him famous. With Bruce remaining quiet, O'Toole continued, 'Sergeant, my career is in your hands. You have the power to damage me irreparably. Haven't you ever had a human weakness over which you sometimes had little control?'

The sergeant listened impassively and then turned to his officers. 'Throw the bag down the sewer and put them back in the cab.'

Another public scandal had been avoided. Yet these incidents reached the ears of Spiegel, leaving the producer fuming. 'You make a star, you make a monster,' he observed. So bad did O'Toole's behaviour become that Lean wrote to a friend, complaining: 'I think it has all gone to Peter's head and already people are getting a bit fed up with him not showing up for appointments. Sam and I did one TV show with him in New York and he was a real dope.' It was the same in London, where reporters regularly complained that they had to scour the pubs of the West End and Soho to snag an interview.

O'Toole himself recognized what was happening. Stardom, he said, was something insidious: 'It creeps through your toes. You don't realize what's happening until it reaches your nut. And that's when it becomes dangerous.' At least one columnist enjoyed O'Toole's shenanigans in the movie capital and lamented the fact he would soon have to return home. 'Too bad O'Toole won't be spending a lot of time in Hollywood – his personality is reminiscent of Errol Flynn.'

Lawrence of Arabia stands as one of the most remarkable achievements in the history of cinema; Steven Spielberg has referred to it as 'a miracle of a film'. Much of its success can be attributed to O'Toole's central performance, he's barely off the screen and carries the drama from start to finish. But it is the vision and maverick genius of David Lean that turns what is essentially a character study into an epic film of rare quality and beauty. It packed out cinemas round the world, raking in $77 million (adjusted for inflation, that's almost $600 million today).

Such is the longevity and esteem in which the film is held that when in 1999 the British Film Institute surveyed a thousand people from the world of British film and television to produce a list of the top one hundred British films of all time, *Lawrence of Arabia* ranked an impressive third, beaten only by *Brief Encounter* (another Lean-directed film) and *The Third Man*. Some would place the film even higher than that, this author included.

TEN

There had been much speculation as to what O'Toole would do after *Lawrence of Arabia*. Just how do you follow one of the most revered and successful films in cinema history? For a time he was linked to the part of Henry Higgins in the Warner Brothers' film version of *My Fair Lady*. Jack Warner was against Rex Harrison reprising the role he played so successfully on Broadway and appeared keen on O'Toole, after Cary Grant had said no. The choice found favour with director George Cukor: 'I think he's our man,' he wrote to a Warner executive, offering to make a test with the actor either in London or Los Angeles. 'That is if he'll make the test at all. I think he might. He really wants the part. He's great.'

Warners opened negotiations with O'Toole's people but baulked at his wage demands. Later when asked about the project O'Toole was rather coy. 'I said that the only man who could and should play Higgins was Rex Harrison,' which didn't really tally with the truth. In the end Harrison was indeed cast.

There was also a desire for Keep Films to make a screen adaptation of *Waiting for Godot*. O'Toole caught a flight to Paris where Samuel Beckett resided with the express intention of persuading the playwright to part with the film rights. 'It took me about eight hours and seven bottles to convince him that *Godot* was never meant to be a stage play at all but was really a film all the time.'

Hoping to both produce and star, O'Toole saw the picture as a small art-house offering, shot over two weeks on the West Coast of Ireland on a budget of just £20,000. To keep costs low he himself would take no fee to play Vladimir, and friends Kenneth Griffith and Jack MacGowran would appear in the other roles. He also asked Tom Stoppard to help with the adaptation. The two had become friends since Stoppard's move from Bristol to London; O'Toole was instrumental in getting the writer his first job and also lent him money when he needed it.

In the end the project collapsed and the film rights reverted to Beckett, who had almost immediately regretted selling them in the first place, firm in his belief that the play was not cinema material, 'and adaptation would destroy it'. He would never make the same mistake again, spurning all future filmmakers, including an approach later in the decade by Roman Polanski.

What O'Toole really wanted was a return to the stage. 'It was the only way I know to get back in touch with what I know I am about. It is the only way I can measure what I have done for the last two years, how I have grown or changed. It gets me back to the freedom I need as an actor.'

Given carte blanche by a West End producer to appear in any play he wanted, O'Toole teamed up with director William Gaskill from the Royal Court with the idea of putting on Pirandello's *Henry IV*. Gaskill admired O'Toole enormously. 'I'd seen him at Stratford and thought he was the actor of our generation, unquestionably.' During early discussions Gaskill raised the alternative of doing *Baal* by Bertolt Brecht. Unfamiliar with the text, O'Toole read it and responded almost immediately, especially to the central character of a wastrel young poet who leaves tattered and broken lives in his wake.

It was certainly a risky venture. 'It's not a crowd puller,' says Gaskill. 'Even with a big star in it, because Peter was riding the crest of a wave.' Brecht's first ever full-length play, written when he was a young student at Munich University, *Baal* had not been performed since 1926 in Berlin and its sordid nature was bound to ruffle a few feathers at the Lord Chamberlain's office, the austere body that still regulated theatre censorship. And that's exactly what O'Toole hoped for, as he wrote to Tom Stoppard: 'I think we will get arrested. It makes Jimmy Porter look like *Mrs Dale's Diary*.' All this was too much for the West End producer, who bailed out, replaced by Oscar Lewenstein, who Gaskill had worked with at the Royal Court: 'Oscar was a very interesting man. He was both a mixture of extremely commercial and really quite left wing.'

During rehearsals O'Toole behaved impeccably and largely stayed off the sauce. 'He was a very dashing person,' remembers Gaskill. 'Tremendously impulsive.' Once he approached Gaskill after a rehearsal saying he needed a lift to Paddington Station. So off they went. 'He was late for the train and so kept instructing me where to go, and we were heading down one-way streets and goodness knows what – "Now go round there!" By the end I found myself driving down the station's entrance ramp, which you're not supposed to go down at all. "That's fine," said O'Toole, got out of the car, kissed me and ran to get his train and disappeared. I can't imagine myself doing something like that, but I did! Peter had great panache, he really did, and you were swept along with it.'

If the subject matter weren't difficult enough (O'Toole had waived his fee), *Baal* opened at the Phoenix Theatre in February 1963 during a bitterly cold winter. When the theatre's heating packed up Lewenstein brought in hundreds of portable heaters to keep the audience warm. Further drama occurred when O'Toole's dresser screamed, 'This show is cursed,' flung the clothes on the floor and fled out of the theatre and into Charing Cross Road, never to return.

Amongst the supporting cast was a young actress making a

very early West End appearance, Gemma Jones, who looks back on *Baal* with nothing but fondness. 'It was an extraordinary production and there was a huge focus of attention on it because of Peter and *Lawrence of Arabia*. It was a wild cast, a lot of drunken Irishmen. Peter treated me with great respect because I was very young and very green.' In their love scene, however, O'Toole did used to unzip the chemise she was wearing so that when she got out of bed she had to wrap the thing around her to stop it falling off.

As it turned out the Lord Chamberlain's office didn't kick up much of a fuss, leaving untouched the play's frank sex scenes, including a three in a bed romp and on-stage nudity. Gemma found herself sharing a dressing room with one of these nubile actresses. 'Guinevere Roberts was her name and she had a very, very luscious figure and the number of actors who would knock on the door by mistake, oh sorry, wrong room, hoping to catch Guinevere in her undies. There was a lot of riotous goings-on backstage to counteract the fact that we were in such a serious piece of drama.'

While it was a courageous move bringing Brecht into the West End, the effort met with a largely indifferent public response. 'If you could keep awake during *Baal* you were a very avid theatre-goer,' remembers David Andrews. 'I didn't like it, I couldn't understand much of it for a start, and all I could see was Peter appearing to indulge himself with it. I'm sure he wasn't but it looked like he'd chosen it because he was never off the stage and I think that slightly demeaned him because he didn't need to be like that, he could walk on with one line and he'd steal the whole bloody thing.'

Even Richard Harris thought it an odd choice, especially coming so soon after his success as Lawrence. Perhaps O'Toole did the play in order to show off his versatility, to look bedraggled and unclean on stage in an attempt to escape the beauty of the Lawrence image. Anyway Harris decided to see it but did so incognito, dressed as a Roman Catholic priest, with rosary beads, hat and collar, the works. 'I went with a mate of mine and we sat up in the gallery and O'Toole was unbelievably brilliant. So I had to go back and tell him he's great, but I couldn't go back dressed as a priest. So my friend and I swapped clothes.' The next day one of the newspapers reported a commotion during the matinee, when a Roman Catholic priest was seen to undress in the gallery. Anyway Harris went to see O'Toole and not a word was said. Fast-forward seven years and Harris had a number one single, 'Macarthur Park', and decided to go out on a one-man concert tour. 'I went up to the north of England, to Scunthorpe where no one could see me break it in. I'm singing a song and I heard a commotion at the back of the hall, so I stopped the orchestra. "What's going on out there?" And a voice said, "I'm Peter O'Toole, I'm here dressed as a nun." '

If the production itself received largely a poor response, O'Toole's acting soared above the play so impressively that one of Brecht's biographers, the scholar Martin Esslin, dubbed O'Toole 'the greatest potential force among all English-speaking actors'. Gaskill, too, was pleased with the performance, having never forgotten how he played Baal's death scene, crawling to the door literally on his fists. There was also one very special rehearsal. 'It was that wonderful moment when the text seems to be coming from the actor, not from the writer, and everyone suddenly went still.'

Midway through the run O'Toole heard that he had been nominated for an Academy Award for Best Actor for *Lawrence*. The picture itself had received ten nominations, an incredible feat. The ceremony was due to take place in Los Angeles and O'Toole found himself competing with Burt Lancaster for *Birdman of Alcatraz*, Jack Lemmon as an alcoholic in *Days of Wine and Roses*, Marcello Mastroianni for *Divorce Italian Style* and the eventual winner, Gregory Peck for *To Kill a Mockingbird*. In the end O'Toole did not make an appearance, as he was still treading the boards in London. Sam Spiegel attempted to buy every ticket for that night's performance of *Baal* so he could fly to Hollywood, but the theatre management said it would be impossible to reach all the patrons for refunds.

Despite the disappointment of losing out to Peck, a popular winner on the night, *Lawrence* triumphed overall, winning seven Oscars, including one for Lean and Best Picture. O'Toole took some consolation in the fact that he won Best Actor at that year's BAFTAs. That he was now on his way to the top was indisputable, but with that expectation came voices of caution. 'A lot of people have talked about being ruined by success,' he said. 'But let's face it, more people have been butchered by failure.'

Baal was only intended to run for a short time, since O'Toole had already committed to his next film. Not long after *Lawrence* began coining in money around the world, Spiegel set about planning O'Toole's future, explaining that his next four films would all be made under exclusive licence to his company, as per the contract he'd signed, the one that Finney had so vehemently refused. It was then that Buck dropped his bombshell. With brilliant cunning and chutzpah he'd managed to put a clause in the contract right under the noses of both Spiegel and Columbia Pictures stating that O'Toole's services did not extend beyond the period of *Lawrence of Arabia*. One of the wiliest operators in Hollywood had been outmanoeuvred and when it was discovered what had happened the shit really did hit the fan and people were fired or resigned. But nothing could be done, O'Toole was a free agent.

He'd learnt that Hal B. Wallis, the famed former head of Warner Brothers, had bought the film rights to Anouilh's play *Becket*, which had caused all that controversy between O'Toole and Peter Hall. For his director Wallis hired Peter Glenville, who had staged the play on Broadway with Laurence Olivier as Becket and Anthony Quinn as Henry II. With those two stars deemed too old for the film version, thoughts had drifted towards O'Toole playing the King when quite by chance Glenville met the actor at a dinner party in London. Before there was a chance to even raise the subject, O'Toole cornered Glenville demanding to be cast. 'Fixing me with blazing blue eyes, he said it was *his* part.' Encountering him in the flesh, Glenville was now utterly convinced of O'Toole's suitability. Here was a man, Glenville observed, 'Full of nervous energy. He is mischievous, sharp witted, uninhibited, extrovert and unquestionably an original.' Glenville, too, was pleasantly surprised to learn that not only did O'Toole know everything about the origins and background of the play and why and how it came to be written, but had already flown to Paris to discuss the part with Anouilh. He had also seen the Broadway production. 'He is not a young man to leave a stone unturned,' noted Glenville.

A dramatization of the conflict between Thomas Becket and King Henry II in twelfth-century England, *Becket* had all the elements of a big, spectacle picture while at the same time was an intimate, literate, witty and adult drama. Amidst all the history, colour and pageantry, there was the underlying conflict of two friends who turn against each other. In their youth Becket and the King pursue wine, women and song, but when Henry appoints Becket as archbishop, his spiritual rise results in his allegiance to God and the Church outweighing any duty to a sovereign. It's a power struggle that ends in tragedy.

As negotiations began with Jules Buck over O'Toole's services, negotiations that Glenville revealed as 'intolerably demanding', thoughts turned to who should play Becket. Several actors were considered including Maximilian Schell, Peter Finch and Laurence Harvey. Glenville's preferred choice was Richard

Burton, which changed to Albert Finney when he heard that Burton was unwilling to appear opposite O'Toole. 'For this I do not blame him,' Glenville wrote to Wallis. 'As by all accounts the latter seems to make mincemeat of any other male actors around him. I do not think this would affect Finney – he has a talent of equal stature to O'Toole and knows it!'

Finney turned out to be busy, and Burton re-entered their thinking when it turned out that he was most eager to work with O'Toole after all. Burton had made no secret of his admiration for this young and thrusting new talent. After seeing him at the Bristol Old Vic he wrote in his diary: 'He looked like a beautiful, emaciated secretary bird. His voice had a crack like a whip. Most important of all you couldn't take your eyes off him.' It was a real casting coup for Wallis, teaming the world's two most exciting stars: Burton, whose notoriety over his affair with Elizabeth Taylor meant his face was never out of the newspapers, and O'Toole, the bright new star of *Lawrence of Arabia*.

Clearly aware of the other's reputation for hell-raising and boozing, the two actors called a truce until they had acclimatized sufficiently to each other and to their respective roles. The film crew, expecting a typhoon to pass through the usually tranquil Shepperton Studios when filming began in the summer of 1963, were left scratching their collective heads as O'Toole and Burton sat quietly between takes sipping tea and doing crosswords. After ten days it was abundantly clear that both actors had the desired on-camera rapport, and putting on his best Irish accent Burton said, 'Peter, me boy. I think we deserve a little snifter.' They drank for two nights and a day. After that Glenville had his work cut out keeping his stars under control; it was not unknown for them to appear on set intoxicated. In the scene where Henry places a ring upon Becket's finger, making him Chancellor of England, O'Toole could barely focus. 'It was rather like trying to thread a needle wearing boxing gloves,' Burton recalled. For an opulent banquet scene O'Toole arrived having drunk solidly for twelve hours.

Often they drank in the small smattering of pubs located near the studio, such as the Hovel, whose eccentric landlord displayed his appendix in a bottle on the bar, along with a shrunken head and a pickled penis. There was also the King's Head, where the landlord, Archie, would greet them with, 'Now is the winter of our discontent made glorious summer by this leg of pork.' These were wild lunches, lasting hours, full of hearty quaffing of champagne and brandy and verbal fencing, both men lobbing Shakespeare soliloquies at each other.

One morning O'Toole arrived in Burton's dressing room with an open bottle of whisky in his hand. Burton declined it and asked what he was celebrating. 'It's an Irish birthday.'

'And what day is that?' asked Burton.

'Any day I say it is.' O'Toole drained the bottle in ten swigs, and fell flat on his back. Shooting resumed twenty-four hours later.

While O'Toole commuted to the studio from Guyon House, the tax exile Burton resided at the Dorchester with Elizabeth Taylor, who came on the set so often that Glenville had a canvas chair made for her with her name emblazoned on the back. Future cult film director Brian Trenchard-Smith remembers being invited to Shepperton as part of the Wellington College film circle and spending several hours there wandering about the sets and watching Glenville directing. In one scene he remembers O'Toole replacing a nude actress under a blanket in his bed with a compliant Miss Taylor just before cameras rolled. When he pulled back the sheet revealing a beaming Liz, Burton didn't find it as amusing as the rest of the crew.

Taking a quick break from shooting, O'Toole spirited a heavily pregnant Siân over to Dublin to give birth to their second child, another daughter, named Patricia after O'Toole's father. Determined that this new child be born on Irish soil, O'Toole made all the hospital arrangements and arrived at Dublin airport dressed all in green (green corduroy jacket, green bow tie – the works). He was treated by the local press like a returning hero.

It was a straightforward birth, a nun administered some chloroform and within seconds Siân was with the fairies. When she woke a baby girl was handed to her and there was a room full of peering faces, some familiar, some not. O'Toole was there, smiling and holding a bottle of champagne, so too Peter Finch and Jules Buck and his wife Joyce. For Siân the celebration was all over in a blur, and O'Toole had vanished, too, back to England to finish *Becket*. But he'd left a gift, the offer of a job on the film. It wasn't a great part, Glenville needed an actress who could speak Old Welsh and sing. Siân was happy to do it.

O'Toole went on record that *Becket* was amongst the happiest professional experiences of his career. 'We laboured like lunatics, but I never laughed so much in my life.' Clearly the bond he developed with Burton over the course of filming greatly enhanced the on-screen friendship between Henry and Becket, with both actors bringing homoerotic undertones to the relationship that was missing between Olivier and Quinn on stage. O'Toole had by far the showier role, full of histrionic colour, while Burton's performance is calm and restrained. O'Toole is like an incendiary bomb turning the King, in the words of the *New York Times* review, 'into a petulant, frightened neurotic'.

Tolerant of their drinking, Glenville called O'Toole and Burton's approach to the film 'sophisticated, well informed and hard working. Each welcomed and admired the expertise of the other.' No wonder he and so many of his fellow directors preferred classically-trained actors, thought Glenville: 'Would there were more of them!' Glenville himself came from the world of acting and the theatre and had decided to shoot the film in sequence, a method rare in cinema but one which O'Toole particularly found

			Registration District	Leeds					
1932.	Birth in the Sub-district of Leeds North				in the County of Leeds				
Columns:- 1	2	3	4	5	6	7	8	9	10
No.	When and where born	Name, if any	Sex	Name, and surname of father	Name, surname and maiden surname of mother	Occupation of father	Signature, description, and residence of informant	When registered	Signature of registrar	Name entered after registration
401	Second August 1932 123 Beckett Street UD	Peter James	Boy	Patrick James O'Toole	Constance Jean Elliot O'Toole formerly Ferguson	General Dealer of 37 Lofthouse Place UD	C. O'Toole Mother 37 Lofthouse Place Leeds	Fifth August 1932	T M Thompson Registrar	

Certified to be a true copy of an entry in a register in my custody.

U. Howard. Deputy Superintendent Registrar

15·10·2014. Date

O'Toole's birth certificate proves he wasn't born in Ireland, as he sometimes claimed, but in Leeds.

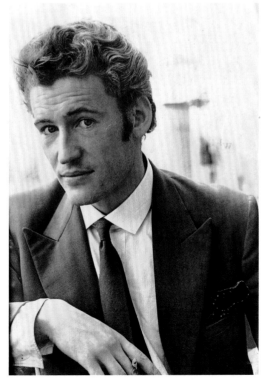

Peter O'Toole, fresh out of drama school and before his nose job.

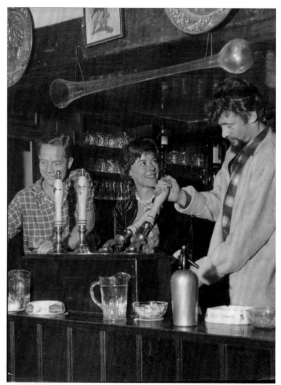

Helping himself at the Dirty Duck pub during his stay in Stratford. Notice the famed 'yard of ale glass' above the bar.

Joining aged twenty-seven, O'Toole was the Royal Shakespeare Company's youngest ever leading man, seen here with his fellow members. Left to right: Paul Hardwick, Frances Cuka, Denholm Elliott, Dorothy Tutin, Peter O'Toole, Patrick Wymark and Jack MacGowran.

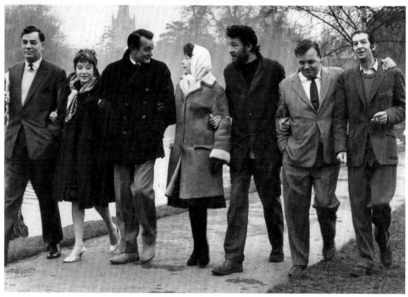

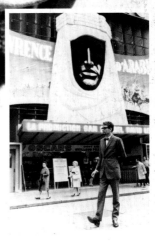

The role of a lifetime: O'Toole was David Lean's choice to play British Lieutenant T. E. Lawrence in *Lawrence of Arabia* after Marlon Brando and Albert Finney turned it down.

The film seemed to follow O'Toole around wherever he went for the rest of his life, sometimes literally.

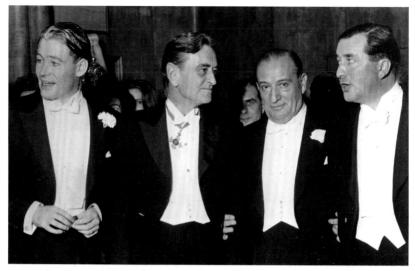

The men who brought *Lawrence of Arabia* to the screen. Left to right: Peter O'Toole, David Lean, producer Sam Spiegel and writer Robert Bolt at the Gala London opening in 1962.

O'Toole's marriage to Welsh actress Siân Phillips was a rollercoaster ride; she would later describe him as a 'dangerous, disruptive human being'.

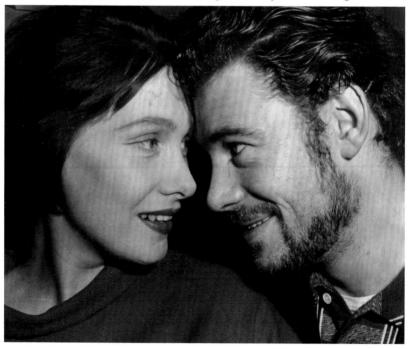

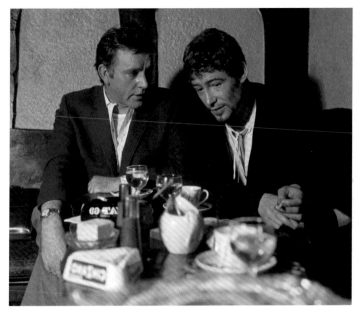

Off duty with Richard Burton during filming of the historical drama *Becket* (1964).

O'Toole (left) parties with Elizabeth Taylor (centre) and Richard Burton (right).

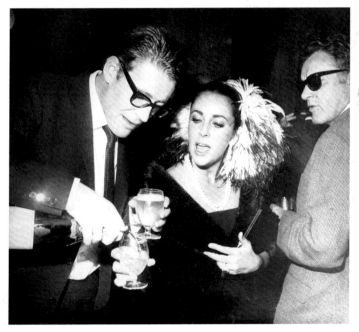

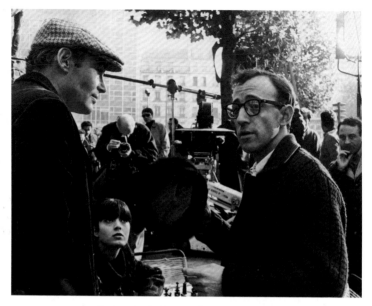

On location in Paris with Woody Allen for
the sex comedy hit *What's New Pussycat?* (1965).

In *How To Steal A Million* (1966) with Audrey Hepburn, who
turned a blind eye to O'Toole's hell-raising on location in Paris.

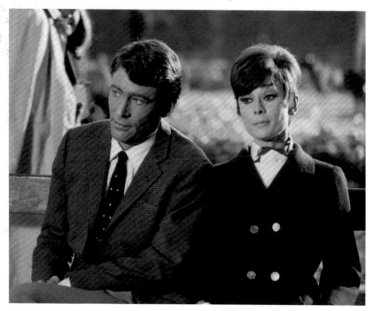

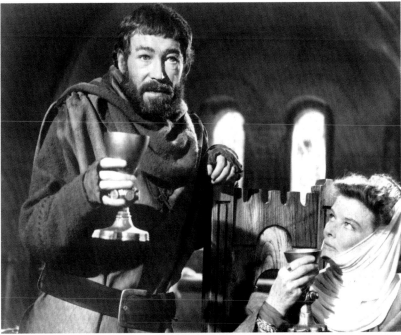

O'Toole met his match while filming *The Lion In Winter* (1968) with Katharine Hepburn, who refused to tolerate his boisterous behaviour.

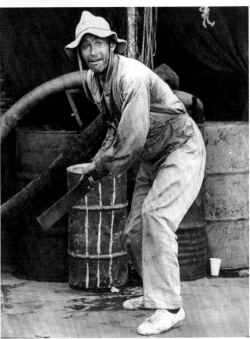

Enjoying an improvised game of his beloved cricket on location in Venezuela for *Murphy's War* (1971).

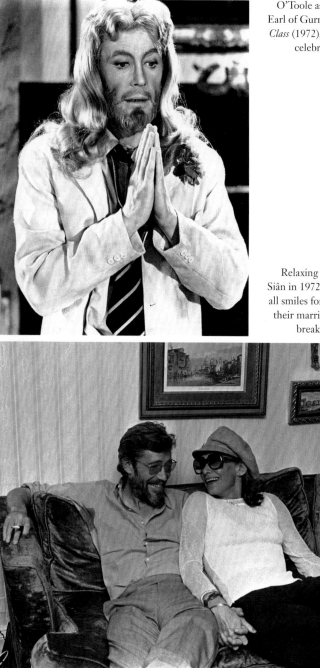

O'Toole as the mad 14th Earl of Gurney in *The Ruling Class* (1972), one of his most celebrated roles.

Relaxing at home with Siân in 1972. The couple are all smiles for the camera but their marriage was at near breaking point.

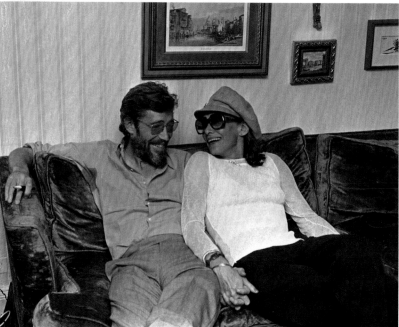

helpful for his performance. It was work 'the disciplined old-fashioned way'. For example, the complicated scene where Becket and Henry meet on horseback on a desolate beach was rehearsed as if it were a play, solidly all morning. When they broke for lunch the studio executives were pulling their hair out that Glenville hadn't shot a single frame of film. Returning to the set Glenville shouted action, and the five-minute scene was wrapped up in a single take.

When *Becket* opened jointly in New York and London it was politely received and did well at the box office. This thinking man's epic was awarded an impressive eleven Oscar nominations, including Best Picture. In the end only Edward Anhalt's screenplay merited a prize. Ironic since O'Toole claimed, 'Practically everything the scriptwriter put in I took out again and got back to Anouilh who, incidentally, approved.'

Again, O'Toole was rewarded with a Best Actor nomination, as was Burton, but he thought it unlikely either would win. 'I think we'll knock each other off in the voting. Perhaps they could cut an Oscar in half.' In the end they lost out to Rex Harrison for *My Fair Lady*. O'Toole did, however, win a Golden Globe as the Best Motion Picture Actor in a Drama.

Back in Hampstead, the O'Toole residence had increased in number significantly, not just the two girls but Siân's mother Mamgu, who had come to live with them. Just days before the London opening of *Lawrence of Arabia* Siân's father died. She received the news late in the evening when O'Toole wasn't there. She'd no idea where he was, a not uncommon situation. That's the way O'Toole liked to live, he hated to be contactable and never took a front-door key. Many was the time when Siân would be woken in the early hours by O'Toole hammering on the door to be let in. 'I wasn't sure if this was a pose or a genuine wish to maintain a measure of liberation in a life that was becoming more and more constrained by approaching fame.'

Leaving Kate with her nanny, and a note for O'Toole, Siân took the train back home. Realizing what had happened, O'Toole dropped all publicity duties and hired a cab to drive him to Wales. His sheer presence seemed to lift the gloom and when things had calmed down it was decided that Mamgu would come and live with them in London. It was a beneficial arrangement all round, Mamgu looked after the children and reigned over the kitchen. She also adored O'Toole and often stayed up late with him talking or playing Scrabble. She'd make midnight snacks for him or cook breakfast for the drunken refugees from the previous night's party.

At this stage Mamgu was oblivious to O'Toole's sporadic drunken rages. Siân never feared for her own safety during these episodes, 'but the noise and the destruction terrified me'. Determined that her mother, and above all the children, never heard them, nor the rows, she had green-baize-lined double doors put in to act as a form of sound-proofing. Siân didn't need anyone telling her these were extraordinary measures, but perhaps recalled the recent words of Kenneth Griffith, 'Do you really think you can sustain being Mrs Edmund Kean?'

ELEVEN

'If you want to know what it's like to be lonely, really lonely,' O'Toole told a reporter once, 'try playing Hamlet.' Burton hadn't much enjoyed the experience either, and over a boozy lunch one afternoon on the *Becket* set announced, 'Let's be masochists. Let's do *Hamlet* again and get it out of our systems.' They drew up an audacious plan, one of them would perform it on the London stage, the other on Broadway. They flipped a coin: O'Toole got London. Next their choice of director, Gielgud or Olivier. Again the decision was made on the toss of a coin. Burton won and chose Gielgud.

In order to fulfil his end of the bargain O'Toole set up a meeting with Olivier at his Mayfair offices. Larry wasn't interested at all in directing O'Toole in a short West End run of *Hamlet*, he had something much bigger in mind. In the last few months he had been chosen as the first artistic director of the National Theatre, an institution a hundred years in the making. Since the late 1800s cultural and political figures from Dickens and Churchill to George Bernard Shaw had bemoaned the fact that Britain had no National Theatre of its own and something really ought to be done about it. In 1962, after several false starts, a board was constituted to run a National Theatre Company and a derelict scrap of land on the South Bank next door to the Royal Festival Hall was earmarked as a perfect site. Nobody was surprised when Olivier was chosen to spearhead the enterprise, given his status and international reputation, combined with the fact that he was the last of the great 'actor-managers', a breed that stretched back to the likes of Kean, Garrick and Henry Irving.

It was also assumed that Olivier himself would headline the company's inaugural production, but snaring O'Toole was too good an opportunity to miss. He would direct O'Toole as Hamlet not amidst the bright lights of London's West End but to launch the new National Theatre. Recognizing the historical import of what was being suggested, O'Toole readily agreed and they shook hands on the deal.

With construction of the new theatre on the South Bank years away (that was officially launched in 1976 with a production of, yes, *Hamlet*, with, guess who – Albert Finney), the governors of the Old Vic in Waterloo, scene of some of Olivier's early stage triumphs, agreed to offer their theatre as a temporary base. Olivier immediately set about making renovations, including putting in a revolving stage and taking out the first two rows of the stalls so that the stage could be extended beyond the proscenium arch. Into this building-site chaos came the *Hamlet* rehearsals. Max Adrian, cast as Polonius, remembered starting work while 'the whole place was still littered with rubble and mortar and there was a bloody enormous hole in one wall which allowed the wind to blow straight in from the Waterloo Road.'

As rehearsals got underway it became clear that O'Toole and Olivier did not share the same artistic vision. 'Peter was like the young buck and Sir Laurence the old bull,' recalls Rosemary Harris, who had been cast as Ophelia. 'Peter had played a very successful Hamlet at Bristol and must have thought, oh I'll just polish it up a bit and do it again, but Sir Laurence seemed to have different ideas about it so they did cross swords a few times. It was clear that they were tolerating each other. But both of them couldn't have been under more pressure.'

One battle was over whether O'Toole, as he'd done at Bristol, should play the role in full beard: 'Why should I be the only man in Elsinore with a razor blade?' Olivier baulked at the suggestion and made his star perform not only clean-shaven but in bleached blond hair and dressed in what O'Toole derogatorily called his 'little Lord Fauntleroy suit'. Olivier also insisted on the uncut version, five bloody hours on stage, as opposed to the cut version O'Toole had so much success with previously.

While O'Toole held Olivier in the highest reverence ('I mean, he's done it. He's sat on the top of Everest and waved down at the Sherpas') he simply refused to bow down and bathe in his living legend-hood. More than anything he resented Olivier's belief that because 'I know my way about the map of *Hamlet* much more than you possibly do' this entitled him to dictate every nuance of his performance. As William Gaskill, who worked under Olivier at the National, observed, 'He tried to make O'Toole act Hamlet as he, Olivier, would have done.' Well, O'Toole was having none of it and fought his corner through sheer bloody mindedness. 'Peter wasn't too keen on changing his performance,' observed Rosemary Harris. 'And I got the feeling that Peter pretty much stuck to his guns and did what he was comfortable with and Sir Laurence in the end sort of shrugged and gave up and realised that there was no point. I thought Peter was giving a wonderful performance, really.'

Years later O'Toole labelled Olivier 'a tiny, strange, vain fucker. He used to lecture me: "Do you think it's a good idea to have a drink after the show?" For fuck's sake!' It's true Olivier could be overbearingly rigid when it came to direction, but he was also capable of kindness and encouragement and had much of the cast eating out of his hands from the get go, simply because he exuded such massive self-confidence from the mere fact that he had nothing to prove to anyone. He was, however, more than capable of coming up with his fair share of crackpot ideas. On *Hamlet*, he wanted the ghost to be a dummy which flew on wires. 'So the actors came on and then this thing would fly across the stage,' recalls Gaskill. 'And we said, "You can't do that, Larry. It won't work." '

In that inaugural company, Olivier had cleverly sprinkled experienced players such as Michael Redgrave amongst a largely unproven group of young thoroughbreds bristling to make an impact: Robert Stephens as Horatio, Frank Finlay as the grave-digger and Derek Jacobi as Laertes. As a lowly spear carrier was twenty-three-year-old Michael Gambon, who described O'Toole as 'a God with bright blonde hair'. Terence Knapp, fresh from the very first Chichester Festival, where Olivier had plucked much of his cast, recalls the general reaction at the news O'Toole was to play Hamlet. 'People were very excited at the thought of what kind of Hamlet he would be. He was already recognized as a very, very distinguished actor, and despite the titled actors like Olivier and Redgrave and Guinness there were many of us who thought that O'Toole was the most exciting actor of the day.'

Hamlet opened at the Old Vic on 22 October 1963. Just as the curtain began to rise Olivier grabbed O'Toole as he waited expectantly in the wings. 'Are you ready?'

'For what?' O'Toole replied.

'For them. They're out there with their machine guns. It's your turn, son.'

It was the critics he was talking about and their opinion of O'Toole was decidedly mixed. 'I don't understand why Peter was criticized,' says Peter Cellier, who played Rosencrantz. 'Because I thought he was a very good Hamlet, most excellent. It was a clear cut, interesting and vital performance. And the audience reaction was ecstatic.' Derek Jacobi has gone on record as saying, 'O'Toole was a smashing Hamlet. There was one rehearsal run-through where he was, I thought, the definitive Hamlet, just wonderful.' In the end O'Toole perhaps fell between two styles, trying to appease Olivier while doing his own thing. Siân, who sat in the front stalls racked with nerves, had to admit that this Hamlet was 'a pale shadow' of the one in Bristol.

As for the production, while not heavily criticized, it was deemed to be lacklustre. 'I think the critics felt, we mustn't knock this new venture too much, we've waited so long for a national theatre we can't kill it at birth,' says Gaskill. 'But I don't think anybody thought it was very good.' Only the set design by the celebrated Sean Kenny was seen as a triumph. Positioned on a revolve, it had the appearance of a snail's shell, beginning life as battlements facing the audience, quite high, before the whole thing slowly turned around to reveal the royal court. 'It was a very clever idea when it worked,' says Rosemary. 'One night it seized up and refused to budge and there was dear Terence Knapp in his pumpkin hose manually pushing this set around and of course it got gales of laughter from the audience.'

The stress of performing the uncut Hamlet six blasted nights a week and two sodding matinees was punishing on O'Toole. At a party, feeling depressed having to play 'the Moody One', a cast member gave him a green pill. 'I was on the ceiling for forty-eight hours. I was cuckooing and crowing from chimneys, hurtling about and gambolling and skipping – and I never stopped talking. I wept at weather forecasts.'

This exhaustion might excuse an amusing lapse that occurred one matinee, at which the cast had been informed that Noël Coward was out front. When it came time for the famous 'To be or not to be' soliloquy, O'Toole was discomforted to hear a bout of guffawing emanating from the front stalls. Undeterred, he carried on. 'Whether 'tis nobler in the mind . . . ' – snigger – ' . . . to suffer the slings and arrows . . . ' another laugh, louder this time. What's going on, he thought. On came Rosemary, and O'Toole put his hand to his forehead and realized he was wearing horn-rimmed spectacles. Just minutes earlier he'd been in the wings with the stage hands picking winners in the *Sporting Life* and had walked on totally oblivious to the fact they were still on. It had been Coward hooting like mad. Now, how to get rid of them. Turning to Rosemary, O'Toole spat the lines, 'We will have no more marriages,' and flung the specs at her.

Luckily for O'Toole's mental and physical well-being, Shakespeare had obligingly provided a lengthy period in the play where Hamlet is not required on stage. Usually O'Toole took this opportunity to visit Rosemary in her dressing room, who having gone mad and died as Ophelia was now just waiting for the curtain call. 'We used to have lovely chats about all sorts of things, but during that time he did drink quite a bit and so he was pretty wild when he came back on stage.' The person who bore the brunt of this was poor Derek Jacobi, who lived in dread of the famous sword fight. During rehearsals O'Toole had voiced his dissatisfaction with the duel as planned and grabbing Jacobi one afternoon said, 'Let's work out our own fight.' He wanted it more 'swash and buckle', jumping up on tables, a touch of the Errol Flynns. So the pair of them came up with a new routine, but during one rehearsal instead of jumping O'Toole ducked and the sword went straight across his face. Clamping his hand to the wound he ran to his dressing room mirror. Luckily Jacobi had caught him with the flat of his sword and there was only a slight mark where there might have been blood. Indeed it was Jacobi who was the more shaken and O'Toole poured him a large brandy to quieten his nerves.

The next day Jacobi was summoned to Olivier's office and told that if he did that again it would cost the company tens of thousands of pounds in insurance money as the makers of O'Toole's next film would be unable to shoot on his face. This did nothing to lessen Jacobi's nerves, nor did the knowledge that O'Toole never stuck once to the agreed routine. 'I was fighting, literally, for my life at the end of the show every night. Peter wasn't always at his most sober, and he'd wink at me across the stage and I knew I was in for it.'

Two of his old RADA classmates, Gary Raymond and Malcolm Rogers, came to see a performance. Since leaving RADA everyone had tried as much as possible to support and attend each other's shows, and there was a sense of real camaraderie. Neither man, however, had enjoyed the evening. 'It was very long and Peter wasn't very good,' recalls Rogers. 'And we weren't looking forward to going to see him in his dressing room. We thought, what on earth are we going to say.' This was always a problem, what to say to a friend after a particularly poor performance. What O'Toole always did on the first night, he would never criticize an actor's performance, it was too sensitive an issue, he'd simply go in and say, 'Spun gold!'

Fortunately, or rather unfortunately, this was the evening of the Kennedy assassination. 'So we didn't have to discuss his performance,' remembers Raymond. 'Peter was in a great state. I'm amazed, actually, that he didn't make some sort of declaration at the curtain call. But he didn't, so when we got backstage we knew nothing about the Kennedy thing, and Peter was in his dressing room anxiously listening to the radio and the news coming from America.'

During all this, the young company looked to O'Toole as a rock to cling to and he gladly led from the front. 'This was the beginning of the National Theatre so we were all very conscious that we were making history,' says Peter Cellier. 'And we would have done anything, we'd have died for one another to make it a success, there's no question.' That O'Toole coped and didn't appear, at least on the surface, to be affected by it all was extraordinary. He even indulged in a few practical jokes, such as the time he filled the main dressing-room showers with ice. 'I must say I took to Peter enormously,' says Terence Knapp. 'It was great fun as well as being a privilege to be on the same stage with him. He was amazingly modest off stage. On stage it was different, he had a tremendous, vibrant, dynamic personality. But off stage he was a quieter, simpler, nicer man.'

Knapp remembers there had been a disaster in Yugoslavia where a beautiful old theatre had burned down. British Equity organized an appeal to rebuild it and as one of their deputies it was Knapp's duty to go round backstage at the Old Vic asking for donations. 'One night after the performance I went into Peter's dressing room and asked if he would contribute and he called for his cheque book and he signed it and gave it to me – and it was blank. I said, "Peter!" He said, "Just round it off, OK." '

This generosity of spirit was often in evidence, especially when it came to his friends. When the actor James Mellor, who had appeared in *Baal*, died aged just forty-three, O'Toole arranged the funeral and then the wake at Gerry's drinking club. There was a memorial event at the Old Vic to raise funds for Mellor's young family, which O'Toole also helped organize. Another anecdote has the actor Tony Selby in the Salisbury having half a bitter, all that he could afford, as he made his way home from the Labour Exchange. O'Toole plus entourage entered and on their way to the snug, where O'Toole liked to drink, he asked Selby to join them. Tony declined pleading a previous engagement to conceal his lack of funds. Just a few minutes later O'Toole came rushing out heading for the exit. Passing Selby he clapped him on the shoulder: 'Good to see you.' When he had gone Selby found that O'Toole had left £50 in the breast pocket of his jacket.

O'Toole's Hamlet came to an end on 4 December, since he was required to start work on a picture. He departed with the gnawing truth that he had far from given of his best on such an august stage. Months awaited him on the other side of the world to search for the reasons why. Perhaps it all stemmed back to that piss-up with Burton, the fact that they both loathed and despised the piece. 'Of course, I think it's the worst bloody play ever written. Actors do it out of vanity. I only did it because I was flattered out of my trousers.'

Just days after *Hamlet* closed, O'Toole called on Rosemary Harris. She was renting a little one-bedroom flat in the Pimlico Road and her two nephews had come to stay the night, bringing along a girlfriend. 'I'd put them all to bed, the boys roughing it in sleeping bags in the lounge, when the doorbell rang, it must have been about one in the morning, and it was Peter standing there with a bottle of champagne in a bucket and a napkin over his arm. "Are you good for some champagne?" I said, "Yes, come on up." ' The bottle was quickly emptied. Rosemary could tell O'Toole was getting drowsy so tucked him into the twin bed next to her nephew's girlfriend, then took an eiderdown and some pillows and fell asleep on the floor. 'The next morning, my nephew's girlfriend woke up and said, "Who is that in the bed?" After a short pause she suddenly exclaimed, "Oh my goodness, oh my goodness, it's Lawrence of Arabia!" Peter stayed there for the next three days, he didn't wake up for three solid days and I had to call Siân to tell her that her husband was fine and that she needn't worry. I mean, he'd had that huge success as Lawrence and he could have thrown his weight around and been obnoxious or difficult but he was a lamb, he was a sweetheart.'

Rosemary kept in touch with O'Toole and they tried to meet up whenever he was in New York, where she now lived. In 1984, when Rosemary's daughter, the actress Jennifer Ehle, was at school in London and O'Toole was appearing on stage in *Pygmalion* she took her and some friends to the matinee. 'I said afterwards, come on, we'll go and see Peter. He had the star dressing room and he was waiting for us in this beautiful dressing gown and he held me in his arms and we gave each other a great big hug, and I looked at all these little girls with their big round eyes and I said,

"You've just seen the oldest Hamlet and the oldest Ophelia in the world." '

Not long after regaining consciousness in Rosemary's flat, O'Toole was pumped full of eighteen inoculations against tropical diseases, then raced to catch a flight to Hong Kong, where he was to start shooting *Lord Jim*. 'The next bloody day I'm in a blazing small boat, wearing a funny hat and paddling like a man possessed.' This was another mammoth *Lawrence*-like epic, with an international cast that included James Mason, Eli Wallach and Jack Hawkins, and a gruelling exercise for O'Toole whose idea of a workout was 'carrying a pint of bitter from one smoke-filled room to another'.

Based on Joseph Conrad's classic philosophical novel, *Lord Jim* was set in the Orient of the nineteenth century and told of a sailor branded a coward who is looking for a way to redeem himself and finds absolution inevitably in his own death. Columbia (the backers of *Lawrence of Arabia*) had given nearly ten million dollars to director Richard Brooks, who had started in the business working with John Huston as the script writer of *Key Largo*, convinced he could deliver an adventure story out of the material.

During his time in Hong Kong, which did not endear itself to O'Toole, 'Manchester with slanted eyes', he dubbed it, the actor got up to his usual antics. Staying in the plush Peninsula Hotel, he horrified the management by personally pulling a rickshaw and its driver into the main lobby at 2am and buying the fellow a drink.

Brooks made extensive use of the city's waterfront, though when it came to filming on a junk the director learned of his star's lamentable time in the Royal Navy and aversion to any sort of choppy water. For the eight days the crew shot on the ocean

O'Toole vomited profusely. 'He'd rush to the side of the ship and heave, and then go before the camera as if nothing had happened,' said Brooks. 'In eight days he must have tried every known medical and non-medical remedy. Nothing worked.'

After six weeks the company left Hong Kong and arrived for the bulk of location shooting in Cambodia. Despite an anti-West ferment brewing amongst the country's populace, Brooks had managed to get permission to shoot in the ancient temple ruins of Angkor Wat, where technicians built school houses, shops, a stockade and a tribal palace. To accommodate the large cast and crew, the studio had to sanction a huge payment to add a forty-seven-room wing onto a little hotel near the location site. 'That hotel!' raged O'Toole. 'More expensive than Claridge's; ten flaming quid a night and a poxy room at that. Nicest thing you could say about the food was that it was grotesque.' Soon everyone was suffering from dysentery and prickly heat rash and being set upon by giant stinging insects amidst insufferable temperatures. When Siân visited, a massive spider fell out of a pristinely folded towel in her hotel bathroom.

Then the snakes arrived. Walking down the middle of a jungle road, O'Toole came face to face with a huge black cobra. 'They say no snake can travel faster than a scared human,' he recalled, 'but I ain't so sure.' When the snake pounced the speed of the thing was dazzling, luckily it went in the opposite direction to a frozen O'Toole. Another time a cobra slithered onto the set and dropped to the floor of the makeshift ladies' toilet. Of particular dread was a snake called the two-step. 'It bites you, you take two steps,' explained O'Toole, 'and then you die.'

In truth the snakes were less of a problem than the local officials, who constantly sought bribes. Brooks was forced to hire Cambodian soldiers instead of local extras, and with half a dozen or so dialects spoken there were translators for the translators. For good reason did Brooks call himself 'a lunatic in the middle of the jungle trying to make a movie'. As for O'Toole, he took enjoyment in the company of the stuntmen, playing poker with them in the evening.

During filming the pulse of political violence beating just below the surface grew louder. Cambodia's pro-China Prince Sihanouk was currently in a war of words with the United States over Vietnam, foreshadowing the horrors that were to come. O'Toole remembers him paying the set a visit. 'He started yelling the usual anti-British crud. I walked up to him and said, "I couldn't agree with you more. I'm Irish meself." '

One day a stranger appeared on the location and advised Brooks to get his company out of Cambodia by 12 March 1964. Deciding to take no chances, Brooks ordered the work schedule to be doubled. Shooting went on seven days a week and from noon until nearly dawn in order for everyone to be safely out of the country. One week later the US and British embassies were attacked by mobs. O'Toole was convinced that some of the trouble-makers had worked on the film. When the Prince denounced the movie company as 'Western imperialist invaders' on national radio, O'Toole took revenge by telling a reporter from *Life* magazine: 'If I live to be a thousand I want nothing like Cambodia again. It was a bloody nightmare.' Not forgetting to mention that he once found a live snake in his soup. When word of the interview reached the Prince, O'Toole was persona non grata.

Once out of Cambodia, O'Toole and Siân flew to Japan for a brief holiday, where they were invited to watch the great Japanese director Akira Kurosawa shoot his new movie with Toshiro Mifune, whom O'Toole insisted on calling 'Tosher'. The two stars seemed to get on, though Mifune could speak no English at all, but that didn't stop them getting roaring drunk that evening. Next the couple flew to New York for the opening there of *Becket*. A nervous flyer at the best of times, 'I can't believe all that tonnage can float in the air', by the time the couple reached the city O'Toole hadn't had a proper kip for thirty-six hours. After the usual press conferences and inane meet and greets, O'Toole hadn't slept for sixty hours when he agreed to go on the *Johnny Carson Show*, one of the most watched TV programmes in America. Three minutes into the interview O'Toole, having been unable to put two words coherently together, collapsed, broke his glasses, excused himself and walked off. The effect was sensational. No one had ever walked off the *Johnny Carson Show* before. 'I came home in a box.'

For years afterwards Carson was asked what really happened in that interview: was O'Toole jet-lagged, drunk or both? Finally, in 1978, O'Toole was invited back and gently reminded of the incident by his host. He decided to come clean: 'We'd left Japan on Monday and arrived in New York on Sunday, which alarmed me. And coming from Japan one stopped at lots of places, Hawaii and all over, and our stopping coincided with the cocktail hour. Everywhere we went it was the cocktail hour. And one doesn't want to be discourteous. So we were pissed, that's true.'

Chosen as a Royal film performance, *Lord Jim* turned out to be a dud at the box office and a critical failure, with the main complaint being that Brooks didn't know whether he was making a full-blooded, no-holds-barred adventure yarn or a psychological study. O'Toole was particularly singled out for attack. *Variety* called his performance 'self-indulgent and lacking in real depth'. Observing the wreckage, O'Toole admitted he suited neither the film nor the role and that it had been an error of judgement. 'I was in danger of becoming known as a tall, blond, thin dramatic actor, always self-tortured and in doubt and looking off painfully into the horizon. *Lord Jim* was my comeuppance. It was a mistake and I made the mistake because I was conservative and played safe. And that way lies failure.' Perhaps, he mused, he should have taken on the challenge of James Mason's villainous river pirate, but of course at that time nobody would have let him, it was not the star part. O'Toole might have scoffed at the idea of himself as a handsome leading-man type, preferring to mould his image into that of a 'star' character actor, but the studios didn't see it that way. He was learning the hard way the limitations and burden of stardom.

Whatever the levels of fame, O'Toole tried desperately to keep his feet on the ground. He was often asked whether success had changed him and he liked to think it hadn't. 'I like having money,' he told one reporter. 'I like to know I can take care of my wife and kids. I've had enough of poverty. I once wrote a poem with the line, "My thighs are bruised by poverty," meaning that pennies are heavy, not like that crisp paper stuff which is what you want. But, of course, success changes other people toward you.'

As often as he could he made trips back to Leeds to visit his parents and retained a small yet loyal group of friends, including Patrick Oliver, now trying to make his way in the art world. Later in the decade O'Toole bought a rather splendid early Victorian house in Potternewton Lane in Leeds with the intention of making it his domicile in his home town. Instead he ended up giving it to Oliver and it became his family home until the mid-nineties.

The two men would often meet up. Oliver's son Richard recalls his father saying how he once arrived at a theatre to see O'Toole perform with a complimentary ticket but without an allocated seat. 'A splendid throne was dragged out of the props room and placed prominent side-stage for him to observe the proceedings from . . . and be observed.' On another occasion Oliver missed a train home due to extended drink-taking by both parties, and O'Toole provided him with a VIP air ticket to get him back to Yorkshire, and a chauffeured limousine to take him to the airport. 'Now, my father was, to say the least of it, visually striking in his younger years with an unforgettable shock of wildly unkempt hair and a beat's disdain for conventional norms of sartorial cleanliness. Apparently the assortment of well-to-do business persons gathered there waiting to board the plane were somewhat taken aback when the immaculate Daimler rolled up, the smart chauffeur opened the passenger door and a wild-looking scruffy tramp with three days' stubble and a red-eye hangover stumbled out, to be escorted to the posh end of the aircraft!'

TWELVE

O'Toole first met the maverick American film director John Huston at Christmas 1959, when he and Jules Buck were invited to stay with him at his home near Dublin. Keen to show off his protégé, Buck waited anxiously to see how the pair got on. Their rapport was instantaneous and O'Toole became a frequent guest for years after.

During one visit the pair planned a hunting trip on horseback but come the morning the rain was lashing down. Huston crept into O'Toole's room, wrapped in a garish green kimono, to announce, 'Pete, this is a day for getting drunk!' Breakfast consisted of a bottle of whisky and as the alcohol flowed it was decided to go hunting anyway. 'John in his green kimono, me in my nightie in the pissing rain, carrying rifles, rough-shooting it – with a shih tzu dog and an Irish wolfhound. Of course we were incapable of doing anything. John eventually fell off the horse and broke his leg! And I was accused by his wife of corrupting him!'

A determined atheist, Huston had nevertheless accepted an offer from Dino De Laurentiis to direct a spectacular epic entitled *The Bible: In the Beginning*, scripted by renowned playwright Christopher Fry. Originally De Laurentiis intended for a host of directors to tackle different subjects of the book of Genesis: Robert Bresson was given creation and the garden of Eden and Orson Welles Abraham, while Visconti and Fellini were also mooted. Ultimately Huston got the whole gig, as well as appearing as Noah. In a star-strewn cast, De Laurentiis hoped Laurence Olivier would play God, but Huston wanted O'Toole and had come up with the audacious idea of having the actor play three identical angels. O'Toole was happy to oblige, keen to work for Huston, and in a film full of overwrought and tiresomely earnest performances his cameo is quite easily the best thing in it, gliding ghost-like through Sodom and Gomorrah in a hooded cloak, unleashing God's wrath with his blazing blue eyes.

Arriving in Rome in the summer of 1964, when O'Toole heard that Richard Harris was to play Cain he joked to Huston that he really ought to re-title his picture 'The Gospel According to Mick'. Another of his co-stars, George C. Scott, O'Toole was less fond. Hired to play Abraham opposite Ava Gardner's Sarah, Scott had an unhealthy obsession with the actress and consequently their love affair was dominated by heated rows that usually ended in violence. One day on the set a drunk Scott went to hit Ava and it took Huston and six crew members to hold him back. When O'Toole heard about the incident it was only Huston's intervention that prevented him from going round and beating the crap out of the Hollywood star.

While staying in Rome, O'Toole had been warned about the paparazzi, who in recent years had become a pest in the city. Resting in his hotel suite, the door suddenly flew open and a gorgeous half-naked blonde fell at his feet. Quick as a flash he darted into the next room before two photographers came bounding in.

It became something of a game between the paparazzi and O'Toole, they'd lie in wait for him, desperate to catch a bit of hell-raising. The fraught relationship reached boiling point at three o'clock one morning on the Via Veneto. O'Toole was hosting a private party at the Café de Paris with Finney and the British-born actress Barbara Steele, who had made a name for herself in Italian horror pictures. As they left to walk to their parked car a young photographer darted in front of them and began snapping away. Bereft of any more patience, O'Toole decked him. The police arrived and the actor, along with Miss Steele, were arrested and questioned in a nearby police station for two hours.

The ordeal was far from over when the police arrived at O'Toole's hotel the next morning informing him that they intended to press charges of assault and were impounding his luggage and passport. Asked to go and fetch them O'Toole had to think fast. Grabbing his stuntman and stand-in, a gentleman by the name of Peter Perkins, O'Toole made him wear his raincoat, cap and sunglasses and sent him down to the lobby and into the hands of the police, while he made a quick dash for it down the fire escape.

The Bible took two years to finally reach the screen, but O'Toole thoroughly enjoyed his short stint with Huston and it was hoped the pair might collaborate again. In the end they never did, but for a while Huston was attached to a project that would have seen O'Toole play Will Adams, a sailor believed to be the first Englishman ever to set foot in Japan, where he became a key adviser to the Shogun. O'Toole stumbled upon the history of this remarkable man during his Japanese visit and once back in London began to research and study it more thoroughly, finally commissioning Dalton Trumbo to write a speculative screenplay. For several weeks O'Toole worked with Huston over the Trumbo draft at the director's house. Anjelica Huston, then just fourteen, remembers busily working behind the bar keeping the men regularly refreshed with vodkas: half vodka, half water for O'Toole, 'He won't notice,' and for her father, just water, 'He won't notice either.' It was scheduled to be shot on location in Japan as a joint production between Hollywood producer Joe Levine and Keep Films, but sadly this ambitious film, which would have co-starred Toshiro Mifune, never materialized.

Other mooted projects around this time included an offer to play the Duke of Wellington opposite Richard Burton as Napoleon in an epic retelling of the Battle of Waterloo. The project resurfaced a few years later with Christopher Plummer as Wellington and Rod Steiger as Napoleon. There was also a planned film version of *King Lear*, which O'Toole hoped to persuade Kurosawa to direct. 'I think he knows *Lear* in his bones, that monolithic feudal thing.' It was an astute observation since Kurosawa did eventually make his own version of *King Lear* in 1985, the critically acclaimed *Ran*.

Unarguably the biggest film role O'Toole was offered at this time came from David Lean, and it was the lead in his next big-budget spectacular, *Doctor Zhivago*. Lean had reservations, fearing the actor was far too extrovert to be ideal casting for the naive and idealistic Zhivago, 'but I would rather suppress his exhibitionism than attempt to coax strength out of a lily'. O'Toole, however, had seen an early draft of the screenplay and made it known that he didn't think highly of it. In the end Omar Sharif won the role. While O'Toole did revise his opinion when he saw the finished film, Lean never forgot his rash early appraisal and the pair apparently did not speak to each other until the early eighties, when Lean offered him the role of Fielding in his adaptation of E. M. Forster's *A Passage to India*. Again O'Toole declined, perhaps his rift with Lean had not altogether healed, and James Fox was cast instead.

With the glorious exception of *Lawrence of Arabia*, O'Toole's most commercially successful film of the sixties derived from a quite unusual source – Warren Beatty's sex life. The Hollywood star had decided to bring his amorous exploits to life on screen, 'the plight of the compulsive Don Juan'. It was called *What's New Pussycat?*, an expression Warren often used when calling up his girls on the phone. He brought in Charlie Feldman as producer, and to write the script sought the talents of a young New York stand-up comic, Woody Allen. 'Warren and Woody thought they were going to make a low-key, Woody Allen kind of picture,' recalls Clive Donner, who'd been hired to direct. 'Now there was no way Charlie was ever going to do that, that wasn't his style, low key pictures, he was into big fucking powerful productions.' Apparently Feldman's advice to Allen was that he 'write something where we can all go to Paris and chase girls'.

Alarm bells started ringing for Beatty when Feldman insisted Capucine play an important role in the film. 'Warren and Charlie were very good friends,' says Donner. 'But Warren just didn't want to act with Capucine. He's a lovely guy, Warren, but deadly serious. So we had a big meeting, it went on and on and on, with Warren trying to get his own way.' In the end he confronted Feldman, it was either him or Capucine; and as she had once been Feldman's lover it was no contest.

Feldman himself came up with Beatty's replacement during a meeting with Donner. 'How about O'Toole?' Donner knew and admired O'Toole, and more importantly knew he was more than capable of playing comedy. As it happened O'Toole was on the lookout for a project with a bit more levity to it. At Bristol he'd particularly enjoyed playing comedic roles but so far on film had barely been allowed to raise a titter. After all, comedy was just as valid as drama. For what was farce, he said, but tragedy without trousers. 'Shoot a man in the stomach and it is drama. Shoot him in the backside and it is comic.' Reading the script, he found it funny, 'wonderfully anarchistic', and reminiscent of the old Aldwych farces. The role on offer also appealed, that of a notorious womanizer who refuses to give up his hedonistic lifestyle to settle down and get married. It made a change, he said, from usually being in love with Richard Burton or camels.

Exerting a bit of star muscle, O'Toole insisted the role of Dr Fassbender, a crackpot psychoanalyst originally earmarked for

Groucho Marx in the Beatty version, be played by Peter Sellers. The pair had almost worked together the previous year when Billy Wilder wanted them to play Holmes and Watson in a film that ultimately broke down due to the lack of a workable script, only to re-emerge in 1970 as *The Private Life of Sherlock Holmes* with a new cast. The problem was Sellers had only recently recovered from a near-fatal heart attack and no insurance company would touch him. In the end Feldman agreed to stump up $200,000 of his own money to cover the possibility of the comedian dropping dead halfway through shooting.

Showing little gratitude, Sellers arrived on the film demanding top billing. The studio were ready to tell him where to go until O'Toole told them he didn't give a damn, 'Let Sellers have what he wants.' It was a bad start, but the two Peters did end up hitting it off. Things weren't entirely comfortable, however, as O'Toole observed. 'It was sometimes downright edgy, but it was the sharp edginess of stimulation and exploration.' They got on so well that O'Toole made a guest appearance a couple of years later in Sellers' overblown Bond spoof *Casino Royale*, playing the bagpipes in a marching band. He later claimed it was a St Patrick's Day joke and didn't realize it would make the final cut.

His relationship with Woody Allen was far more strained. Allen had worked for months on the screenplay, his first, only to watch chunks of it re-written by Sellers, Donner and O'Toole, or scrapped altogether. Allen's grumblings aside, Donner remembered the general mood on the set was good. O'Toole was particularly delighted to hear that Burton and Liz Taylor were shooting interiors for their dreary romantic film *The Sandpiper* in the same Paris studio. One afternoon he snuck onto the set and replaced one of the actors playing a drunk who disturbs Liz and Burton's amorous coupling on a beach. When the director called action, on pounded O'Toole who let forth a torrent of bad Welsh, cursing the bewildered Burton. Not to be outdone

Richard insisted on a small cameo role in *Pussycat*. The pair of them bump into each other at the bar of a swish nightclub. 'Give my regards to what's her name?' asks O'Toole.

O'Toole and Burton made good use of their time together in Paris, drinking in various establishments without serious incident. It was one evening when O'Toole was alone that he allowed the darkness within him to take hold. Returning to his hotel from filming one night he saw two policemen roughing up a prostitute. His revenge took place several days later at a nightclub he regularly frequented where at the close of the evening a policeman (not one of those he'd seen earlier) always arrived to be plied with alcohol by the customers and dance until he fell over. In the midst of these activities O'Toole weaved through the dancing throng until he was over his prey and jumped him, knocking the man to the floor and roughing him up. 'By the time I'd finished with him I don't think he was in any condition to whack any poor old whore around the head for a night or two.'

Finishing *Pussycat* in the early spring of 1965, O'Toole returned to London to discover Siân was the talk of the West End, having just opened to rave notices in Tennessee Williams' *Night of the Iguana*. Siân's casting in the play may have had something to do with an event the actor Bruce Montague witnessed some months before at the Salisbury pub. 'There was a big chair at one end of the Salisbury in those days. At some point, we were impressed to see Tennessee Williams sitting in it. We were astonished to see Peter O'Toole get on his knees at the feet of the great writer and cajole him into talking about the casting of *Night of the Iguana* due to be presented at the Savoy Theatre. Whatever was discussed it must have worked because Siân Phillips ended up in the production.'

No matter how well or badly a play had gone, it wasn't unusual for Siân and O'Toole to spend hours the following day pulling the performance to pieces, working out how to make it better.

Siân later admitted that O'Toole was better than any drama school she went to. A good example was the time she was struck down with flu after being cast in a West End play and O'Toole coached her through it, going over every line of her dialogue. With virtually no rehearsal Siân was able to give a commendable performance.

O'Toole saw *Iguana* and enjoyed it enormously. He invited Siân's co-star Mark Eden for dinner at Guyon House. The drink flowed and as the evening wore on Siân excused herself to go to bed. 'From then on things began to go downhill rather quickly,' Eden recalls. 'Peter started pouring alarmingly large brandies, and like a fool I tried to match him drink for drink. It was to be my undoing. When I finally lurched to my feet to leave, I fell flat on my face and passed out.' Eden faintly remembers being carried up the stairs by O'Toole who had him over his shoulder in a fireman's lift. 'How he was still able to climb the stairs was a miracle, never mind carrying a 175 pound drunken actor on his back.'

Next morning Eden woke with a horrendous hangover but still managed to drag himself to the theatre for the matinee. 'Peter was there waiting for me with a glass of what looked like muddy water. "It's my own remedy," he said, handing me the glass. 'Great for hangovers – if you can keep it down." It tasted absolutely vile, but it did the trick and I was able to get through the rest of the day – just.'

Not working, O'Toole could indulge in hanging out with his drinking pals, people like James Villiers, Ronnie Fraser, Philip Bond, Bryan Pringle. For O'Toole the pleasure of drinking wasn't the effect, it was the company. 'I like being around men with jars in their hands. Sober people, they're not for me.' They'd start off at the Cranbourne Tavern (now long gone), next to the Arts Theatre, and slowly drift towards the Salisbury. Acting would rarely come up as a topic for conversation, instead they'd be sharing the latest gossip, chatting about women, drink and sport. Any talk along the lines of 'Did you see my Lear?' was instantly frowned upon.

Most of them were followers of sport and always made a special effort to attend the Middlesex Sevens, an annual rugby tournament at Twickenham. It was a glorious piss-up that went on all day. This year, O'Toole picked everyone up in his Roller and as they arrived at the stadium car park who should they almost bump into but Robert Shaw, driving in his Rolls. The wine and beer flowed, but when the event finished around six the obvious next question was, where shall we go now for a drink. Philip Bond knew a member of the committee over at Rosslyn Park Rugby Club in Roehampton, so everyone piled into the two Rolls and off they headed. Allowed into the club's private bar the drinking carried on until O'Toole announced he needed to be in the West End as he'd promised to pick up Siân. Again, off they all went and news was sent for Siân to meet them in such and such a pub. After several more hours' drinking it transpired that O'Toole and Shaw had challenged each other to a race in their separate Rollers down to Brighton. Everyone piled outside to wave them off. No one saw either of them again for three days.

That June, O'Toole began rehearsals for a new play, David Mercer's *Ride a Cock Horse*, which dealt with intense adult relationships. It appealed for a number of reasons, a desire to return to the stage, to do something contemporary, and to work with Mercer, whose intellectual weight of writing he respected. O'Toole took no fee until the production costs had been met. Above all, this was a star vehicle, requiring O'Toole to be on stage virtually the whole time as he juggles a wife, a girlfriend and an older mistress. It was a real marathon and at one point O'Toole demanded Mercer make cuts, only to learn that the deleted scenes meant a young actress in the cast had practically no character left to play. O'Toole insisted everything was put back in.

They opened for previews in Nottingham and were completely sold out. By this time Siân had joined the cast at short notice when the actress playing the older mistress had to leave, only to be largely left to her own devices by the director and O'Toole. Just managing to keep her head above water in the role, Siân hated every minute of the run, feeling she had been treated rather shabbily. She was just at the point of hating O'Toole when he managed, as he so often did, to pull an ace out of his sleeve. Many years before, moving house after a failed relationship, Siân had misplaced her mother's complete set of Charles Dickens, which she had read avidly since childhood. On the opening night of their West End engagement, as Siân sat panicking and vomiting in her dressing room, a huge package arrived from O'Toole, a beautiful collection of Dickens' works.

Playing at the Piccadilly Theatre for a limited engagement, *Ride a Cock Horse* broke the theatre's attendance record. O'Toole gave a tremendous performance and was highly praised, even if the play itself received lukewarm notices. Kenneth Tynan came more than once to see it. But the strain was taking its toll and O'Toole began to suffer abdominal problems. Never having missed a performance through ill health he was determined to press on, despite having to perform sometimes in agonizing pain. He suffered intense nose bleeds, too, and there would be blood all over the stage. Thanks to an already healthy box office, it was decided to pull the play two weeks early. O'Toole immediately took Siân off for a relaxing break in Venice and on his return booked himself into a nursing home to get his battered body back into shape. He was told by doctors to ease off the drinking, as he had been during his tenure at Stratford. Again, he ignored them. He simply refused to accept he had a drink problem, later admitting that he never suffered a hangover until he was thirty.

Poor Siân though had become exasperated by her husband's hell-raising image, an image he had begun to revel in and play up to. Stories about him were turning up regularly in the press. Sometimes it was difficult to decipher what was truth and what was Fleet Street fancy. Typical of these tales was one which had him arriving late for a ferry back to Ireland and he was refused entry by the captain. Undeterred, O'Toole chartered a plane to Dublin, then hired a taxi at the airport and raced to the harbour. When the ferry arrived there was O'Toole waiting on the dock to challenge the officer to a fistfight. Did this actually happen? The public didn't care, they lapped it up with their morning coffee and toast.

He certainly got up to all sorts, that's true. 'We were silly and young and drunken and making complete clowns of ourselves. But I did quite enjoy the days when one went for a beer at one's local bar in Paris and woke up in Corsica.' For O'Toole it was all about having fun. Alcohol wasn't an addiction, it was just a fuel, it was in addition to what was going on, which was leaping and shrieking and saying: why not? Robert Bolt, who wrote *Lawrence of Arabia*, remembers a dinner with O'Toole at this time when they were joined by *Carry On* star Kenneth Williams. The booze flowed and they all went on to a nightclub afterwards. In the morning both Bolt and Williams woke up with horrendous hangovers. It was an experience that compelled Bolt to write to Williams: 'Evenings with Peter always extend into the early morning don't they? It's this quality in him which you diagnosed of making every occasion a holiday. I wonder if it feels like that to him. It must be lovely if it is so.' Indeed it was, most of the time. As O'Toole explained to Tom Stoppard once, having fun for him was 'a deep philosophical attitude'.

After *What's New Pussycat?*, O'Toole looked for another project that would further avoid him being typecast as an actor who played tortured types, à la Lawrence and Lord Jim. He wanted to surprise people, to avoid a set pattern. This was something he'd been taught in theatre. 'If you wanted to be a proper actor, if you wanted to be a Larry Olivier, or a Michael Redgrave or a John Gielgud, you had to have versatility.' He found what he wanted in *How To Steal A Million*, a romantic/heist comedy shooting that autumn in Paris that gave him the chance for 'a touch of the Cary Grants'. It also gave him his most glamorous co-star yet in Audrey Hepburn.

With Siân in London and Hepburn's husband Mel Ferrer at home in Switzerland, inevitable rumours surfaced of an affair between the stars. In truth nothing happened, though both got on extremely well, with great mutual respect for each other's abilities. Audrey loved O'Toole's zany antics, which included the Irishman getting the actress plastered on set for the first and only time in her career. It was a cold morning and the scene required Audrey to do nothing more strenuous than drive down a street. O'Toole suggested a shot of brandy to starve off the chill, but one glass became two glasses which became three until finally when she was required on set Audrey bounded out of her trailer, waddled towards the car, got in and drove straight into five huge arc lights, totally demolishing them. Luckily nobody was injured.

Frawley Becker was the dialogue coach on the film and got to know O'Toole quite well, well enough to discern with his trained ear that the actor's everyday speech did not always consist of the theatrical tones he often expressed himself with, but there were distinct traces of his working-class heritage there, too. Becker saw O'Toole as 'the common man who became the crowned King'.

The film was shot at the Studios de Boulogne in the west of Paris under the supervision of William Wyler, a director responsible for a cavalcade of Hollywood classics from *Roman Holiday* to *Ben-Hur*, but who was now operating past his prime and in somewhat poor health. Wyler was under no illusions about O'Toole's hell-raising reputation, bluntly referring to him as 'a drunk'. As far as Becker could tell, O'Toole behaved himself on set, waiting until the very last shot of the day before opening a bottle of Dom Perignon, which he invariably shared. Off set things were a little different as O'Toole was a frequent visitor to the trendiest Parisian night spots. 'But whatever he did in the evening never seemed to affect his performance during the day,' recalls Becker. 'The lines around his eyes sometimes gave him away, and Audrey once remarked to me, as Peter appeared on the set, all smiles and removing the dark glasses he frequently wore, "What *does* he do with his nights." '

Obviously Audrey never read the Parisian newspapers, which delighted in reporting some of O'Toole's drunken disturbances. One night he became involved in some fisticuffs with a gentleman who turned out to be a French count. Although he logged a complaint with the police of wilful assault, the incident was hushed up and O'Toole was never charged.

On his forays into the Parisian night O'Toole was often accompanied by Peter Perkins, the assistant cum bodyguard who began to work for him on the *Bible* shoot. Perkins had the constitution of a wrestler, having begun in the film business as a stuntman, notably doubling Sean Connery as James Bond in the classic fight aboard the Orient Express in *From Russia with Love*. Becker and many on the crew found the pair an odd match, the effortlessly sophisticated O'Toole with what looked like a fifth-rate Soho bouncer. Becker was even less enamoured of him after one encounter during a break in filming at the studio bar. 'I give Peter three more years,' said Perkins. 'Five at the most. It'll do him in, you see, his drinking. He'll lose his looks. It'll show up on the screen, in his face. Like I said, three to five years. And that gives me just a few years, too, to make my fortune.' However sadly accurate Perkins' prediction was to prove to be, it was still a callous assessment, especially by someone who was obviously doing well out of his association with the star. By the end of the decade, though, the two men parted company.

Deliberately lightweight, *How to Steal a Million*'s chief attraction is the double act of Audrey and O'Toole. During the heist sequence, the two actors had to hide in a tight broom cupboard. Waiting for Wyler to call action O'Toole commented, 'This must be what death feels like when you're in your coffin.'

'Are you afraid of dying?' whispered Audrey. O'Toole said it petrified him.

'Why, Peter?'

'Sure, there's no future in it.'

Audrey exploded into a fit of giggles, loud enough to concern Wyler, who asked what was going on. In the end Audrey had to retire to her dressing room to lie down in order to compose herself to continue the scene.

Becker found O'Toole polite and cheery company, also bright and alert. Between set-ups the actor would often sit quietly by himself doing crossword puzzles. Becker was particularly impressed by his astonishing memory. He recalled being in Wyler's caravan along with O'Toole and co-star Eli Wallach going over a scene the director wasn't happy with. It just didn't work. 'Why don't we go back to the original,' O'Toole piped up. 'We all looked at him,' recalls Becker. 'Nobody had the original script any more, we were probably on script number five at that point, and Peter delivered the entire scene by heart. Wyler laughed and said, "That was good, why didn't we use that." And it went back into the picture. Peter had memorized the entire first script and despite all the changes that had been made it was all still there, in his head.'

At O'Toole's insistence Becker was hired as dialogue coach on his next film, *The Night of the Generals*, about a high-ranking Nazi who is also a crazed sex-killer. Again shot in Paris, the film reunited O'Toole with Omar Sharif and also involved location work in Warsaw, the first time a Western film unit had been allowed behind the iron curtain since 1945. A less enjoyable reunion was with Sam Spiegel, who acted as producer, but incessantly interfered both with the script and the shooting. It got so bad that Spiegel was even telling his director, Anatole Litvak, where to place the camera. According to O'Toole the script was rewritten and changed on an almost daily basis and he later laid the blame for the inadequacies of the finished film solely at Spiegel's door, believing that had the original material been left untouched the picture would have been far superior.

This proved the last time O'Toole worked with Spiegel. Indeed their paths rarely even crossed again. There was a twinge of sadness, however, when O'Toole heard of his death in 1985, especially upon learning of the circumstances. On the set of *Lawrence*, Robert Bolt had asked how he thought Spiegel would meet his end. Almost without pause O'Toole answered, 'Spiegel will die in two inches of bath water.' And such was the case, on New Year's Eve, Spiegel died from a sudden heart attack, alone in his hotel suite, falling into his bath.

Halfway through filming in Paris, O'Toole was given permission to fly back to England to attend the bicentennial celebration of his beloved Bristol Old Vic, so long as he promised to be back on the set by at least noon the next day. Bringing Perkins along for the ride, O'Toole chartered a plane and ordered the pilot to land in London, so he could wet his whistle first at the Salisbury. Ordering a crate of champagne, the two men jumped into a hired car and off they drove to Bristol, arriving late for the ceremony. The Duchess of Kent had already been presented on stage along with some hundred and fifty former students, so O'Toole made his silent way backstage and slunk on at the end of the line. Afterwards the throng made their way to Harvey's Cellars, the home of the famous Bristol sherry, for a private function. There O'Toole held court, and if anyone so much as looked as if they wanted to leave his table, Perkins forcibly sat them back down again. 'If anyone goes,' announced O'Toole, 'he's a poof.' It had been a return to his alma mater that those who attended were not to remember with much fondness.

As for the journey back, only the most optimistic crew member believed that O'Toole would arrive on time. Word reached the film unit at eleven that the plane had indeed landed at Orly airport and that he and Perkins were en route to the studio. Relieved, Litvak began to plan that day's scene, one of the most crucial in the film, where Sharif arrives to arrest O'Toole's General. When the car arrived, the news was that O'Toole was in no fit state to work. Becker quickly made his way to O'Toole's dressing room to find him being helped inside the door by Perkins. O'Toole looked up and saw Becker. 'He put his arm around me and I was instantly engulfed in all the fumes of all the fetid pubs of England.' As O'Toole staggered into the room and into the arms of his make-up people Becker was told to come back in half an hour.

Becker was shocked, he'd never seen O'Toole in such a state before. Apparently he'd been so drunk at the airport that he was manoeuvred from the plane to his car in a wheelchair because he could barely stand upright. Half an hour passed and Becker returned. 'Come back in an hour. He's sleeping,' shouted Perkins.

Litvak did not take the news well, but decided to press ahead with the scene, making up the time shooting close-ups of Sharif. It would be three hours before O'Toole was in any fit state to perform and five o'clock before he walked onto the set dressed in his army uniform. 'Everyone went still as he walked up to Litvak,' Becker recalls, 'and in almost heart-breaking contrition said, "Tola, I'm so sorry!" Litvak's anger dissolved instantly, his eyes went moist, and then the two of them embraced. I swear they both were sniffling before Peter broke away and apologized to Omar and the crew.'

THIRTEEN

While they never reached the dizzy heights of Burton and Liz Taylor, the O'Tooles were still seen very much as a glamour couple, complete with the obvious trappings of stardom: nannies, au pairs, secretaries, gardeners, cleaners and a chauffeur for O'Toole, who had given up the driving lark, but whose collection of cars now included a Daimler, a Rolls-Royce, an imported American Chevrolet and a Mini Cooper.

There was the occasional dinner party, and stars such as Peter Sellers or Rudolf Nureyev often dropped in. Burton and Taylor owned a house in the neighbourhood and Peter Cook lived just across the road. The local pub would deliver crates of booze to the cellar at the start of every week and invariably by Friday it was all gone. He was also involved in local politics in a minor way, ordering the entire household to vote Labour in the 1964 General Election. There were even reports of a unique campaign strategy that saw O'Toole hire a coach with Guinness on tap to travel around the local pubs promising Labour voters a 'free drink and ride' to the polling station.

Over the years Guyon House had been expensively furnished, a tasteful mix of antique and modern, mainly chosen and bought by Siân. O'Toole's main influence was seen in his study, his hide-away den christened the Marcus Luccio's Room, an in-joke for Shakespearean scholars, for he is a character in *Othello* talked about but never actually appearing. O'Toole populated the room with all manner of theatrical memorabilia: the walls were covered with theatre posters, and tucked away were the gloves once worn by Sir Henry Irving and Edmund Kean's ring, a gift from Kenneth Griffith.

O'Toole's other interest in the house was a steadily growing collection of paintings and *objets d'art*. There were a number of Jack Butler Yeats paintings, hung in the drawing room, including his father's favourite, *The Emigrant*. A Bonnard hung on a wall opposite the couple's bed, there was a Picasso in the hallway and a Jacob Epstein bust that Kate used as a makeshift place to hang her discarded knickers.

O'Toole's passion for archaeology and collecting antiquities began on *Lawrence of Arabia*, and was happily satisfied with each new far-flung location. He once confided to the photographer Bob Willoughby that he smuggled a pair of precious Greek earrings through customs by hiding them in his foreskin, resulting in some minor discomfort that lasted weeks. Dotted around the house were Noh masks from Japan, a bejewelled Persian chest and his particular favourite – pre-Columbian art. Going off on excavation digs, O'Toole explained to Malcolm McDowell on the set of *Caligula* that the best way to find Etruscan jewellery was to locate the drains in the tombs, and then to sift through all the grime with one's fingers because as the bodies decompose all the artefacts deposit themselves into the channels: 'The thought of Peter O'Toole on his hands and knees in an Etruscan catacomb makes for a lovely image.'

Many of these finds he gave to Siân, who built up such a grand collection of Etruscan jewellery that she was advised that many of the pieces were so valuable they needed to be in the Louvre in Paris. One afternoon she raised the issue. 'O'Toole [it wasn't unusual for Siân to address her husband in conversation using his surname, a revealing habit since it illustrates something of her attitude towards him – apparently both distant and hero-worshipping], do you want this to go to the Louvre – I don't mind, really.'

'Do I fuck. It's yours.'

The house tended to revolve around O'Toole, its atmosphere entirely linked to the moods of the owner. Siân called life there 'intermittently ecstatic or unbelievably dreadful'. It was certainly never dull. Beside a chair he took to keeping a box of ping-pong balls which he used to throw at the television set when something came up he didn't like or didn't agree with. It was apparently Siân's idea after the occasion he was so incensed about something he threw a portable TV through the screen of their larger television.

As for the children, he was delighted and happy and madly in love with them, but he didn't necessarily want them under his feet the whole time. 'My father decreed that we were to be neither seen nor heard unless specifically invited into the presence,' remembered Kate. She and her sister, along with their nanny, lived on the top-floor nursery, a self-contained flat that had a small balcony and looked out over the London skyline dominated by an unhindered view of St Paul's Cathedral. It was a place that O'Toole rarely ventured, if a story of Siân's is to be believed. One evening both parents came up to see Patricia, who was ill in bed. A couple of days later the young girl confessed to not recognizing the man Siân was with and asked who he was. Concerned about O'Toole's lack of presence in their children's lives, coupled with his constantly changing appearance, Siân began to leave stills of him around the house in whatever role he was currently playing.

Life at Guyon House went in cycles, when O'Toole was working and when he was not working. Preparing for a job, O'Toole was a moderate, benevolent presence. 'I lock myself away for a month, before any film or play, and I absorb every word and every moment.' Things changed dramatically when filming started. 'I walk around like a ghost not talking to anyone,' he confessed. When the work and the role were discarded there was a new change as he became almost a different person. 'Erratic and unpredictable,' claimed Siân.

It was a rollercoaster ride quite often, coming to an end only when another project came along.

During the peak years of the 1960s, as one of the biggest stars in the world, O'Toole's time was precious and he was in huge demand. François Truffaut wanted him to play the lead in his adaptation of Ray Bradbury's classic science-fiction novel *Fahrenheit 451*. O'Toole passed and Truffaut chose Oscar Werner. For a time Robert Bolt wanted him to play Henry VIII in the film adaptation of his hit stage play *A Man for All Seasons*, a role that went instead to his sometime drinking competitor Robert Shaw. O'Toole was also first in the frame to play Fagin in the big-screen version of Lionel Bart's hugely successful musical *Oliver!*. Indeed he claimed to have been personally promised the role by Bart himself. However, when a press release was issued linking Peter Sellers to the part O'Toole fell out with Bart and they didn't speak to one another for years.

In early 1967 he began work on the screen version of George Bernard Shaw's comedy *Great Catherine*, playing a very prim and proper British military attaché to the court of the sexually uninhibited Catherine the Great of Russia. It was the third co-production with Keep Films after *Becket* and *Lord Jim*, and something of a personal project, given his love of Shaw and the fond memories he still had of his success in a production of it during his RADA days. He and Buck managed to assemble top international names in Jeanne Moreau and Zero Mostel, and O'Toole insisted on a role for Jack Hawkins, his first screen appearance after an operation to remove his larynx due to cancer. It was a lovely show of affection and loyalty to his old friend. When O'Toole first heard that Hawkins could no longer speak due to throat surgery he sent him a card. Inside he wrote two words, 'Shut up.'

The film was thrown into chaos when the original director, Elliot Silverstein, who'd made his name with *Cat Ballou*, quit due to creative differences with O'Toole; in other words he wouldn't do what O'Toole told him. 'I didn't want to become a star's lackey,' said the American. O'Toole was adamant that he wasn't going to have anyone messing around with his film. 'If it's going to be wrong, I want it wrong my way.' In the end Gordon Flemyng, who'd collaborated with O'Toole on *Ride a Cock Horse*, was brought in.

It was shot at Shepperton, and when O'Toole's services were not required he often waddled back to his dressing room to rest, maybe check over his dialogue or crack open a bottle of champagne and chat to Perkins, whose job was to drive the star everywhere and get him home safely after a night on the sauce. One particular afternoon, when the unit were finally ready to shoot, Flemyng dispatched an assistant to fetch O'Toole. He knocked on the dressing-room door. No reply. He knocked again, still no reply. Walking inside, the place was empty, only a television set blasting out the horse racing from nearby Sandown Park. The assistant's attention was drawn to the image on the TV screen, a close-up of the crowd in the stands, and there was O'Toole gamely cheering on the nags. The assistant rushed over to Flemyng. 'Peter's not in his dressing room. He's at Sandown races.'

Flemyng looked puzzled. 'How do you know that?'

'I've just seen him on television.' The errant actor was told to return immediately to the studio.

Against his better judgement, O'Toole had agreed to make a picture on location in Switzerland for producer Martin Poll called *The Ski Bum*, playing a misfit ski instructor who gets mixed up in shady dealings thanks to his girlfriend, played by newcomer Katharine Ross. He was never happy with the script and at the last minute declared it totally unworkable and refused to make the movie. Far from aggrieved, Poll merely sent O'Toole another script and this one met with almost instant approval.

James Goldman's witty and literate play *The Lion in Winter*, a dramatization of the personal and political conflicts of Henry II of England, his wife Eleanor of Aquitaine and their three sons, all fighting each other to inherit their father's kingdom, had been a recent smash on Broadway. Poll had quickly snapped up the film rights and hired Goldman to adapt it to the screen in the belief that it was a perfect vehicle for Burton and Elizabeth Taylor, a sort of *Who's Afraid of Virginia Woolf* in ermine. What had O'Toole hooked, besides the obvious brilliance of Goldman's words, was the intriguing idea of playing a character he had already essayed in *Becket*, this time an older and wiser version.

Once committed, O'Toole sought to make a high-class production. It was his suggestion that there was only one actress formidable enough to play Queen Eleanor, and that was Katharine Hepburn. Scribbling a quick note to her, O'Toole sent the script to Martha's Vineyard, where she was holed up, still grieving the recent loss of her beloved Spencer Tracy. A week later the phone rang and a voice said: 'I might as well do it before I die.'

With backing from heavyweight producer Joseph E. Levine, the search began for a suitable director. O'Toole had seen a short film called *Dutchman* made on a shoestring budget in a week at Twickenham Studios by debutant Anthony Harvey. It was about a woman preying on men in the New York subway and had O'Toole so excited that he sent a print over to America to show Katie Hepburn. 'I don't quite know what a murder in a subway's got to do with Henry II,' she replied. 'But if you trust him let's go ahead.' Anthony Harvey has never forgotten the enormous debt of gratitude he owes Peter O'Toole for *The Lion in Winter*, which effectively launched his career as a director. This was a major motion picture and for O'Toole to insist on a newcomer was a huge gamble that had it backfired would have reflected badly on his judgement. Even Harvey himself wasn't quite sure the right decision had been made and took the script over to the Boulting Brothers, for whom he was currently working as an editor, and asked, 'Do you think I really could do this?' The film-making pair, responsible for some of British film's finest comedies (*I'm Alright Jack*, *Carlton Browne of the FO* et al.), replied, 'Are you crazy. You can do it. Pull yourself together!'

To play Henry's three bickering sons O'Toole and Harvey went against the wishes of the American producers in casting complete newcomers: Nigel Terry, John Castle and Anthony Hopkins, none of whom had made a film before. Hopkins was with the National Theatre Company when his agent called to say that he was in line to play the young Richard the Lionheart. Hopkins was a huge admirer of O'Toole, having seen his Jimmy Porter at Bristol – 'He was the most extraordinary actor I'd ever seen' – but arriving at the production office in Eaton Square was determined not to put his reverence on display. Handed a script Hopkins read the part, with O'Toole giving lines off-camera. Afterwards there was a short pause and discussion. 'Right, you've got the part,' said O'Toole and ordered him to get out of his National Theatre contract. When Olivier proved obstinate it was O'Toole who personally rang him up to plead Hopkins' case, that here was an actor with real potential for the cinema. It did the trick.

For the remaining key roles, again O'Toole and Harvey opted for new talent. Timothy Dalton, just a year out of drama school, was cast as the King of France, and Jane Merrow played Alais, Henry's young devoted lover. Jane had some experience in pictures and was appearing in a London play when O'Toole spotted her. Arriving for her audition perhaps too full of self-confidence, right in the middle of their scene together O'Toole held up his hands. 'I don't believe a word you're saying.' Jane was mortified, but quickly composed herself and began again, 'A bit slower this time and not so full of myself.'

Work began late in November 1967 with a two-week rehearsal period at the Haymarket Theatre in London, to help bed in the largely inexperienced cast. For Harvey these rehearsals were both extraordinary and invaluable. 'There was something about being on that stage, in that particular theatre, the cast found the magic in the writing right away.' The Plantagenets were an extraordinary group of people and Henry perhaps the most extraordinary of them all. O'Toole, at thirty-five, was much younger than the real Henry, who at around fifty was heading towards the end of his life during the time these events took place. Because of the age discrepancy, Harvey recalls the actor 'was always rolling in the dust wherever we went to try and make himself look worn out'.

Henry's life is being completely torn apart by these terrible children: Richard is a war lord and very much aligned with Eleanor. Geoffrey, played by John Castle, is a nasty, devious piece of work, typical middle son, and Nigel Terry's John is the runt of the litter. Henry and Queen Eleanor are pitted against each other but the fierce love they once shared still smoulders in a dark corner somewhere. For Jane, everyone in that cast adopted a little bit of the characters they were playing, which often happens if the script is good. 'I know I had a crush on Peter. I thought he was just the bee's knees. And I think he had a slightly fatherly attitude to the rest of us. And the relationship he had with Kate was fascinating. I mean, he really did adore her and held her in a certain awe.'

What became instantly apparent to everyone when shooting began at Ireland's Ardmore Studios in December was that lightning in a bottle was happening with O'Toole and Katie Hepburn.

Harvey remembers during one highly charged exchange, where they're tearing emotional lumps out of each other, he was so overwhelmed that he literally couldn't say the word cut.

The common perception of Katie Hepburn is of a slightly masculine woman, due to the sort of roles she played, but this really wasn't the case, she was a very feminine woman and had a thing about all her leading men. 'And Peter was no exception,' reveals Jane. 'She adored him, and was quite possessive of him.' It was at times a love–hate relationship, with Katie insisting on calling O'Toole 'pig'. 'Hello, pig,' she'd cry out each morning as she arrived at the studio. Often she'd berate him in front of his fellow actors and the crew. 'Peter, stop towering over me. Come and sit down and try to look respectable.' She'd also bring up his drinking, telling him he was in danger of throwing his talent away. So concerned did she become of his general state of health that she bought him a bike and ordered him to cycle to and from the studios. He'd met his match, no doubt about it.

In return O'Toole christened Katie 'nags' and once deposited a load of empty spirit bottles into her car. It did get feisty a few times. When O'Toole kept her waiting on set because he was still in his caravan playing cards, she stormed in shouting: 'You are a real nut and I've met some nuts in my day.' She then punched him, rather hard. A couple of hours later he meekly knocked on the door of her dressing room to apologize profusely. 'Don't worry, pig,' she answered. 'I only hit the people I love.'

On one occasion Jane Merrow was with O'Toole in his trailer going through some lines when in stormed Kate, red in the face, almost uncontrollably full of rage. 'She walked up to Peter and whacked him round the head and screamed, "You son of a bitch, don't you ever keep the make-up and hair people from me again – ever!" There was a deadly silence and I sort of shrank in the background. Peter sat there with his mouth open and then she stormed out again. I thought, oh bloody hell, now all hell's going to break loose. Well, Peter just burst out laughing.'

In fact, O'Toole was quite innocent of the charge, the make-up and hair people were simply delayed on their way to the set, but the crew feared that this misunderstanding could spell the end of relations between the stars. Jane explains what happened next: 'Peter got the first aid man to come in and dress him up with a sling and a crutch and a bandage round his head, and he went back onto the set and of course that broke the ice and Kate and everybody fell about.' Years later O'Toole was not stinting in his praise of his legendary co-star. 'Many of us were a little bit . . . tired . . . in the morning, she'd give you about sixty seconds in which to recover and if you weren't there – zip! She'd cut your head off. I adored the girl.'

After a brief Christmas break, filming resumed on location at various castles in France. Unlike the Broadway play, which Harvey felt was played more for laughs, here he wanted complete authenticity, what it actually must have felt like to live in a damp, dank castle. This approach chimed perfectly with O'Toole, who arrived with reams and reams of research material on Henry Plantagenet and everything to do with that period. Impressed by such dedication, Harvey remained apprehensive about directing O'Toole. 'I thought he was going to be bloody difficult.' Instead he found a highly intelligent man, full of constructive ideas, with a solid grasp of contemporary cinema and, thank God, a great sense of humour. What was most surprising was the discovery that O'Toole was an intensely private man who found revealing aspects of his personality difficult. Harvey tells one story of when they were staying at a hotel in Dublin. 'About two in the morning my bedroom door suddenly burst open and there was Peter quite insanely excitable and he threw something into the room and said, "Happy birthday," and then disappeared. I turned on the light and lying on the floor was a painting in a beautiful frame with broken glass all over the place. In the morning I was a bit more with it and saw that it was an etching of Picasso. I was so overwhelmed I said to him on the set first thing, "My God, Peter, what a wonderful thing." And he looked at me and said, "I don't know what you're talking about." ' Harvey is convinced it wasn't the drink blurring his memory, that he did find it hard to be openly generous in some ways.

O'Toole had promised Katie Hepburn that he would stay off the drink during the shoot. 'That was one of the conditions of her doing the film,' confirms Jane Merrow. And for the most part he kept to his word. Jane herself can recall only one serious lapse, when he disappeared for half a day. 'The next morning he dropped to the floor grovelling and apologizing to Kate.'

Much drinking went on in the evening however at the numerous restaurants the cast frequented. One night Nigel Stock, who played Captain William Marshall, was delighting everyone with tales of his time with Wingate's Chindits in Burma during the war. O'Toole took umbrage at this, probably because for once he wasn't the centre of attention, and began belittling the famous guerrilla force, calling them 'tin soldiers'. Stock was incensed and a violent argument broke out between both men which ended in Stock having to be restrained from attacking O'Toole.

There was also a bizarre accident during the shooting of the scene where Eleanor arrives at the castle in regal style aboard her barge. O'Toole paddled out to discuss something with Katie but managed to catch a finger between the barge and the rowing boat. 'Bloody agony it was, took the top right off.' The unit doctor wasn't around so O'Toole carried the tip of his finger back to shore, dipped it into a glass of brandy for safe keeping and then stuffed it back on, wrapping it up in a poultice. Three weeks later he unwrapped it and there it was, all crooked and bent and frankly disgusting. 'I'd put it back the wrong way, probably because of the brandy which I drank.'

On another occasion he awoke at four in the morning to discover his bed was on fire; the result no doubt of a misplaced Gauloise. For a moment he thought it was a dream, then reality kicked in. 'At first I tried to put the thing out myself, but I couldn't read the small print on the fire extinguisher. By the time the first fireman arrived I was so glad to see him I kissed him.'

Remarkably, it had only been five years since his breakthrough as Lawrence, but amidst upstarts like Hopkins and Dalton, O'Toole felt positively middle-aged! At the start of filming he'd told them all – 'The gloves are off. I'm out to steal every scene. Stop me if you can.' On set they watched him like hawks while he in turn couldn't help but impose upon himself a certain fatherly position. 'They looked to me for advice, for bloody guidance!' When they dared each other to swim from one bank of the river Rhône to the other, it was O'Toole who stepped in to throw the book at them. 'The problem was keeping a straight face. I'd done exactly the same thing when I was their age. In Switzerland I'd swum across one of the lakes. In evening dress, as I remember.'

For the young cast this had been an education, Hopkins regarded the advice he received from Hepburn as some of the best he was ever given about film acting, but for him the one all-powerful, charismatic figure he never forgot was O'Toole.

O'Toole had high hopes for *The Lion in Winter*. 'If this one doesn't come off, then I shall hang up my jockstrap and retire.' For Harvey, too, 'I never enjoyed making a film in my life like that.' Jane Merrow called the shoot, 'Bliss. One of the highlights of my life. Peter was extraordinary to work with, just his energy, his total involvement in what he was doing.' The only sour note came when Levine threatened to withhold O'Toole's fee due to 'disgraceful conduct', which had added to the film's costs, including being booted out of two hotels when he became excessively drunk. O'Toole sued the producer and won the case.

A commercial success, *The Lion in Winter* opened to mixed reviews, with some complaining that Harvey had reduced a major historical event to the level of a soap opera. Yet it is precisely this aspect of the film that has kept it fresh and relevant for modern audiences. Here is a literate script handled intelligently, an all-too-rare thing in a mainstream Hollywood movie. The entire cast are superb but the film belongs utterly to O'Toole and Hepburn; O'Toole's playing is especially magisterial, yet at the same time heartbreakingly vulnerable, like a mighty tower that can crumble if just one brick is removed. It earned him yet another Best Actor Oscar nomination; this time he lost out to Cliff Robertson's performance as a man with learning difficulties in *Charly*. At least he took pleasure in Katharine Hepburn being named Best Actress, though she didn't take the honour at all seriously. Harvey recalls visiting her some six months later and searching for a bite to eat found the Oscar tucked away unceremoniously in one of the kitchen cupboards.

The Lion in Winter made quite an impression on a young would-be director called Roger Young, who in 2003 cast O'Toole as Augustus Caesar in an epic TV movie. 'It was an amazing performance. I asked Peter how he arrived at that character because it flies all over the emotional map but never for one second is it melodramatic or overdone. Peter replied: "It was in the script, my boy, in the script." I doubt that any script could be that good. Peter made that film into something beyond film, beyond theatre. It was a combination of the best of both.'

Siân had always thought it strange that O'Toole found it difficult to compliment her work to her face, it rarely if ever happened, yet would go around telling friends what a great actress she was and how much she meant to him. Over the years she had learnt to live with the mass of contradictions at the centre of O'Toole's personality, that he was the kind of person who would casually forget birthdays, not remember visiting times at hospital, but was always there for the big important things.

She had even accepted that her career had been largely put on hold in order to be mother to O'Toole's children and that the energies of Keep Films and Jules Buck were the exclusive territory of her husband. Yet she did regret that the few occasions they had worked together tended to end as bitter and crushing experiences. The latest was no exception. She had been cast by director Herbert Ross to play a flamboyant actress in his remake of *Goodbye, Mr. Chips*. O'Toole was playing the kindly headmaster, a role made famous by Robert Donat in the classic 1938 film. Siân sensed that her presence in the picture was against O'Toole's wishes and during a large party scene he point blank refused to rehearse with her, preferring to sit alone on the set some distance away. Ross would later say it was like sending into space astronauts who didn't know each other. Then, when a reporter asked how she combined her busy private life with a career, O'Toole answered on her behalf, saying how she didn't have a career as such, only jobs.

Besides these aberrations the shoot was idyllic. The film company rented a charming cottage for them to stay in near Sherborne in Dorset, where most of the picture was shot, and the girls were able to come down and enjoy a few weeks in the sun.

In a role originally earmarked for Audrey Hepburn, Petula Clark was cast as the music-hall actress Mr Chips falls in love with and marries. They met for the first time at a lavish reception for the press at the Savoy Hotel in June 1968 and Petula was uneasy about the encounter. 'It's always a little tricky when you admire somebody very much and suddenly you're going to meet that person, you hope you're not going to be disillusioned. And of course, he was absolutely charming and funny.'

Their second meeting was very different, taking place in Dublin, where Petula got to know O'Toole much better. 'After dinner word must have got out that Peter was in town because suddenly all these people came out of the woodwork – to have a drink with him. I finished up just as tiddly as everybody else. And that was the shape of things to come; the film seemed to me like a huge party with a bit of acting thrown in.' On location in Dorset she'd often visit O'Toole and Siân at their cottage, which had the added bonus of a croquet lawn. 'Of course the croquet parties used to turn out hysterical and boisterous,' remembers Petula. 'Croquet is supposed to be a polite little game, but with Peter it didn't go that way at all.'

O'Toole had accepted the job largely because of his respect for playwright Terence Rattigan, on whose screenplay it was based. This latest version, however, was to be a musical with songs by Leslie Bricusse and would require O'Toole to sing, something he'd not done since *Oh! My Papa* in 1957. He'd certainly never sung on screen before. 'Although when I went out with Peter we'd finish up the evening with him singing at the top of his voice,' recalls Petula.

This was to be no ordinary musical, 'where everything stops for five minutes while some bloke yells the place down', quipped O'Toole. Rather the songs were unobtrusive, with O'Toole performing them not in his own voice, but the slightly cracked voice of the ageing schoolmaster he was playing, 'a voice full of chalk and reflections'. Alongside musical director John Williams, O'Toole found it tough laying down his tracks in the studio, at one point joking that out of nearly forty-nine takes of one particular song they might be able to salvage one tuneful note. 'I thought he pulled it off,' says Petula. 'He was superb.'

O'Toole had promised Herbert Ross that he would abstain from the sauce during working hours, but in the evenings he was hitting the bottle just as hard as ever. 'Every morning I would see him drinking this weird thing which I'd never seen or heard of before,' says Petula. 'Fernet Branca, a digestive bitter liquor made of herbs and goodness knows what else. I asked him eventually what it was and he said, "My dear, I can't start the day without this." Of course, I had to taste it, and just once was enough. And then he would be on the set giving this beautifully controlled performance. The rest of the time, when he could anyway, he was out having a great time.' George Baker, who had a small role in the film, often joined O'Toole on these boozy nights out and recalled the only thing that would calm him down if he started to get out of control was Mendelssohn. O'Toole had a thing for Mendelssohn, so if you talked about the composer you were at least in with a chance.

When the unit came to Elstree to shoot interiors, O'Toole took Petula out for a meal at his favourite restaurant in Hampstead. 'As usual, the meal turned into a boisterous occasion and I finished up sitting on Peter's shoulders walking down the high street singing at the top of our voices. And people were leaning out of windows telling us to shut up. I remember at one point Peter yelling, "Do you realize who we are. You should be paying for this!" '

For a week the crew filmed in Pompeii, marking the first time O'Toole had worked in Italy since his disagreeable bust-up with the paparazzi. Just to be on the safe side he took boxer Dave Crowley with him to keep any prying lenses at bay. Being in Pompeii was too good an opportunity to miss and he often disappeared on hunting trips for Etruscan treasures, often with Petula's husband Claude, both sometimes not coming back until the following day. 'He was always trying to get his hands on some valuable piece of pottery,' recalls Petula. Several ceramic pots were packed and sent back to London, save for one large and valuable second-century Apulian pot that was deemed too delicate. Instead O'Toole organized a chauffeur-driven car to transport it all the way across Europe, but during its trip the driver had to brake suddenly and the pot was destroyed.

When *Goodbye, Mr. Chips* opened it didn't quite resonate with audiences, for whom perhaps the memory of the sparkling original was still too strong. It didn't help matters that former Broadway director Herbert Ross was making his feature debut with such a large-scale picture. 'I had the feeling that Herbert was a bit overwhelmed with Peter,' claims Petula. 'In fact, Peter took over quite a lot of the directing.' Critics weren't too impressed, either. Vincent Canby of the *New York Times* singled out O'Toole as the film's only redeeming feature. Indeed, he was once again nominated for an Oscar, losing out this time to John Wayne for *True Grit*. Age has been kind to the film though and today it is fondly remembered by many. Perhaps the prime reason is the relationship between the two leads, whose romance is believable and tender. 'That's how we felt about each other,' says Petula. 'We genuinely loved each other, not romantically, we really did feel for each other and that's something that I don't think you can fake.'

Petula rarely saw O'Toole again, living and working as they did in different spheres of the same business. The last time they met was in the early eighties when O'Toole was appearing on the London stage in *Man and Superman*. 'That was the real Peter because he was in total command of the stage. That seemed to be his place, the theatre.'

After the curtain came down Petula made her way to his dressing room. He had just come off the stage and was exhausted. 'I don't think he was in great health and looked extraordinarily thin. He would push himself to the limits, in many ways. We hardly spoke, we just both sat on these hard little chairs, sitting opposite each other, knee to knee, and wept. I don't quite know why, maybe they were such wonderful memories of our time working together and he had a feeling we wouldn't have that experience together again. It was just a moment between us that only we could share.'

FOURTEEN

Since the mid-sixties O'Toole had been taking Siân across the water to visit the town of Clifden in Connemara, real O'Toole country, with hundreds if not thousands of people bearing that surname dotted about the place. He first arrived there alone on a cold October evening in 1964. Billy Foyle was with some of his friends in the smoke room of the Clifden Bay Hotel, as it was known then, when this knock came at the door. 'And this big, tall, lanky stranger was standing there with an English accent and he wanted to get a room for the night.' Although they were closed Foyle invited him in. With not one cinema in Clifden nobody had seen *Lawrence of Arabia* nor had the first clue who Peter O'Toole was. 'He came in and my friends were having pints of Guinness and I introduced him and we got talking and we got drinking, and drinking, and drinking perhaps more than we should.'

O'Toole wanted some cigarettes so he and Billy Foyle walked to the pub across the street. There had been a funeral that day and the place was heaving with mourners and the drink was flowing. 'We stopped to have a few pints and Peter got to know everyone and he bought drinks on the house. As the revelry started they all sang rebel songs for all the people that died for Ireland. You could almost hear the bullets going into the wall. And Peter was delighted and egging them on.' Somebody then suggested Peter have a go at a song. He made a few grunts and then got up on a table. This bar had a very low ceiling and he was almost bent over. 'And it sticks in my mind forever this day,' says Billy Foyle. 'Now, to appreciate what he did, the atmosphere in that pub that particular night was heated, these were all Irish rebels dying for Ireland every five minutes. And I heard this song coming across and I was certain I knew it but I thought it was an out of tune Irish ballad he was singing. It must have taken about ten seconds before I realized the song he was singing was "God Save the Queen". I grabbed Peter and yanked him off the table and he hit the floor with a moan. Then I bundled him out of the door and into the street. "For Christ's sake run, Peter," I yelled, because they'd have beaten me up more than they would have beaten O'Toole up.'

Both men ran back to the hotel and into the safety of the smoke room. Inside O'Toole delighted in telling everyone what had happened and suggested to Foyle an encore the following evening. 'I'm sorry, Peter, I'm very busy tomorrow. But if you do go out, for God's sake don't sing that song again.' He did go out, starting off in several pubs before going to a private house party, where he brought all the drink, bottles of whisky, gin and vodka. Sometime in the night there was the obligatory singsong and O'Toole was asked to have a go. 'Of course, what did he do,' says Billy Foyle. 'He sang "God Save the Queen" again, only this time I wasn't there to save him and they kicked seven kinds of bejesus out of him. The next morning I was going across the road to get the newspaper when I saw this image come up the street. He said, "William, old boy." I said, "Peter, is that you? What happened?" I thought I'd saved him once. And he was so proud, he had a broken nose, his eye was black and blue and there was congealed blood. I don't know where he slept that night. He didn't sleep at my hotel. I took him in and cleaned him up and then sent him on his way.'

A few months later O'Toole was back, saying he wanted to

trace his ancestors. Although for all the time he knew O'Toole, Foyle can't recall him ever managing to locate a single one. 'I think he was probably hoping he wouldn't find any. But when people asked, what are you doing over here, he'd say, I'm looking for my relations.' What did happen was that O'Toole fell in love with the wild and desolate beauty of this piece of Ireland, battered by the torrents of wind that sweep off the Atlantic. He told Billy Foyle that he wanted to build a house for his family there and to let him know when he'd found the perfect plot of land.

It was partly by accident, partly by design that O'Toole's next film was made in Ireland. He'd seen James Kennaway's play *Country Dance* at the Hampstead Theatre and become fast friends with the author. When Kennaway tragically died in a car accident, driving back from O'Toole's home, the actor was determined to bring some kind of permanence to the work and make it into a film, changing its Scottish locale to Ireland. In it he plays a crazy alcoholic who has an incestuous relationship with his sister, played by Susannah York. It was a controversial premise and on the first day of filming O'Toole told producer Robert Ginna, 'You know we're not going to make a buck on this, don't you? But let's have a bloody good time.'

Bringing his usual diligent research to bear upon a role, O'Toole got regularly smashed. It was not uncommon for him to be absent Monday mornings in order to sleep off the exertions of the weekend's festivities. Filming at Ardmore Studios, county Wicklow, he often drank at the nearby Harbour Bar and donated a large moose head (a prop from *What's New Pussycat*) as a gesture of gratitude to the owners for making sure he was returned in one piece to his hotel each night.

One evening O'Toole took some of the crew out on one of his customary pub crawls through Dublin which ended in a restaurant at 3.30 in the morning. When things got a little too boisterous for the owner he asked them to leave and when they refused brought out his Alsatian dog to reinforce the point. When O'Toole demanded more drinks and was bitten for his trouble he punched the landlord in the face. It just so happened that an off-duty policeman observed the whole incident and O'Toole was arrested. In the end the landlord refused to press charges, though O'Toole still humbly accepted a fine of £30 the next morning in the Magistrates' Court.

Another night in Dublin he got into a fight and arrived on the set the next morning sporting a black eye. 'We had to rejig the shooting in order to hide it,' remembers co-star Michael Craig. 'He didn't seem to take much notice of it really, it was just one of those things that happened in his daily life.' Craig went with O'Toole one afternoon to the Curragh Racecourse in nearby Kildare, where they met up with a whole gang of film people who had been in Ireland for months working on *Ryan's Daughter*. 'I remember I lost £700 on the day and I never saw a horse race because we were in the bar all the time. Then we went back to our hotel in Dublin and Peter insisted on staying up all night and carrying on.' After that experience, and a couple of others, Craig decided not to go out on the booze any more with O'Toole. 'I knew there would come a point when the pub would shut and he'd be looking for somewhere to make on to, and I'd be thinking, I should get my head down because I've got a call at six in the morning, but that didn't bother him.'

O'Toole's drinking was yet again a cause for concern and the effects it was having on his general health. He'd taken to recording his morning cough for posterity, so impressively repulsive was it. Siân told of one distressing incident when her husband turned up at the theatre where she was performing only to pass out drunk in the corridor backstage requiring the actors to step over his crumpled form in order to get on the stage. Medical opinion was once again sought and the same advice delivered, lay off the drink, which prompted the same reply as before – he wouldn't, despite a recurrence of his stomach pains.

That October, Burton and Liz Taylor saw O'Toole quite by chance in the paddock of Longchamp Racecourse outside Paris. In his diary that night Burton did not paint a very flattering portrait of his old friend: 'We were standing there when suddenly a tall man appeared emaciated and ill and stubble-faced and smiled a lot and was quite incoherent, and had a right hand which was burned to the bone between the index finger and the next. It was Peter O'Toole.' Other friends and colleagues were equally concerned. Phyllida Law, who had acted with him at Bristol, was one: 'To be quite honest, at one point in his life I seriously didn't think he'd live. I'd see him about looking as white as anything and thin. He did look so ill that I used to think, he'll never make it, he can't live.'

When *Country Dance* finished filming in the autumn of 1969 (it would eventually meet with an uninspired reception in cinemas), O'Toole and Susannah York remained in Dublin since both had been invited to appear in a production of Shaw's *Man and Superman* at the Gaiety Theatre. O'Toole was reprising the role of John Tanner that he had played years earlier at Bristol. Directed by his old mentor Nat Brenner, it ran for only fifteen performances and demand for tickets was extraordinarily high. 'The finest thing I've ever seen,' remarked fellow cast member Nigel Stock. Brenner remembers being alone in his office one night and the telephone ringing. It was the Irish Prime Minister trying to get tickets.

There was talk of a London transfer but O'Toole had already committed that December to appearing in a production of *Waiting for Godot* at Dublin's Abbey Theatre, once again playing Vladimir. Appearing opposite him was another Irish drinking pal, Donal McCann. When in London, McCann was a regular visitor at Guyon House. Siân remembers one extraordinary episode when McCann, on his second bottle of vodka, fell asleep in an armchair in the drawing room and somehow managed to set fire to his hair with a cigarette. Calmly, by now used to such eccentricity, Siân walked over to the drinks cabinet, picked up a soda siphon and drenched his head with it. McCann merely blinked, then held out his empty glass for a refill.

Godot lasted just eighteen performances, since O'Toole was due to start shooting a new movie. An offer had arrived to appear in a film directed by Peter Yates, then a hot talent after helming the Steve McQueen classic *Bullitt*. The location was South America, a part of the world he'd never been to before and was keen to explore. The money was good too, a quarter of a million dollars. He quickly accepted.

Murphy's War was based on a novel by Max Catto about the sole survivor of a British merchant ship sunk by a German U-boat who becomes obsessed with sinking the submarine to avenge his companions, shot as they floated in the wreckage. When the film rights were snapped up by Paramount, producer Michael Deeley and Yates were handed a list of ten actors and told to make their choice. Amongst the usual suspects were a couple of left-field choices, chief amongst them O'Toole. A Sean Connery or a Lee Marvin would have given a perfectly fine bravura performance, but Yates was aiming for something a bit more quirky than your regular war movie. In that regard O'Toole was the perfect fit, though after reading the script he insisted on playing the part as an Irishman, necessitating a slight rewrite.

Deeley and Yates had hired O'Toole fully aware of his reputation, but came up with a cunning plan to keep him under control. In a film that was distinctly macho, there was just the one female role, that of a nurse who befriends Murphy. 'Because of one's fear that Peter might be unreliable, pissed out of his mind or something,' says Deeley, 'we decided to cast Siân to play opposite him. Of course she's a great actress, but stuck in the jungles of

Venezuela, we thought she would be our insurance. In the event it was totally unnecessary. Actually, he was the glue that held that film together.'

For Deeley, *Murphy's War* remains a particular favourite, it was fun and challenging but also the most hazardous film he ever worked on. The location was an absolute killer. Shooting on the Orinoco River, the unit were miles from any kind of civilization and surrounded by hazards – piranha fish in the shallows and poisonous snakes everywhere else. 'It was a dangerous location because if you fell into the water you'd be dead.'

To make matters worse the Belfast to Liverpool ferry that had been converted to accommodate the film crew, having crossed the Atlantic, got stuck on a sand bank as it approached the mouth of the Orinoco, a mile short of the location site, demanding the use of small flat-bottomed boats to move everyone back and forth. One morning a party that included O'Toole and Siân, along with Deeley and his wife, were halfway across when the weather turned bad and the sea began to cut up rough. 'The fella who was driving the boat suddenly had hysterics and got down on his knees and started praying,' Deeley recalls. 'The boat was now completely out of control. Luckily our stunt arranger Bob Simmons knocked the guy out, seized the wheel and took over. But it was very nasty for a moment.'

This, as everyone soon discovered, was par for the course on *Murphy's War*; if something could go wrong it invariably did. O'Toole, at times non-communicative and grumpy, due to more stomach problems, persevered, indeed flourished in the hostile surroundings, living it like some kind of adventure. 'Peter was the absolute soul of the picture,' confirms Deeley. 'And I've never seen this with an actor before.'

After a couple of weeks O'Toole and Siân were re-housed in a hotel in the town of Puerto Ordaz and a helicopter took them into the rainforest for filming. The chopper was manned by a

French stunt pilot called Gilbert Chomat and on weekends O'Toole would command Chomat to pilot him round the area, landing on mud banks to search for pre-Columbian artefacts. O'Toole was determined to explore the region, having read up on Eldorado, pre-Columbian art and the revolutionary Simón Bolívar.

One weekend they passed near the famous Angel Falls, the highest waterfall in the world. It was a spectacular sight and when the pair met later in the hotel bar they began a long discussion about the possibilities of landing the chopper directly on the falls, on a flat-topped plateau just above where the water flows out in a huge gush and drops for about a mile; an aerial feat so far as they knew never attempted before, probably for good reason. 'We had a few more drinks,' remembered O'Toole. 'And it became infinitely more sensible.' They decided to do it the following weekend.

Chomat had the chopper stripped down, leaving just the skeleton, and O'Toole brought along Siân and the photographer Bob Willoughby. Once at Angel Falls the helicopter began its ascent up this sheer wall of water until Chomat had it hovering over the top. Carefully he eased the machine down until it gently but uneasily settled on what was little more than a smooth patchwork of rock. Everyone got out, save for Chomat who kept watch for any sudden change in the weather that could spell disaster. Willoughby took some pictures for posterity, Siân collected a few wild flowers, while O'Toole lay prostrate on the ground, looking over the edge, down at this mile of water. It could only have been minutes when Chomat urged everyone back in the chopper. It was time to leave, clouds were coming in.

While the landing had been tough enough, their exit was white-knuckle stuff. Chomat couldn't start the engine for fear the helicopter might shudder off the rock out of control. The trick was to fling the craft off and as it hurtled down like a rock the rotor blades started and Chomat piloted them all to safety. It was a masterful piece of flying.

Following the river for some distance they came across a compound owned by a former German officer, 'who clearly decided not to hang around after the war was over for fear of his record emerging', says Deeley. 'The crew often went there. It was amazing. My wife and I were walking down to his hut one night when a huge anaconda wound its way out of a tree into one's path.' It was that kind of place, and the man himself a genial host, despite being eaten away by leprosy. This was where Chomat landed and O'Toole and his party spent a riotous evening. 'We drank every single drop the man had had stored for over a year,' the actor reported. 'And then we had a shooting competition.'

When location filming wrapped, O'Toole and Siân had some spare time before they were required for studio work back in England. O'Toole had made his mind up to track down some Yanomami Indians, which entailed a long and deep trek into the jungle. Siân was once again game, Willoughby too. Chartering a boat, and hiring a couple of guides, off they went up the Orinoco, into the wilds of the Amazon basin, the land of head-hunters and goodness knows what. After just a couple of days' travel, one of the guides refused to go any further, and nerves were tested again when a Greek missionary working at a small settlement they passed through advised them all to go back. Still they ploughed on, up river, in blasting heat and then torrential rain.

After another day O'Toole spotted a young child playing on a beach and they pulled in. Far from displaying shyness or fear the girl ran up to O'Toole, took his hand and pulled him into the jungle. They ran further and further inside as Siân and Willoughby tried desperately to keep up, arriving eventually upon a large encampment. They'd found their Indians. It was a once in a lifetime experience as they were invited to eat, play and rest with the tribe and exchange gifts. O'Toole even embarked on a spot of archery, his sheer ineptitude drawing merriment from the men of the village. It was only after making it back they learned they'd managed to get four hundred miles further up river than a recent BBC documentary team who travelled in a hovercraft with armed guards.

The gruelling circumstances *Murphy's War* was made in certainly paid dividends on screen as the film is wholly authentic, and O'Toole delivers a whimsical and hard-edged performance. But it didn't fare particularly well with the public or the critics. Deeley himself feels the film is flawed due to Peter Yates' insistence that O'Toole's character be killed off at the end. 'Yates had this passion to make a picture which mattered, but this was not a film which mattered, it was a film which was meant to be a lot of fun, an adventure movie. Yates wanted to have this great sad ending, this anti-war message or something, which is such shit.'

On his return from Venezuela, O'Toole was exhausted and recuperating in hospital when director Peter Medak paid him a visit. In spite of strict instructions that he was not to drink, Medak was surprised to see O'Toole sat up in bed eating caviar and downing vodkas. Medak had recently seen Peter Barnes' scurrilous new play *The Ruling Class*, which gleefully laid into the decaying institutions propping up Britain's rotten Establishment, and thought it would make an ideal film. As for the dazzling central role, that of the 14th Earl of Gurney, who is clearly out of his mind, first believing himself to be Christ and then Jack the Ripper, it was made for O'Toole.

At Medak's insistence O'Toole saw the play and was so captured by it he instructed Jules Buck to buy the film rights without delay. Promising Medak that he could direct him in it, there followed a worryingly lengthy period of inactivity as O'Toole busied himself on other projects. Worried, Medak would think the film was on, only for it to get bogged down or cancelled.

'Finally, one night we came back from seeing *Waiting for Godot* at the theatre. And to go home with O'Toole meant stopping at every pub between Soho and Hampstead, and it didn't matter that it was after closing hour because he would knock on the door and just say, "Peter's here," and every door opened for him. So about three o'clock in the morning we staggered into his house and he said to me, "Come on, let's do *Ruling Class*." And I said, "You say you're going to do it but then nothing happens, it's like *Waiting for Godot*." I ripped into him a little bit. I said, "You will never make this fucking film." And he leapt out of his chair across the room and jumped on my lap and picked up the phone and called Buck and said, "I'm with the crazy Hungarian and I know I'm drunk but I give you twenty-four hours to set this movie up, otherwise I'll never make another film." '

In order for the deal to happen, according to Medak, O'Toole had to agree to make the musical *Man of La Mancha*. 'They wanted him to do *La Mancha* first,' claims Medak. 'And we said, no, no, no, first we do *Ruling Class*.'

Before filming was due to begin O'Toole wanted Medak to fly with him to Ireland to work more on the script. 'I remember the plane for some reason couldn't land,' recalls Medak. 'And it made three passes, we thought we were going to fucking die.' Finally landing, they were picked up by a chauffeur and driven to Clifden, where O'Toole had rented a cottage. 'We were alone there for a week in this cottage. One night he said, "Come on, let's go to the pub." We hopped in the car, I don't think he had a licence any more, we drove and I didn't think I was going to be alive the time we got to this pub. And we sat in this wonderful little pub and everybody was the missing link to the IRA, and everyone was listening to Peter telling all these wonderful stories. We used to spend hours there. But then we also worked through the script, read it to each other and talked it out.'

Medak had learnt all about O'Toole's relationship with alcohol and come to the opinion that because of the sheer amount of drink he consumed it often only needed a small amount to put him over the edge. This was only too apparent on the occasion Peter Barnes came over and all three of them went to this quiet restaurant in Dublin. 'We were having lunch and in deep discussion about the film when the waiter arrived. "No, no, no, no drink for me," says O'Toole. Nothing. He didn't touch a drop. When I asked for the bill the chef came over to our table with a bottle of champagne, "With the compliments of the restaurant." He opened it and Peter just took a sip. I turned away to pay the bill and when I turned back he wasn't there any more. I looked around and he'd fallen all the way down these stairs, he just went, whoops!'

Filming began in May 1971 at Twickenham Studios, where O'Toole was largely a detached presence, some might have interpreted it as aloof. Actress Carolyn Seymour found him to be intensely private, happy to tell stories about himself ('They all involved bars and pubs, and a lot of them were chauvinistic'), but never revealing any of his emotions or feelings. There was always a barrier. He'd been quite different at her audition. Carolyn arrived absolutely terrified only to be put immediately at ease by O'Toole. 'He gave me everything at 150% and supported me throughout; it was quite an intense screen test. Then he found out that I'd already started a relationship with Medak and he never really looked at me again. He wasn't a playboy or anything, Peter, he didn't play around, but he liked to know that if he wanted to, the ingénue was available.'

There may have been other contributory factors since O'Toole was at the height of his alcohol addiction. On an average day Medak was lucky to get four or five hours out of his star. He wasn't much use very early in the morning and even worse after lunch. It probably didn't help that O'Toole installed his own bar in his dressing room. 'But in those days everybody was drinking,' insists Medak. 'Each of us used to drink a bottle of wine at lunchtime at the studio and I don't know how we went on working after that, but that was the culture.'

What is interesting is that even in this state O'Toole was capable of putting together a performance that was later Oscar nominated (losing of course, this time to Marlon Brando for *The Godfather*). 'That is the measure of his talent,' says Carolyn. 'And being prepared. He was always prepared. For somebody who was so un-sort of put together in his personal life, he was incredibly professional.' Certainly he never drank on the set, but at the end of the day off he would go drinking with co-stars James Villiers and Michael Bryant.

It was a long and strenuous shoot that lasted fifteen weeks and wore pretty much everybody out. 'Peter was incredibly intelligent and bright, on a genius level,' says Medak. 'He also had a photographic memory so it took him only one reading to remember a script, and everybody else's lines. Working with him wasn't easy though. Sometimes he really got upset with people but it was always for a reason. All these great actors were incredibly demanding but once they knew that the person directing them is not a total idiot then you can get anything done.'

Carolyn, too, has never forgotten the experience: 'O'Toole was one in a million, they don't come along very often, that talented. He could have read the phone book and I think everybody would have fallen on the floor.'

When *The Ruling Class* opened it divided opinion amongst critics, some loved it, some despised it. In London at an early screening Carolyn remembers, 'All the Sloane ranger types got up in a block and walked out.' The *New York Times* thought the film acquired another dimension by O'Toole's mere presence. And *Time* magazine believed O'Toole's performance to be of such intensity 'that it may trouble sleep as surely as it will haunt memory – funny, disturbing, finally devastating'. While it flopped badly on initial release (O'Toole took no salary and put money into the film and lost out quite heavily), *The Ruling Class* has gained admirers over the years and is today widely regarded as a minor classic.

By the early seventies O'Toole's career was in pretty poor shape, *The Ruling Class* was his fourth commercial flop in a row and there was a sense he was drifting out of fashion with little prospect of ever again attaining the fame he commanded in his sixties heyday. The emergence in recent years of a new breed of American actor typified by Dustin Hoffman, Gene Hackman and Al Pacino had rendered O'Toole's theatrical performance style almost prehistoric and certainly affected the kind of films he was being asked to appear in. O'Toole never had much truck with 'gibberish spouting' Method actors. He knew nothing of the Stanislavski school, nor did he wish to know anything about it, that kind of introspective style of acting he felt did not fit in with what he believed to be the actor's main job – the telling of a story.

As promised, O'Toole had signed on to play Don Quixote in the film version of the hit Broadway musical *Man of La Mancha*. Based on the seventeenth-century novel by Miguel de Cervantes, it told the story of an eccentric Spanish knight and was essentially a play within a play performed by Cervantes and his fellow prisoners as the writer awaits trial before the Spanish inquisition.

O'Toole's *Becket* collaborator Peter Glenville had agreed to direct the film provided the original Broadway script by Dale Wasserman was jettisoned in favour of one by British writer John Hopkins. He'd then set about surrounding O'Toole with top talent, Sophia Loren as the cliché whore with a heart of gold, and James Coco playing Sancho Panza, Cervantes' manservant. Setting up the movie in Rome, Glenville heard that United Artists intended to go back to the Wasserman treatment, since the

Hopkins script, which leant heavily on the Cervantes book, would necessitate a much higher budget. Glenville walked and the project was thrown into temporary disarray. As he waited for the studio to sort itself out, news reached O'Toole that writer/director Andrew Sinclair had acquired the rights to Dylan Thomas' classic 1954 radio drama *Under Milk Wood*, about the day in the life of an imaginary Welsh fishing village and its curious inhabitants. O'Toole knew Sinclair slightly, their paths having crossed around the time of *The Long and the Short and the Tall* when John Osborne and Tony Richardson wanted O'Toole for the lead in a planned musical version of Sinclair's first novel, *The Breaking of Bumbo*, a satire on the modern military. While nothing came of the idea, O'Toole and Siân did travel up to Cambridge to meet Sinclair, who was then sharing a grotty flat above a cafe with future satirist John Bird. 'O'Toole sang songs all night in Gaelic, or thereabouts,' Sinclair remembers. 'When a policeman came up the stairs towards dawn to stop us disturbing the peace, O'Toole persuaded him to drink whisky from his helmet and join in the choruses. Peter always had enough charm to steal the brass off a bobby's badge.'

Dylan Thomas was something of a hero to O'Toole and Burton and both men had tried without luck to bring *Under Milk Wood* to the screen. Now, Sinclair was offering O'Toole the chance to play Captain Cat, a part he'd performed years before in a RADA production. He couldn't resist the idea and committed immediately to the venture. By a stroke of good fortune Burton and Liz Taylor just happened to be in the country. 'And once he heard O'Toole was on board and it was going ahead, Burton had to do it,' says Sinclair. 'How could he not do it.'

A few days later Sinclair was sat in his office when the phone rang. It was Jules Buck. 'Andrew, you're a lucky bastard. You haven't got the two biggest stars in the world, you've got all three.' Elizabeth Taylor had consented to appear.

'But what bloody part,' said Sinclair, rather ungratefully. 'It's *Under Milk Wood*. She's not Welsh.'

'Your problem,' said Buck. 'You've got her or no picture.'

Incredibly, O'Toole, Burton and Taylor agreed to appear for a paltry fee of £10,000 each, although their representatives demanded a hefty chunk of any potential profits. But Sinclair was going to have to work fast, with Burton and O'Toole only available for five days each, and Elizabeth even less, just the two days.

Fishguard, a charming fishing town in Pembrokeshire, had been selected to act as Dylan's mythical village and Sinclair brought with him the *Debrett's* of Welsh thespian talent: Glynis Johns, Ryan Davies, Victor Spinetti and also a young David Jason. Siân Phillips also appeared, wearing her own wedding ring. Burton arrived in grand style in his Rolls-Royce but indisposed. The next morning he collared Sinclair. 'I am not drinking on your film, Dylan was one of my greatest friends.'

'What's sober mean, Richard?'

'That's only two bottles of vodka a day, not four.'

O'Toole made much the same promise and remained the ultimate professional, insisting on wearing milky-blue contact lenses to play the blind Captain Cat, taking them out after half an hour when the pain became unbearable. 'If he had not been capable of five-minute takes hitting an unseen mark without a wrong word, we could never have completed the shots on him without his sight,' says Sinclair. 'He played the whole part word-perfect literally as a blind man. Absolutely stunning.'

Once work was finished for the day it was a different story, with O'Toole leading the nightly singing and dancing at the Fishguard Bay Hotel. Sinclair remembers it was 'The Cuckoo Song' that was his favourite. 'In the middle of a line of a dozen cavorting grave men, who had all dropped their trousers, he high kicked and belted out the words like a soubrette.'

Midway through the shoot Sinclair had to dash off to the Lee

Studios in London to film the few scenes involving Elizabeth Taylor, who due to continual back problems hadn't been able to travel to the Welsh location. The role of Rosie Probert, the sailors' whore, had been assigned to Elizabeth and her main scene would be played with O'Toole. Arriving on the set that morning Sinclair was informed that Elizabeth would not be making an appearance for several hours. With time short (the Burtons had to leave the country by midnight the next day for tax reasons), Sinclair braced himself and went to her dressing room. There before a mirror, slapping on the rouge and big eyelids, was Elizabeth, every inch Cleopatra. 'That won't do,' said Sinclair. 'You're a Welsh sailors' whore of the fifties. You can't look like that!'

'I always look like Cleopatra,' said Elizabeth and waved the director out of the room.

It was noon before she arrived on the set, and there was O'Toole as the young Captain Cat, all eager beaver on a brass bed ready to make hay with his Welsh whore. When Elizabeth snuggled in beside him, he lifted his shirt and there scribbled across his stomach in biro was the legend: 'I love you Rosie Probert.' Elizabeth burst out laughing.

After three takes the scene was done and everyone broke for lunch. As Sinclair sat in his office making preparations for that afternoon, O'Toole popped his head round the door. 'You've lost your filum, Andrew,' he said, in a matter-of-fact tone. 'Liz is not appearing after lunch. But for what I am about to do for you, I deserve the Victoria Cross and bloody Bar.'

All that was required of Elizabeth was to stand in front of a microphone and dub her lines but she had resolved not to do it. 'So off they went, O'Toole, Burton and Taylor, and they all got drunk from one till four over lunch,' says Sinclair. 'They must have drunk six bottles of wine, and in the end O'Toole and Burton carried a dead drunk Elizabeth into the studio and held her up between them, an arm over each shoulder while she read out her dialogue. In that moment O'Toole saved the film.'

Sinclair liked O'Toole, without his initial and continued commitment the film would never have been made. He judged him to be amongst the most intelligent and witty men he ever met. 'And irrepressible, unpredictable and daring. Of all the stars I worked with he was the greatest by a long way. He had a terrific life-force, an incredible inner charisma which made him a meteor.'

After a brief rest O'Toole flew to Rome in January 1972 to begin preparations for *Man of La Mancha*, which now had a new director in Arthur Hiller. To his utter delight O'Toole discovered he was sharing a hotel with Burton, who was in the Italian capital working. One evening Burton had arranged a quiet meal at a discreet restaurant with a young actress. Suddenly O'Toole burst in, making something of a grand entrance. Not to be outdone, Burton leapt onto a table and broke into a song in Gaelic. O'Toole leapt atop another table and sang the second verse, and on it went; so much for a quiet, unobtrusive meal.

They met up several times after that for the odd snifter, activity frowned upon by Elizabeth, who was trying to keep her wandering husband on the wagon. One evening assistant director Norman Priggen received a call from Liz explaining that Burton would not be working tomorrow. 'Why's that?' asked Priggen. 'Well, you'd better get back to our hotel and look in the bar and see for yourself.' Priggen drove quickly to the hotel and found Burton and O'Toole, both as drunk as lords, lying on the floor fondly embracing each other and singing 'Happy Birthday'. They had been there since lunchtime.

It was exactly this kind of hell-raising that Liz hoped to put an end to. When Burton had a place in Hampstead, O'Toole would often be round or Burton would pay Guyon House a visit. 'And then we'd carry the other home,' explained O'Toole. 'Elizabeth wasn't keen on that. She probably thought I led him astray. I don't know. She didn't approve. That was a bone of contention between me and Richard.'

One afternoon O'Toole put a call through to Burton's suite at the hotel. As always a secretary answered. Mr Burton was busy, could he try again later. For two days Burton didn't return his calls until finally a member of his entourage came with a message and led O'Toole to a clandestine meeting in the corner of a dark bar tucked in the back of the hotel. 'Elizabeth,' said Burton, in a meek voice, 'does not approve of our racing around together.' And that was pretty much it. 'I didn't see him again for many years,' claimed O'Toole. 'Poor soul.'

Henceforth O'Toole referred to Elizabeth Taylor only as 'That Woman', though according to Andrew Sinclair hostilities between the two dated back to the days of *Becket*. O'Toole told Sinclair that he was in the back of a limo with Liz and Burton on their way to London from Shepperton Studios. Also in the car was Eddie Fisher, Liz's ex, who was attempting a reconciliation. They were all crammed inside when O'Toole nodded to the chauffeur saying that he was the only one here who hadn't fucked Elizabeth Taylor. 'I was thrown out of the car,' O'Toole told Sinclair. 'Somewhere towards Twickenham.'

When filming began on *Man of La Mancha*, O'Toole quickly made an impression on Hiller, the director who had made 1970s box office hit *Love Story*, having immersed himself in Cervantes and the historical period. 'I didn't do very much directing because he was so well prepared.'

The pair had very nearly worked together before. In 1959, when Hiller was in London with his wife, they'd gone one evening to see *The Long and the Short and the Tall*. 'About ten minutes into the first act this private came on stage and sort of took over, and I was just bowled over. I took out a piece of paper and I wrote down – Peter O'Toole. Of course, not long after that he was in *Lawrence of Arabia*.'

What surprised Hiller the most about O'Toole was a reluctance to interact socially with the other members of the cast. He was very private and kept himself largely to himself on the set, save for the odd game of poker with his co-stars. Despite his gregarious nature, O'Toole had always loved being alone, relaxing in his own company, but in recent times had started to become a much more introverted person, something that Siân had noticed. Over the years O'Toole had become much more withdrawn, not a recluse by any means, but certainly spending more time alone than he had done. This was to be largely the pattern for the remainder of his life.

As for his relationship with Sophia Loren, cast as Dulcinea, whom he playfully took to calling 'silicone', it was complex. To the press O'Toole was generous in his praise for the actress, but Hiller remembers one incident in particular that struck him as rather odd. One afternoon, as the cameraman was setting up a shot, a visibly distressed Sophia walked over to him. 'What's wrong?' said Hiller, taking her hand. 'Don't worry, Sophia, you're playing the part just right.'

'I'm not talking about that! I'm talking about Peter!'

'What about Peter?'

Sophia caught her breath. 'Every time you say ready and you're going to say action, Peter says to me – "What makes you think *you* can act." '

'Sophia,' said Hiller reassuringly. 'He's just trying to get your adrenalin up for the scene.'

Sophia shook her head. 'I've been acting long enough to know when somebody's trying to get my adrenalin up, or when they're trying to put me down.'

'I'll speak to him if you want, but it would be much better if you can show him that it doesn't bother you.'

'Easy for you to say,' Sophia replied. 'Not so easy for me to do.'

Hiller had a quick think. 'I'll tell you what to do. The next time he says it you smile and say – "Fuck you!" '

About twenty minutes later Sophia came running over to Hiller, her face beaming. Hiller guessed what had just happened. O'Toole never said it to Sophia again.

It was odd behaviour to be sure, especially since O'Toole was genuinely impressed by Sophia's professionalism. And yet friction was never far from the surface. They'd sometimes play poker between takes. After one match Sophia playfully accused O'Toole of trying to cheat as she took the winnings and put them in her expensive Gucci bag. Amidst a torrent of abuse O'Toole grabbed the bag and ripped it to shreds. Calmly Sophia sat back down and dealt out the cards again – and won.

One of the film's most touching moments is when Sophia holds the wounded O'Toole in her lap. For her close-up, Sophia had expressly asked for O'Toole not to be present, he might distract her, and she wanted to focus totally on the marker representing her eye line that had been positioned at the base of the camera. As luck would have it O'Toole waltzed into the studio that morning asking what was happening. Hiller told him and O'Toole offered to stay.

'No, we don't need you. It's fine. Sometimes when you have a mark you prefer the other person not to be there.'

'She'll want me!' boomed O'Toole.

'She doesn't. I asked her,' said Hiller flatly.

'We'll see about that!'

O'Toole began to make strong strides towards the set when Hiller grabbed hold of him. Sophia was huddled in a corner alone working on her emotions. 'This is not the time to get into a discussion about this,' advised Hiller. O'Toole finally saw sense and turned away, making towards the camera crew instead and asking where Sophia's mark was. An assistant showed him and O'Toole took off a shoe and placed it right on the camera base before leaving. This was no prank, or laddish jape, believes Hiller, but a deliberate act of sabotage. 'He meant that to disturb Sophia, to say – you don't need me, but I'm there.'

In spite of admitting that his singing voice was akin to 'a broken bottle going under a door', *Man of La Mancha* was O'Toole's second film musical in just a few short years. This time, however, he realized that his voice was not up to the task of singing most of the songs, including the standout track, 'The Impossible Dream', and that he would have to be dubbed by a professional singer, Simon Gilbert. The usual procedure for this was for the actor to lip-sync the singer's version on the set, but Hiller was keen to use O'Toole's artistry and asked the actor to give his own version of each song, even though it wouldn't be used, so Gilbert could achieve the same level of emotion.

Man of La Mancha flopped at the box office and received such poor reviews that Hiller was personally affected by it: 'I couldn't work for eight months. I kept thinking, what had I done wrong?' Analysing the film today, Hiller believes he didn't quite get the mix of reality and fantasy right. O'Toole himself received mixed notices, too. David Robinson of *The Times* thought he had turned into 'a very strange performer, spitting and mouthing his lines with the excessive vowels of a twenties stage juvenile', while Arthur Knight in the *Saturday Review* thought he played Cervantes' hero 'with extraordinary delicacy and restraint'.

One doubts O'Toole read the reviews; according to Hiller he never even saw the film. By the end of its production he had grown disenchanted with the filmmaking process and with the film industry itself, principally the people behind it – the suits, the executives who'd no creative bone in their bodies. 'The business is run by the cornflakes men,' he grumbled. 'And they're only in it for the girls. You used to join amateur dramatics to get at the crackling. These men buy up studios to achieve the same end.'

Mostly though he was tired and fed up with acting, he'd been at it since Bristol, 'twenty years of it in one uninterrupted lump', and he wanted a rest. His fortieth birthday seemed as good a time as any to reassess what he wanted out of life and where he was going. Right now his life was drawing him back to Clifden, where preparations had begun on his dream home. Taking Siân and the kids with him, nothing would be heard of O'Toole for the next twelve months.

FIFTEEN

In the last few years O'Toole had been back many times to Clifden, sometimes with Siân and the kids, sometimes alone. Always he would make the effort to see Billy Foyle, and sometimes he'd bring a little showbiz sparkle to the town. Foyle will never forget one occasion, when O'Toole arrived for lunch at the little restaurant he owned on the high street with Federico Fellini in tow and an entourage of ten of the most beautiful women anyone had ever seen. People in the town still talk about it.

As he'd promised, Foyle had been looking for a perfect piece of land for O'Toole to build on and had finally found the ideal spot, up on the picturesque Sky Road a few miles outside Clifden. It was totally isolated and barren, looking out over the Atlantic. 'And really he shouldn't have got planning permission,' confesses Foyle. 'But I knew some of the lads in the planning office, this was how things were done back in those days, I had a few words with them and greased their palms so to speak and Peter had no problem.'

Over the next couple of years the house slowly began to take shape, with both O'Toole and Siân often working alongside the builders, digging ditches for the sewage or planting trees, flowers and vegetables in the garden, which due to the battering they received from the harsh wind off the Atlantic had repeatedly to be replaced. 'Plants must be sturdy to survive here,' O'Toole pointed out. 'Just like the people.' Until it was completed the family all crammed into a three-roomed cottage which had no phone or television and just a Calor-gas stove to cook on, while the entourage (nanny, chauffeur, tutor and minder) were installed in the best hotel in Clifden with all the mod cons. 'They had swimming pools and tennis courts,' remembered Kate. 'We had brown water from the well and warm milk from the cow. We loved it.'

When it was completed the house was very much an extension of its owner. 'There was a coldness about it, I thought,' says Billy Foyle. Very few people really got to know who Peter O'Toole was. 'With Peter,' says Billy, 'you never really got inside of his head. He wouldn't come out and say, "Billy, I feel bloody awful," or "This marriage has gone on the blink." He would never confide in me. I know he trusted me, but he would never confide in me about his personal life.' It was the same with Johnnie Planco, who represented him in America for over thirty years. 'Peter rarely talked about his personal life beyond his children.'

O'Toole's Irish bolt hole was the complete antithesis of Guyon House, which was warm and inviting. And it is no coincidence that Siân was responsible for buying and furnishing their Hampstead home, while O'Toole took the lion's share of the decision-making at the Clifden property. Inside it was basic and about as far removed from a film star's house as it was possible to get. For one thing there were no carpets, instead the floors were made from slabs of stone. When Robert Shaw, who had his own home in Ireland, paid a visit he scratched his head before complaining that the O'Tooles must have been mad, bypassing luxury in favour of impersonal functionality.

In other ways, though, it was impressive. The outside walls were made entirely of stone from a local quarry. Inside it was spacious, with high ceilings and wood-panelled doors and walls. The drawing room was built to O'Toole's own specifications with a large stone fireplace with a turf fire that was never allowed to go out and two large windows looking out over the sea. Often he'd stand for hours just looking out across the vast blueness, taking in the wildlife and the smattering of islands that lay off the coast, inhabited mostly by fishermen, as they had been for centuries. But the rooms were all plain, almost anonymous. 'You could go in and out of that house ten times and you'd ask me to describe it and I couldn't,' says Billy Foyle. Yet O'Toole lived blissfully quietly there for many years. It became an anchor in his life, a place of sanctuary and refuge to disappear to and be at peace with himself and his surroundings. He'd go off on long walks along the coastal roads or up into the mountains or drop down into Clifden. The small town represented the perfect antidote to his frenzied lifestyle in London, with its one main high street and two prominent churches either end, one Catholic, the other Protestant. 'I don't attend either,' O'Toole told a reporter. 'I go to Frank Murphy's pub.'

Predictably O'Toole was a regular in the town's numerous bars and was often spotted out and about. He was treated with respect and courtesy by the community, who came to regard him as one of their own, rather than a film star. 'After a while they loved him,' says Foyle. 'He became more Irish than the Irish themselves. He kept boasting about the O'Toole name and friends to this day ask me, "By the way, did Peter O'Toole ever find his roots?" No, I'd say, but there was more joy in looking for them than finding them.'

Although the house was secluded, lying off the road, the O'Tooles were always happy to receive invited guests and even threw the occasional party. 'We had some jolly old evenings up there,' remembers Foyle. For many summers Michael D. Higgins, a future President of Ireland but then a Labour Senator, with his wife Sabina and their children, would hole up in a small cottage just down from the main house. Old friends, too, would call upon them. One afternoon the girls, who had been playing in the front garden, ran inside the house crying, 'Mummy, Daddy. There's an old tinker woman coming up the drive.' When they opened the door Siân and O'Toole were delighted to see Katharine Hepburn, dressed in a black raincoat, her face half covered with a shawl. She'd come to see O'Toole about a possible film and ended up staying several days. Before leaving she wanted to know if living in the wilds of Connemara O'Toole wasn't only escaping the film world but civilization as well. 'Hell, no,' he answered. 'This *is* civilization.'

The movies hadn't entirely been left behind, scripts continued to arrive, were dutifully read and immediately forgotten. For a while he contemplated writing a novel or perhaps a play, there was even talk of doing some academic study, having always been self-conscious of his lack of formal education. Instead it was an approach from the Bristol Old Vic that prompted him to leave his Irish idyll and return to the world of acting.

By 1973 the Bristol Old Vic was in trouble. In recent years the theatre had been modernized and turned into an arts complex, but audiences were dwindling. A plan was needed to bring the public back, a marquee name. Nat Brenner, now principal of the Old Vic school, was convinced he could persuade O'Toole to return. Just recently the actor had set up a scholarship at the school to help one pupil every year. The very first recipient was a certain Pete Postlethwaite and it was Brenner's suggestion that it might be a nice gesture if O'Toole came to the school to meet him. What happened next became one of Brenner's favourite O'Toole stories. Pete Postlethwaite was called out from class and asked to go to Brenner's office and there was O'Toole sitting in the corner. After a few minutes of polite conversation, O'Toole suggested they all go for a drink. It was the middle of the afternoon and the drinking carried on until closing time. 'Nat,' said O'Toole. 'I think we should go to Joe's.' Brenner shot his old colleague a quizzical look. 'We can't drive to London, that's ridiculous.' 'I don't mean Joe's in London,' said O'Toole. 'I mean Joe's in Dublin.' Hailing a cab they drove to Bristol airport and hired a plane to fly the three of them out to Dublin to carry on drinking for another four hours or so, after which O'Toole put the pair of them back on a plane to Bristol where they arrived first thing in the morning and Postlethwaite went back to his classes.

Very little persuasion was needed in the end for O'Toole to come to the aid of his beloved Bristol, and the plan was to perform three plays: Chekhov's *Uncle Vanya*, *The Apple Cart* by Shaw and the first full-scale professional stage revival of the Ben Travers farce *Plunder*. The Old Vic was unable to afford the wages of a star actor, so O'Toole offered his services for free, with Bristol providing him with accommodation, a pleasant house in Clifton, for the three months he would be there. O'Toole did insist on hand-picking much of the company himself, old friends like Edward Hardwicke and Nigel Stock, along with a smattering of new up and coming talent – Judy Parfitt, Sara Kestelman and Penelope Wilton, who became one of his favourite actresses.

O'Toole knew it was going to be hard work and he took the venture seriously, after all this would be seen as a theatrical return of sorts, his first performance on the British stage since the mid-sixties. 'I imagine that he might have been feeling quite anxious,' says Sara Kestelman. 'Although he would never have let you see that because he was a proud man, an aggressively proud man.'

Rehearsals began on *Uncle Vanya* with the theatre's artistic director Val May in charge. They did not go well. 'In the rehearsal room O'Toole was arrogant and he was selfish,' remembers Sara. 'He didn't listen and he didn't really pay respect. He didn't respect Val May at all, he despised what you might describe as Val's rather pedantic way of working: This is where you pick up the pen and this is where you put it down. Many in the company didn't really want to work in so prescriptive a manner, certainly O'Toole didn't want to work like that, and it was crazy to assume he would want to. Why would anyone want to offer him that kind of detail, except in the most helpful way, which is no doubt how Val meant it, but it came across in a schoolmasterly way and put O'Toole on the back foot from the start.' And so he very much pursued his own route, arriving on day one with a prepared performance that he did not intend to alter in the slightest.

Despite the problems, *Uncle Vanya* was a triumph when it opened in October 1973, with O'Toole receiving a standing ovation every night. 'It was a completely brilliant piece of work,' confirms Sara. 'His Vanya, when we opened, was astonishing. It was terribly moving, and it was very funny and touching and dangerous. But as the run went on he got practised in it, he knew the moments that would work and he moved towards them, so it wasn't as good, but it was still a very fine performance.'

Since part of the reason that O'Toole had returned to Bristol was out of loyalty to his old mentor Nat Brenner, it was baffling that when Brenner came in to direct the second play of the season, *Plunder*, O'Toole turned on him so viciously. 'He would humiliate him in front of everybody,' recalls Sara. 'And it was a shocking thing to behold.' Like Val May, Brenner was another prescriptive director, no doubt due to having worked for many years with students where you have to be very specific about how you elicit a performance as opposed to a professional who might be able to interpret it in a very different way with more expertise. 'But I wasn't expecting O'Toole to be so damaging to him and so cruel,' says Sara. 'And because he was a very strong man you couldn't, unless you wanted to risk having a bop on the chin, you couldn't really intervene, and Nat didn't really know how to protect himself, because he wasn't expecting it. And it was pretty consistent throughout rehearsals. Whatever Nat would say Peter would belittle immediately, he'd say, "We're not going to do that," or he'd just deliberately ignore it.'

Again, a troubled rehearsal period seemed to have no effect on the finished production and *Plunder* was well received by the public, who came to see it in droves.

During the run of *Plunder* it was clear that O'Toole was not in the best of health. He was suffering again from stomach pains, at times excruciating. He took pills but they didn't seem to work and physically he looked thin and pallid. Siân was there most of the time to lend support, but that didn't stop O'Toole openly flirting with some of the actresses. 'Certainly there were little liaisons during the season,' claims Sara.

The season closed with *The Apple Cart*, a production Sara refused to appear in due to her aversion to Shaw. It was a decision that incurred the wrath of O'Toole and she left the company feeling bitter and miserable. She had enjoyed working with him, despite the challenges, but came away from the experience with the opinion that here was a highly manipulative individual. 'He was maddening because he insisted that he was right and wasn't actually interested in what anybody else had to say unless it complimented some intellectual concept that he had and then you could have a big intellectual discussion with him. He was a bit of a bully. And he didn't suffer fools gladly. If he saw somebody who wasn't pulling their weight or giving a performance that he didn't approve of, he'd belittle them.' O'Toole had a very quick tongue and could lash out in a subtle way, or a not very subtle way, just to put a person in their place. One was always reminded that this was all about him and that he was the centre of it. 'He was a star,' says Sara. 'He dazzled, and he knew that he dazzled. He wasn't an ensemble man.'

Yet it was O'Toole's star power that had brought huge crowds back to the Old Vic. 'He saved our bacon,' said Val May. 'We never looked back after that.'

*

Having not made a film since *Man of La Mancha*, O'Toole had given instructions to Jules Buck to find suitable projects for him to star in. In the summer of 1974 Robert Mitchum was cast in a kidnap drama about Palestinian terrorists called *Rosebud*, but arrived on location in Corsica drunk and over the next few days appeared not to sober up very much. Finally director Otto Preminger confronted him, they shook hands and he walked. When Buck, an old friend of Preminger's, heard of Mitchum's departure he called the director and suggested O'Toole as a replacement. Just forty-eight hours later O'Toole landed in Corsica ready to begin work.

Some questioned Preminger's logic replacing one drunk with another. When Mitchum heard the news his response was, 'Hell, that's like replacing Ray Charles with Helen Keller.' Preminger knew he was taking a risk but for once alcohol wasn't the problem, O'Toole was desperately ill. In London he'd complained of extreme stomach pain and was so unwell he couldn't be moved and was forced to lie in bed for a month, where he would flit in and out of consciousness and when awake had to endure terrible pain. His doctor was at a loss for an explanation and when O'Toole was able to get up and move about the hope was that this mysterious illness had been defeated. According to Tony Gittelson, an assistant on *Rosebud*, O'Toole arrived in Corsica, 'Looking totally dissipated, at death's door.' Sure enough, while shooting in Paris the stomach pains returned and he was taken to hospital and the film was delayed by several days.

O'Toole had barely returned to work on the film when there was another emergency. The crew were filming in the Parisian apartment of an American journalist and when O'Toole arrived early that morning he discovered a note addressed to him, 'Personal and Confidential'. He opened it and couldn't believe what he was reading. It purported to be from the IRA, accusing him of being a 'so-called Irishman' and traitor to the cause for performing in a film that was critical of their terrorist brethren in Palestine, and that a bomb had been planted on the set which would detonate at noon. Taking no chances, Preminger ordered the building cleared. 'This was the height of the bombings,' O'Toole later recalled. 'Bloody Friday, Bloody Sunday, my fore-bears were getting together and blowing things up. You had to take these things seriously.'

As it turned out the whole thing was a hoax. A dinner party had been held in the apartment the previous evening and one of the guests, the critic Kenneth Tynan, had written the note as a prank. Preminger wasn't laughing, nor was O'Toole, who learnt of Tynan's whereabouts in the city and with two burly crew hands went over and viciously beat him up. Once friends and keen admirers of each other's talents, O'Toole and Tynan never spoke to one another again, but no charges were brought.

Rosebud is one of those globetrotting thrillers beloved of seventies filmmakers: Paris, Berlin, Tel Aviv, the French Riviera, Hamburg all make cameo appearances. O'Toole plays a CIA agent masquerading as a journalist trying to track down five kid-napped women, including a young Isabelle Huppert and in her film debut, Kim Cattrall. O'Toole gamely fleshed out the charac-ter, bringing a burned-out raffishness and eccentricity to the role, although according to Erik Preminger, Otto's son, who wrote the screenplay, the actor didn't think much of the project. 'Or the script. I always got the feeling that basically he was doing it for the money. But you wouldn't know it from the level of his professionalism. He was always on time ready to go. And very nice to me, considering how bad the script was.' O'Toole did, however, insist on bringing his own writer in to redraft all of his dialogue scenes. He also rarely socialized, after filming he went back alone to his hotel.

As for the formidable Otto Preminger, O'Toole found him a delightful character, and the feeling was mutual according to

Erik. 'Otto loved British actors because British actors did what they were told to do and that's exactly what Peter did.' Erik recalls no arguments between the two of them or disagreements. 'Maybe Peter felt that the picture was a lost cause from the very beginning so why argue about it.' Other members of the cast weren't so lucky and fell prey to Preminger's legendary temper, including Erik himself, who agreed to play a small role on the proviso that his dad didn't shout or yell at him. Well, when Erik didn't hit his marks on a couple of takes Preminger blasted him in front of the whole crew. 'I remember though Peter rubbing the back of my neck to take the tension out of the situation.'

When *Rosebud* finally opened it was clobbered by the critics and quickly vanished from cinemas. O'Toole's film comeback had been inauspicious to say the least. His next screen role fared little better, a new version of the Robinson Crusoe story, *Man Friday*, based on a play by one of his Hampstead friends, the poet, playwright and novelist Adrian Mitchell, who wrote passionately about nuclear war, Vietnam and racism. O'Toole had seen the play and liked it enormously, enough to persuade Jules Buck to produce it under the aegis of Keep Films, with financial backing obtained from television tycoon Lew Grade.

For director O'Toole chose Jack Gold, an accomplished filmmaker, and the pair got along fine, with Gold learning pretty quickly that you didn't so much direct O'Toole as let him loose. 'Peter came with a fully realized portrait in his own mind of what Crusoe was like, and the style in which he was going to play it, and my first awareness of it was when the camera was running. It didn't evolve during the process of the filming, he'd got a conception of it and there it was, presented.'

The five-week schedule in Puerto Vallarta in Mexico passed off smoothly, save for the occasion O'Toole inexplicably went to sleep on an ant farm and developed a throat infection as a consequence. There were long, luxurious lunches and games of football on the beach and O'Toole enjoyed working with Richard Roundtree, the American actor best known for playing Shaft, who had been cast as Friday. Gold also discovered he and O'Toole shared a love for Max Miller. 'We used to do some of his old routines between us while we were waiting to shoot.' As for booze, O'Toole was dry for the most part. Actor Peter Cellier, who last worked with O'Toole on his 1964 *Hamlet*, remembers getting a phone call on Christmas Eve asking if he could fly in on Boxing Day. 'I arrived and there were six tequilas on the bar waiting for me. "You're late," said O'Toole.'

One evening O'Toole invited Gold and Roundtree to join him for dinner with his old friend John Huston, who lived not too far away. One of his idols, Gold never forgot the experience. 'He was old and arthritic by this stage and wanted to go to bed early, nothing like the roaring days, but the warmth was still there between him and Peter. It was a bit like memory lane for them, while I just sat there the whole evening with my mouth open.'

As the film geared up for release news broke that it had been chosen as the official British entry for that year's Cannes Film Festival. However, this did little to appease the critics, who largely dismissed the film, and thanks to a limited release the public ignored it, too. Gold thinks the poor response was due to the fact that audiences expected another traditional Crusoe/Friday story, not this critique of imperialist attitudes. 'It wasn't intelligent white man and ignorant savage, it was intelligent white man with a very intelligent and cultured, in his own way, black man,' says Gold. 'The roles became inverted. There was a strong moral and philosophical thread running through the whole piece.'

O'Toole's own performance was criticized in some quarters for being too extrovert. Katrine Ames of *Newsweek* complained that while there was no actor better at playing contained madness, 'once he lets it out he turns into a ham'. Gold argues that the performance fitted the piece, which contained broad strokes in that there were elements of song and dance and slapstick comedy. 'It also had to have great touches of sensitivity and self-examination. I thought it was fascinating. He could do the gamut, there's no question how efficient Peter was.'

SIXTEEN

O'Toole hadn't been long back from Mexico when all the stomach problems that had plagued him for years and his reckless drinking conspired to almost put him into an early grave. Repeatedly he was warned that the amount he was drinking was unhealthy but O'Toole had been born with extraordinary restorative powers and always seemed to come out of the other end of a drinking binge seemingly none the worse for wear. When he shared a flat with Kenneth Griffith in Belgravia, Siân learnt that some nights O'Toole would sit there drinking Scotch from one glass and white ulcer medicine from another, while alternately puffing on Gauloises.

Was all this drinking a death wish, as some have suggested? Highly doubtful. On the night he returned to Guyon House after an evening boozing and complained of stomach pains evidently greater and more acute than any he had hitherto experienced, Siân could see the worry etched out on his face. When their local doctor arrived he decided that O'Toole should be immediately hospitalized and called an ambulance to take him to the nearby Royal Free.

Curiously among the first things that happened to him was a vigorous shave. O'Toole had grown a handsome beard to play Judas in Lew Grade's TV mini-series *Jesus of Nazareth* and went to remonstrate with the nurse given the task of removing it: 'Hey, don't do that. I need it.' No he didn't, he could barely walk let alone act. So ill was he that he couldn't keep solid food down and pure water had to be fed directly into his stomach through a pipe.

As tests began Siân was kept away, they wouldn't even let her see him until the next day. When she walked into the room he was hooked up to so many machines that it looked like his life force was being drained away. When the tests came back inconclusive his team of doctors decided to carry out exploratory surgery. It was to be the first of several serious operations. 'I suggested they put in a zip, they were opening me up so often,' O'Toole later joked.

Inevitably the press found out and began to speculate that O'Toole had alcohol poisoning or something wrong with his liver. They didn't know the full story, only Siân, the doctors and Jules Buck knew how perilously he was clinging on to life. The children, who were luckily on holiday in Ireland with Siân's mother, hadn't been told and together Siân and Buck tried to keep the media in the dark as much as possible, though it didn't help that Siân was sometimes called at home by journalists asking if she'd help update her husband's obituary. Siân knew things were bad when talking to the ward sister one day, 'It will get better, won't it?' she burst into tears and fled the room. For the weeks that O'Toole lay in that hospital in a comatose state Siân stood a lonely vigil by his bedside, watching as the man she loved 'hovered between life and death'.

With some convinced he wasn't going to pull through, O'Toole finally opened his eyes, looked across at Siân and gave her a lopsided grin, before ripping out the tubes stuck in his body and demanding to be fed. Shortly afterwards Jules Buck arrived, beaming. 'He'll outlive us all, kid,' he said.

Discharged, O'Toole was gingerly taken back home and placed in bed to convalesce. Bored after a week, he fancied recuperating somewhere a bit more exotic than his own bedroom. Siân tried to reason with him, that doctors had urged him to rest and stay put. O'Toole would not be dissuaded and they booked a month in a hotel in Positano on the Amalfi coast that in the end did him the world of good.

Returning to London, O'Toole was open to a barrage of press intrusion about his time in hospital but refused to comment. 'My plumbing is nobody's business but my own.' American tabloids reported that his pancreas was removed, other rumours were that he'd got stomach cancer, but O'Toole denied them. What was true was that he came as close to dying as you can do without actually snuffing it. 'It was a photo-finish, the surgeons said.' However, there was now so little of his digestive system left that even the smallest amount of alcohol might kill him. He was ordered off the booze. And this time he heeded his doctor's advice, while at the same time insisting the wine cellar at Guyon House remain fully stocked, as indeed was the drinks cabinet in his study.

In 1980 on the set of the American TV mini-series *Masada* O'Toole confided in his co-star Barbara Carrera about his operation and the consequences of his years of drinking. 'You know,' he said, 'I've got to tell you I've got no stomach, my whole stomach has been removed because of alcohol. And if I were to drink a mere spoonful of alcohol it would kill me.' Barbara was so shocked that every one of those words she's never been able to forget. 'Then he unbuttoned his shirt and showed me this scar that went from his chest to his abdomen. It was horrific.'

It's very easy to stop drinking when your actual life depends on it. But what's it like for someone who made virtually a career out of it, an ex-hell-raiser, to no longer be the rip-roarer of old? 'The pirate ship has berthed,' is how he put it. O'Toole simply stopped playing the bad boy, cut out the wild antics, no more binges, no more lost weekends, no more taking his two daughters into pubs under his coat just as his father had done with him. 'It was all becoming a bore. The pleasure wasn't worth the pain.' But what remained was a ravaged shell of a man, and the loss of his looks too early in life. Yet he remained unrepentant till the end, telling a US magazine in 1989, 'I wouldn't have missed one drop of alcohol that I drank.'

He was actually coping quite well, having been prescribed plenty of vitamins to chew and hefty doses of Valium, though still chain-smoked his Gauloises using a long black holder, equipped with a filter in a concession to health. Such was his devotion to the habit that a friend once complained. 'Peter, you smell like a French train.' Actor Michael Craig recalls a strange incident when the two of them were making *Country Dance* in 1969. 'We both smoked Gauloises, Peter smoked his without filters then and I smoked filtered ones. And he got in a terrible rage. "What's the matter with you, bloody filters!" And he took my fags and broke all the filters off. "Now have a proper cigarette," he said.'

After giving up the booze O'Toole had little patience with drinkers, even if they were friends, or so it seemed. One of his closest acting buddies was Donal McCann, who took great pride in his association with O'Toole. 'He idolized O'Toole,' claims Billy Foyle. 'He was a god to Donal.' Visiting the Connemara area, McCann got in touch with Foyle asking if O'Toole was around and if they could set up a meeting. O'Toole's number was ex-directory, Foyle was one of the few people who had it, so he called the house. After a short pause O'Toole spoke, he wanted to know if McCann was drinking. Foyle said he didn't think he was. In fact, unknown to Foyle, McCann, who was an alcoholic, had been seen drunk in Clifden, something that O'Toole soon discovered after making a few phone calls of his own. When Foyle and McCann arrived at the house O'Toole was down near the beach exercising a pony on a long rope. The two men rested on the gate to watch. O'Toole ignored them. McCann was holding a stick and put a white handkerchief on the top and started waving it. O'Toole continued to ignore them. Fed up, Foyle went down to O'Toole to tell him in no uncertain manner what he thought of him. O'Toole returned his glare. 'You told me McCann wasn't drinking.'

'He's not drunk,' said Foyle.

O'Toole's face remained impassive. 'I didn't ask you that. I asked was he drinking!' Things got a bit heated and Foyle ended up telling O'Toole where he could go and left. 'Poor McCann was very upset that Peter wouldn't see him,' says Foyle, 'and spent three days in the town drunk until they got him out. You know, there's nothing so pure as the reformed whore, and O'Toole not being the drinker and McCann still at it, I thought Peter would have shown a bit more generosity and sympathy, but he didn't.'

SEVENTEEN

In spite of all the problems in their marriage, O'Toole had always been happy for Siân and the children to visit him on film locations. Now, as he packed for a stay shooting in Mexico in mid-1975 for his next film, he wouldn't countenance the suggestion of Siân accompanying him. Faced with a brick wall of intransigence she did something she'd never done before, she pleaded to come with him. O'Toole waved her protestations away and headed to the airport leaving Siân rejected and isolated.

What was behind such behaviour? Was it the need to be alone and independent again, not to be fussed over and nursemaided, to get on with his life after so very nearly losing it? Or was there another reason? During the filming of *Man Friday* O'Toole had begun an affair with a local waitress and budding actress more than twenty years his junior, Malinche Verdugo. Siân's suspicions had been raised after coming across what looked like a love letter amidst the correspondence O'Toole left lying about. Her anxieties weren't helped by the fact she hadn't heard anything from her husband for weeks since his departure, not a letter or a phone call, nothing. She hadn't even been given a telephone number that she could reach him at. It's true that O'Toole had an aversion to telephones, finding conversations on the blasted things cold and emotionless, but this total lack of any communication was troubling.

Siân was kept busy appearing in a play in the West End and

mid-way through the run, to her immense surprise, shock and delight, began a passionate affair of her own with one of the cast, a young actor by the name of Robin Sachs. He was exciting, attentive and generous in his feelings and emotions, the complete opposite of O'Toole, who had always kept his emotions in check, that included with friends, family and work mates.

In August 1975, O'Toole returned from Mexico and life seemed to carry on as usual at Guyon House. The film he had made, *Foxtrot* with Charlotte Rampling, ended up being of absolutely no consequence, not even theatrically released in Britain. In it he played a jaded aristocrat who deserts Europe at the end of the Second World War to live on an island. Its reception was indicative of the poor choices he'd made since returning to the cinema, which the actor blamed on a dearth of good material coming his way, a situation that was beginning to wear him down. Ironically, it was now Siân's career, so long in the shadow of her husband's, that was blossoming, having won a major role in the BBC's adaptation of *How Green Was My Valley* with Stanley Baker. O'Toole accompanied her to the Welsh location and for one scene playfully dressed up as a collier and milled around in the background as an extra. After that was finished she was asked to play Livia in another major BBC drama series, *I, Claudius*, the role for which the actress remains best known.

With a paucity of good film roles on offer, O'Toole took to writing poetry and did a lot of reading, just trying to fill every moment of the day with activity; perhaps to keep his mind off alcohol. He also kept himself busy by putting in hours at the Belgravia office of Keep Films, even though his relationship with Jules Buck had begun to unravel over the past year and would soon end. The American had always taken pride in the fact that he above most other people was able to read O'Toole, keep him under some kind of control. 'It depends what sort of mood he's in. If it's Peter's Yorkshire mood then it'll be all right. He's sensible and makes all the right decisions. But if he's in his Irish mood. Duck.' Now they had grown apart and were no longer of the same mind on too many things. Maybe the partnership had just run its course. Maybe O'Toole blamed him for his string of film failures.

Siân was around for the most part, still secretly seeing Robin Sachs, but also looking after the house and the children, almost sleepwalking through her role of wife, a role she found increasingly hard to sustain. To all intents and purposes she was already lost to O'Toole and he didn't know it, to him the house and those in it, wife, children, mother-in-law, maid, etc., still revolved around his presence.

At last a quality script arrived, written by Frederic Raphael and based on Geoffrey Household's 1939 novel *Rogue Male*, about an English aristocrat who tries to assassinate Hitler just before the outbreak of the war. The book had been a favourite of O'Toole's youth and he quickly accepted. Over the years the work had achieved cult status and when the word was out it was being made by the BBC, agents inundated the corporation with requests for their clients to be in it. O'Toole himself was clocked by Harold Pinter at a cocktail party asking to play the role of the solicitor. And Alastair Sim, literally on his death bed, crawled out, saying to his distressed wife, 'Peter will need me to play his uncle.'

It was a gruelling six-week shoot on locations in England and Wales requiring a great degree of physical action, leaping from cars, hurdling gates and the like. Particularly tough was the torture scene, where the would-be assassin is captured by the Nazis and has his fingernails torn out. 'Peter found that excessively difficult,' recalls Michael Byrne, who played the chief interrogator. 'Because as he told me that was the moment, finishing a tough and painful scene, when he would have loved to have had a drink, and of course he couldn't.'

Something that surprised Byrne, given O'Toole's flamboyance, panache and devil may care behaviour, was how conscientious he was about film acting. He especially emphasized the importance of the moment just before the director calls action and how it shouldn't be wasted, that whether you were standing on a cliff top or freezing in a studio tank pretending it was the sea, you had to be truly in that moment. 'Before a take he would hold my look,' says Byrne. 'And if there was a hold up in the filming and we should have been going in about thirty seconds but in fact we were four minutes late, he would hold that look throughout that four minutes, not let it go, and then we'd start the scene.'

Once, on location in Wales, O'Toole asked Byrne if he minded coming to lunch with him. 'I'm seeing a Mrs Jones.'

'Where?' asked Byrne.

'In her house.'

'Is it appropriate I come?' Byrne thought something might be afoot. But for propriety's sake O'Toole wanted him there.

'This was so typical of Peter,' says Byrne. 'He'd bumped into this woman in the street, this ordinary housewife who lived in a little two up, two down, and she'd invited him to lunch and he'd said yes. So there we were, it really was most bizarre. And Peter was really playing up to it, but he was also delightful with her. He knew exactly the effect he had on her but wasn't taking advantage of it in any way, he was not being condescending. Though he was obviously delighting in this little frisson that was happening.'

Rogue Male was shown on the BBC in September 1976, ironically the same week as the first episode of *I, Claudius*. With the shows vying for the prestigious cover of the *Radio Times* it was O'Toole who won. When he visited Siân on the *I, Claudius* set, where they were still busily filming, he remembers being 'about as popular as a pork sausage in a synagogue'.

A week later he was flying to Rome to begin work on his own toga epic, having agreed to play the Emperor Tiberius in what would turn out to be one of the most controversial films in cinema history, *Caligula*. Financed by Bob Guccione, the proprietor of sex magazine *Penthouse*, and directed by Tinto Brass, who specialized in avant-garde and erotic films, what began life as a serious examination of how all power corrupts, with a script by Gore Vidal, quickly spiralled out of control into a visual assault of the senses with decapitations galore, rape, incest, buggery, orgies, murders and torture.

O'Toole found himself in prestigious company. In the title role of the debauched Caligula was Malcolm McDowell, and there were Helen Mirren and John Gielgud. When O'Toole first encountered Gielgud on the set he greeted him with the words: 'Hello, Johnny! What is a knight of the realm doing in a porno movie!?' Nothing at all could be taken seriously, bored looking at all the naked bodies on display they began comparing operation scars. As for McDowell, he dressed for the most part in a nice gold lamé number, so O'Toole dubbed him 'Tinkerbell'. McDowell adored O'Toole, spending hours in his trailer going over lines but mostly listening to his stories. He remembers one particular night shoot as they waited for the set to be dressed. 'Peter was smoking and it certainly wasn't tobacco.' When they were finally called onto the stage the sight before them was of a mass orgy with every kind of perversion going on with dwarfs, amputees and giant dildos. O'Toole said a line, paused, looked over into a corner and then asked McDowell, 'Are they doing the Irish jig over there?' For one shot O'Toole had to ram a sword beneath the breast plate of a Roman guard, piercing a rubber bladder concealing blood. 'But by this time he was so ripped, he could barely grasp it,' revealed McDowell. The sword went under the plate with such force it hit the poor actor in the face and knocked him out.

According to Guccione, O'Toole disliked Tinto Brass on sight, who he delighted in calling Tinto Zinc. On the first day of shooting O'Toole was asked, 'How you like to be paralysed in picture?' He thought about it and replied, 'Anything you like, smiler.' So O'Toole got himself a naked Sumerian girl to lean on from start to finish. 'She became known as Betty the Collapsible Crutch.' Nor did the actor endear himself much to Guccione when he told the producer of his intention to launch a girlie magazine of his own to rival *Penthouse*. It was to be called *Basement* and would include such features as 'Rodent of the Month' and 'Toe Rag of the Year'. Much later Guccione got his own back in an interview revealing that he never once saw O'Toole sober. 'He doesn't drink any more, or at least he wasn't drinking then, but he was strung out on something. From time to time it took a little longer than usual to get him on the set.' Whatever O'Toole's condition, he managed to deliver an extraordinarily deranged performance, soaked in maliciousness and perversion as the syphilis-ridden Tiberius.

For a while Siân and the children visited O'Toole in Rome. Siân was appalled at the profligacy and ineptness on display and even more appalled by the script, which had been rewritten to such a degree that Gore Vidal would eventually demand his name be taken off the picture. Over the next two years, as legal wrangling prevented the film from being released, McDowell and others also tried to distance themselves from it, especially after Guccione inserted some choice slabs of hard-core porn to spice things up. O'Toole wasn't impressed. 'As for being erotic, I'd say it was about as erotic as bath night on HMS *Montclare*.'

Back at Guyon House, O'Toole and Siân had withdrawn from each other. Siân saw it as a 'gulf that had opened between us'. There were long periods of silence and non-communication. Siân had also discovered O'Toole had acquired some land in Mexico with the intention of building a house there and was taking Spanish lessons. After months of this situation dragging on she moved out in February 1977, when O'Toole learnt of her liaison with Robin Sachs. It was decided that the children, who were still at school, should remain behind, as would Siân's mother, who was now a permanent fixture at Guyon House and pretty much ran the place and whom O'Toole affectionately called 'the old Welsh cow'.

He was also adamant that the press should not find out about the separation for as long as possible. With Siân working on a BBC film, O'Toole insisted that the studio car still collected her each day from the pavement outside their house in Hampstead, rather than the flat she had taken in Chelsea. All of which necessitated Siân getting up at the crack of dawn to make her way across the capital to Hampstead to be picked up. It was madness.

O'Toole bought Siân out of the house, but she received almost nothing else, certainly none of the beautiful jewellery that had been given to her over the years, that was sold at Sotheby's. She was too embarrassed and defeated to contest the decision in court. The joint bank account was closed, her allowance stopped, her medical insurance cancelled; it was a complete severing. O'Toole and Siân were scarcely ever to cross paths again. Elizabeth Harris, who knew the couple, recalls great animosity between both of them after the separation. 'I never remember seeing them together after the divorce.' When Siân left she was fully aware that this would be the case. 'O'Toole prided himself on his resolutely unforgiving nature.' He was a supreme narcissist, capable of great warmth and generosity, but also capable of shutting people out of his life without seemingly ever wanting to get them back again. As Jane Merrow observed, 'He respected people for a long time and then they showed their feet of clay and that was the end of it.'

To the press O'Toole was philosophical about his own inadequacies that had helped consign the marriage to the waste bin. 'Ooh, I was a hopeless husband. Hopeless. I'm a loving man, but not a particularly well-behaved one.' Even to close friends he put up a bold front, saying, 'It's been a good canter.' But in private Siân's desertion and betrayal, for that's what he saw it as, cut him to the marrow. He was devastated. It wasn't necessarily an emotional loss. O'Toole was an ego-driven man and how he ran his life, from the very beginning of his marriage to Siân, was demanding and selfish and expectant of everything to go his way. For Siân to pull away from that would have come as both a shock and a big surprise, a case of 'How could anyone leave me; and especially for a younger man?' And yet Siân didn't leave O'Toole for Robin Sachs, she had already ended the affair. Only later did they reunite and marry, when her divorce finally came through at the end of 1979. Rather, Siân left O'Toole simply to get away and be on her own, having finally had enough of his behaviour. Siân was by nature quiet and refined, and out and about with O'Toole, or simply at home, she was always nervously waiting for the next thing to happen, for the fireworks to start. Not for nothing has she described O'Toole as a 'dangerous, disruptive human being'. And yet she loved him to distraction. 'He did and does fascinate me,' she said years later. 'But I can't claim to understand him.' This from a woman who was married and lived with the man for almost twenty years.

Asked once if anyone in the world really knew him, O'Toole laughed his high laugh before seriously contemplating how he was going to answer the question. 'I think probably my mother and father had a better hint of the plot than anyone else. My sister once turned round to the very famous actress I was about to work with for a lot of months and said to her, "At the end of the picture, will you tell me who my brother is? What goes on in there, in the fucking thing he calls a mind?" '

Within months of Siân leaving, Malinche Verdugo was installed at Guyon House. The first Siân heard of it was during a lunch with her mother when she explained matter-of-factly how she intended to look after Malinche as though she was her own daughter. Siân was completely lost for words. With O'Toole's help Malinche had also been accepted on a stage-management course at the Bristol Old Vic under the tutelage of Nat Brenner.

The circumstances of recent years had indeed been a trial for O'Toole: 'Heartbreak House wasn't in it,' he complained. 'The things that happened to me were almost biblical.' There was Siân's departure, his near-death illness, his association with Jules Buck finally coming to an end and then the recent death of his father at the age of eighty-six. He was struck by a car while coming out of a bookie's and crossing the road to go into a pub. 'They took him to hospital and found he had nine mortal injuries. Nine! When we went to the hospital we found a form which said – The patient discharged himself. Discharged himself! Christ, he should have been dead nine times over.' Remarkably, O'Toole senior lasted another three months and died at home. 'But it took a car to take the old bugger away.'

As far as work was concerned, O'Toole was still not receiving the big movie offers, so low had his marquee value slipped. For a while Nicolas Roeg did consider him to play the alien Thomas Newton in his spellbinding science-fiction film *The Man Who Fell to Earth*, a role that eventually went to David Bowie. Instead O'Toole accepted an offer from a young writer/director called Martyn Burke to star in his film about a military coup, called *Power Play*. Invited to Guyon House for preliminary talks about the script, Burke couldn't help but notice how wounded an individual O'Toole was. 'He talked about Siân with a real sense of pain and what came through was that they must have had some terrible battles, and that he was impossible, and yet I felt the pain and the regret so strongly I walked out of that house almost having to brush it off.'

Burke is convinced that the recent marriage break-up was directly responsible for O'Toole taking on the film, since his role as an army colonel had him seducing and stealing the wife of an older colleague. This was a scenario that clearly resonated and one that perhaps O'Toole felt if he acted out might be purged from his psyche. 'But the odd thing was,' says Burke, 'the weakest scenes in the film are where O'Toole is with this actress, he was somehow stiff, like he was afraid. I tried to work him through it but he never loosened up.'

Another reason for taking on the film was the realization that his career was in trouble, especially after his involvement in *Caligula*. 'He was despondent over having been in that,' confirms Burke. He saw working in Canada with a new young director as representing a fresh start. His arrival in Toronto certainly caused a stir. As he disembarked from the plane he was greeted on the tarmac by a detachment of Royal Canadian Mounted Police, the Mounties, famous for always getting their man. Amongst their number was one of the first female recruits. O'Toole spotted her straight away, took one look and said to her, 'Darling, I hope you always get your man.'

The first read-through Burke remembers as 'electrifying'. Besides O'Toole, top English stars David Hemmings and Donald Pleasence had been hired but the rest of the cast were largely young Canadian actors. 'And when Peter walked in the room there was just an electricity in the air that was almost palpable and everybody in one way or another was trying to raise up to his level.'

During the shoot O'Toole was helpful and encouraging, although if anyone loosened the reins through unprofessionalism, ill preparedness or just general laziness, he would eat them alive. This was Burke's first feature, he had no track record, but O'Toole saw he was hard working, he saw that he hoped and prayed that he knew what he was doing and had a vision. 'There was something in Peter that wanted the film to work for my sake, and I've always been enormously grateful to him for that. But there were times when I had to push him physically, you could tell something was starting to go wrong with him.' Burke puts this down to drug use, though he never found out exactly what O'Toole was taking. 'But I could see there was a physical haggardness that had started setting in, the make-up people had to work a little harder.' He was a man in his late forties but looked ten years older.

One extraordinary encounter Burke had with O'Toole came not long after they worked together, when he was invited one evening to Guyon House, along with the Irish actress Marie Kean. O'Toole traipsed around the place wearing a full-length fur coat, even though the heating was on high and the weather was mild. O'Toole invited his guests upstairs to what he referred to, as far as Burke can remember, as the Etruscan Room. It was wonderfully lit, tastefully panelled, filled with beautiful Etruscan art. It was a long room and sparsely furnished, a chesterfield sofa stood at one end, and a slightly raised platform with a throne-like chair at the other. 'We went into this room and I almost fell over from the heat, it must have been eighty-five degrees, it was brutally hot. Marie and I sat on the sofa, while Peter sat on this throne-like chair at the other end, still dressed in this fur coat. Suddenly he stands up and says, "Nobody knows the trouble I have seen," throws off the fur coat, stands there arms outstretched, crucifix-like, stark naked. And Marie and I were wondering what exactly did he want us to look at. And then we realized, peering through the light that was shining on him from overhead, the scars across his stomach and his abdomen, you could see them from where we were some thirty-five feet away. It was a truly bizarre moment. And then he puts the fur coat on again and grins that crinkly grin as only he could do, sits back down and says, "Well now, where were we." '

Whilst filming *Power Play* in Toronto, O'Toole was introduced to Ed Mirvish, a Canadian businessman and theatrical impresario who persuaded him to undertake a season at the city's prestigious Royal Alexandra Theatre. Seized by the chance of a return to the stage, O'Toole asked Nat Brenner to set up the deal since he was scheduled to fly with Malinche to Cape Town in the spring of 1978 to start work on the Douglas Hickox directed *Zulu Dawn*, a prequel to the classic 1964 film *Zulu*. He had agreed to play Lord Chelmsford, the arrogant commander of British forces in South Africa who presided over one of the British army's greatest military defeats at the Battle of Isandlwana, an engagement that occurred the day before the heroic British stand at Rorke's Drift.

Zulu Dawn proved to be a handsomely mounted production, shot in the kind of terrain that O'Toole thrived in, right in the middle of the African bush, ten miles from the actual battle site, now a memorial. It must have reminded O'Toole of his days on *Lawrence*, since everything had to be built from scratch including roads, wells and a runway for small planes. At one time 250 crew members and 6,000 extras were living on location. Given the logistics involved, shooting passed relatively smoothly, though O'Toole had trouble with his horse. 'It threw him several times,' recalls the film's producer Nate Kohn. 'In the end, though, he came to love the horse and asked if he could have the animal. We shipped it to him in Ireland. After being thrown one time, he required a tetanus shot. The nurse gave it to him in his trailer. She swooned when she left the trailer and fainted.'

Kohn liked to think he got to know O'Toole quite a bit during the filming. 'He was among the most intelligent actors I've met. He was also funny, quick-witted and didn't seem to take himself seriously. I was particularly struck by his diction. He is the only actor I've worked with who was able to actually improve his performance in looping' (the re-recording of dialogue by actors during post-production). One morning O'Toole came into Kohn's office to discuss his character. They talked for about an hour. 'His insights and suggestions were brilliant and we incorporated them. He was very focused on doing the best possible job.' As he was leaving, O'Toole paused in the doorway, 'By the way, I won't be showing up on set until I'm paid.' The production company had run into financial troubles and owed some of the members of the cast money. Needless to say, they were able to rustle up the required sum surprisingly fast.

In the film O'Toole looks, even for him, haggard and gaunt, and Kohn was fully aware of the actor's recent surgery: 'Something about removing his spleen, about which he joked, so he didn't drink, although I think he did experiment with the local weed.' Kohn also confirms that O'Toole did not get along terribly well with his co-star Burt Lancaster. 'Coming as they did from different schools of acting. They only had one scene together, but it proved to be extremely powerful.'

Finishing his commitments in Africa, O'Toole returned to Toronto in September 1978. The plan was to perform two plays directed by Nat Brenner, *Uncle Vanya* and Noël Coward's *Present Laughter*. After Toronto the productions were to go on tour in the United States. Rehearsals did not go well. Canadian actress Nonnie Griffin arrived on the first day with high expectations. That all changed when she caught sight of O'Toole. 'I thought, three months of this tour he's going to be dead. His face was the colour of puce and he was all skin and bone, it was awful.' Slowly, Nonnie began to see things unravelling, the plays were poorly prepared and many of the actors had in her view been miscast. Most of all O'Toole was behaving irrationally, one minute charming, the next ranting and raving. 'I think he might have been on some kind of drug, maybe it was cocaine, because he changed so much, total change, which can only be explained by drugs. You could see what a sweetie pie he could be but then his mood would suddenly alter and he'd be in a rage just like that. He could turn on you and destroy you in seconds.'

The prospect of staying with the show for three months was

filling Nonnie with horror and she decided to leave. 'It was with regret,' she says, 'because Peter and I had great chemistry, we just sparked, but he was truly a mental case during that production.' Later on she heard some stories from the play's run, one involving the Canadian actor James B. Douglas, who played the role of the manservant in *Present Laughter*. 'Jimmy was quite an adept actor and he used to get great laughs and Peter became enraged on the stage with him, he'd say things like – fuck you! He was having a breakdown, I think.'

Martyn Burke and his wife had been invited to the opening night of *Uncle Vanya*. 'I hadn't seen him for maybe four or five months and when the curtain came up and Peter stepped onto the stage there was an audible gasp throughout the entire audience. People were so shocked at the way he looked. Physically he looked devastated, gaunt, haggard, barely recognizable as Lawrence of Arabia, just a totally physically destroyed human wreck.' It was no surprise to Burke that O'Toole could not carry the play and gave a performance that fell back on his stock mannerisms. He was going through the motions and it was sad to see. The production and O'Toole particularly were savaged by the critics.

After Toronto the company embarked on its tour of the United States, which marked O'Toole's debut on the American stage. Over the years he had been courted by several Broadway producers but was always wary of making such a heavy commitment. 'The prospect of signing to do one play for a year absolutely terrifies me.' Playing in Chicago and the Kennedy Center in Washington, audiences were delighted and dismayed in equal measure as his performances ran the gauntlet from slurry to exuberant, enjoyable and yet at the same time unnerving. Midway through the run no one was surprised when an exhausted O'Toole revealed he was quitting the tour early.

EIGHTEEN

O'Toole found himself at a Hollywood party, not drinking but doing somersaults in the middle of the floor (this was apparently something he did quite often when bored at parties, that and hide behind curtains to pop out and surprise people, just to liven things up), when he was approached by a director called Richard Rush. This meeting was no happy accident, Rush was a huge admirer of O'Toole. 'He defined the outer limits of the art of acting for me.' For several years Rush had been working on a script about an imperious film director who hires a criminal on the run as a stunt man on his new movie. 'At the beginning you recognize him as a benefactor, who gives this young man a place to hide and shelter. But by the last act of the picture you have to believe that this man is going to kill the kid in order to get it on film, and there aren't many actors who can handle that kind of subtle transition and still remain fascinating to the audience.'

Rush cornered O'Toole and they chatted happily for half the evening. 'But I never brought up the screenplay because it seemed like such a tacky thing to do at a party. When he walked out the door I remember saying to myself, "You chicken shit bastard, why the hell didn't you mention it!" ' Then fate interceded. O'Toole came dashing back inside and grabbed Rush. 'Somebody just told me you directed *Freebie and the Bean*. I'm crazy about that picture.' Rush seized his chance. 'Well, I've got a screenplay for you.' A week later O'Toole had read the script of *The Stunt*

Man and identified it as the best he'd seen in quite some time, and the role of maverick director Eli Cross was without question the best since *The Ruling Class*. He called Rush. 'I'm a literate and intelligent man, and unless you let me do your film I will kill you.' Rush thought that was about the best answer one could possibly get.

The financing for the film wasn't quite in place and the inclusion of O'Toole's name above the title didn't exactly help. 'It was not easy casting Peter because the Hollywood money men didn't rate him high enough box-office wise,' recalls Rush. 'So it was a battle. But there was no chance of yielding on my part. Once O'Toole said yes the picture had to go with him as far as I was concerned.' Eventually the budget was raised thanks to investment from a shopping-mall magnate and filming began on location in California towards the end of 1978.

Before a foot of celluloid was taken Rush was warned about O'Toole's reputation for being sometimes difficult on set, but as it turned out he was no trouble at all. 'You couldn't ask for a more perfect working companion. It was like having a Stradivarius to play that was quite willing to be played.' In turn, O'Toole loved working with Rush, rating him amongst the best directors he ever worked with.

In the role of the young fugitive Rush had hired Steve Railsback, then best known for playing Charles Manson in the 1976 TV movie *Helter Skelter*. As he prepared for his first scene with O'Toole, Railsback felt under pressure. 'When you work with somebody like a Peter O'Toole, when you're working with what I considered greatness, you'd better step your game up or you'll get destroyed.' O'Toole wasn't out to deliberately intimidate the young actor, he was just doing what he did naturally, taking the moment by the scruff of the neck and flying. That's when Railsback started to climb, he had to. 'That night I went to my trailer and there was a bottle of wine with a ribbon and a card and it said: "Steve, for being unintimidatable – love Peter." I still have that card.'

As the shoot went on, Railsback and O'Toole grew close. Between takes they'd wander off and just talk, talk about the work, about acting, about themselves. Railsback listened to O'Toole's roaring stories about the past. 'And that man could tell a story, you would visualize everything he was saying, you could see it. There was something about Peter, even when he wasn't telling a story, you were transfixed. God, what a pleasure it was to be with that man.'

When the unit landed in Sacramento to shoot over the course of a few days, Railsback's hotel room was right next door to O'Toole's. Out back in the yard the owner kept some ducks and every morning at 2 a.m., without fail, O'Toole would wander out onto his balcony and recite Shakespeare to them. 'And I would get up to make sure I was listening.'

O'Toole displayed no hang-ups, he wasted no time with prima-donna behaviour, he was relaxed and free and the mood on set remained upbeat throughout. 'We couldn't wait to get to work every day,' confirms Railsback.

Given the role he was playing was a crackpot and tyrannical movie director, the suggestion was that O'Toole had used his old *Lawrence* collaborator David Lean as inspiration. In truth, the character didn't change much from Rush's own conception, although O'Toole was certainly instrumental in refining the role, for example carefully selecting the right costume. Every morning he'd go to Rush with a new set of clothes. 'One day Peter came to me and said, "How's this?" And I said, "That's it, that's exactly the look I've been after, the Americanization of Peter O'Toole." What I didn't realize was that he was dressed exactly like me and it wasn't until noon that day that I finally figured that out.'

It wasn't just his choice of costume, O'Toole brought an enormous amount to the film. 'Mostly the magic of turning those words on paper into a living and breathing reality,' says Rush, who also had a hand in the screenplay. 'Which had all the subtlety and virulence that one could hope for, and on top of that the extra O'Toole power that he delivered.' There was something else, too, which the director interpreted as being traditional in the English theatre, of the leading man being a sort of father figure within the company. Whenever there was some little problem developing in relationships between the cast, Rush could always rely on O'Toole to help solve them.

As he waited for what he was sure would be an enthusiastic response to *The Stunt Man*, O'Toole took on two television projects. First was *Strumpet City*, a seven-part serial based on James Plunkett's bestselling novel about the 1913 strike known as the Dublin Lockout, where workers were threatened with losing their jobs if they refused to sign a pledge not to join a union. It was the most ambitious television project RTÉ, Ireland's national broadcaster, had ever undertaken and O'Toole excelled as James Larkin, an Irish trade-union leader and activist. Appearing in only a handful of scenes, O'Toole was proud enough of the production to help flog it at the Monte Carlo television festival, where he was lauded and invited to dinner with Princess Grace at the Palace.

His second venture was far more taxing, involving several months of hard slog on brutal locations in Israel. *Masada* was an eight-hour American TV miniseries based on a true event, when nine hundred Jewish zealots held out against a vast Roman legion on a mountain-top fortress. At $21m it was the most expensive miniseries ever made. O'Toole played a Roman general commanding an army seemingly made up purely of British thespians. The producers had cast Americans to play the Jewish renegades. 'And the Americans were very health conscious,' recalls Peter Strauss, who played the leader. 'Eating carefully and doing smart things about the sun. And the Brits would be up till five in the morning collectively singing and enjoying the local libation in the hotel. And the Brits never got sick while all the Americans came down something awful.'

During long camera set-ups O'Toole would invariably wander off into the desert on his own with just an umbrella for company. 'Once he meandered off and no one could find him for the rest of the day,' recalls Strauss. 'And to this day I don't think anybody knows where he went. He had this Lawrence-like adoration of the desert and seemed much more comfortable in it than the rest of us.'

O'Toole did seem to distance himself as much as possible from the rest of the company, taking his privacy seriously. While the bulk of the cast stayed in the same hotel, O'Toole rented a private house some distance from the location and when work was done for the day would return there alone. 'Peter was not an actor you got close to on the set,' confirms Strauss. But he was always pleasant and once again arrived having done his usual meticulous research. 'No one can ever say to me that Peter O'Toole was not the best prepared actor on the set,' says Strauss. 'He would have his cigarettes, and once in a while he would partake from this little snuff box, and God only knows what that was all about. He would come on the set and very quietly listen to the director's instructions regarding staging, and then you would just sit there in awe as he delivered a thirty-page speech without hesitation and impeccably prepared.'

In one of the film's most important roles, that of a slave girl who is the lover of O'Toole's general, director Boris Sagal had cast the Nicaraguan-born former supermodel Barbara Carrera, who had been acting for only a few years. When she heard she would be playing most of her scenes opposite O'Toole, Barbara got a friend of hers to run a print of *Lawrence of Arabia*. 'And I was blown away by the beauty of this man, he was overpowering.' When Barbara arrived in Israel she thought a nice way to introduce herself was to invite O'Toole over for lunch at her rented villa. He arrived in a convertible driven by Malinche, determined it seemed to make a good first impression, wearing a grand hat and cape as if he were going to the opera. When Barbara opened the door to greet him she was momentarily stunned. 'Because he looked so different, it was not the young man whom I saw on that screen, it was someone who was looking more like his father. But his eyes, my God, his eyes were amazing, so bright blue. And I liked him from the first moment I met him.'

Barbara was scheduled to begin work the next day, but due to difficulties ended up waiting around in her trailer and not being used. When O'Toole heard what had happened he was visibly upset. Exactly the same thing happened the following day, Barbara was left waiting and they never got around to shooting her scene. The next morning O'Toole arrived to say good morning. 'Did they get to you yesterday?' he asked. Barbara shook her head. 'What!' Grabbing Barbara's hand, O'Toole pulled her out of the trailer and onto the set. 'There must have been two thousand extras there dressed as Roman soldiers,' she recalls. 'And everyone looked at him as this great General. And he was holding me by the hand, I felt like a five-year-old, and he got the attention of all these people and said, "Never, in my twenty years of acting, have I seen such an abominable treatment of a leading lady. If she were Sophia Loren they would have to go to Rome to bring her back." And I was fine, I was not at all upset that they didn't get to me. But that was Peter, he demanded his fellow workers be shown respect.'

Until the end of shooting O'Toole took Barbara under his wing, teaching her how to survive the extreme desert heat by drinking water every ten minutes and sharing his supply of salt tablets. In return she was to call him her 'mentor'. She was still relatively inexperienced as an actress, and O'Toole guided her and helped her enormously, going through every scene they shared together. He'd take her to one side and say, 'This scene is a close-up, Barbara, so you must stay very, very still. There is tremendous power in stillness.' He would direct her almost. 'He educated me and I was a willing pupil. He told me that I should always look for the greatness in a character. And it didn't matter how lowly they were, find the greatness in the lowliness.' Barbara also remembers being told that every evening before going to sleep he took the script and re-read his entire part. In that way he was able to keep entirely in the character.

Often the two of them would sit together between set-ups and O'Toole would regale her with wild stories, usually revolving around drinking and his fellow hell-raisers like Harris, Finch and Burton. 'And you know, Barbara, we would meet wherever we were working, we would meet up on weekends and we would spend the whole weekend just drinking. We would go twenty-four hours just drinking.' Sometimes it would be longer. O'Toole, Harris and Trevor Howard paid Burton a visit in England when he was shooting *Where Eagles Dare*. They left on the Friday night on a plane for Paris. 'You will be back Monday?' the producer Elliott Kastner asked Burton. 'Oh, don't worry,' said Burton. They turned up on the Wednesday.

At these moments O'Toole took a modicum of pleasure goading one of the producers, with whom he had struck up a disagreeable relationship. The second assistant director would come over to them asking, 'Mr O'Toole, Miss Carrera, we're waiting for you on the set.' This was O'Toole's cue to turn to his personal assistant and ask for some coffee. 'And then he would begin another story,' recalls Barbara. 'A long story, and of course he would always embellish it.' After something like fifteen minutes the first AD would show up. 'Mr O'Toole, Miss Carrera, we're ready for you on the set.' O'Toole would just ignore him and turn to Barbara, 'Don't move, my dear, sit there, don't move.' The coffee would arrive and he'd continue with his story.

This went on until finally the director himself showed. 'Peter, didn't they tell you that we're ready for you on the set?' With an expression of pure innocence O'Toole would reply, 'Why didn't somebody tell me?' According to Barbara this happened quite often and the reasoning behind it was quite plain. As O'Toole explained to her, 'I do this to delay them, because delay is money. Damn producers. Get them by the truss.' Then he would get on the set and pow, away he'd go. 'And every time he worked you could hear a pin drop.'

Eventually the heat and the physical discomfort in Israel led to a decision being made to take the film back to Hollywood and finish it there. Many of the actors felt a huge emotional loss no longer playing at the base of the real Masada, in the real desert, instead shooting in the Hollywood Hills, with the freeway noise rushing by; it just wasn't the same.

There was an obligation, recalls Strauss, that anything to do with O'Toole had to be done before lunch. That invariably left Strauss, dressed in Judean garb, having to play his close-ups in the afternoon with O'Toole standing behind the camera giving him his lines dressed in an impeccable three-piece suit. Still, Strauss would do his best. At the end of perhaps their most pivotal scene together Boris Sagal called, 'Cut, print, I'm fine, let's move on.' As the crew began to dismantle the lights, O'Toole lent over to Strauss and whispered, 'Ask to do it again.' Strauss looked at O'Toole. 'Why?' O'Toole looked deep into him. 'Because you can do it better.' Some actors would have taken umbrage at this, but Strauss knew that O'Toole was simply being encouraging. When Strauss called over Sagal to say he wanted to do another take the director looked flustered. 'Why? I've got what I want.' Strauss insisted and so they went again. 'And I tried to do it better. And perhaps I did.'

NINETEEN

It was always 'the Scottish Play', never *Macbeth*. O'Toole simply would not countenance its name being uttered. Whether he took the curse that is supposed to haunt productions of this piece seriously or pandered to the old theatrical superstition, who knows, but he did take it to extremes. Frawley Becker, the dialogue coach, remembers arriving at O'Toole's trailer on the set of *Night of the Generals* in 1966 on a sunny but cloudy morning in Warsaw. Taking inspiration from the fluctuating weather he thought a quick burst of Shakespeare was in order: 'So foul and fair a day I have not seen.' Pleased with himself, Becker watched as O'Toole's face recoiled in horror, as if some horrendous spirit had just passed over the threshold. 'Do you not know that you must never quote the Scottish gentleman?'

'You mean *Mac* . . .'

'*The Scottish gentleman!*' O'Toole blasted, giving even more theatrical bent to his voice than usual. 'He must never be named! And never a line from that play may be spoken, except in the theatre where it is being performed or rehearsed.'

'What happens if *Mac* . . . ' Becker stopped himself just in time. 'If the play is quoted?'

'Great misfortune follows,' said O'Toole. There was an uncomfortable silence before he spoke again. 'I forgive you because you are American, and as such I assume you do not know the traditions of the English stage!' O'Toole then went on to explain that the last time lines of dialogue from 'the Scottish Play' had been quoted on one of his film sets, *Lord Jim*, a boat full of extras capsized in a river. Becker never did find out if anyone drowned.

By the close of the seventies the Old Vic theatre was heading for financial ruination, rumours abounded that it might have to close down. What it needed was a box-office attraction to bring the crowds back through the door. O'Toole had last performed on the London stage in 1965 and in a newspaper interview spoke of his desire to return, somewhere like the Old Vic, a theatre that held a very special place in his heart. It was where, as a drama student, he had come to watch the likes of Guinness and Olivier ply their trade, 'All working for buttons.'

Reading these comments with interest was Toby Robertson, head of the Old Vic Company. Getting in touch, he wanted to know exactly what the actor had in mind. There was a long-cherished ambition to do *Macbeth*, a play O'Toole believed to be the precursor of practically all gothic literature, a text that positively crackled with evil, and in his opinion Shakespeare's greatest achievement. Perhaps it could form part of a short season that might also include another favourite, *Uncle Vanya*, which O'Toole fancied having a crack at directing himself. Robertson was in no position to refuse and O'Toole was hired in early 1980. He was also granted associate director status, with his own office on the premises.

Very quickly doubts spread about O'Toole's health. Would he be capable of playing such a physically demanding role as Macbeth night after night, while at the same time preparing another play? It was not an unreasonable concern, but when it was raised at a meeting O'Toole reacted angrily and stormed out. In the end he was forced to bow to pressure and *Uncle Vanya* was dropped.

While he was away filming *Masada* events took a dramatic turn. Robertson was unceremoniously sacked by the Old Vic's board and replaced as artistic director by the actor Timothy West. Pragmatic by nature, West was nervous of O'Toole's reputation and that the actor's contract at the Old Vic allowed him total artistic control over the *Macbeth* production. He feared a disaster.

For weeks O'Toole was holed up at his house in Clifden carrying out his customarily methodical research and preparation. Running along the beach in front of his house carrying heavy logs of wood, chanting the lines of the play, trying to get the rhythm of the speeches right, he was like a prize fighter getting into shape, fully aware that this undertaking brought with it huge risks and expectations. That was fine. He was fully committed.

For director, O'Toole asked Jack Gold, having worked well with him on *Man Friday*. But Gold had been offered a movie and decided he'd be on safer ground doing that. 'Peter was very much his own man when he got into a part, particularly on stage; it was difficult enough on film. And I think I was much too inexperienced in stage work to direct a major piece like that.' Gold is under no illusions that he made the right choice and was never tempted to watch the final result. 'I couldn't bring myself to see it.'

With directors proving either unavailable or scared off by O'Toole, actor turned film director Bryan Forbes was eventually chosen, a man who had never pretended to be anything other than an actor's director and who once said: 'In the last analysis, everything has to be subservient to the actor.' Music to O'Toole's ears to be sure.

Together O'Toole and Forbes assembled a large cast that mixed established players such as Dudley Sutton and Brian Blessed with rising talents such as Clive Wood and Frances Tomelty, chosen to play Lady Macbeth after O'Toole's suggestion of Meryl Streep was rejected as being impractical. Rehearsals began in August 1980 in a blaze of publicity. Christopher Fulford, in his first professional job as an actor, remembers O'Toole arriving for the press call and walking onto the stage to the accompaniment of a band of Irish pipers. But already storm clouds were forming. Kevin Quarmby was another young actor not long out of drama school, who had long idolized O'Toole, but what he saw on that first day of rehearsal shocked him. 'Here was someone in his late forties but my immediate thought was, my God this guy looks old. Incredibly lined, and thin. Let's say O'Toole didn't look like he was in the peak of health. But he was amazingly imposing – you were scared shitless.'

It was a strange rehearsal period. O'Toole had arrived already word perfect and had asked Forbes not to give him any direction until the third week. 'To a great extent he had already set his performance,' claimed Forbes. But doubts were raised very early on about the path O'Toole was taking. In the opinion of Quarmby, who now writes and lectures on Shakespeare, O'Toole's delivery was tortured, idiosyncratic and laboured. 'It was like listening to a mature public schoolboy being forced to recite Shakespeare in class.' Christopher Fulford, however, remembers things differently. 'Peter did his soliloquies holding his coffee mug and cigarette, and did them I thought brilliantly. There was a sense of grandeur to his performance, even in rehearsal.'

Over the coming weeks many in the company hoped that some concession to contemporary naturalism in Shakespeare performance would creep into O'Toole's delivery. In fact it evolved not a jot, according to Quarmby. 'I can still hear him doing every line, because I was on stage practically all the time, and the delivery was absolutely the same from the moment of rehearsals right to the very last night. His exclamatory style remained firmly rooted in the tradition of the lead actor controlling the stage, as exemplified by Donald Wolfit's post-war touring Shakespeare productions.'

Other creative decisions were also coming under scrutiny, not least the madcap suggestion of employing inflatable scenery. O'Toole had an interest in an Irish company that had invented a revolutionary concept in stage design, scenery that could be erected and then dismantled to fit into the boot of a car. A demonstration was called for on the Old Vic stage, but all West and his fellow board members could see was what looked like an assortment of black bin liners haphazardly stuck together inflated by a generator producing enough noise to rival a 747 jet engine. Even O'Toole had to admit defeat and booted the inventor and his contraption out of the stage door.

Forbes quickly took the decision to hire a film-set designer with no theatrical experience, one of many film buddies that were coming in; jobs for the boys. The most dangerous of these was the fight director, who was an Irish stuntman O'Toole had befriended on *Zulu Dawn*. Quarmby has never forgotten his first fight rehearsal when he was given a spear and told, 'Right, now Kevin, get this spear and you thrust it at the bastard, just thrust it at the bastard.' Within two minutes Quarmby had accidentally pierced the jeans of his opponent, who cried out, 'Stop, I am not working like this. I refuse to work like this.' Everyone was a little more wary after that. 'But we did have very realistic fights,' says Quarmby. 'Because there was absolutely no proper stage chore-ography. It was, let's make it look as dangerous as possible by making it as dangerous as possible. It was pretty scary.'

Backstage, too, swords were drawn. From the off O'Toole and West appeared to be poles apart in both temperament and in their approach to theatre. It didn't help that O'Toole kept refer-ring to West as 'Miss Piggy'. Theirs was a relationship Forbes described as like that of a warring husband and wife ripe for divorce living under the same roof. Paranoid, O'Toole believed West was out to sabotage his production and banned him from rehearsals. West in turn was worried about O'Toole's erratic behaviour, not helped by his drug use, a situation the cast were fully aware of. 'Let's say he was sailing very close to the wind,' says Quarmby. Actress Susan Engel saw it first-hand. 'He was stoned out of his mind, seriously stoned. And that's tragic.' Susan, who had worked with O'Toole years before at Bristol, had been asked to play Lady Macduff, a role she didn't care for much, but went to see O'Toole anyway. 'And he was non compos mentis. He was very excited about the play and had all these completely mad ideas but I couldn't actually follow what he was saying. It was very sad.'

By now even Forbes was beginning to harbour a few misgivings, particularly over his star's obsession with making this the bloodiest *Macbeth* on record. 'Do you know how many times the word blood appears in the text, old darling?' O'Toole said to Forbes one day, before volunteering the information that, 'If you stab a living man, blood spurts seventeen feet.' There was also the double-handed sword he was having made of the finest Toledo steel for his duel with Macduff. When this fearsome weapon finally arrived at the theatre his co-star visibly paled. In the end it proved too heavy and O'Toole armed himself instead with a flimsy aluminium sword to conserve energy, which after each encounter became increasingly bent, not helped by his sometimes using it to practise his cricket swing.

Oddly, HRH Princess Margaret paid a visit to one rehearsal and during a break the subject of blood came up yet again in conversation. 'What you need is some Kensington gore,' the Princess volunteered, the stuff deployed in the old Hammer horror films. 'We use it all the time in St John's Ambulance demonstrations. It's very realistic.' Forbes saw O'Toole's eyes light up.

Red appeared to be the production's motif, since O'Toole had insisted his dressing room be painted blood red from floor to ceiling. He also had a lumbering Irish minder posted outside at all times. 'This guy would have killed anyone for Peter, there's absolutely no doubt,' says Quarmby. Christopher Fulford, too, has memories of this gentleman, who rode shotgun with O'Toole at all times. 'He was very genial to me and not at all unpleasant. But there were all sorts of rumours flying around about him.'

It was fairly obvious that Forbes was helpless when faced with this ego-driven onslaught, and so O'Toole's personal vision for the play went gloriously unchecked, with members of the cast simply not used to being mere satellite figures to O'Toole. Enquiring what they should be thinking when Macbeth raves at the ghost of Banquo in the banquet scene, O'Toole's sharp reply was: 'You should be looking at me, dear, I'm the star.' As Quarmby describes it, 'His sole purpose for being in the play was to be *the* star. There wasn't a vision for the play, there was a concept of Peter O'Toole is a great star and everything must be done to ensure that all focus is on him at every moment.'

As a result rehearsals became factionalized, with individuals discussing and answering amongst themselves questions of character, motivation and textual nuance. In essence it had become an unbalanced production, in that you had the principal actor playing one thing and the majority of the company playing something else and they were so far apart that nothing would make them gel. 'It was an inevitable car crash that was going to happen with a huge star of the old school,' says Quarmby. Forbes put it simpler. 'It was an imbalance between Peter and some of the less experienced actors, some of whom were understandably in awe of him.' There were those in the O'Toole camp and those firmly outside of it.

One decision of O'Toole's that Forbes was powerless to overturn was the abandonment of the traditional portrayal of the three witches as hideous old crones and instead having them as voluptuous sirens dressed in silken robes. The fact that O'Toole was having an affair with the young actress playing the first witch, after the recent collapse of his relationship with Malinche Verdugo, almost certainly had no influence upon his decision.

Her name was Trudie Styler and she and O'Toole were the subject of much gossip amongst the cast.

From the start O'Toole wanted to create a sense of occasion and a sense of adventure and had tried to get to know each one of the cast on a personal level. In the middle of rehearsals Christopher Fulford recalls being invited to Guyon House and told to prepare a sonnet. 'We had chilli con carne in his kitchen and before that we'd sat in his study. He'd got me a couple of beers, he wasn't drinking, and he had me doing this sonnet with a clock to my ear to get the rhythm of the sonnet. And as far as I know he'd done something similar with everyone in the company.'

As the opening night approached, relations between O'Toole and West had deteriorated so badly that they were now only communicating through intermediaries. Barred he may have been from rehearsals, but West insisted on his right to watch the first dress rehearsal and was appalled by what he witnessed. It wasn't just that it was hopelessly old-fashioned, but there seemed to be absolutely no artistic vision either, no concept, least of all anything imaginative or relevant in O'Toole's performance, who delivered the lines as if his foot was tied to iambic pentameter. He pleaded with Forbes that radical changes needed to be made to avert a full-scale disaster but the director felt that to confront O'Toole now 'would provoke an explosion that could destroy us all'. After West tried and failed to get a meeting with O'Toole he insisted on a brief statement being inserted into the theatre programme declaring that this *Macbeth* was under the direct artistic control of Peter O'Toole and not the Old Vic; in other words he'd washed his hands of it.

On the opening night, 3 September 1980, as the audience took their seats with twenty minutes to curtain up, Forbes walked into O'Toole's dressing room and was stunned to find him stark naked except for a Gauloise in his mouth. 'Peter, old son, aren't you leaving it a bit late to get into costume?'

'Can't wear them, darling,' replied O'Toole. 'They're hopeless.'

'Ah!' Forbes exclaimed, with a rising sense of panic. 'We don't have much alternative, do we? But let me see what I can do.'

Outside, Forbes grabbed Brian Blessed, who was playing Banquo. As a loose friend of O'Toole's he was Forbes' only hope.

'Do you think his bottle's gone?' said Blessed.

'God help us if it has,' said Forbes.

'Leave him to me. Can't promise what he'll look like, but I'll get him on.'

By some miracle O'Toole got onto the stage, haphazardly dressed though he was, including for some bizarre reason jogging trousers and baseball boots. The costume designer was so disgusted that she was seen later that night scratching her name off all the posters outside the Old Vic. 'There was madness in the theatre that night on both sides of the curtain,' Forbes said. At first the audience were bewildered by what they were seeing, then as the play went on the giggles began. By the time of O'Toole's much promised bloodbath they could contain themselves no longer. Traditionally Macbeth returns after the off-stage killing of the King with the actor having merely soaked his hands in blood. Not O'Toole. 'In the wings was a tin bath with about a foot of Kensington gore inside it,' recalls Quarmby. 'Peter would stand in it and douse himself from head to foot, walk on stage with everything dripping, looking like Carrie, and say, "I have done the deed." The effect produced on the audience wasn't the uncomfortable laughter of people who are not sure whether something is being sent up or not, it was the laughter of disbelief and theatrical horror.' As Forbes later confessed, 'From that moment onwards the play was doomed.'

Absurdity followed absurdity when stage hands came on the stage to mop up the fake blood because the actors complained they were slipping in it. When the safety curtain came down some members of the audience instinctively got up to leave, requiring Forbes to announce over the tannoy, 'Ladies and gentlemen, this is not an interval. I repeat, this is not an interval.' Something had to be done and it was put to O'Toole that perhaps he had overdone it slightly. Fulford clearly remembers hearing O'Toole shouting from his dressing room: 'No blood! No show!'

In the audience that first night was O'Toole's old Bristol pal Patrick Dromgoole, by now a top television executive. Like the rest of the audience he watched with mounting incredulity. 'In my view, Peter hadn't got an angle on the part at all. He didn't know what he was doing, it was incredible.' Afterwards Dromgoole went to see him in his dressing room and there he saw a man, his old friend, not only physically laid low but emotionally teetering on the edge. 'But not admitting it.' Dromgoole brought his car round the back of the theatre and got O'Toole out, past a baying mob of journalists shouting, 'What's it like to be laughed at, Mr O'Toole?'

In the following morning's newspapers the critics did not hold back. 'The performance is not so much downright bad as heroically ludicrous,' said the *Daily Mail*'s Jack Tinker. 'The voice is pure Bette Davis in her Baby Jane mood, the manner is Vincent Price hamming up a Hammer horror.' The *Sunday Times*' critic called it 'a milestone in the history of coarse acting. Mr O'Toole's performance was deranged.' Perhaps *The Times*' Irving Wardle hit the nail on the head when he said that O'Toole's performance evoked the kind of thing one got from Sir Donald Wolfit on a bad night. 'I view it almost like it was the closing volleys of the barnstorming actor/manager type,' says Quarmby. 'The death of the Wolfits. One actually felt that you were at the funeral of that style of performer and acting.'

O'Toole realized that something was wrong when his housekeeper told him there was a scrum of journalists outside the front door. 'What could I do?' he later joked. 'My shaver is electric so I could not cut my throat.' Like the rest of the cast arriving at the theatre that night, O'Toole had to fight his way through TV crews and crowds besieging the box office for tickets that had already sold out. Although the overall mood amongst the cast was one of despondency, with many looking at each other for some kind of reassurance, O'Toole made a point of visiting every individual member of the company in their dressing room prior to curtain-up to present them each with a red rose and a private rallying cry: 'We've had some bloody awful reviews, but I'm firmly committed to this production. I absolutely believe what I am doing is right. We do not change a thing. We don't listen to those bastards. We carry on!'

While there was certainly an element of everyone rallying around and getting on with it, having to go on night after night knowing that many of the audience were there for the wrong reasons, like motorists stopping to gawp at a car accident, was a demoralizing experience. 'There was a real sense with many of us that it was like we were going through a sort of trench warfare,' recalls Quarmby. 'And we were being sent over the top every night and the general leading us hadn't got a pair of glasses and didn't know that we were firing in the wrong direction.' The hope remained that there would be an attempt to at least put some of the problems right. But there were no further rehearsals, nothing. 'It was farcically, scarily organized, or disorganized,' says Quarmby. 'It was a trial.'

O'Toole continued to give the impression that it was all like water off a duck's back, revelling defiantly in the controversy and criticism. 'There has to be danger in theatre or it doesn't work,' he'd once said. 'You can't play safe.' But inside it was tearing him apart. In a cry for help he wrote a revealing note to Patrick Dromgoole which read: 'I've forgotten how to do it.' He did feel terribly betrayed by the critics, who seemed hell-bent on giving him a really good kicking. 'I was terribly upset for him because he was absolutely crucified over *Macbeth*,' says Dromgoole. 'And any lack of love was agonizingly painful to him. He loved being loved.' Remarkably, out of sixty-odd performances of *Macbeth*, O'Toole did not miss a single one.

Friends rallied round. Katharine Hepburn phoned with the advice, 'If you're going to have a disaster, have a big one.' Burton called, too. 'I hear you've had a bit of stick from the critics.'

'Yes,' O'Toole replied.

'How are the houses?'

'Packed.'

'Then remember this, my boy, you are the most original actor to come out of Britain since the war and fuck the critics.'

'Thank you,' said O'Toole.

Burton went on, 'Think of every four letter obscenity, six, eight, ten and twelve letter expletives and ram it right up their envious arses in which I'm sure there is ample room.'

'Thank you,' said O'Toole, no doubt touched.

Halfway through its London run *Macbeth* embarked on a short tour, playing Liverpool, Leeds and Bristol. The Liverpool Empire, a barn of a theatre seating around two thousand and usually reserved for mammoth musicals or rock concerts, was packed every night and the roars of laughter were even louder. In Bristol, Nat Brenner, who had just left his post as Principal of the Bristol Old Vic Theatre School, showed up one night and news filtered backstage that his opinion of the production was unsympathetic to say the least. 'The word was that Nat really destroyed Peter with his comments,' reveals Quarmby. 'And I don't know if it's just in retrospect or whether I do remember Bristol being the only venue where one sensed a sort of crestfallen Peter. And I'm pretty damn sure it was after Nat came to see it.'

Christopher Fulford recalls that the play seemed to receive a more favourable response from provincial critics. And his own opinion of O'Toole's performance hadn't changed. 'When I had my moments on stage with him I thought he was fantastic, absolutely fantastic. I remember coming on stage once and he had something going on in his head that was so in the moment you almost reeled back from the force of it.'

Playing Donalbain, Fulford was required to wear a wig because his own hair was too short. By the time of the tour his hair had grown sufficiently long enough that he didn't think he needed it any more and went to see O'Toole. Knocking on his dressing-room door he entered and there was O'Toole doing press-ups on the floor. 'Absolutely, no problem, get rid of the wig.' He then looked at Fulford intently. 'But you know something, you've got to get it a bit thicker, yes, a bit thicker.'

'OK,' said Fulford.

'You know what I use?'

'No, what's that, Pete?'

O'Toole was dressed in his Macbeth costume and in his dressing room was a large circular table containing every conceivable spirit, plus mixers. They weren't for him, but for guests who might pop in. On the middle of this table was a large carton of orange juice. 'You know what I use, Christopher, orange juice.' With that he poured some of the juice out into his cupped hand and splashed it onto his hair. 'It's marvellous. Marvellous,' he said as he rubbed it all in. 'And then he approached me to put some of the juice on my hair,' recalls Fulford. 'I said, "It's all right, Peter, I've got some upstairs, it's fine." And he looked at me seriously, because he was a terribly sincere, wonderful man. I really admired him and liked him enormously. He said, "And do you know what's so marvellous about it, Christopher?" I said, "What's that, Peter?" He said, "It brushes out." '

Installed back at the Old Vic, *Macbeth* continued to play to sell-out crowds until it finally finished its run just before Christmas. For the cast there was no cathartic release or sense of elation. 'One really just felt so bloody relieved that it was over,' says Quarmby. 'Just absolute relief of being able to close the door on that chapter.'

For O'Toole, however, the reverberations would last for years. In the short term his position at the Old Vic was untenable. Yes, *Macbeth* had made money, lots of money, but the bad publicity had damaged the reputation of the theatre and O'Toole, who had hoped to stage a production of *King Lear* next, had no choice but to resign his position as associate director and walk away.

Months later, as the scandal died down, O'Toole was able to look back more philosophically on the event and recognize it for what it was – a total fuck-up. 'My nose starts bleeding the minute I even think about the reviews.' It had been a chore, 'without any question, the most difficult thing I've ever done.' Not helped by the fact he'd had to deal with the emotional stress of losing his mother, who died in January 1981. 'It's odd to feel like an orphan at forty-eight,' he said.

Forbes, too, was hurt by the play's reception and the effect on O'Toole, of whom he had grown fond: 'For I admire nothing more than true talent.' In the end, Forbes put it all down to 'a tragi-comedy of good intentions'.

TWENTY

One ironic result of the disaster of *Macbeth*, which made headlines around the world, was that it put O'Toole back into the international spotlight and turned him into a saleable commodity again. Hurriedly he was rushed over to Hollywood to help with the publicity push for *The Stunt Man*, which after over a year on the shelf had found a willing distributor and was earning rave notices. At first no one would touch it. 'It didn't fit into the wrapper that the distributors had prepared that they send their hamburgers out in,' complains Rush. 'They would always say when they saw the film, "What is it, is it a comedy, is it a drama, is it an action adventure? Is it a satire?" And of course I would say, "Yes! It's all those things." ' Rush was also under pressure from his financiers to re-cut the picture; it got so bad that he suffered a heart attack.

All this time O'Toole stood by the movie, remaining positive and always full of great ideas. When Rush sent him a copy of the poster art, of a devil figure sitting on a director's chair looking through a camera, O'Toole called back to say that he took one look at the picture of this devil with that massive tail thrusting forward between his legs and his only comment was: 'How did you know?'

The Stunt Man remains one of the best movies about making movies ever produced. By turns crazy, sophisticated, surreal and base, it is a thoroughly entertaining jigsaw puzzle that demands repeated viewings. The cast are uniformly excellent but this is O'Toole's gig. He dominates every scene he's in and brings to bear upon the role his enormous intelligence as an actor, sharp sense of humour and boundless energy. Also that quality that all great actors must have, an enormous sense of danger. It's there in so many of O'Toole's performances, this ability to keep an audience off balance.

O'Toole's performance in *The Stunt Man* resulted in his sixth Oscar nomination for Best Actor. 'Peter was staying at my house at the time of the Academy Awards,' says Rush. 'And he came out of his room that morning and said, "I am a movie star!" He was getting in the mood for the ceremony.' He failed to win yet again, this time losing out to Robert De Niro for *Raging Bull*.

Cursing his luck, O'Toole took solace in a new relationship in his life. He and Trudie Styler had parted, though remaining on friendly terms. Since his separation from Siân, O'Toole hadn't really been looking for a long-term relationship and certainly didn't think he would marry again. 'I love company. I'm very gregarious. But I love to be alone. Always have. It would take an exceptional woman. I have an open pair of arms and an open mind. And low expectations.' On relationships he once told reporters that any woman contemplating marrying him ought to be led gently to a place of safety. It was during a recent stay in Hollywood, however, that O'Toole met Karen Brown Somerville, an American former model fifteen years his junior. They began dating.

After a tough few years things were beginning to look up on the professional front, too. He was preparing to start work on a film that would prove to be one of his most enjoyable and popular, a project that came his way through the generosity of his old RADA chum, Albert Finney. *My Favorite Year* was produced by Mel Brooks' company and based on his own experiences as a young comedy writer on a TV show in the fifties when he was drafted in to keep Errol Flynn sober and out of trouble until he'd made his guest star appearance. To many, O'Toole seemed perfect casting for the role of a sozzled and faded Hollywood film star, but Brooks' co-producer on the film, Michael Gruskoff, first sent the script to Finney. He got an unusual reply back. 'Albert read it and said, "You've got the wrong guy, Michael. Peter would be better for this part than me." ' Finney even made sure that a copy of the script made its way to O'Toole, who upon first reading it knew this was something he could have fun with.

O'Toole also took to Richard Benjamin, an actor making his debut as director, when they met in New York for talks. Benjamin recalled the very first day of shooting in Central Park. The light was fading and there wasn't any energy in the scene, it was too slow, especially O'Toole. Then it hit him, he was now going to have to direct Peter O'Toole. As he walked over, all Benjamin could see was Lawrence of Arabia and Lord Jim and Henry II, and any second he was going to have to tell this legend to raise his game. 'Peter, er, it's really good, it's all good, but—' O'Toole interrupted. 'You want it faster and funnier, is that it?' Benjamin looked relieved. 'That's it. You've got it!' After that Benjamin rarely had to do more than three takes with O'Toole. The only thing O'Toole insisted upon was not being called from his dressing room until he was absolutely required. 'He just wanted you to be ready,' said Benjamin. 'And boy, he'd come out there and it was like howitzer shells.'

It was much the same with Mark Linn-Baker, a young actor from a largely theatrical background who had been chosen to play the writer given the task of looking after O'Toole's matinee idol, Alan Swann. Baker had done a few small roles in films but this was his first lead and his relationship with O'Toole in many ways paralleled that of the characters they were playing. 'Peter very kindly took me under his wing. He gave me pointers all along the way, just little practical points of craft that you don't know till somebody tells you. Anything I know about film acting I learnt from what he told me and from watching him in those few months.'

Playing an Errol Flynn type swashbuckler, O'Toole was required to be fairly nifty in a couple of scenes with a rapier, so Gruskoff scheduled three two-hour fencing lessons. 'Michael, we simply can't do this,' he said when told of the plan.

'What do you mean?'

'In order for me to pull this off I need at least ten lessons.' He didn't miss a single one.

However, O'Toole's professionalism did come into question on of all days the singular occasion Mel Brooks showed up to watch filming. Ironically, the scene was Swann arriving late at the TV studio. The call time was 8 a.m. Brooks was there, Benjamin was there, the crew were setting up, but O'Toole was a no-show. 'He must be a real Method actor,' Brooks was heard to mutter. After an hour there was still no sign of him. 'I'm going to his hotel and see what the hell is going on,' Gruskoff told Brooks. When he arrived, the woman at the front desk told him that O'Toole had been on the phone for four hours with his daughters in London, there was some family problem he had to deal with. Finally a message came down that O'Toole didn't want to see Gruskoff, he would see him later on the set. 'At twelve o'clock he arrived,' Gruskoff recalls. 'The first thing he did was to come over and see me. "Gruskoff," he said. "Sorry I'm late, but from here on in I'm carrying you on my back and we're going to bring this movie home." '

Not everyone on the film was aware that O'Toole no longer drank, but one incident confirmed how even a drop of alcohol passing his lips could prove dangerous. There's a scene in *My Favorite Year* where Swann wakes up in bed with a stewardess and immediately downs one of those airline-size mini-bottles of Scotch. A whole case of little bottles had been prepared, each one emptied of liquor, washed and re-filled with coloured water. Somehow a real bottle slipped through by mistake and, according to Mark Linn-Baker, who was on set at the time, 'Peter got immediately sick.' It was several hours before he was well enough to continue work.

There was caution too about just how much of the physical comedy O'Toole could manage, given his rather perilous state and frail frame. Quite a lot as it turned out, O'Toole was game for anything. In one scene he falls, dead drunk and rigid, against a bathroom wall so that his forehead strikes the tile. He did the take twenty times without complaint, thumping his head against the tile again and again. In another scene O'Toole and Baker gallop on horseback through Central Park. Before the first take O'Toole took Baker to one side. 'Dear boy, there's only two things to remember working on a horse. If I start to fall off, let go of me. The second thing is, if you start to fall off, let go of me!' Two different animals had been brought in, a running horse and a horse that reared on command, the command being simply to brush one's leg on its haunch. For the shot of them galloping over a bridge no one had seen fit to tell Baker they were using the rearing horse. 'So we're both on the horse, they're getting ready for the shot, and I move my leg and the horse starts rearing and we're falling off – and I let go. But we're both still falling off. And as I'm falling my thought is, oh my God, I've killed Peter O'Toole! I land on my back on the ground. It looks like Peter has landed lightly on his feet and has a cigarette already lit and is staring down at me. "Dear boy, are you all right?" '

When it opened, *My Favorite Year* did modest enough business but over the years has grown in reputation, something Gruskoff puts down to O'Toole's performance. 'He made the movie what it is – a semi-classic.' It is a master class in physical comedy and timing. And met with near-universal acclaim. The doyen of American film critics Pauline Kael raved: 'O'Toole is simply astounding. I can't think of another major star, with the possible exception of Ralph Richardson, who would have the effrontery to bring this sly performance off.'

Early on the signs were clear that O'Toole would bag another Oscar nomination, and so it was. This time he lost out to Ben Kingsley for *Gandhi*. Gruskoff puts the blame squarely on the shoulders of backers MGM, a company then heading for bankruptcy. 'You need money to win an Oscar, to put the ads in the trade papers, and MGM didn't have the financial clout to compete with the other companies. Had they had the money Peter might have stood a better chance.'

Much of *My Favorite Year* was shot on location in New York, with interiors done in Hollywood. O'Toole had always preferred New York to Los Angeles and was beginning to spend more time there and so was eager to find some kind of representation in the city, having an agent back in London, Steve Kenis, and one in Hollywood. Johnnie Planco had been a successful agent since he joined the famed William Morris Agency in New York in 1972, staying there until 2000. In those twenty-eight years he became the youngest department head and senior vice-president in the agency's history, representing among others Tom Hanks, Richard Gere, Rock Hudson, Michael Douglas, Susan Sarandon and John Cassavetes. Planco was asked to drop by the set of *My Favorite Year* to meet O'Toole. Directed to his trailer, Planco knocked sharply on the door. No answer. He knocked again, then repeatedly until it was opened. 'Yes,' said O'Toole.

Planco introduced himself. 'Yes,' said O'Toole.

'We talked about my dropping by to see you.'

There was another short pause. 'Yes. Now's not a good time,' and with that the door was firmly closed. It was not a successful first encounter. 'But then when I got to know him,' says Planco, 'I knew that's exactly how he treated somebody he didn't know.

But then we took off like a rocket and he came to New York quite often.'

Very early on in their relationship Planco knew he was dealing with someone who was much more than a mere star. People like Robert De Niro can sit in a cafe and you'll never notice them, but there are stars who when you meet them in real life are so much bigger than they are on the screen. 'And Peter was one of those. He would just stand in the doorway, and every head in the room would whip around. It was the way he carried himself. And his voice. There was no sneaking him in and out of anywhere. He had it. And a lot of famous people don't.'

O'Toole remained in America in the spring of 1982, having agreed to appear in a made-for-television movie entitled *Svengali*, a modern twist on the George du Maurier novel published in 1894 and which had been filmed several times, most memorably with John Barrymore. O'Toole plays a mercurial voice coach who discovers Zoe, a young singer (played by Jodie Foster), performing in a seedy night club and agrees to accept her as a student. There was nothing very original in the material, the real story for many was what was happening on location in New York. *Svengali* marked the first time Jodie Foster had stepped back into the limelight after she was the unwitting motive in an assassination attempt on President Ronald Reagan. When John Hinckley gunned down Reagan it was to prove his warped love for the actress, after becoming infatuated with her ever since she'd played a prostitute in *Taxi Driver*. Anthony Harvey, who O'Toole had insisted direct the film, recalls that press interest was intense. 'We were always being followed in New York when we went from one location to another by reporters who longed to get some dirt on us. We were always running round corners trying to escape from them.'

The pair struck up a touching friendship on set, with O'Toole mischievously nicknaming the actress 'midget'. 'He gave her enormous encouragement,' remembers Harvey. 'And the chemistry between them was amazing. He had a gift for making people feel comfortable.' By the end of filming Jodie wrote in an *Esquire* article that the making of *Svengali* had helped her fall back in love with acting. 'It cured me of most of the insecurities. It healed my wounds.'

Inevitably in this type of 'star is born' scenario, the young artist falls in love with her teacher but the way in which the subject was approached, and in O'Toole's performance, it never came across as offensive. 'There he was with Jodie,' says Harvey, 'who was far younger than he was, and the love scenes he did with such enormous originality that you never felt this is a dirty old man. It was a very moving relationship between an older man and a young girl.' Harvey also sensed a change in the older O'Toole, some fifteen years after they worked together on *The Lion in Winter*, a definite mellowing. 'The anger was still there, of course, but there was a gentleness, an inner strength.'

After filming *Svengali*, O'Toole returned to the peace and isolation of Clifden where he quietly celebrated his fiftieth birthday with family and friends. He was in the process of converting some farm cottages near his property into homes for his daughters. Eventually, both Kate and Patricia would have homes nearby. 'This is Zulu-style living,' he was to call it. 'The family lives in the same spot, but each family member has his own dwelling. I think it's a very sensible arrangement. It keeps the family together but the fuck away from one another at the same time.'

At his house, O'Toole had put up a greenhouse and employed someone local to act as his gardener and odd-jobs man. One day this chap was standing there with O'Toole looking at this strange and wonderful plant. 'Jesus, Peter, they're mighty plants. What kind are they?'

'Ah, they're fantastic non-flowering tomato plants. They're my pride and joy.'

They were in fact marijuana plants, O'Toole having been given some seeds by a friend. Unaware of this the gardener took special care of them when O'Toole went off filming, lovingly nurturing and fertilizing them. All hell broke loose on his return when he saw that the plants were now almost as tall as the house. Paul D'Alton was a friend of the family and was up at the house with a few other people the day O'Toole came back and recalls with humour his reaction. 'He went absolutely mad. We thought this was great craic. I must have been seventeen or eighteen at the time, and Peter was yelling, "I can end up in fucking jail over this, you fuckers. You've got to get rid of it." And we were literally putting it in bags and hiding it in people's houses around the town. The whole town had dustbin bags full of the stuff. It was like *Whisky Galore!* hiding it from the authorities. People in the town still talk about it.'

Paul D'Alton attended school in England but during the holidays always came back to Clifden, where he worked in the bar and restaurant that his uncle Frank Kelly owned on the High Street. Frank Kelly was a great friend of O'Toole's and it was through that association that D'Alton became a friend of the family, particularly with O'Toole's youngest daughter Patricia, seeing as how they were the same age. D'Alton was one of the very few people allowed inside the inner sanctum of O'Toole's Irish home, often just sitting around drinking beer, watching the actor and his uncle play snooker. Looking back now, D'Alton realizes how privileged he was to observe the private O'Toole, the real person behind the movie star as he relaxed and could be himself at home. He was surprised that O'Toole never liked to reminisce. At home the film-star persona was firmly switched off, and he felt free from any obligation to put on a 'performance'. He wasn't a great one for saying stuff like 'The first time I met Orson Welles.' Instead he talked about current events, sometimes rugby. O'Toole and Frank Kelly often read *The Times* together and discussed politics. 'He was also a great lover of young people,' says D'Alton. 'He loved being surrounded by the young, he was very contemporary in that sense, he would know about the music of the time and things like that. He wasn't an old luvvie sitting in a chair recalling his great Hamlet. Although he could be extremely luvvie-ish when he turned it on. But he wouldn't be in real private company.'

O'Toole would drive into Clifden most days, usually to see Frank Kelly in his bar, and they'd sit in there and chain-smoke for hours shooting the breeze. 'He was never hassled on the street or anything like that,' confirms D'Alton. 'It would mainly be the tourists who might come up and ask for an autograph.' At other times you wouldn't see him in town, he'd be holed up alone in his house not seeing anyone for days. 'At times Peter could be intensely, almost pathologically private,' says D'Alton. 'At others, a ribald, daring attention-seeker. He arrived in town once with this London taxi. I said, "Peter, you're supposed to be low key here, you're driving around the place in a fucking London taxi!" And he said to me, "Well, darling, it'll give the feckers a thrill." And we were driving along sharing a joint in the back seat and him waving like the Queen Mother to the astonishment of tourists. There was a dual personality there.' Many people identified this strange quirk in his personality. 'He was a contradiction,' says actress Amanda Plummer. 'Private and then very gregarious, and then very private, isolated, and then totally out there.'

One summer Sting came to visit. O'Toole and Sting had got quite pally during the *Macbeth* run, with the rock star then married to Frances Tomelty, who played Lady Macbeth. He was to leave her, of course, to marry O'Toole's former girlfriend Trudie Styler. Sting had rented a house in nearby Roundstone and was often seen roaring through Clifden on a vast motorbike on his way to see O'Toole. It was a holiday cut dramatically short when one lunchtime Sting barged breathless through the door of Frank

Kelly's bar shouting: 'I have to go! I have to go! Where's everybody? Where's Peter?' After a moment of what seemed like blind panic Sting was off, never to be seen again. His disappearance remained a mystery until O'Toole himself showed up that evening saying that Sting had upped and legged it back to England because he'd received death threats from the Provisional IRA. 'Really?' asked Kelly, somewhat sceptical. O'Toole broke into a wide grin. 'Did they fuck, those feckers down in Roundstone couldn't stand him so they ran him out!' It was an admission that was met with resounding laughter from everyone in the bar. 'IRA my arse!' O'Toole roared.

TWENTY-ONE

The time had come to lay the ghost of *Macbeth* and make a return to London's theatreland. For what some commentators were calling his stage rehabilitation, O'Toole was taking no chances, choosing a play he loved and knew well, Shaw's *Man and Superman*, and another very theatrical star role in John Tanner, and asking his old friend Patrick Dromgoole to direct. The two men had kept in touch over the years since Bristol, 'sort of'. 'We could have rows, not speak for years and when we met he'd completely forgotten we'd ever had a cross word.'

If O'Toole was anxious or had misgivings about what lay ahead he wasn't showing it. As for his state of mind, well that was highly changeable. 'It really depended how he was when you caught him,' says Dromgoole. 'If you caught him on a high then he could be as jubilant and bubbly as ever. But he was at times pretty low.' Often O'Toole simply didn't turn up for rehearsals and stayed in bed, forcing Dromgoole to go round to Guyon House to lay down the law and if possible get him up, which sometimes entailed a bout of singing. 'I used to do that when we were in the flat together in Bristol, he'd be asleep and I'd go and sing very loudly until he got up to chase me out of the room. I'd sing cockney songs to him, tunes like "My Old Man's A Dustman" or "Any Old Iron".'

What was made very clear from the off was that O'Toole had no intention of taking direction. 'Peter was not a man who was obedient to a director or obedient to anybody,' says Dromgoole. While he took and used some suggestions here and there, O'Toole was determined to do it his way and play John Tanner, political firebrand and confirmed bachelor, as a man of huge attractiveness and tremendous charm. According to Dromgoole it was an approach that worked splendidly. 'When you have a character talking about marriage and relationships and the male/female principle, it can be a bloody bore, but Peter made the guy so lyrical, so when he advanced his theories or explained things he kept the audience with him all the time.'

The play opened in Birmingham first, then travelled to other cities before arriving at London's Haymarket Theatre in November 1982. As the first night approached, O'Toole grew increasingly nervous, well aware that the press were waiting for him. At least he could take solace in the fact that this time the whole company were on his side. According to Lisa Harrow, who played Ann Whitefield, everyone, not least herself, was in complete awe of him. 'Sometimes I'd just look across the stage and go, oh my God, I'm on stage with Lawrence of Arabia. It used to rivet me to the spot.'

There was no need to worry, his performance was mostly well received. O'Toole had now perfected an acting style of such power and idiosyncrasy that it was a phenomenon to be savoured for itself alone. 'He sometimes used to soar and it was thrilling to watch,' says Lisa. 'He was a master, even if it was sometimes all out of control. He was just pure theatre and there are very few of them around.' Here was somebody who now had utter command of his craft. 'He was technically brilliant,' recalls Michael Byrne, who was in the production. 'His technical ability vocally on stage was just extraordinary.'

Some commentators, however, complained that he had turned into a self-indulgent ham. O'Toole's style of acting had always looked back at the musty world of the barnstorming actor managers represented by Henry Irving and his hero Edmund Kean. He knew there was a mesmeric presence when Kean was on stage and he was always aiming for the same kind of effect. If that was interpreted by some as scenery chewing so be it. 'I think a critic once said he went over the top at a certain stage of his career and liked the view so much he never came down again,' jokes Dromgoole. 'And that's not entirely unfair. He was a barnstormer, both as a theatrical presence and as a person.'

He could sometimes be impossible to act with. When in a clinch with Lisa Harrow, he wasn't averse to directing her live on the stage, telling her, 'No, no, no, wait, wait, wait, wait – now say the line.' Michael Byrne recalls that O'Toole would stand back and give him a wink whenever he got a laugh. There was without doubt an element of playing to the crowd. 'He was an actor who absolutely adored his audience and they adored him,' says Byrne. 'I remember, he would sometimes take a speech so fast that he'd trip himself up and he would stop and he would say to the audience, "Oh, I'd better start that again." And of course they loved it.'

He did look fragile, though. 'I think he only had half a pancreas at that point,' believes Byrne. And rumours were flying around that he was still taking cocaine. So when, halfway through the limited run, O'Toole dramatically vanished people were understandably concerned. Lisa Harrow remembers O'Toole's daughter Patricia, who was working as the stage manager, coming into her dressing room with the news that the understudy was on. 'Something had gone wrong with Peter. It was never really properly discussed but it sounded like he'd had an overdose of something really bad and he was just not capable.' As far as she could tell, O'Toole had gone into one of his black depressions. He wanted Siân and she wasn't there.

O'Toole was missing for five days before he finally turned up at the theatre. 'I'll never forget it,' claims Lisa. 'He crawled into my dressing room, literally crawled, and he had the make-up from five days before still on his face. This is Peter O'Toole we're talking about. And he put his head in my lap and apologized. That was so shocking.'

Whilst on tour Lisa had discovered she was pregnant by her partner, the actor Sam Neill. Delighted, Neill was present for those early shows, indeed filled her dressing room on opening night with flowers. As the London run came to an end prior to Christmas, the couple suddenly split up, leaving Lisa shattered. Somehow she made her way to the theatre that evening, speaking to no one about what had happened, but in a terrible state. At the close of the first act Lisa had one of her most important scenes with O'Toole, about how successful her character was going to be at getting the man she wanted, precisely the opposite of what had just happened in real life. 'As I began my lines I totally collapsed, tears just poured out of my face, I couldn't speak for sobbing, and I thought, this is the moment I leave the English stage because I can't go on. Acting with Peter, usually you hadn't a clue where his mind was. He was just so big and out there that the idea that he would actually pay attention to what was happening to you, well, you didn't even think about that. But he walked slowly towards me without his eyes leaving mine for a second, and he literally forced me to turn and face the audience, and pull myself together and carry on.'

When the curtain hit the deck O'Toole grabbed hold of Lisa. 'Baby, what's wrong?'

Lisa broke down again as she told him that she was pregnant and was no longer with Sam. 'I don't know what I'm going to do,' she sobbed, her make-up running.

'Lisa, you don't need a man, you don't need us. You're perfectly capable of doing this yourself. You're a strong, good woman. Just love the child and get on with it.'

It took a few seconds for the words to hit home, but when they did it gave Lisa pause. O'Toole then gave her a huge kiss and that was that. 'He didn't have to do that. He could have left me wallowing, but he saved me. I'll always love him for that.'

Of course, now O'Toole knew Lisa was pregnant she never heard the last of it. 'I would walk on stage and he used to hit me in the belly and say, how's the baby, and I'd be going, oh God, Peter, don't do that.'

By a strange coincidence, O'Toole went on stage every night aware that his girlfriend Karen was pregnant with his child and that he was going to be a father again, at the age of fifty. The birth occurred, serendipitously, on St Patrick's Day, 17 March 1983, in Dublin, of course. Delighted, he called his friend John Standing, announcing loudly down the phone in the early hours of the morning: 'A boy. On St Patrick's Day! I shall call him Lorcan – Irish for Lawrence.' When Standing's wife Sarah asked, 'Were you there at the birth, Peter? What was that like? Bit gory?' O'Toole replied, 'A piece of cake, baby. Piece of cake. To be honest, I've seen far worse things come out of my nose.'

O'Toole wholeheartedly embraced late fatherhood, after two daughters he was overjoyed with the birth of a son and told friends in Clifden: 'The only thing I want more than life itself is to have him raised an Irishman.' But Karen had not taken to the lyrical isolation of the Connemara coast. 'Karen was a lovely woman and always very charming,' says Paul D'Alton. 'But she just wasn't part of the "craic agus ceol", as we say, the craic and the music kind of thing in Ireland. She was very softly spoken and quite reticent and reserved so she didn't really take to life in Clifden, it was just completely removed from her world. She didn't understand it, she didn't feel that she was accepted, which was true, not because people were snobby or cliquey, but if you're not part of the culture there, then they are going to turn their back on you.' When she was staying with O'Toole at Clifden,

O'Toole (pictured here with Malcolm McDowell, left) was later to regret his appearance in the infamous and debauched *Caligula*, which was filmed in 1976 but not released until 1979.

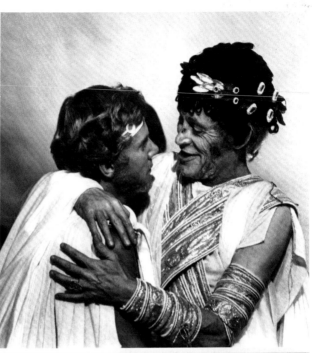

With his youngest daughter Patricia and girlfriend Malinche Verdugo.

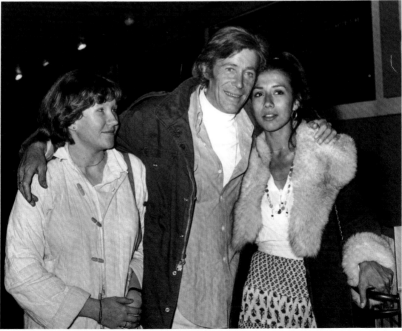

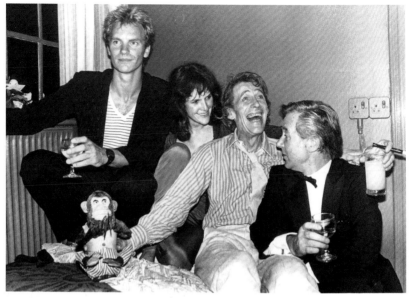

O'Toole (second from right) backstage at the Old Vic during the infamous *Macbeth* production, with Sting (far left), Frances Tomelty (who played Lady Macbeth, second from left) and director Bryan Forbes (far right).

As maverick film director Eli Cross in the cult classic *The Stunt Man* (1980).

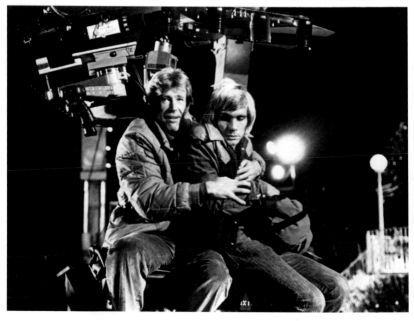

O'Toole steals the show with a great comedic film performance in *My Favourite Year* (1982).

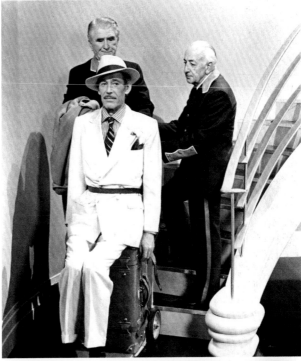

In 1982, with daughter Kate (left) and his girlfriend at the time, former model Karen Somerville.

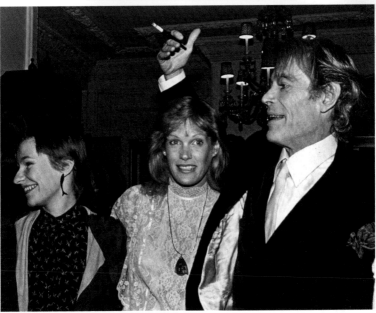

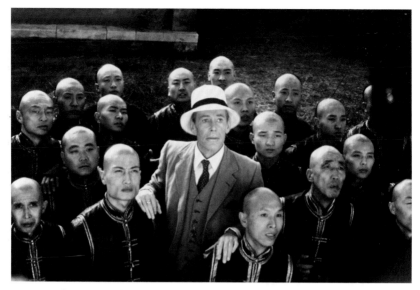

After a string of flops and forgettable films, O'Toole finally won plaudits for his role in *The Last Emperor* (1987).

O'Toole had a passion for breeding horses and regularly attended the annual Connemara pony show.

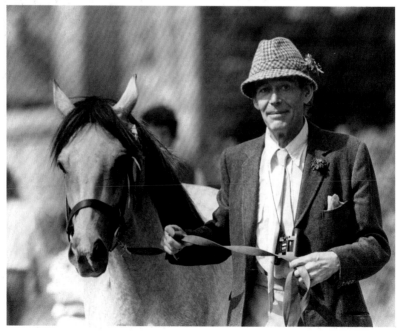

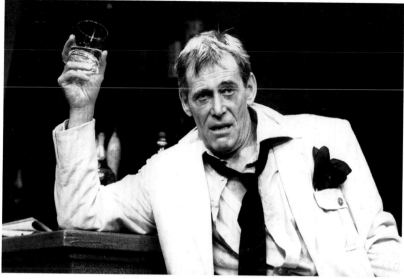

O'Toole in one of his greatest triumphs on the London stage, *Jeffrey Bernard is Unwell* (1989).

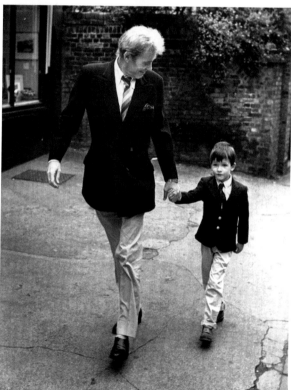

With Lorcan, the son he had always wanted.

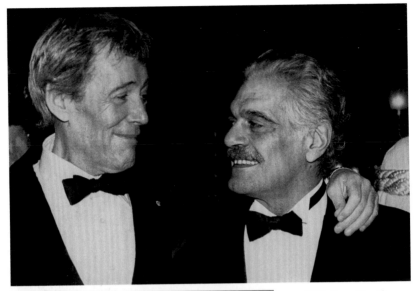

With Omar Sharif,
a lifelong friend.

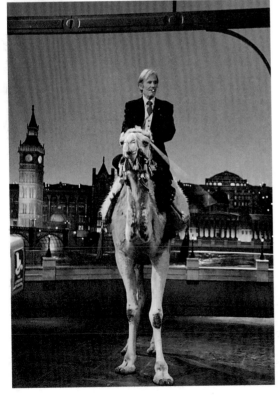

O'Toole makes a grand
entrance on a camel in an
unforgettable appearance
on *The David Letterman
Show* (1995).

Meryl Streep presents O'Toole with his honorary Oscar in 2003.

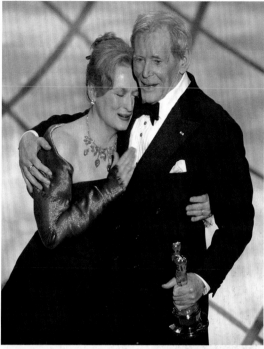

Embracing the new generation, with Eric Bana and Brad Pitt at the launch of *Troy* (2004).

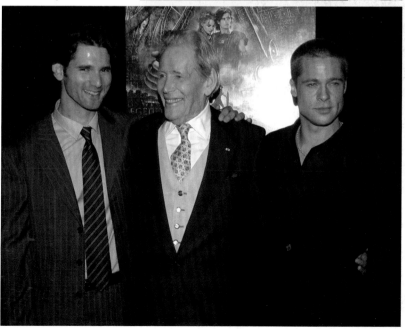

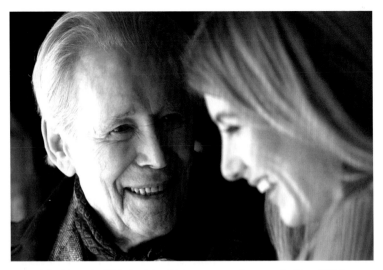

A final hurrah: O'Toole giving his last great performance in *Venus* (2006), for which he received his eighth and final Oscar nomination for Best Actor.

A proud father, with son Lorcan and daughter Kate.

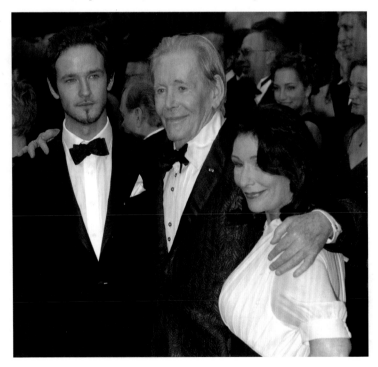

Karen tended to stay in the house and not mix socially in the town.

Other fractures were beginning to open up in their relationship, too, and by the middle of the year they had separated. Perhaps they were never truly suited to each other, although Karen did share many similarities with Siân Phillips. Both women were beautiful and charming but also quite reserved in their nature, neither was a roaring, laughing, screaming, drinking Irish country woman for example. As Paul D'Alton observes, 'It's strange that for such a gregarious, when he wanted to be, and flamboyant man, the two women that Peter had the most important relationships in his life were very different to him, they were reserved women, quite studied. I don't know whether he got that from his mother, but he was attracted quite obviously to that kind of solid, quite reserved woman. He wasn't going for the fiery type.'

When Karen returned to her home in New Jersey with the infant Lorcan, O'Toole was furious and desperate to get the child back. His desperation, however, clouded his judgement and with ruthless cunning and precision he plotted to kidnap his son. What he was contemplating was a criminal act and those helping him knew it. 'There was a slight Irish/mafia streak to Peter where if you crossed him you got two barrels blazing at you,' says Paul D'Alton. O'Toole arranged to take Lorcan on a few days' holiday, with the hidden intention of smuggling him back to Ireland. There was even talk of father and son stowing away on a fishing vessel and landing in secret on the Connemara coast. Instead, O'Toole and Lorcan, with a nanny in tow, ended up in Bermuda.

Karen's first reaction was that Lorcan had been taken by professional kidnappers and that a ransom note might be pushed through her letterbox at any moment. On learning the truth she alerted authorities to prevent O'Toole taking the child off the island. Police and officials arrived at the hotel just as O'Toole was preparing to leave for the airport and he was forced to hand Lorcan over.

O'Toole always denied that he was trying to snatch his son. All Karen said on the subject and of her former partner was, 'Let's just say that he is not a predictable man.' Heartbroken, O'Toole returned home alone, the son he had always craved was thousands of miles away, more out of reach than ever.

On the professional front 1983–1984 turned out for the most part to be rather dismal. There was a poorly conceived performance as an Indian monk in a television adaptation of Rudyard Kipling's classic story *Kim* and an erratic cameo in the box-office turkey *Supergirl*.

He also courted controversy at the gala re-opening of the Gaiety Theatre in Dublin. Asked to do a reading, O'Toole chose Jonathan Swift's satirical essay of 1729, 'A Modest Proposal', in which he suggested that the Irish should eat their children to avoid starvation. O'Toole said the piece had 'a little something to offend everybody', and so it proved when the cat-calls began, followed by a mass walk-out of dignitaries. Congratulated by a reporter on the mayhem he caused, O'Toole laughed heartily. That's what he enjoyed about it – challenging the stuffy audience and the constraints of convention.

The only bright spot of this period was a well-made Canadian television version of *Pygmalion*, which saw O'Toole as Professor Henry Higgins opposite Margot Kidder as Eliza. It was a role he would soon be asked to perform on the London stage by playwright Ray Cooney, famous for his Whitehall farces, notably *Run For Your Wife*. Cooney had recently created the Theatre of Comedy Company, together with thirty leading actors, directors and writers. They took out a lease on the Shaftesbury Theatre just off London's West End with the ambition to present the very best of British comedy writing. Many discussions took place about what plays should be done and the type of actors recruited. *Pygmalion* came up as an option and Cooney believes it was John Alderton who put forward the suggestion that O'Toole and only O'Toole should play Higgins. Everyone agreed the idea was a splendid one and negotiations began. Immediately O'Toole wanted to know who was directing. 'Ray would love to direct you in it, Mr O'Toole.' Big problem. Of course O'Toole knew who Cooney was, and indeed was impressed with his résumé, but was nevertheless extremely apprehensive that he hadn't done any of Shaw's works before.

Cooney pleaded his case, that he had read the play now three or four times and loved it. 'The thing that really impressed me with Peter,' remembers Cooney, 'was that not only did he know *Pygmalion* backwards, but he knew everything about every play Shaw had ever written. He was so knowledgeable about it all.' The meeting was a success and O'Toole signed on. As rehearsals began Cooney believes that O'Toole quickly realized that although they heralded from different theatrical backgrounds, they essentially spoke the same language and ended up getting on well. Although Cooney did make the mistake of asking if he was happy with his dressing room. Very sweetly O'Toole replied that he'd actually like everything to be crimson, and if possible by the first preview. 'Over the following weekend my wife Linda and I slept overnight in the theatre while she hung these huge red curtains she made herself and I laid the crimson carpet! There was also a divan in the dressing room which we covered in about twelve red cushions.'

As Cooney remembers, it was a happy atmosphere for the two-month run that spring and early summer of 1984 and O'Toole the glue that keeps a company together. 'He was very much like Donald Sinden in that respect. Donald would come into the theatre and go round every dressing room every single night and go, "Hello darling, how are you, we're going to have a great show tonight, never mind the bloody weather, it's going to be fantastic." So when the curtain went up you felt great. And Peter had that same effect with a company.'

Pygmalion played to packed houses and was well received by the critics. 'Peter was terrific as Higgins,' says Cooney. 'He had this wonderful rapport with the audience. He was a brilliant comedy actor. And he and John Thaw, who played Doolittle, got on like a house on fire.' O'Toole also took immense pleasure in appearing opposite Joyce Carey, who played Mrs Higgins. By that time Joyce, who'd had a wonderful career appearing in many of the West End hits of Nöel Coward, was eighty-six and suffering from early Alzheimer's. However, she was absolutely delightful, except that she did have trouble remembering her lines. 'Peter was amazing with her,' recalls Cooney. 'Whenever she dried he would gently put his arm round her and give her a warm gentle smile. If Joyce could still not recall her lines Peter would ad-lib and, still smiling, lead her back to the script. The scene was supposed to last about four minutes. It usually went on for nearly ten with Peter looking gently into Joyce's eyes and never losing his loving smile.'

Again, O'Toole's dressing room became a haven for friends and admirers, wishing him well and full of congratulations. His *Stunt Man* co-star Steve Railsback happened to be in London at the time and managed to catch a performance, bringing along with him the actor Patrick Stewart, who was keen to be introduced to O'Toole. 'It was a breathtaking performance. Peter was at home on a stage. Every time I would see Peter it would always be open arms and that laugh, that wonderful laugh he had.'

That August, O'Toole heard the terrible news that his old friend Richard Burton had died. He was just fifty-eight. It was a genuine shock, although theirs had been a rather distant friendship since Elizabeth Taylor's severing of it in that Rome hotel way back in 1972. 'Richard lost touch with a lot of people when he was married to Elizabeth Taylor,' says Sally Burton, Richard's widow. 'Yes, there were some rollicking times in the fifties and sixties but there was no friendship towards the end of Richard's life. I think had they happened to be in the same restaurant at the same time they would have fallen upon each other with great amusement. I do know that Peter O'Toole did not attend the funeral in Switzerland.'

Not long after Burton's death, O'Toole and Richard Harris met up in a London pub and talked into the night about their recently departed friend. 'Burton once told me,' Harris said, 'that we spent a third of our lives drunk, a third with a hangover and a third sleeping.' There they sat quietly in a corner, two of the biggest hell-raisers of all, sipping their rancid tonic water. 'What I wouldn't give for one glass of red wine,' pined Harris, himself now off the booze. 'Just one.' A friend was sharing the evening with them and O'Toole picked up the man's glass of Muscadet, held it to his nostrils and took in the bouquet before replacing it untouched back on the table. 'Aaah,' he moaned, in fond remembrance of drinks past.

Burton's sudden death had also brought their own mortality into stark question, that and the realization that perhaps both of them were lucky to be still alive. There had been long periods during their hell-raising heyday when they made a deliberate choice not to see each other, 'Because if we did, we'd kill us both,' said Harris. 'We always brought out the worst in each other.' Elizabeth Harris remembers an occasion at a rugby match in Wales where O'Toole was with Ronnie Fraser in the hospitality room, 'And Richard told me afterwards, "No, I didn't speak to him. I just didn't feel in the mood." Richard wasn't drinking then and he knew that if they got together they'd be off for weeks. And they didn't want that, neither of them wanted that.'

Curiously this reluctance to see each other carried through into the eighties as well, when both were on the wagon. Johnnie Planco knew Harris and always thought it odd how they would always ask after each other: How's Peter, how's Richard, did he say anything about me? And yet Planco could never get the two of them in a room together. O'Toole called Harris 'The Mixer', since he was the type who'd turn up at a social do or dinner party and say, 'So you're William, you're the one who doesn't like Louise, right.' He would set people off at each other and that would drive O'Toole crazy. 'Peter loved Richard,' says Planco. 'He said he was one of his best friends – "If I don't see him." If he saw him it had the potential to go downhill.'

O'Toole was on the *David Letterman Show* when Harris decided he was going to walk out in the middle of the interview and surprise him. Planco showed up at the studio to see O'Toole in his dressing room. 'Listen, Harris . . . '

'I know,' said O'Toole. 'They told me. He's not going to show up, you know.'

'He's going to meet me here, we're going out to eat afterwards, he's coming.'

O'Toole shook his head. 'Have you any English money on you?'

'No,' said Planco. 'Why would I, I'm in New York.'

'I'll bet you five English pounds he doesn't show up.'

'OK, you're on.'

The Letterman team were well organized and had a walkie-talkie link-up with Harris' limo. In the dressing room, Planco and O'Toole listened in as it made its progress through the Manhattan traffic. 'Harris has got in the car,' a voice crackled. 'He's on his way.' O'Toole looked nonchalantly over at Planco. 'He's now on 60th Street. He's on 55th Street. He's turning west.' O'Toole sat there listening, while Planco rubbed his hands, I'm going to win this. Suddenly a raised voice came through. 'Wait,

Harris just jumped out of the car. He's running down the street.' O'Toole just smiled. 'He didn't say anything,' remembers Planco. 'He just looked at me like, you lose.'

Following two poor film choices, *Creator*, about a neurotic university scientist who yearns to clone his deceased wife, and the Robin Williams comedy *Club Paradise*, O'Toole must have felt back at home at the Theatre Royal Haymarket in another George Bernard Shaw play, *The Apple Cart*, at the start of 1986. His co-star was Susannah York, who experienced a couple of his eccentricities. 'Onstage, Peter lay back and closed his eyes just as I was about to make a speech. I was utterly enraged. I forced his eyes open and screamed the speech in his face. Another time, he closed his eyes and opened his mouth as if he was about to snore. I was so furious I went over and poured a glass of champagne straight into his mouth!'

That August, O'Toole was approached to appear in a mammoth international co-production charting the extraordinary true-life story of Pu Yi, the last Emperor of China. The role on offer was relatively small but pivotal, that of Reginald Johnston, a diplomat, a scholar and most famously tutor of Pu Yi, who later wrote a book about his experiences inside the Forbidden City. He was a remarkable man, and director Bernardo Bertolucci and producer Jeremy Thomas knew he was a vitally important element of the story. In essence Johnston was the Western link into the film, being the only Western character who appeared. After briefly considering Sean Connery, the filmmakers zeroed in on O'Toole. 'Peter was really the obvious choice,' says Thomas. 'He was the symbol of Western style, in a top hat and tails, and very statuesque with a great clarity of speech. And he loved the character and was very enamoured with the idea of working with Bertolucci, who he called Bert O'Lucci.'

Before O'Toole landed in China to begin work, his dresser

arrived with a large trunk of effects, things O'Toole liked to have around him on location. Other duties included checking out the accommodation and where he was going to be working, just making sure that everything was in proper order. 'Peter had been unwell,' recalls Thomas. 'I think he had had some surgery a few months before so he was quite delicate and frail but he got much stronger during the movie. He used to stride around the Forbidden City and Tiananmen Square. He became extremely engaged with being in China, enjoying the food and the jasmine tea. He loved all the different makes of teas.'

There was very definitely a lack of star treatment on the film, no Winnebagos, no nothing, in fact everyone stayed in the same hotel, simply because there wasn't another one in Beijing. O'Toole was given the best suite, luxurious by Chinese standards but fairly basic as seen through Western eyes. Still, O'Toole coped, after years of expertise he knew all about making a film location a bearable experience. There were barely any cars around either, only bicycles. 'Now, outside that hotel there is an eight-lane highway,' reveals Thomas.

On each floor there was a houseman to look after the guests, though Thomas assumes this person was most likely a government official. 'He knew everything that you did, checked your room the moment you went out, and maybe photographed anything that looked suspicious. Definitely everybody was under surveillance.' A strange situation since the authorities had given Thomas and Bertolucci permission to shoot in the country, extremely keen for the story of Pu Yi to be told, this man who was the Emperor, son of heaven, lord of 10,000 years who died happily as a humble gardener; there can be no better example of 'the way' than that. 'And they helped us from a government level down,' says Thomas. 'To get into the Forbidden City, to shoot in the Hall of Supreme Harmony, to go into Manchuria to shoot where Pu Yi's palace was, built by the Japanese, to do everything with ease, rather than putting up barriers. We shot with complete freedom.'

The incredible logistics involved, however, meant that the unit was always under huge pressure and strain. Thomas admits he wouldn't dream of tackling such a production today. Being a predominantly Italian crew, it was all very sociable, everyone would have their meals together, with Bertolucci and O'Toole at the head of the table. During these meals Thomas doesn't remember O'Toole talking much about filmmaking. 'We would talk culture. I think probably the theatre was more of a love of his than movies. I think movies were just a means to an end, and that his heart was in the theatre.' In the evening O'Toole was invariably the first to go to bed. 'He was a very private man,' says Thomas. 'A will-o'-the-wisp sort of character. He didn't really want to be known.'

Michael Gruskoff, who produced *My Favorite Year*, remembers being in a New York restaurant around the late 1980s with Albert Finney and Roger Moore when O'Toole came in with a young lady and they sat at a table. 'Then he saw us and came over to say hi. We had a little chat and Albert asked, "Where are you staying?" And Peter said, "I'm staying privately." And he went back to his table. We got such a big laugh out of that.'

This is something Basil Pao, one of the assistant directors and an acclaimed photographer, picked up on. Often he'd chat with O'Toole on the set about Chinese history and the current political climate in places like Hong Kong, where Pao was from. But most of the time O'Toole kept his own counsel and his own company. 'He'd talk to people he was interested in,' says Pao. 'But he was definitely a man who lived in his own private world by choice.'

At one point during filming Terry Gilliam turned up in Beijing to talk to O'Toole about the possibility of him playing Baron Munchausen in a big-budget adaptation of the famous German stories. According to Pao they spent some time discussing the film, he even caught sight of the actor on walks brandishing a twig as if it were some imaginary sword. Though Gilliam deemed O'Toole 'perfect for the part', which indeed he was, there were concerns whether or not he would be strong enough to endure the long months of filming and the physically arduous role. John Neville was cast instead.

When O'Toole's time on *The Last Emperor* came to an end he decided to return to England by way of the Trans-Siberian Express. The ticket was bought and he saw that he had several days before the train left. He was eager not to waste them. Whilst playing Reginald Johnston, a Confucius scholar, O'Toole had become increasingly interested in the philosopher's teachings and declared an intention to travel north to Qufu, the birthplace of Confucius and where his body was laid to rest. It was a long journey and Basil Pao was assigned to accompany him. They travelled by sleeper train arriving early the following morning. Given a tour guide, and with scarcely another soul around, O'Toole and Pao wandered quietly, almost solemnly, through the barren cemetery finally arriving at the gravestone. In the terrible days of Chairman Mao and the cultural revolution the teachings of Confucius were banned and the Red Guard had smashed his tomb to pieces. Now it stood whole again, although the vandalism of the past was clear to see in the pathetic way the stone tablets had been put back together using iron brackets and cement. 'Peter stood in front of that grave holding a wild flower he'd picked with tears in his eyes,' Pao remembers. 'It was quite a touching moment. But also very depressing, the senselessness of the destruction, the human stupidity of it and the effort to now commercialize the place after what they'd done to it.'

Feeling sorry for themselves, O'Toole and Pao went to a nearby hotel. It was beginning to get cold, winter was just setting in, and Pao decided to have a shot of brandy in his coffee to warm himself up. 'I'll join you,' said O'Toole. As the evening progressed they moved on to sweet Chinese wine and well lubricated made their way to the train, carrying a few bottles which they happily shared with their fellow passengers on the way back to Beijing. It had been a memorable experience.

O'Toole had recently gone back on the drink, just the odd glass of wine and perhaps the odd binge. It was during a trip to Moscow. He found the Russian capital truly ghastly. 'There were all these people queuing for cardboard shoes and everyone with forms and clipboards. I found a tea bar where they served sly vodkas. What else could I do.' A little over ten years ago the booze had almost killed him. It was a remarkable recovery, a wonder of modern medicine, but the O'Tooles were made of strong stuff.

TWENTY-TWO

In April 1987, O'Toole accepted an offer to reprise his London success as Henry Higgins in a Broadway production of *Pygmalion*. It proved to be his first and only appearance on the New York stage and was not an altogether happy experience. The show ran till August, during which time O'Toole was felled by illness and poor health, resulting in him missing something like twenty-two performances. His understudy, Ivar Brogger, has never forgotten that first phone call from the stage manager: 'Mr O'Toole has lost his voice – so you're on.' That was towards the end of the first month, after which O'Toole never managed to play a full week again. 'He just could not bounce back,' says Brogger. 'So he would do a few shows and then he'd be out maybe for one performance, maybe three, it depended on how he was feeling.'

The rumour mill went into overload that O'Toole's cocaine use was to blame. But Brogger firmly believes it was nothing to do with drugs or alcohol. 'I think Peter physically was at a place where if something happened it was hard for him to recover easily or quickly.' At one point Brogger confronted O'Toole's personal assistant to ask if there was anything going on. 'No,' she said firmly. 'He is not doing anything. When he comes home after the show he has a glass of warm milk and then goes to bed.'

When the producers began insinuating that O'Toole wasn't really sick, that he just didn't fancy doing eight shows a week, the hospital called to confirm his illness. 'I found out many years later that Peter was really sick, that he could have passed away,' confirms Johnnie Planco. 'It was something to do with intestinal pain or internal bleeding. It was serious, no doubt about it.'

The effort and strain O'Toole exerted to get himself through that run Brogger saw first-hand. Often he was invited to his dressing room, where they sat and talked for hours, sometimes about acting. Brogger recalls O'Toole telling him about how one day he wanted to play King Lear. 'I'll never forget this particular night, Peter was really low, he wasn't feeling good. He was about to get ready to go on stage and I think it was looking like Mount Everest to him. He was sitting in his chair in front of his make-up mirror. I put my hand on his shoulder and thought I'd get him onto a subject he might enjoy talking about so I said, "Tell me about your ideas for Lear." And he put his hands over his face and said, "Oh Christ." Then he looked in the mirror: "Just let me get through tonight." '

Besides being understudy Brogger was also cast in the small role of 'sarcastic bystander', who gives Higgins something of a hard time in the opening scene set in Covent Garden. At an early rehearsal O'Toole called Brogger to one side. 'Ivar, do you know, I had some thoughts about the sarcastic bystander, and I think perhaps he slouches a lot, perhaps with a fag hanging out of his mouth and a cap on his head, hands in his pockets, never really stands up straight.' Brogger's face registered a degree of scepticism. It didn't take long for a wry smile to emerge on O'Toole's face. 'Well, you see,' he said. 'The fact is, I want to appear very tall on stage and you and I are of the same height . . .' Brogger cut in. 'It's perfectly OK, Peter, it gives me something to play as the sarcastic bystander, and if you want to be taller than me on stage that's cool.' O'Toole was nothing if not very canny.

After Brogger had appeared for O'Toole a few times he was called into his dressing room one night and asked how he was enjoying it. 'Peter, I have to tell you, it's a great role, and I appreciate the opportunity, but it's not an unalloyed joy going on for you.'

O'Toole looked aghast. 'What do you mean?'

'Well, I've never been in a situation where just my very presence is a disappointment to hundreds of people.'

O'Toole looked at Brogger, a veneer of sympathy on his face. 'I know, dear boy. I know.'

'He knew he was a star,' says Brogger. 'He accepted it like you need water to live.'

In the role of Eliza Doolittle, O'Toole had insisted upon Amanda Plummer, the actress daughter of Christopher Plummer. O'Toole and Christopher Plummer had been friends since the sixties and delighted in each other's company. 'They never worked together,' says Johnnie Planco. 'But boy when you saw them together they were like long-lost brothers. Whenever I used to bump into Chris the first thing he'd say was, "How's Peter?" '

An enormous fan of O'Toole, Amanda had flown from New York to London just a few years before, when O'Toole and Albert Finney were appearing in separate plays at the same time in the West End. 'I calculated that I would only have a few pennies left after this trip, but I went, fuck it, I've got to go see this, I don't care if I don't eat for a year.' After one show she went backstage to see Finney and he took her out for a meal. 'Wow – that was so friggin' generous, unbelievable. I didn't quite get the courage up to go see Peter backstage. But then to end up working with him – shit!'

Before the read-through Amanda took it upon herself to invite O'Toole to dinner at her apartment. 'I was in extreme awe of him, which is like the kiss of death, so I had to overcome this aweness. God I was trembling. Ding dong – oh shit, I could hear him coming to the door – oh my God I can't talk.' Graciously O'Toole put Amanda at ease, he had huge admiration for her abilities and became extremely fond of her. On stage the pair clicked. Amanda marvelled at O'Toole's ability to change things from performance to performance, to make what was light, dark, to make what was dark, light and play with all the greys in between. But above all it was his energy. 'Playing with Peter and looking in his eyes, it was magic, the energy around him – you just let go.'

Sadly, Amanda herself came down with an illness and had to take a break from the show. O'Toole took pleasure in playing nurse maid, putting her in his guest bedroom and making her drink a concoction of his own devising. Looking at it Amanda wasn't so sure and wanted to know what was in it. 'Don't ask,' she was told.

When Amanda's understudy, an English actress, took over, O'Toole didn't think she was up to the job. One night during the opening scene she said her line only for O'Toole to turn away to face Brogger and say, 'Oh Christ, she's acting again.' O'Toole's goading did not stop there. 'Another night,' recalls Brogger, 'she said a line to him and he said – "What!" – and made her repeat it. She repeated the line and he said – "WHAT!" – and made her say the line a third time. This was on stage, in front of an audience.' After the famous tea-party scene, where Higgins shows off the transformed Eliza to his mother, O'Toole literally shooed the actress off the stage like you might shoo off a bunch of chickens. Brogger confronted him about it. 'But she does nothing,' O'Toole said in his defence. 'So I have to do everything!'

While in New York, O'Toole was able to have Lorcan come and live part of the week with him in his Manhattan hotel. Brogger remembers that O'Toole often talked about Lorcan and it was so very evident that he doted on the boy. 'Lorcan was the apple of his eye. He loved Lorcan. To see him light up when Lorcan came into the room was wonderful.' Even at the age of four, Brogger could see a little of O'Toole in the precocious lad.

'There was the occasion when Lorcan arrived at the theatre all dressed up because they were going on somewhere after the show. Preening himself he announced, "These are my smashing clothes." Another time he wandered a bit too far backstage and one of the stagehands had to tell him not to walk any further because then the audience would be able to see him. Lorcan turned around and looked at the stagehand and there was a mischievous twinkle in his eye like, oh yeah, you mean I could just walk over there and everyone will see me.'

While business was brisk, reviews for *Pygmalion* were mixed. Amanda Plummer herself thinks the production was too conservative and safe. The supporting cast were very much of the old school: Lionel Jeffries as Pickering and John Mills playing Doolittle. There was also Joyce Redman, best known for the eating scene with Albert Finney in *Tom Jones*, playing Higgins' mother. According to Brogger, O'Toole doted on Joyce throughout the production. 'He loved her, and no wonder. She was seventy-five years old but walked like – I still got it.'

O'Toole's own idiosyncratic performance, according to Brogger, divided the Broadway theatrical community: 'I think a lot of people thought he was drunk or they were not overly receptive to what he was doing. Then there were others, and I'm certainly in that camp, who thought he was so original in that role that he was a joy to watch.' When he was not nominated for a Tony Award, O'Toole defended himself in his usual manner. 'Not knowing what a Tony was until I had not been nominated, I wasn't disappointed.'

When his time on Broadway was at an end O'Toole returned to Clifden and his beloved house and garden and his trips into town. 'When we were making *The Stunt Man*,' recalls Steve Railsback, 'Peter told me that when he was in Ireland he would go to the pubs and he would just recite poetry. This was his life. What a wonderful thing.'

He had also found a new passion, something that perhaps gave him a sense of locality and identity, breeding the famous Connemara pony. He owned three or four of them, which he'd enter in the annual Connemara pony show, held in Clifden every summer. This was like Oscar night for O'Toole. There he would be every year, always the centre of attention in his tweeds. 'Peter was funny because at home he would come in with a dirty old rain mac and a pair of chinos and a jumper,' says Paul D'Alton. 'But then in the Connemara pony show, because he was then on stage, as it were, he'd dress up and it was hilarious. Although he always said he was an Irishman and patriotic, he'd dress like the full English country squire, the tweed outfit was perfectly pressed. It was like a Silicon Valley millionaire going shooting in Scotland, the Barbour jacket wouldn't have been handed down and dirty and torn like all of ours, it would be spotless.'

According to D'Alton, O'Toole didn't really know very much about horses, 'and was nearly decapitated when his stallion Dr Slattery half dragged him across the show field at the Connemara pony show as we died laughing'. O'Toole thought he was on to a winner with Dr Slattery, telling everyone who'd listen what a great stallion it was. When it failed to win the top prize one year that was the last anyone heard or saw of the beast.

By the end of the year he had accepted another movie role, in the comedy *High Spirits*, playing the owner of an Irish castle in danger of repossession who decides to turn the place, with the help of his staff, into a haunted house for the tourist trade. The studio wanted Sean Connery, but when he pulled out director Neil Jordan replaced him with O'Toole. It was his first lead in a film for several years and it was now plainly obvious that he was no longer first choice in many Hollywood producers' minds. In truth, his box-office status had been waning for more than a decade now, but his name and presence could still add gravitas to any production.

Jordan pulled together an impressive cast. Joining O'Toole were Steve Guttenberg, Daryl Hannah, Ray McAnally and Liam Neeson, whose girlfriend of the time was hovering around the set most of the time, a young actress by the name of Julia Roberts. Filming began with interiors at Shepperton and O'Toole's dressing room quickly turned into the social hub of the movie, coming as it did with a well-stocked bar. Most of the Irish actors, once made up and in costume, hung out there, drinking and playing cards. O'Toole held court, either talking about cricket or studying the papers and putting bets on the horses. Often he was in raconteur mode. 'He told us lots and lots of drinking stories,' recalls actress and singer Mary Coughlan. 'About when he was in the desert with Omar Sharif and they hired motorbikes from a local guy and just fucked off for three days.'

On set O'Toole was friendly and amusing, and Guttenberg has always appreciated the one piece of advice he was given. 'He'd say, always do something different, whenever you're acting, whenever you're creating, always pop out from another hole.'

One day on set Guttenberg talked to O'Toole about the frustrations of the profession, that it had the capacity sometimes to make you so angry you got home and kicked the dog. 'How do you avoid kicking the dog?' O'Toole thought for a while before replying, 'Don't have a dog.'

During location filming around Limerick, O'Toole took Guttenberg to a rugby match, one presumes it was Munster, the team both he and Harris followed. It was a memorable experience for the American, the passion of the crowd and being with someone whose love of the game was matched by his knowledge of it.

Although *High Spirits* was panned by critics and flopped at the box office, Mary says it was 'absolutely great craic to make'.

Guttenberg, too, enjoyed his time on the film and working with O'Toole. 'He was so theatrical in himself. When he was ordering tea he was Peter O'Toole, he couldn't help the equipment he was born with.'

In Limerick his room was directly below O'Toole's and every morning he could hear him methodically going through his vocal exercises. 'Even after being in the business for so long and having done all those movies, every job was important to him.'

Over the last few years Lorcan had been shuttled back and forth between his mother and father in England and America. It must have been an intolerable situation for O'Toole and Karen, and a deeply unsettling one for the young Lorcan, having continually to say goodbye to one or other of his parents. 'There were always tears and it was hard for me. Sometimes I think the happiest time was sitting on the plane that took me across the Atlantic because I was midway between them.'

It had now come to the point where the joint custody arrangement, set up when Lorcan was a baby and under which both parents alternated custody of him every three months, had become unworkable and both parties were arguing for a change. In April 1988, O'Toole allowed his judgement to be clouded once again when he refused to release Lorcan after his visit was over. Karen immediately ordered the courts to force him to return the boy. He refused. Tough New York lawyers threatened O'Toole with a daily fine of $1,000 from his earnings on *The Last Emperor* if he failed to hand over Lorcan to his mother. Karen then upped the stakes even higher, getting her lawyers to ask a US federal judge to issue an arrest warrant and a ruling that O'Toole was in contempt of court, which meant he could be arrested the moment he entered the United States.

A month later, O'Toole and Karen sat barely thirty feet apart from each other in London's High Court, the two former lovers refusing to even look each other in the face. It was an appearance before the world's press that O'Toole could well have lived without, he looked frail and nervous. The judgement, when it came, was a devastating setback. The son he adored had to return with his mother to America pending a further court hearing when it would be decided once and for all which parent should get sole custody.

Visibly shaken and in tears, O'Toole knew his gamble had failed. He returned with Lorcan to Guyon House and together they packed his small suitcase and for a while played in the garden, perhaps for the last time as father and son.

In July, O'Toole and Karen renewed their legal fight in a New Jersey court. O'Toole testified behind closed doors, giving what was described as 'fairly emotional' testimony. Karen too was emotional, accusing O'Toole of using her as a 'brood mare' to produce a longed-for son. Both parents claimed the other had violated the original joint custody agreement.

At issue, primarily, was the welfare of the child. 'It's a lifestyle question,' explained Karen's attorney, Raoul Felder. 'One parent is an international movie star, and the other is a homebody. She wants her son brought up as a typical American boy.'

Just days before the verdict was due to be given, Johnnie Planco was at home in New York with his wife Lois and young family. O'Toole rarely ever called him at home, so when the phone rang that evening and it was O'Toole, Planco thought something was wrong. 'What are you doing?' O'Toole asked.

'There's a baseball game on television I'm going to watch, why?'

'Oh, mind if I come over?'

'We haven't got anything fancy for dinner or anything, Peter, we're just watching the game.'

'It'll be fun,' said O'Toole. 'I love baseball.'

O'Toole came over and almost immediately Planco sensed he

was on edge and nervous. He tried talking about the game but O'Toole was somewhere else. 'Then our son came in, he was just a baby at the time, and when Peter saw him he just took off like a rocket and started playing with him. They must have played together for hours, myself and Lois could have left the house and he wouldn't have known. Then he profusely thanked us and left.'

When the verdict finally arrived it was good news, the judge had ordered that the boy be allowed to stay with his father and carry out his schooling in London. He would live with his mother during the holidays. 'Peter went through the roof,' confirms Planco. 'He was so happy. The court gave him a whole list of things he had to do to keep custody of Lorcan, he had to agree not to work certain times of the year, he had to stay at home and look after Lorcan and lots of other things, and he did it.'

For this most private of men, who only consented to interviews out of necessity and had always shunned the glitzy media spotlight, to have to live out this personal trauma in the glare of the public was an agonizing ordeal. But the reward was sweet and the remaining years of Lorcan's childhood that O'Toole was now able to share brought out the very best in him. 'Lorcan had a particular significance for Peter,' says Planco. 'It wasn't just a father and son relationship, he saw something in Lorcan that made his whole life worthwhile.'

Having won a great personal victory, O'Toole was in the summer of 1989 on the cusp of one of his most spectacular professional successes on stage, with *Jeffrey Bernard is Unwell*. Based on the real-life columnist of the *Spectator*, whose weekly accounts of disasters caused by booze, women and horse racing became cult reading, Jeffrey Bernard was a proper London character, his stomping ground the pubs and drinking dens of Soho. Written by Keith Waterhouse, the story has Bernard waking up to find that he's been locked in his favourite pub, the Coach and Horses, after closing time and spends the night reflecting on a life of dissolution with the help of people and faces from his past. Waterhouse saw his play as not just about one man, but about drinking, about friendship and failure, vulnerability and coming to terms with the person you are.

Once finished Waterhouse sent a copy to his friend Ned Sherrin. They agreed that their perfect Jeffrey was John Hurt, a close friend of Bernard's and fellow habitué of Soho's drinking clubs. To their surprise Hurt turned it down, saying how he thought it might work as a radio play but didn't think it was right for the theatre. A year later when it was a triumph Hurt bumped into Sherrin at a party and admitted, 'God, you were bloody lucky you didn't finish up with me!'

A little disappointed by Hurt's rejection, the very next day Waterhouse biked a copy of the play over to O'Toole's house. The rumour was that O'Toole had a season of three classical productions planned for the West End, so Waterhouse was careful not to raise his hopes. Returning home that evening Waterhouse saw there was a message on his answer phone. It was O'Toole: 'Keith, you bastard, you have screwed up my fucking life. I had this whole year mapped out and now I have to change all my fucking plans. I hate you. Love Peter.'

At the press launch, held of course at the Coach and Horses, O'Toole told Bernard that he had no intention of doing an impersonation of him. 'Just as well,' replied Bernard. 'I've been doing an impersonation of you since we met thirty-odd years ago.'

According to Sherrin, the pair were introduced when Bernard was a stage hand and they were rivals over a girl. Stumbling to remember anything through the blurred mists of time, O'Toole conceded that Bernard had won that particular round. 'No, you won,' said Bernard. 'I married her.'

The play was in rehearsal for three weeks with Sherrin

proving the ideal director, especially when it came to O'Toole. 'He did nothing, absolutely nothing,' reveals co-star Royce Mills. 'Laziest director you can imagine. He had nothing to offer, but he let it happen. He had very good judgement.' According to Sherrin, O'Toole had recorded the entire script on tape in order to learn it prior to rehearsals. 'In this way he likes to arrive on the first day word perfect, and expects the other members of the cast to have done likewise.'

O'Toole rarely if ever brought his script to the theatre but on the one occasion he did Royce Mills was able to take a sneak peek at it and was amazed by what he saw. 'It was like music, every movement, every gesture, every inflection was marked. And that's the extraordinary thing about him, he made it fresh and new, but he'd worked it all out. I found that amazing, however methodical he may have been about something, if the emotional part of it overtook him suddenly he'd just run with it.'

Prior to its London engagement, the play opened at Brighton's Theatre Royal in September 1989. As a treat the entire cast went for a day at the races, accompanied by Jeffrey Bernard, who proved such a nuisance that he was put on the first available train back to Victoria. 'We gave him twenty Benson and Hedges and a quarter bottle of something,' recalls Mills. 'He was smoking in the carriage and then put the cigarette in his trouser pocket to smoke later. Unfortunately by the time he got to Hayward's Heath station he was on fire and his trousers had to be put out.'

After its successful debut, the play moved to the Theatre Royal Bath and met with a similarly enthusiastic response. Staying in the historical city, someone suggested everyone have afternoon tea in the famous Pump Room. 'Oh fucking hell,' declared O'Toole, deeply uninspired by the prospect. In the end he was persuaded to go and had a bit of trouble walking through the city centre, being followed by a party of Japanese tourists who kept hiding behind lamp posts. He finally made it and joined everyone at a table. 'The place was packed,' recalls Mills. 'At one point this Irishman came up to our table and said, "Excuse me, now which one of you is Peter O'Toole!" '

In spite of the positive reactions to the play it was obvious that it was too long and cuts were needed. O'Toole certainly had his own ideas what should go, delighting in whispering to members of the cast whilst playing certain scenes, 'This one's a corpse.' Royce Mills was perhaps the most experienced of the supporting cast, famous for his TV comedy appearances with the likes of Morecambe and Wise and Frankie Howerd, all of which did not impress O'Toole in the slightest. 'He didn't trust me at all.' They had in fact already met many years before, when Mills appeared in a play with Siân. 'And Peter used to spend the evening in my dressing room. He had no recollection of it.'

One afternoon Mills suggested his own ideas for where a sizable cut should be made. 'You know that three or four pages you do about Jeff as a stage hand at the Royal Opera House, Peter. I think most of that can go. It's not very funny.'

'Oh, do you. Mind your own fucking business.'

For the following day's matinee performance a car had been sent to bring Nat Brenner down to see the show. Afterwards Mills overheard Brenner chatting to O'Toole. 'I see you've got Royce with you then. He was at the Bristol Old Vic, you know.'

'Was he,' said O'Toole.

'Yes,' Nat went on. 'Played leads and everything.'

When Mills arrived at the theatre for the evening performance he was passing O'Toole's dressing room and heard a voice booming out from the half-closed door. 'Come in here for a moment.' Mills entered. 'You went to the Bristol Old Vic.'

'Yes.'

'I think we understand each other, don't we,' said O'Toole. 'Put the cut in.'

Jeffrey Bernard is Unwell opened at the Apollo Theatre in

October and was a massive success. In the *Financial Times*, Michael Coveney wrote: 'Waterhouse and O'Toole present one of the greatest comic creations of our day.' It was agreed by almost everyone that O'Toole gave a tour de force performance of which few actors would have been capable, bestowing a Beckettian melancholy upon this anti-hero and pub philosopher. There were standing ovations every night, sometimes lasting the length of four long curtain calls. And there was the added spectacle of the man himself, Jeffrey Bernard, propping up the bar in the royal circle, basking in the adulation and free vodkas.

Many friends and colleagues came to see the show. Andrew Sinclair thought O'Toole exceptional. 'It was the most marvellous, spectacular performance.' Johnnie Planco flew to London to see it and after the performance was taken to the Groucho Club for a small celebration.

At one point who should walk in but Jeffrey Bernard. 'And he looked just like Peter in the play,' remembers Planco. 'It was quite scary. And Peter goes, "There's Jeffrey," and ran over to him and introduced me, and the guy was obviously barely standing. But that was so freaky to meet Bernard right after seeing Peter do it, and then realizing how brilliant he was, because he did become that guy.'

O'Toole was a hit back on the London stage, but his film career was faltering badly. He was starting to make pictures that went either unwatched or unreleased, like *The Rainbow Thief*, which at least reunited him with his old *Lawrence of Arabia* co-star Omar Sharif. Filming a dangerous stunt, Sharif almost drowned on the set of a flooded sewer. O'Toole naturally saw the funny side of it. 'Come on,' he said. 'There's nothing funnier than an angry, wet Egyptian.' The two men had managed to remain close friends over the years, seeing each other periodically in a bid to relive their golden heyday. 'The last time Omar and I were together was in Cairo a few months back,' he said in the early nineties. 'And we misbehaved ourselves all over again. Even though we're venerable gentlemen, we can still misbehave ourselves appallingly, only perhaps marginally more slowly.'

Another misfire was *King Ralph*, about a brash American who becomes King of England when the entire Royal Family are killed in a freak accident. O'Toole knew he was slumming it. 'The film was meant to be a light-hearted, quick little frolic that suddenly turned into this dull, plodding nightmare.' At least he found pleasure in the supporting cast of fruity British thespians. 'The only thing that got us through was that John Hurt and James Villiers were in it, so at least we had a decent poker school.' The star was John Goodman, who during a break in filming, asked to borrow an ashtray. With characteristic flair O'Toole flicked his ash on the floor: 'Make the world your ashtray, my boy.'

TWENTY-THREE

While he confessed to friends that it was tough bringing up a son on his own, O'Toole still wholeheartedly embraced late fatherhood, believing it to have been a positive in his life. 'I think Lorcan's birth provided a pivotal, stabilizing and important turning point for O'Toole,' said family friend Sarah Standing. 'It gave him a second chance. It tethered him.' Certainly he was taking his responsibilities seriously. Back on the booze as he was, his drinking was measured, he only accepted films that fitted in during school holidays when Lorcan was with his mother, and when appearing in *Jeffrey Bernard is Unwell* insisted that the curtain went up no earlier than 8.15, so he could put Lorcan to bed.

It had also meant leaving the costly and now far too big Guyon House and moving to a more moderate though still large home in Brondesbury, in north-west London, turning most of the back garden into a functioning cricket pitch. 'There was a proper twenty-two-yard strip and I think there might have been a net at the end,' recalls friend Michael Neilson. 'He used to practise bowling against Lorcan, and batting against Lorcan's bowling. He was passing on his cricket knowledge to his son.' O'Toole had enjoyed a lifelong passion for the game. He'd played in the streets as a kid in Leeds, with a lamp post for a wicket, planks of wood for a bat and a round stone for a ball. During the filming of *Lawrence of Arabia* he and Sharif, himself a keen cricketer, would partake in a few sessions in the 120 degree desert heat.

The watching Bedouin tribesmen never quite got the hang of the game, more interested in the potential of the ball as a weapon.

While appearing on the *David Letterman Show* in the mid-nineties, top American baseball pitcher Mark Langston of the California Angels was a fellow guest and Letterman, talking about the differences between cricket and baseball, thought it might be fun afterwards for Langston to pitch a few to O'Toole and see if he could hit them. 'They all went to a hallway,' remembers Johnnie Planco. 'And this guy Langston threw at something like a hundred miles an hour, you couldn't see it, and Peter smashed it. Everyone was astonished. And they kept doing it over and over again and afterwards Peter said, "Well, that was fun." '

O'Toole classified himself as an opening batsman and off-spin bowler with a really special delivery. 'It does absolutely nothing. From leaving the hand to pitching – nothing at all. This confuses many batsmen.' He also liked to field at slip, 'for observational purposes'. He was particularly proud, and often brought it up, that the Irish beat the West Indies in 1969 when they were in the country on tour. Only because, so the story went, the Irish took the West Indian team to the Bushmill's whisky factory first and got them absolutely plastered and then managed to beat them in a little one-day friendly game.

Around 1986, to put his cricketing prowess to good use, O'Toole founded his own cricket team, the Lazarusians. He joked it was named after Lazarus who rose from the dead, something he himself felt he had done not so many years before. It consisted of a few acting buddies like John Standing, his godson Timothy Ackroyd, and another young actor called Michael Neilson. Kenneth Griffith was club president. 'It took off very quickly,' recalls Neilson. 'A lot of teams wanted to play against us.'

O'Toole had proper cricketing caps made for everyone and

also provided a suitable mascot. 'It was a life-size plastic vulture,' recalls Neilson. 'This vulture was called Lazarus and before each game, it was Peter's idea that we all encircle Lazarus and give our team chant of "Lazarus, Lazarus, you fucking beaut." This was the typically theatrical and very naughty touch that Peter brought to everything. We won more games than we lost, but the main thing was to enjoy the match. Peter was always more interested in having fun than winning. We never took the cricket seriously. That wasn't the aim of it.'

On Saturday match days everyone would meet early outside Lord's, where a coach would take them to wherever they were playing. Sometimes if they arranged a second game on the Sunday they'd stay overnight. They were a wandering side with no home ground, playing amateur and charity teams all around the country in places like Kew in West London, Ampleforth College in North Yorkshire and Lustleigh, down in Devon, O'Toole's favourite cricket ground. They even played at the invitation of Earl Spencer at Althorp. Playing once in Northampton, O'Toole was at the crease batting when a drunken spectator ran out onto the pitch and poured a can of beer over his head with the words, 'You like a drink, don't you, mate.' O'Toole ignored it and carried on batting. When he came off Neilson went over to him. 'God, Peter, if that happened to me I would have chinned the bloke.' O'Toole looked over with a resigned expression on his face. 'Michael, I can't hit him because the following day in the papers it would just say – Peter O'Toole hits spectator.' It was then that Neilson realized what it must be like to carry that amount of fame around.

Not that O'Toole couldn't handle himself when things got physical. 'He always looked extremely fragile,' says Neilson. 'But he was quite tough. He'd get hit by a cricket ball at the crease and he'd shrug it off. He was made of strong stuff.' And while some drinking went on, Neilson once wandered to the crease to umpire a match drinking cans of Foster's, he doesn't recall ever seeing O'Toole with an alcoholic drink in his hand. 'Although he used to get through three packets of Gauloises a day.'

It wasn't unusual for O'Toole to sometimes counsel the young actor. 'He always used to say to me, it's nine-tenths tenacity and one-tenth talent.' And during a discussion about acting one day he told Neilson: 'You can't get away with what I got away with these days. When I was a young actor theatres and movie companies were run by artistic people, but the trouble is now, Mike, the business is run by accountants and that's a very different ball game. An accountant won't let you come to work with a hangover.'

The Lazarusians carried on into the early nineties until one Saturday, having arranged to play at Lustleigh, a long trip from London, only six people turned up. 'What happens in cricket teams is guys grow up,' says Neilson. 'They get married and they have kids, they can't go gallivanting off on a jolly with the lads any more. So it became obvious we couldn't as a team continue like that. And we couldn't get new players in all the time. So it just faded away. But they were happy days. It was just eleven blokes having a laugh and really enjoying being in each other's company.'

Due to his friendship with the MCC's head coach Don Wilson, O'Toole was also a regular visitor to the nets at Lord's, once facing an over from Imran Khan at full tilt. But he took greater satisfaction in helping children developing their skills at Brondesbury and Cricklewood cricket clubs, and was never happier. Approaching his sixties, O'Toole had decided to become a qualified cricket coach. It was a way of putting something back into the community, sharing his love of the game with a new generation and a way of relating with his son. 'I wanted Lorcs to know I still shared his sense of adventure – a merriment. I was an older father and I had to keep up without conscious effort.'

For Lorcan's birthday, again O'Toole had looked to do something in the local community. He'd heard that the sports centre at the Royal Free in Hampstead, the hospital whose staff had saved his life years before, put on children's parties. One afternoon he decided to pay it a visit. Keith Hunt, who ran the sports centre, was sitting quietly in his office when there was a firm knock on the door, followed by the unmistakable figure of Peter O'Toole waltzing into the room. Hunt was astonished, since this wasn't the first time the two of them had met, though plainly O'Toole had forgotten. Back in the late sixties Hunt worked as a barman at the Old White Bear, a popular pub just round the corner from Guyon House. Naturally O'Toole was a regular and Hunt would have to sometimes escort him home when he'd had a little too much to drink. The White Bear was run by a fearsome landlady who frequently banned O'Toole: 'But then she'd forget she'd banned him and he'd drift in and then when he got a bit boisterous she'd ban him again.' Hunt always found O'Toole the perfect gentleman, never offensive, even when loaded.

Over the course of four years Keith Hunt organized Lorcan's birthday party at the hospital's sports centre and witnessed firsthand the special relationship between father and son. 'He adored Lorcan. He loved that boy. It was such a beautiful bond between them, an incredible bond. It was such a closeness that you really felt it.' The parties were either football-themed or made use of the centre's swimming pool and O'Toole always attended, wearing his trilby hat and with the collar turned up on his camel-hair coat. 'He wafted into a room and the room changed, totally,' Hunt says. 'Even youngsters who might not have heard of him went – wow.' As Lorcan and his friends had fun, O'Toole would sit quietly at the side, content to be left alone, but also happy to talk if approached, happy to reminisce about David Lean or whatever subject came up. 'He always had time for people,' says Hunt. 'If someone said, "Can I have your autograph please," he'd say, "Why do you want an autograph of me, I'm nothing now." Although I think he still preened when people recognized him.'

After the first party O'Toole got in touch with Hunt to send him tickets to see *Jeffrey Bernard* as a thank you. The invitation also included a visit to see him backstage. 'He had a room with a bar, which was for his guests, and he just sat there drinking water. Smoking, always. He used to say to me, "I've been told by my doctor I've got the lungs of a twenty-year old." ' A little while later O'Toole heard that Hunt took regular trips over to New York to see the Broadway shows that he loved and so always made sure that the hottest tickets in town were made available to him. 'He paid for the use of the sports centre for Lorcan's birthdays, very generously, that was all he needed to do, but then he'd call me saying, "I hear you're going to New York next week, what show do you want to see?" '

However, Hunt's most remarkable encounter with O'Toole was yet to come. One Saturday afternoon at the centre Hunt saw a couple of football fans playing at the pool tables and calmly and politely told them that as this was a members' only club he was sorry but they'd have to leave. 'One of the guys got out a razor. I ducked but he just caught the top of my head and as with any head wound there was a lot of bleeding. Out of panic I think the two men ran off.' The incident made the local newspaper and the next day O'Toole called Hunt's office. 'Are you OK? I've just read the report.'

'I'm fine, thanks, Peter, except when I see a razor blade now I go all cold. I can't even wet shave myself any more. I just can't do it.'

There was a pause on the other end of the line. 'When did this happen?'

'Last Saturday.'

'What time?' asked O'Toole.

'About two thirty.'

'Right, you and me will wet shave by the pool table at two thirty on Saturday afternoon.'

'No, you don't have to worry about it,' said Hunt.

'No, I remember something like this happening in Ireland and it worked.'

Sure enough, the following Saturday at two thirty O'Toole arrived and together the two men had a wet shave and afterwards Hunt felt fine about using a razor again. 'When I said, "Thank you so much," afterwards he went, "I haven't done anything." '

TWENTY-FOUR

Since O'Toole had a sizeable investment in the *Jeffrey Bernard* stage production he was keen for it to continue after his stint in it came to an end. First Tom Conti took over the role, still playing to packed houses, then James Bolam. In early 1991 O'Toole contacted Waterhouse and Sherrin with a view to reviving his celebrated performance as Bernard, this time in a bigger venue. They settled on the Shaftesbury Theatre. Again it was a huge success over its limited two-month run, and the offer came in to take the play on tour to Australia. O'Toole said he'd do it on the condition that Royce Mills came as well. It was agreed. 'But then Australian Equity objected to me,' recalls Mills. 'They said, "We know who Peter O'Toole is, but who's this Royce Mills? Never heard of him." So Peter turned round and said, "Fuck them, I'm not doing it." ' Dennis Waterman was cast as Bernard instead.

Coming off yet another triumph as Jeffrey Bernard, O'Toole sniffed around for another potential stage hit and was certain he'd found it in John Osborne's new play, *Déjà Vu*, a sequel to his landmark *Look Back in Anger*, which saw a middle-aged Jimmy Porter still ranting and raving against the world. Osborne had spent the best part of two years trying to interest producers and theatres into taking it on, encountering a barrage of rejections, including from the Royal Court itself which had produced the original. Still, O'Toole was enthused, writing to Osborne: 'It feels like old times. We could stir up a hell of a fuss.'

The two met that July to begin discussions, with the biggest stumbling block the play's sheer length. Having timed the whole thing at around the four-hour mark, which would necessitate two intervals, O'Toole told Osborne, 'Sing it, hum it, shout it, speak it, rapidly recitative it, exit and entrance it on golf carts or bumper cars, when act two is uttered out loud it lasts for approximately one hour and 45 minutes. That is five minutes less than the entire playing time of *Jeffrey Bernard is Unwell*.'

Osborne went off to make forty-five minutes' worth of cuts, but O'Toole was still not happy and left the production shortly before rehearsals were due to begin. 'As I understood it,' recalls Tony Palmer, who was installed as director, 'Peter and John had a tremendous row, things had been thrown and I think they'd finished up with almost blood on the floor. They were both fairly fiery characters. After that Peter said he absolutely wouldn't do it. But I thought he was such an extraordinary actor and such ideal casting that I wanted to try and persuade him to come back.'

Palmer got in touch with O'Toole and set up a meeting that lasted three hours, during which they went through the text carefully together. O'Toole was still adamant that in its current form the thing was undoable, since no one went to the theatre any more to see what was a three-act play. He also seemed anxious about his age, that he was too old for the part. 'Well, no,' said Palmer. 'Rather more importantly I think you have that absolutely right feeling of having had a life very well used.' Palmer waited to be hit but instead the actor merely raised half an eyebrow.

There were more reservations. Some of the speeches O'Toole thought were full of Osborne's own private hang-ups and that he'd lost the trail of what it was he was trying to say with the play. Palmer remembers there was one bit O'Toole thought was completely bonkers where suddenly Jimmy Porter is talking about all the Australian nurses that he hated. 'That's got no relevance to Jimmy Porter,' blasted O'Toole. 'It probably has a great deal of resonance to John Osborne, but there's simply no point in including this tirade about Australian nurses.' Palmer felt some loyalty to Osborne but couldn't help but agree with O'Toole's objections and got a promise from him that if he managed to persuade Osborne to do some more major revisions he would look at it again. Palmer left the meeting quietly confident. The next problem facing Palmer was getting Osborne to cut three acts into two. 'And that was not easy.' Once accomplished the 'revised' script was sent to O'Toole, but nothing was heard again. So what could have been amongst the theatrical events of the nineties, Peter O'Toole back as Jimmy Porter, was never to be. The play did open six months later with Peter Egan in the role, an excellent actor, but not quite the same thing, and as a result *Déjà Vu* did not make the impact it might have done and quietly disappeared.

Instead O'Toole teamed up again with Keith Waterhouse and Ned Sherrin for *Our Song*, a play about an illicit love affair between a successful middle-aged married advertising executive and a destructive young woman in her twenties, played by Tara Fitzgerald. It opened in November 1992 at the Apollo Theatre where it was greeted warmly by audiences and favourably by critics, but came some way short of making the same kind of impact as *Jeffrey Bernard*.

Classifying himself now as a jobbing actor, offers of work continued to come his way, although he had become more prickly in the way he conducted himself, according to Johnnie Planco: 'If he arrived on a movie set and he liked the way he was treated, he had respect for everybody, he'd do anything. But if he walked on and somebody might just say good morning the wrong way, all through the shoot he'd be miserable. Either way he'd remain professional right the way through, but it was either a joy and a comfort or it was a trauma.'

The most rewarding recent jobs were from television. He had a small role in the acclaimed Lynda La Plante drama serial *Civvies* with Jason Isaacs, about former soldiers struggling to come to terms with civilian life, played the Emperor of Lilliput in a lavish mini-series based on *Gulliver's Travels* and was asked by BBC producer Verity Lambert to headline a television adaptation of the P. G. Wodehouse comedy *Heavy Weather*, also starring Richard Briers and old friends Bryan Pringle and Ronnie Fraser. A fan of Wodehouse, O'Toole was also delighted to be working with Jack Gold again, who'd been brought in to direct. 'Peter loved playing the Earl, he entered fully into the spirit of the production.' His was truly a dotty performance and a welcome return to comedy. Again Gold found O'Toole creative and inventive to work with. 'He was frail, though. But he had enormous will power. There was a great joie de vivre about Peter. He enjoyed life all the time, it seemed to me.'

In the cinema, the work on offer was of an inferior quality. Typical of these was *The Seventh Coin*, an action adventure made on very little money ('It was put together with string and chewing gum and sleight of hand,' admits its producer Lee Nelson), but at least there was the allure of location work in Israel and it gave O'Toole the chance to play a villain, something he was rarely asked to do and the reason why he accepted the offer.

His arrival at Ben Gurion airport, according to Lee Nelson, was like that of a visiting deity. 'They literally stopped the plane on the runway to allow Peter to leave and get into a private car, then the plane carried on to the arrival terminal and everybody else got off.'

Nelson was apprehensive though when his star arrived. Such were the budgetary restraints that the production could not afford the kind of amenities and behind the scenes comfort that a star of O'Toole's stature was used to. 'The trailer that he had to change in was quite frankly embarrassing, but he could not have been more thoughtful, loving, approachable, prepared, and ready to go every day.'

At the end of every busy day O'Toole's ritual was to wander back alone to his trailer on the set, strip and take a sponge bath. Lee Nelson knocked on the door one time asking about something. O'Toole called him in. 'So I open the door and he's standing there full frontal, totally naked, nothing on at all, he couldn't have been more blasé.'

One of the clauses that O'Toole insisted upon having in his contract was that he stay at the American Colony hotel in Jerusalem, situated in the West Bank. It was an old Ottoman-style building, a beautiful boutique hotel with a guest list that was legendary, including T. E. Lawrence himself. 'When I saw he'd put that in his contract,' says Nelson, 'of course I said, "Well, I'm staying there, too." So we'd meet sometimes in the bar and have a drink. He told me that on *Lawrence of Arabia* he and Omar Sharif when they were filming in Jordan and wanted to get some booze they would hire a little boat and sail over to Israel. One night they were intercepted by the Israeli Navy who thought they were gun-runners!'

O'Toole knew he'd been living on borrowed time for years, watching all his drinking pals from the sixties go under the turf one by one. 'The common denominator of all my friends is that they're dead,' he once said. He became a fully paid-up member of the 'hip-flask mob', standing around open gravesides in the shivering cold, downing warmth-giving shots of the hard stuff. 'They're dropping like flies, it's the end of an era. I've played all the graveyards: Kensal Green. Putney Vale. Golders Green.'

One passing, in 1997, particularly shook him, that of Ronnie Fraser. The outpouring of grief at his funeral in Hampstead was testament to how beloved he was. O'Toole was one of the pallbearers, sharing the duty with Simon Ward, Chris Evans and Sean Connery. For years O'Toole and Ronnie had not just a deep friendship but a special relationship going on, as fellow actor Bruce Montague reveals: 'I lived a few houses away from Ronnie Fraser in Belsize Park. Ronnie was fond of strange substances – "African woodbines" as they were sometimes called. Ronnie was one of Peter's regular suppliers. The transactions were strangely formal. Although I knew what was going on, I was sent to the kitchen while a plastic bag was handed over and Peter placed a wad of notes under a cushion of the sofa. Then I was summoned back into the sitting room and conversation continued as normal. At one point Ronnie couldn't find his weed and he phoned the police, with whom he was on friendly terms. "Have you got any sniffer dogs in Hampstead?" he said. "We could lay our hands on one. Why do you ask, Ronnie?" said a constable. "Well, could you send it round? I seem to have mislaid my stash." '

Just a few short months later James Villiers died, again another close friend gone. Not long after the funeral O'Toole asked Villiers' widow Lucy if she would come and work for him as his assistant. She ended up staying with him and looking after his day-to-day professional business right up until the end. 'They were really close,' confirms Planco. 'He took her everywhere with him. She ran his life. I would talk to Lucy probably as much as I talked to Peter.'

After Villiers passed the grey clouds descended once again. 'Peter got very depressed during that period,' claims Planco. 'He was saying things like, "Why am I surviving? Burton's gone, Finchie's gone, Fraser's gone, they've all gone. Why am I still here?" '

Harris was still around and they occasionally met up at the odd rugby match, usually Harris' beloved Munster, and reminisce about the old days. During one sporting afternoon O'Toole suddenly said, 'Ah, Jesus, I miss waking up in fucking places that you never knew you'd been to.' Harris smiled. 'I know. I used to love going to the shop to buy a packet of cigarettes and not coming back home for a month.' Both men burst out laughing. As O'Toole recalled, 'We were two old codgers trying to watch a rugby match and stay sober!'

During one lunch Harris said to O'Toole, 'Chaps like us, after all we've done, we should be dead, shouldn't we?' O'Toole looked at his old friend and said, 'But, Richard, we already are!'

O'Toole's next film, *Fairy Tale: A True Story*, was loosely based on the Cottingley Fairies hoax of 1917, when two young cousins took photographs that purported to be them interacting with real fairies. O'Toole played Sir Arthur Conan Doyle, the creator of Sherlock Holmes and a keen spiritualist who accepted the photographs as genuine and pitted his credibility against the cynicism of his friend, the escapologist Harry Houdini, played by Harvey Keitel. According to director Charles Sturridge the two actors spent most of their time talking about bars they knew rather than worrying about any clash of acting styles. Co-star Paul McGann recalled his first meeting with O'Toole as strictly bizarre. After the obligatory, Hello, how do you do, O'Toole changed tact completely. 'Now – disease. I've been meaning to talk to you . . .' And off he went about typhus, the Irish potato famine, the Battle of the Somme, the Weimar Republic and the rise of Hitler.

O'Toole flew next to America to make *Phantoms*, a sci-fi/horror movie, a genre he'd never tackled before, which was part of the reason for taking it on. Director Joe Chappelle's first contact with O'Toole was in a conference call that also included the producers and Dean Koontz, who'd written the script based on his own novel. 'Over similar calls I've had with actors subsequently over the years, they all want to give notes and have changes made, some quite major. Not so with Peter. He did not want *any* changes. For him, the concept of pink pages [i.e., script revisions] was "daft".' For much of his career, O'Toole saw himself, the actor, as the author's advocate.

Chappelle finally met his star at the home he was renting in Georgetown, Colorado, the film's principal location. 'Not surprisingly, I was nervous going in – his larger than life reputation preceding him. Would he be drunk? Bombastic? Rude? He'd worked with David Lean, William Wyler, Bertolucci, garnered countless Academy Award nominations and I was a virtually unknown director coming off *Halloween 6*.' Chappelle needn't have worried. O'Toole was gracious and welcoming and it turned out to be a memorable evening. They had dinner together, watched a Denver Broncos football game on TV and O'Toole recited Irish poetry and Shakespeare sonnets. 'It was like my own private *My Favorite Year*.' One of the most difficult shots in the film required O'Toole to perform a long speech during a heavy snow fall. It took all night to shoot. 'And Peter nailed it,' recalls Chappelle. 'When the dailies came back, however, the moisture in the air had somehow messed with the camera and the image was out of focus. Expecting the worst I said, "Peter, we have some bad news." As soon as he detected where the conversation was going he simply said, "Done." '

The young cast Chappelle had assembled, which included early roles for Liev Schreiber and Ben Affleck, all adored O'Toole, handling him at first with kid gloves; Affleck would for example help him across the street like an invalid. O'Toole liked Affleck, knowing they'd get on well together after overhearing the young actor quote the nineteenth-century English poet A. E. Housman to the first assistant. For his part, O'Toole tried to keep up with his young co-stars in what was a fairly physical role. 'I thought he was quite spry for someone who had a reputation for carousing over the decades,' recalls Chappelle. 'One time when things were slow going and we were trying to work out some technical issue he said, to no one in particular, "Children, we must get going." But that was the only time I heard him say anything less than 100 per cent positive.'

Phantoms proved a moderately effective thriller, but did no business at all. 'I just wish the movie had been a success,' laments Chappelle. 'So, if for no other reason, it would have instigated yet another comeback in Peter's career. He was only sixty-six at the time and could have played parts that went to the likes of Anthony Hopkins, Ian McKellen, etc. – all terrific actors, but not Peter O'Toole.'

It was back on the London stage where O'Toole was a guaranteed box-office smash, especially in the persona of Jeffrey Bernard. The play's latest revival had much to thank Hollywood star Kevin Spacey for, then a trustee of the Old Vic. O'Toole had recently seen Spacey in a production of *The Iceman Cometh* at the theatre and bounded into his dressing room to grab hold of Spacey's head with both hands and unleashed a flood of compliments: 'Funny, brilliant, hilarious, quick, fast, clever.' But as he was doing that he was banging the back of Spacey's head with his hand. 'I literally thought I was going to be knocked out. But I didn't care. Peter O'Toole was bashing my head in with compliments, and it was fine by me. I thought, That's a way to die.'

The subject of performing at the Old Vic naturally came up. Spacey wanted to know why he hadn't appeared there for so long. 'You should be on this stage. What the fuck are you doing?'

'Fuck off,' blasted O'Toole.

After a great deal of pestering and badgering by Spacey and the Old Vic board, *Jeffrey Bernard is Unwell* opened at the theatre in the summer of 1999, for forty-eight performances only, to sell-out audiences and fulsome praise. It had been ten years since the original production and Bernard himself had died and all but been forgotten, it was now all about O'Toole returning to the role he had made his own. 'It fitted him so comfortably,' says

Royce Mills. 'And this time he managed to push it and pull it so it was even better still.'

The first night was a sensation, with several curtain calls. 'Somehow the performance had become even richer,' recalled Sherrin. 'Peter seemed happier to investigate the darker, more sardonic side of Jeff than he had been when he was alive and might drop in.' Keith Waterhouse agreed: 'He has managed to improve a performance that we thought could not be improved upon.'

Kevin Spacey had secretly flown in from the States and after the performance gate-crashed O'Toole's dressing room. The actor was sitting on a chair, drained, but sat bolt upright and cried, 'Spacey! What have you got me into now! I'm exhausted and it's only opening night!!!' It was the beginning of a loving friendship. In 2003 when Spacey became the Old Vic's artistic director O'Toole was one of his keenest supporters and never missed a production. That didn't stop him from time to time making his opinions known. When Spacey put on the comedy *National Anthems*, O'Toole came backstage afterwards. 'It's a wonderful play, funny, fast. But I have a complaint.'

'What's that, Peter?' said Spacey.

'You cannot do comedy without legs!'

'What are you talking about?'

O'Toole continued his point, his voice rising all the time. 'There are two couches on stage that you stand behind all night long – you cannot do comedy without legs!'

The couches were removed. Another time O'Toole appeared in Spacey's dressing room during a show's interval, he stared long and hard into his face before spitting out the words – 'Absolutely appalling' – then leaving.

By this time O'Toole had called a halt to his theatre career. During the Old Vic run of *Jeffrey Bernard* he felt that while the love affair was still there he no longer had the appetite to take on and sustain a large role in a long theatrical run. 'It was an ideal play to bow out on,' he told reporters. 'I was dreading saying goodbye on the last night at the Old Vic. Dreading it. But it turned out OK. I just thought, well that's it. The stage days are over.'

TWENTY-FIVE

O'Toole didn't do very much of anything for the next two years, save for living quietly. Every Sunday evening without fail he would dine with Lorcan and Lucy at his favourite restaurant, La Gaffe, a stone's throw from Guyon House. It had been a haunt of his since the late sixties and he had become friendly with its proprietor, Bernardo Stella, who never worried about his famous client's hell-raising reputation. 'There is a saying, never shit on your doorstep, so in my establishment he was always very well behaved.' Bernardo remembers one evening a customer asked O'Toole to stop smoking. 'He turned to her and said simply, "Fuck off." But it was done in such a way that it appeared almost elegant.'

One lunchtime Bernardo Stella introduced O'Toole to Martin Bell, a former BBC war reporter who had recently become an independent Member of Parliament, well known for wearing distinctive white suits. After that the pair would regularly meet at La Gaffe for lunch. 'He smoked. We talked. He never had more than one lager. He was great company,' recalls Bell. 'And like many actors he had an acute interest in politics. He used to quiz me about various wars and what was going on in the House of Commons.' Politics was one of O'Toole's abiding interests. 'When he talked about politics you were sitting with a master,' says Johnnie Planco. 'One time he was invited on the *Jon Stewart Show* in America and he started talking about the Middle East, he knew the tribes, he knew the leaders and explained why America's involvement in Iraq will never work. And he was absolutely right. He was astoundingly well informed.'

There were also trips over to his beloved New York, where he would always see Johnnie Planco. Over these last few years, however, Planco had seen a marked physical deterioration in his friend. 'If we were at the Players Club for example and somebody he wanted to meet walked in he would bound up to greet them. But I noticed it was getting really hard for him to get up.' One day they were leaving the Players and heading back to the Chelsea hotel. It was about a distance of five blocks but O'Toole insisted on walking. 'About half a block into it he got really angry, "We should be taking a cab." '

At the 2002 Telluride Film Festival, O'Toole seemed to be back to his old self, engaging in several outdoor pursuits including shooting and biking whilst staying at the Colorado resort town. The festival was holding a celebration of his career, culminating in a Q&A on stage with renowned film critic Roger Ebert, who O'Toole had never heard of. It proved a memorable evening with O'Toole and Ebert engaging in a bout of one-upmanship by topping each other with quotations from Yeats. Coming off stage that evening to thunderous applause and a standing ovation planted the seed of an idea in O'Toole's mind. Back in London he called Planco. He wanted to do a one-man theatre show where he would talk about his career, show film clips and take questions from the audience. He got in touch with comedian and comedy writer Barry Cryer, a fellow Leeds lad who he had known off and on for several years, to help write the show. 'Peter said, "You'll be uncredited, Baz, and amply rewarded." And he had a marvellous idea for the opening. He said, "Let's get it out of the way, straight away, theme from *Lawrence of Arabia* full blast and the lights go up and there's me, an old man with a drink on the stage." I thought, what a marvellous opening. Boy, would that have sold out – an evening with Peter O'Toole!' According to Planco the project was quite advanced, 'until I got a call from him to say he wasn't interested in doing it any more.'

That August, news reached O'Toole that Richard Harris had been taken ill. He was a resident for some years at the Savoy Hotel, and when his family had heard nothing from him for days Elizabeth, who had divorced him in 1969 but remained on friendly terms, managed to gain access into his suite to find him lying on the bed drifting in and out of consciousness. An ambulance was immediately called. The director Peter Medak heard from friends what happened next. 'When they took him away to hospital the lobby just completely stopped, and Richard sat up on the stretcher and shouted, "It was the food! Don't touch the food!" '

Moved to the University College Hospital in central London, Harris was diagnosed with Hodgkin's disease. He was registered under an assumed name and the press never got to know he was there; O'Toole was one of the very few people other than family members allowed to see him. 'Peter used to come in endlessly into the hospital and sit with Richard,' reveals Elizabeth. 'And Richard used to enjoy Peter's visits. It was wonderful seeing these two old rebels sitting there together.'

When Harris died on 25 October 2002, aged seventy-two, the effect on O'Toole was profound. 'Peter was in tears for I don't know how long,' reveals Elizabeth. 'He was so shocked.' At his memorial celebration Andrew Sinclair bumped into O'Toole, having not met for several years. 'He was very frail by this time, incredibly frail. He was sticklike almost and walking with grace but difficulty.' Inevitably the topic of conversation was Harris. 'Both of them, Peter told me, had lost their gizzard, their spleen and their lights because of the gargle, and they had to give it up.' As the conversation drifted on O'Toole confessed, 'A lot of my plumbing is gone.'

One of Harris' boys came on the podium and said, 'Peter's coming on after this, but I must just tell you a story. There's my father coming out of Claridge's one afternoon, and there is Peter weaving down Brook Street. And Harris said, "O'Toole, look at you. Are we not members of Alcoholics Anonymous." And O'Toole replied, "Indeed. I am trying to find my way to the next meeting." And Dad said, "But are you observing the rules." And O'Toole answered, "It is very difficult. You see, every bar I enter, I have to give a false name." '

Having not given a single thought to work for almost two years, O'Toole resumed his career with renewed vigour. There was a cameo role in Stephen Fry's directorial debut *Bright Young Things*, a telling appearance as von Hindenburg in the TV miniseries *Hitler: The Rise of Evil*, and a rare starring role in *The Final Curtain*, a satire on modern television from the writer of *Shallow Grave* and *Trainspotting*, John Hodge.

The producer Jeremy Thomas, who last worked with O'Toole on *The Last Emperor*, also got in touch. He and renowned director Peter Brook wanted to make a film of the book *The Mind of a Mnemonist*, which told the true story of a distinguished Soviet psychologist's study of a young man who was discovered to have a literally limitless memory. O'Toole had made it known that he was interested in playing the ageing psychologist, mainly because it would offer him the chance to work with Brook, whom he admired, and so a meeting was set up near Chelmsford. 'We'd planned to meet somewhere and go to a pub,' recalls Thomas. 'I was driving Peter Brook and we were on a dual carriageway when I saw Peter driving at incredible speed in a silver estate car on the other side of the road coming from London. He spotted us and instead of going back to a roundabout he did the most amazing U turn I've seen in my entire life. He mounted the central barrier, took off, flew through the air, landed on our side of the road and then accelerated towards us. It was his way of getting to us the fastest way, which had included virtually ripping off the underside of his car. Peter was absolutely oblivious that he'd done anything wrong.' Sadly Thomas never managed to raise the finance and the film wasn't made.

O'Toole did agree to play Augustus Caesar in an American TV movie entitled *Imperium: Augustus* directed by Roger Young. When it came time to begin filming O'Toole's scenes Young couldn't find the courage within himself to give the star any piece of direction for three full days. 'I could barely ask him to do a second take. Finally, on the fourth day he said to me, rather loudly, so all could hear, "Darling, call me Peter. And tell me what you want." I'm not sure I can impart what a privilege that was. *Peter O'Toole* just said, "Direct me." *To me!* So began one of the most enjoyable shoots I ever had.'

About a quarter of the way through filming, O'Toole got sick. 'We thought it was serious,' says Young. 'I visited Peter in hospital. I was afraid for him. The next day we started planning how to shoot around him. He was obviously going to be out for weeks. The day after that, he was back on the set! No little illness was going to stop him. He worked every day after that. If anyone showed concern for his health he simply waved them off. He was a strong man.'

Still, Young remained concerned about his star's fragile health, particularly as the role required considerable stamina. In one scene Caesar faints on the hard concrete floor of a temple. O'Toole insisted on doing it himself, waving away the stunt man. 'I don't want you to take that fall, Peter,' said Young. 'Oh, darling, I'll be fine. Let's try it.' Young cried action and O'Toole collapsed in a heap on the hard floor. Getting up he looked over at a concerned Young. 'Want me to do it again?'

That kind of dedication seemed to sum up O'Toole for Young. 'It's an experience I'll never forget, sitting around talking about his films, David Lean, cricket, women, his children, various directors, Kate Hepburn, his books, and more cricket. I asked him to explain cricket to me one day and he said, "Oh dear boy, it would take months." '

O'Toole remained in historical garb for his next film, *Troy*, which at $175m was one of the most expensive films ever made, and boasted an impressive cast led by Brad Pitt. O'Toole appeared as Priam, the father of Paris played by Orlando Bloom. When Johnnie and Lois Planco visited O'Toole on the film's Mexican location he gave them a personal tour of the sets, which he thought were terrific. 'That evening we were supposed to have dinner and we kept getting a phone call from his room from Lucy saying, he's going to be ten minutes late. Now he's going to be another ten minutes late. He's going to be half an hour late. Then he's not coming at all.' Planco assumed maybe O'Toole had been drinking and was in no fit state to socialize.

Ever since he'd begun representing him, Planco had noticed the strange relationship the actor had with alcohol and his hell-raising image, how on occasions he liked to play up to it. There was one evening in the Players Club when O'Toole made a big show about ordering a certain type of Martini. 'I want it up and very cold and very dry.' He went on and on. 'When it arrived,' says Planco, 'he kept taking the drink and putting it to his lips, but the drink never went down. And when we left the glass was still full but people in the bar were saying afterwards, "Boy, he staggered out of here last night." And I'm like, he didn't drink anything!' From the Players they both headed to P. J. Clarke's on Third Avenue, which O'Toole loved, the place was something of a New York institution and where they shot scenes for the film *Lost Weekend*. 'We go in and the bar tenders all know him, "Oh my God, O'Toole's here!! You want the usual." And they make that same giant Martini, and Peter's walking around saying hello to people he doesn't know and the Martini's spilling over him.

And this time I really paid attention, he never drank a sip of it. I guess he needed that drink like it was a prop. Then I thought, maybe he just wants to continue the illusion. But then sometimes I would see him and know he'd had something to drink.'

After almost twenty years of largely indifferent film work, it was a low-budget independent British movie that brought O'Toole back into the limelight, garnering him his eighth and last Oscar nomination for Best Actor. Ironically, he wasn't first choice. Director Roger Michell first offered Paul Scofield the part of Maurice, an actor in the twilight of his years, who finds himself increasingly attracted to a brash teenager called Jessie, the daughter of his friend's niece. Scofield sent a charming letter to Michell politely declining. He'd been somewhat of a long shot anyway, having virtually retired from acting. Michell was a little more hopeful about his second choice, O'Toole, although the actor required some tracking down. 'He was very elusive, even to his own agent,' recalls Michell. Eventually the script of *Venus* by Hanif Kureishi was sent over.

At last O'Toole agreed to meet with Michell but on home ground, the Garrick Club near Covent Garden. It was the day of John Mills' memorial service in April 2005 and as Michell waited on the first floor the place began to slowly fill up with a fabulous array of actors over seventy, all struggling up the grand staircase. O'Toole arrived soon after, looking his usual dapper self and led Michell into the bar where he ordered a whisky for himself and a mineral water for Michell. Michell made his pitch. O'Toole smiled. 'No one better for a dirty old man who falls for a sluttish young woman.' The plotline, however, had caused some concern with the film's main backer, Miramax. Michell had done his best to reassure them that his story was much more about death and yearning and damage, 'and absolutely not a perverts' paradise'.

*

After several weeks of toing and froing O'Toole pledged his commitment, in principle, to the project. He had also begun to make some demands of his own, primarily more money and a hand in the casting. He strongly objected, for example, to Michell's choice of Ian Holm as Maurice's friend Ian, whose great-niece he's trying to seduce, preferring instead Paul Scofield. Since Scofield had already turned the film down that was a bit of a non-starter, besides, 'We don't want two Hamlets in the bloody film,' thought Michell.

O'Toole also voiced a preference for Penelope Wilton over Eileen Atkins, Michell's preferred choice to play Maurice's ex-wife. 'This is slightly bollocks,' Michell wrote in a diary that he kept throughout the production, which this chapter draws heavily upon, offering as it does a unique insight into the day-to-day experiences of working with O'Toole. In his view Penny Wilton was far too young for the role. 'That presumably is Peter bigging himself down age-wise.' The request was an early warning that O'Toole was looking to exert a greater influence over the film than his status merited, a film that he had yet to fully commit to doing. 'My instinct is to tell him to bog off,' Michell wrote.

Out of the blue O'Toole requested another face-to-face meeting. Michell popped round to his local Morrison's to buy a bottle of whisky and waited for O'Toole to waltz in. The evening was a long one. The two men talked for hours, O'Toole mostly about theatre in the fifties, his conversation liberally sprinkled with profanities as he ranted and rambled amusingly about some of his peers. 'He is hilarious and funny and a rogue and lovable,' Michell noted. 'And terribly indiscreet about some of his contemporaries: Holm, "We called him Ian Gnome." Atkins, "Spent the first thirty years of her career trying to persuade herself she had any talent at all." And Osborne, "Couldn't write shit on a shutter." ' By the end of the evening Michell had reached the opinion that O'Toole was 'a big old eccentric luvvie who will either be marvellous or quite, quite ghastly.'

Much got done that evening, yet O'Toole still voiced disapproval over the choice of Eileen Atkins, putting Michell in a tight spot since he'd already offered the role of the wife to the acclaimed actress. 'Well, I am very sorry, dear boy. It's either her or me, it's as simple as that,' O'Toole decreed. 'He is so funny,' wrote the director. 'So alive, so right for Maurice that it fills me once again with courage and pleasure.'

The Eileen Atkins issue disappeared when she took a job on Broadway. Michell offered the part to Vanessa Redgrave and this time O'Toole approved. 'Big Van,' he called her admiringly.

In mid-September Michell received an encouraging email from O'Toole declaring his positive reaction to the redrafted script: 'It's expanded a touch but has been deepened not swollen. Your construction and pacing startlingly good. Characters alive. Facets galore. Human and real. I'm thrilled.' There were a few reservations but O'Toole insisted these were minor. Michell breathed a huge sigh of relief, only to hear that O'Toole was spitting blood that his email was not replied to immediately. 'I think he genuinely is crazed or massively old,' Michell concluded. 'It's like dealing with a six-year-old and we haven't even started on the hard bit yet.'

More ghastly rumblings emerged, a precious attitude about doing a medical, hesitancy over the choice of the young actress to play the girl, vehement opposition to any rehearsal period ('Feature film rehearsals I find not constructive. I relinquished amateur status more than half a century ago'), ongoing haggling about money and generally posturing in a massively unhelpful way. So much so in fact that Michell was left pondering, 'Shall we fucking ditch him.' It was a tempting thought. In his diary Michell expressed how he had scarcely encountered anything like it: 'He is clearly under the illusion that he is a genius. Alas his last good film was twenty years ago. He is his own worst enemy and I am taking him on. Can I face it?'

On 8 October another face-to-face meeting with O'Toole to discuss the script quickly spiralled into a series of grumpy stand-offs. Kureishi was present, acting almost like a referee at times: 'What I think Roger means is . . . What I think Peter's worried about is . . .' Most of O'Toole's script points were well thought out and constructive, but on those Michell disagreed with he would explode, 'I'm not asking for much!' During what turned into another marathon meeting, the three men would be laughing, telling stories, gossiping and working well together, 'then another dark squall would scud across the table and the raging fury be unleashed again', wrote Michell.

At the close of the meeting the possibility of Ian Holm playing Ian was once again raised. That did it for O'Toole. 'You're like a fucking barnacle!' he shrieked. 'You won't let go!' Michell was left to ponder just what it was about Holm that upset O'Toole so much. 'He simply doesn't like Ian. Or is jealous of him. Or feels he will steal the picture from him.' Leslie Phillips was eventually cast.

However difficult the meeting had been, Michell convinced himself that progress was being made. He was wrong. A few days later he received an email in which O'Toole took issue with many of the new changes made to the script. 'Maurice's spare, simple dialogue has sprouted bow ties and lumps of flab. Please be aware of altering what persuaded my interest in the first instance.' This directly contradicted O'Toole's earlier positive reaction to the changes. Michell was now at the end of his tether and wrote to Kureishi and his producer Kevin Loader. 'Don't see the point of juggling yoghurt with this mad fucker any longer. Can we please dump him and find a proper collaborator?'

By the following morning Michell had calmed down, having managed to convince himself again how spectacular O'Toole could be in the part, only for another incident to drag him back into the depths of despair. The concept behind Maurice's wardrobe was to use O'Toole as he really was, a scruffy, careless dandy; frail, often unshaven, slightly frayed at the edges. Michell chatted long and hard with O'Toole about this approach, to use minimal make up and for him to wear his own clothes, and it was all agreed. At the actor's wardrobe fitting, however, O'Toole whipped out a notebook and began dictating his needs to the costume designer, Natalie Ward, which included handmade shirts and trousers, cravats and handmade suits, everything to be fashioned from silk or cashmere. Next he waved away any notion of attending the week's rehearsal that Michell had planned, explaining that he would attend for just the one day.

It was at this point O'Toole stopped answering his emails and became uncontactable by phone. It was also his intention to royally fuck off to Mexico for two weeks, 'So he would return the day before rehearsals looking like Bob Monkhouse after his Florida holidays,' complained Loader. Worse, they had still been unable to get him to sign a contract. Loader began to worry that O'Toole might have lost his bottle.

Meanwhile Michell was contemplating the nuclear option, contacting Daniel Battsek, President of Miramax, about replacing O'Toole with John Hurt. Other names bandied around included Jim Broadbent, Michael Gambon, Michael Caine and Ian Holm. It was time to panic, with shooting due to begin in just over two weeks. Michell could now see only three things happening: Miramax advocating the parachuting in of Hurt, O'Toole caving in to all their demands or the film collapsing.

In the end O'Toole caved in, apparently telling his London agent, Steve Kenis, 'Oh, well, I knew I'd never win that battle with Roger.' For all his fear and frustration Michell was relieved by the news. 'No one else on our list was quite as good . . . no, as perfect, as O'Toole.' Looking back today, Michell admits it was an overreaction wanting to replace him. Miramax would never have countenanced it anyway. 'Battsek told us that O'Toole was key to the film, that he wasn't going to fund the film without him.' But an important lesson had been learnt, that unless Michell told O'Toole to go fuck himself every now and then, and really meant it, he risked the actor walking all over them. Still, Michell and Kureishi admitted to feeling intimidated by their star. 'We feel him peering over our shoulders whilst whispering "Amateur!" into our shell-likes. We feel, in short, compromised as artists.'

Just a few days later Michell was walking back from the National Gallery on a location recce, 'When who did I see sailing benignly down the Strand, driven by Lucy, in their battered and battle-scarred white thunder-bus, but OT himself. The man, the miasmic spectre, the proverbial white elephant. Our eyes met momentarily and shifted: he thinking fuck I'm supposed to be in fucking Mexico and there's that cunting director: me thinking fuck he's supposed to be in fucking Mexico and there's that cunting actor.'

Now it was established O'Toole was back in the country, if he had ever left it, and that his complexion appeared unburdened by sunlight, Michell awaited his arrival on the Monday for the start of rehearsals. The first day passed off wonderfully with O'Toole in good spirits, full of enthusiasm and ideas. 'Peter smiles and the room lights up,' Michell wrote. 'He laughs and giggles and wheezes and splutters, but is like a weather-cock, spinning in the breezes of his moods and anxieties.' As rehearsals entered the third day Michell became even more impressed. 'He goes from strength to strength. He has it all at his fingertips.'

The first day of filming was due to begin at 6.15 in the morning; bets were on whether O'Toole would be a no-show. He did arrive, albeit late, and the first day was completed without incident. By day three everything was going to plan. 'O'Toole getting more and more confident in us, and in me,' wrote Michell. 'And thus more adventurous and up for the risk and the fun of it. He really is marvellous, and funny and amazing . . . put simply, a star.'

Michell can't really fault O'Toole's professionalism on the set, investing as he did totally in the no Hollywood frills, guerrilla-style shooting Michell liked doing. At his request a one-man shelter resembling one of those manhole marquees used by telephone engineers travelled with him from set to set, with a chair and a Calor-gas heater inside to keep him warm between takes. As for booze, O'Toole laid off it. Only once did he confess to Michell that he'd had a little snifter because he was freezing his nuts off shooting outside the British Library.

The mornings were undoubtedly the worst, 'when he is fractious and odd and insecure . . . and *late*,' wrote Michell. 'But then he bucks up and is up for anything. My respect for his gifts and his spirit grows every day. He takes ideas and notes ravenously, gets them instantly and throws back such astonishing and profoundly moving emotions that I am shocked as I squint into the tiny monitor in front of me.'

O'Toole's relationship with his fellow actors was equally complicated. After the first day of rehearsal he'd taken aside the actress chosen to play the teenage girl Jessie, newcomer Jodie Whittaker, and said to her, 'Darling, I can't understand a word you're saying. You're going to have to tone your accent down.' This was totally against what Michell wanted from her. 'How unnerving for an actress to be taken aside by a senior actor like that and given that kind of note,' says Michell. 'It's almost unheard of.' Michell told Jodie to carry on the way he'd instructed her. 'In the end I think Jodie found him wearing.'

Leslie Phillips also found the working relationship difficult, arriving at the conclusion that O'Toole was self-regarding and dominant. Phillips was almost ten years his senior and yet, in some ways, seemed a lot fitter. 'As the weeks went on Leslie did get more and more exasperated with Peter,' says Michell. 'Particularly as Peter's entourage got larger and larger, and Leslie's entourage never started. I think Leslie found Peter infuriating. It was perhaps a bit of ego bouncing off each other. Peter would tease Leslie and sometimes tell him to just fuck off.'

Of course, Michell faced the obvious difficulty of working with a cast made up almost entirely of near-octogenarians. The most pain-numbing scene was set in a cafe. 'Richard Griffiths was a narcoleptic and would fall asleep during takes, through no fault of his own. Leslie would really battle to get through the scenes. And then Peter, who would sit there absolutely stoically knowing every one of his lines perfectly, if he said he was going for a slash, game over, because that would take an hour! So I'd be sitting at the back with my monitor basically throwing a noose over the rafter thinking, how the fuck am I going to get through this?' Amazingly it all cut together in the finished picture.

By the second week O'Toole was really hitting his stride and fearlessly engaged in it all, even happily improvising and relishing interaction with the public when out on location. 'I am now utterly devoted to him,' wrote Michell. 'And very very lucky to have him around.' After the moment when Maurice falls through the door into the art class where Jessie is modelling, O'Toole told Michell, 'I loved doing my stunt. It made me feel young again. Just for a little moment, of course.'

Naturally his energy levels did tend to flag towards the end of the day, sometimes early in the afternoon. Filming the scene where Maurice throws stones up at a window was a simple shot, but the conditions were cold and wet and when Michell called for another take the message came back that O'Toole was unwilling. Michell found him, 'knackered and panting like an old seal, back pressed to a radiator, rheumy-eyed, buggered.' Michell called it a day. 'He is terrified of the cold and of getting a cold.'

Michell always knew when O'Toole was growing tired, he'd reel off his lines at rapid speed to get the scene finished.

Filming wrapped for the Christmas break on 23 December. On 2 January Michell heard that O'Toole had taken a nasty fall at home on Boxing Day and cracked a hip. Doctors recommended a hip-replacement operation requiring almost a month's rest, which put the film dangerously behind schedule. While in hospital O'Toole picked up a nasty chest infection and had to be put on a course of antibiotics. On 7 January he returned home for a period of quiet convalescence.

By the end of the month the film was back up and running again but Michell was worried about his star, especially a nasty wheezing and gasping for breath; the infection he had caught in hospital had obviously not been fully eradicated. All went well the first day back until three in the afternoon when it was clear O'Toole couldn't continue. 'He collapsed into his horridly sinister medical chair and sat there fighting for breath, fighting to stay alive, clearly shitting himself, clearly struggling, eyes bulging, terrifying to behold.' O'Toole was immediately sent home and it was agreed that a paramedic be on set for the remaining three weeks of the shoot.

Over the next few days O'Toole improved slightly but remained very hit and miss. He tottered delicately to the set on sticks, fearful of any potential hazard, like a crease in a carpet, that might cause him to fall, and would occasionally go into paroxysms of spluttering, clearly in considerable pain. A harassed Michell wrote: 'He is too fucking knackered and ill and slow and fragile. And I *must* finish the fucking film at all costs before he croaks or breaks another bit of himself or contracts MRSA.' It had reached the point where O'Toole not only had a dedicated paramedic on standby, but a dresser, make-up man, shaver, face massager, his own car and driver, and a physiotherapist on loan from the MCC. When Leslie Phillips also began to develop various chest colds and the like, Michell felt it was like 'a competitive geriatric ballet of attention-seeking conducted in the slowest motion known to man'.

By the final week Michell had grown weary of O'Toole's irascibility, the endless waiting around, his ever-expanding entourage, and was now willing the end of the shoot. Like all true stars O'Toole had found a way of making the entire film revolve around him and Michell resented the daily ritual of sitting with him in the morning in his dressing room laboriously taking him through the day's work, shot by shot, while the crew stood outside anxiously waiting. 'He's a cunt. But a cunt with a lion's heart, and that great ferocious rage shines through his performance in the most surprising and glorious way.'

O'Toole could often be difficult on set, as we have observed, and take against some of his fellow performers such as Sophia Loren and the understudy in *Pygmalion*, but for the most part directors and colleagues enjoyed the O'Toole experience. So what made Michell's encounter with him so very different? *Venus* was O'Toole's first leading role in a film of substance for almost twenty years and the fear of failure must have been enormous, enough to put him on edge right from the start. There was also the realization that with Maurice he would have to reveal more of himself than he had ever done before on screen, which must have caused him some anxiety. Maurice is as close as we've ever got to seeing the real Peter O'Toole. There was such a vulnerability in that character which O'Toole the man never dared show.

As the end of filming drew nearer everyone on the crew had their own private intimations of mortality, O'Toole especially. When Michell began to describe how he intended to shoot Maurice's death scene, a long panning shot around to the sea, O'Toole burst into tears. 'He really is the most disarming old gruff.' When it was all a wrap O'Toole's relief that it was all over was palpable. 'God knows what reserves of strength and will power and bloody mindedness he has burrowed into to get through these last three weeks. The acting has benefitted hugely: frailer, more uncertain, and yet raging at the weakness and the mortality.' For a few moments both men sat outside in the winter sunshine then O'Toole shook Michell's hand. 'Mission accomplished,' he said and walked way.

When they met again that June for the dubbing session Michell thought O'Toole looked 'sprightly and fit'. He was cheerful, too, and during clips of the film was either roaring with laughter or pummelling and stroking Michell with affectionate approval. Then, having agreed to promote the film, O'Toole backed out at the last minute from attending the Toronto Film Festival, blaming an attack of 'gastric nasties'. He did, however, show up for a gala screening as part of the London Film Festival that October.

More doom and gloom followed when Michell was notified that O'Toole's doctor had insisted he carry out no press work this side of Christmas, which rather scuppered things since that's when the movie was opening in America. Michell joked that the least O'Toole could do now was pop his clogs, 'Thus providing a wonderful synchronicity of obits and the PR flourish the film has been waiting for.' Then O'Toole rallied, flying to New York in January to appear on several television chat shows and conduct a wealth of newspaper and magazine interviews. His publicist there reported that he had been a dream, completed every last interview, charmed every single reporter and was a real trooper. The hope was that this late flurry of publicity would help his Oscar chances. There had been significant buzz that O'Toole wasn't merely up for a record-breaking eighth nomination for Best Actor, but had a real opportunity to win it. Everyone knew it was his last chance, but O'Toole simply refused to be part of the Hollywood charm offensive. 'He was very ambivalent about it all,' says producer Kevin Loader. 'He could have won that Oscar, but he said to us, "I'm not going to be paraded around like a prize heifer!"' Forest Whitaker won in the end, for *The Last King of Scotland*.

On the eve of its release in the UK, after a successful US opening and rave notices, O'Toole sent Michell an email in which he called *Venus* a good picture, 'a Roger Michell picture', but then proceeded to lambast some of the cuts that had been made, the shortening and rearrangement of scenes, standard practice in post-production. Sadly Michell had really come to expect this. 'The old cunt has made the whole process of making this film as utterly miserable as possible from practically the first moment. But even I didn't anticipate this particularly vicious endgame.' He contemplated sending a reply but didn't bother. Kureishi thought, 'The man is mad,' and that Michell should 'totally disregard his poisonous ramblings'.

On 22 January 2007 Michell attended the London premiere. 'O'Toole true to form tottered around twinkling with that great self-deprecating leer he has perfected over the years, rather like the wolf in granny-clothes in the fairy story.' Afterwards in the foyer, O'Toole shouted Michell's name and made a great play of shaking his hand, but as the director caught a cab in the cold London night he could think of only one thing, 'How pleased I am to be almost certain of not having to see him again.'

Looking back on the experience today Michell is marginally more warmly predisposed to the actor. 'We were very lucky to have made a film with him, and I think we were right to make the film with him.' Without any doubt the role of Maurice was O'Toole's last great performance, and one of the most revealing he ever gave, full of self-reflection and drawing on his last forty years as a star. 'And that's the reason why the film works so well,' says Michell. 'When you see that picture of him in the obituary it's terribly affecting to see this stunning young man looking back at you.'

TWENTY-SIX

While O'Toole knew it was highly unlikely he would get to play such a challenging role as Maurice again, especially as he was now in his mid-seventies, and looked at least ten years older than that, offers of work were still arriving. Largely these were for supporting parts, as had been the case now for several years, or cameos which added gravitas to a production, such as his appearance as the King in director Matthew Vaughn's fantasy *Stardust*. There was also a recurring role as Pope Paul III in the major television series *The Tudors*.

One offer so intrigued O'Toole that he agreed to do it without reading a complete script, something he'd never done before. *Ratatouille* told the story of a rat who dreams of becoming a great French chef, and hailed from the animation studio Pixar, responsible for recent hits such as *Toy Story*, *Finding Nemo* and *Monsters Inc*. He had been asked to voice the character Anton Ego, a cynical restaurant critic. 'There's only one voice in my head when I'm writing this,' director Brad Bird claimed. 'And it's got to be Peter O'Toole.'

O'Toole's vocal performance was recorded in London over the course of six sessions, whenever a relevant section of animation had been completed. Before each session O'Toole always wanted the script pages a couple of days in advance so he could prepare properly. 'He seemed to really enjoy the process,' remembers producer Brad Lewis. 'He always had that twinkle in his eye. You could tell by the end of the session sometimes he got tired but he always came in with a fantastic energy. I remember the very first session he walked in and asked the crew, "Anybody watching the cricket?" I think pretty much the general response was no, and he looked at us all and said, "Heathens!" '

One thing Brad Lewis has never forgotten is that after twenty minutes, on every session, O'Toole would let rip with this tremendous roar, like a lion, several times between takes. 'At one point I said to him that he might want to be careful, just because he might tire out his voice. And he said, "Do you know who I learned that from? You'll never guess." We didn't guess and he said, "Audrey Hepburn." I don't know whether it was a throat clearing or head clearing exercise, or whatever, but it truly was a roar, and it was the roar of a twenty-year-old.'

When it opened in 2007, *Ratatouille* was a huge box-office hit, taking over $600 million around the world. Brad Lewis flew to London with a healthy bonus cheque for O'Toole. 'Peter gave me the biggest and wettest kiss on my cheek that I've ever got.'

O'Toole was increasingly spending his time now in London. His trips to New York had virtually dried up; he had sold his house in Clifden and according to Paul D'Alton rarely returned now to Ireland, except to see his daughters, who retained homes in the country. O'Toole was proud of his children. Kate, who adored her father and had inherited his sense of humour, had gone into the acting profession, something Lorcan was also trying his hand at, while Patricia was a business education and arts training consultant. All agreed their colourful upbringing had helped immeasurably in their adult life. 'Dad introduced us to a vast range of actors, writers, alcoholics, crooks, you name it,' said Kate. 'And he gave us great freedom to believe we could do what we wanted to do.'

In London O'Toole rarely went out, but was a pretty permanent fixture at the annual Oldie of the Year Awards held at

Simpson's-in-the-Strand, where he'd bump into friends Martin Bell and Barry Cryer. O'Toole loved the *Oldie* functions. 'And he was lionized there,' says Bell. 'Top table, of course.' At one *Oldie* lunch not long after the release of *Venus* Leslie Phillips was with him. Standing up to make a speech, Phillips looked over at O'Toole. 'It was great fun, wasn't it, Peter, making that film.' With a deadpan expression on his face O'Toole replied – 'No!' 'He loved wrong-footing people,' says Cryer. 'Saying something they didn't expect.'

The last time Barry Cryer saw O'Toole was at one of those *Oldie* lunches. 'His legs had gone, he had to be helped up out of his chair. He was so frail – but his mind wasn't frail.'

Over recent years O'Toole had worked in films shot across the world: in America, in China on the TV mini-series *Iron Road*, in Mexico playing a martyred priest in *For Greater Glory*, based on the true story of the Cristero War of the 1920s starring Andy Garcia, and in Kazakhstan, appearing briefly in an action film called *The Whole World at Our Feet*. While in Kazakhstan, O'Toole picked up a nasty viral infection in his lungs and bladder. While he inevitably bounced back, this latest illness, along with all the other minor ailments and injuries he'd picked up over the years, forced him to reach the decision that filming overseas, even America, was now out of the question. 'I can no longer walk from the check-in desk to an aeroplane, that's a fucking journey in itself.' His knees were particularly bad, one of them dreadfully swollen, 'looking like a sack full of dead babies.' He refused to have his cruciate ligament done, or knee reconstruction, because he was in no pain. But he did have trouble putting on a jacket due to his once proud bowling arm being 'completely buggered'. Indeed, he had recently given up cricket altogether, playing and coaching. 'I knew I was finished when I could hardly see the bloody ball.'

One offer of work that came his way only required a short trip to Pinewood Studios. For years first-time director Michael Redwood had been looking for finance for his Roman epic *Katherine of Alexandria*. In the hope of interesting private investors he sent the script to O'Toole and a host of other veteran British thespians. O'Toole was the first to respond, telling Redwood: 'If anyone alters this screenplay other than to add a full stop, shoot the bastards with my permission.' With O'Toole on board the likes of Edward Fox, Steven Berkoff and Joss Ackland signed up and the money quickly followed. Few guessed at the time, though, that it would prove to be O'Toole's final performance.

Redwood had his services for just six days and neither he nor his crew were aware of how poorly he was. 'If he was ill, he was hiding it really well because he brought a crackling energy on set with him.' The bulk of his scenes were completed on the first take. Before the cameras rolled O'Toole would ask Redwood what was required, listen intently, pause for something like five seconds and then say, 'You've got it.'

However frail and failing his body might have been, the mind was still alert and capable. 'His memory was like a computer,' confirms Redwood. ' He was always ten paces ahead of the crew.' Almost up until the end of his life O'Toole retained an astonishing memory. The last time his old RADA classmate Gary Raymond saw him was a couple of years before his death at the Garrick club. 'I went to speak to him and he knew immediately who I was and he was talking about things from way back, and he was totally there, although he looked a wreck. And it was wonderful.'

There were, of course, lapses. Playing a scene with Berkoff, on 'action' O'Toole began speaking only to stop and for nothing else to come out of his mouth. A few seconds passed before the continuity lady broke the silence and gave him the rest of the line. 'How fucking dare you,' he said, a stony glare in her direction.

'Cut,' shouted Redwood. 'How fucking dare you,' repeated O'Toole. Berkoff interrupted, 'Don't you know what a Mackenzie pause is, you idiot?' Later that day Redwood collared O'Toole and asked him what the hell a Mackenzie pause was. 'It means, for the uninitiated, I've forgotten my fucking lines.'

The one characteristic that Redwood found the most endearing about O'Toole was his infectious sense of humour; he was always up for a giggle, to have fun. 'He would make the whole crew laugh. If he was filming a scene, he would say things afterwards like, "You've fucked that up and I'm going to tell everybody." '

While the other actors travelled to and from the set from their dressing rooms elsewhere in the studio, O'Toole insisted on installing a large tent on the floor itself, where Lucy looked after his every whim. 'They were quite close,' observed his co-star on the film, Nicole Keniheart. 'Peter did feel very secure with her around. You could see that Lucy did take care of him.' He took breakfast early each day before the rest of the cast, and it was always the same, steak and porridge to give him energy. 'And he worked till he dropped,' confirms Redwood. 'From eight am till six pm on the dot. There wasn't a minute he wasn't ready and available.'

Towards the end of his time on the film O'Toole complained of stomach pains and Redwood went to see him in his dressing room. 'Peter, your health comes first, I'll bin this scene.'

Though visibly in distress O'Toole was having none of it. 'You can't do that.'

'Look, your health comes first. Tell me what's wrong.'

'Fuck it,' said O'Toole. 'We're going to do it.'

TWENTY-SEVEN

On 30 April 2011, O'Toole was joined by friends and family, including Kate and Lorcan, as he had his hands and feet enshrined in cement on the famous Hollywood walk of fame. It was a great honour and he was genuinely touched by the gesture.

In July 2012, not long before his eightieth birthday, O'Toole announced his immediate retirement from acting. He'd always said that one of the lovely things about being an actor was that you can go on for ever. 'Although I have no intention of uttering my last words on the stage in fucking Macclesfield or something. No thank you. Room service and a couple of depraved young women will do me quite nicely for an exit.'

Typically, he penned the press release himself: 'It's time for me to chuck in the sponge. To retire from films and stage. The heart for it has gone out of me: it won't come back. My professional acting life, stage and screen, has brought me public support, emotional fulfilment and material comfort. It has brought me together with fine people, good companions with whom I've shared the inevitable lot of all actors: flops and hits. However, it's my belief that one should decide for oneself when it's time to end one's stay. So I bid the profession a dry-eyed and profoundly grateful farewell.'

Not long after this statement was released O'Toole's friend Sarah Standing asked if he had any regrets about the decision. 'I'm not bloody Edith Piaf you know,' he answered. He did admit that he would miss the companionship. 'We all had such larks. Yes, it was hard work but the friendships and the genuine respect we had for one another, that side I shall miss greatly.' Other things, particularly the getting up at the crack of dawn bit, he wouldn't miss. 'And getting the old vocal equipment up to concert pitch at eight-a-fucking-clock in the morning, and keeping at concert pitch until eight at fucking night.' In later life he'd taken to wearing a watch on each wrist so if he forgot which wrist it was on he would still be able to tell the time.

So, that was it. He'd done his bit, been a leading man for half a century. 'That's enough.'

What was he going to do now was the question. O'Toole had already produced two critically well-received memoirs, chronicling his childhood and his experiences at RADA. Certainly he took great care over them and was enthusiastic and dedicated to getting it right, as is vividly illustrated in a letter he wrote to his editor at Macmillan at the very beginning of the venture. It reads:

'It is a tricky old lark this scribbling, isn't it? Beginning being a particular bugger and it is finding and sustaining a tone which is mine, though you are right, the inky prattle of my letters is me, not a studied composition and that voice is hard to find when addressing no one in particular. I have found it though and the words are gently dropping off my pen. More, thus far I am enjoying this extraordinary adventure.'

Written in a Joycean stream of consciousness that some readers did find difficult to comprehend and follow, these jottings of a 'demented poet', in the words of Sheridan Morley in his *Sunday Times* review, were intensely personal to O'Toole. So personal in fact that he did have trouble letting go of it. He hated being edited. The rumour from those who worked on the book was that he argued over virtually every comma that was put in or taken out.

When it came time to produce an audio book of both volumes O'Toole was mortified to discover that they had been abridged. In a fierce letter to the publisher he let them know exactly what he thought of the situation. His letter ended with: 'I shall now vomit.'

There was talk that now he had retired he would focus his attention on a third volume of memoirs, detailing his early film career and rise to fame. It was never to materialize. He also spoke of a desire to record all of Shakespeare's sonnets. 'They live at the side of my bed and are my constant companion.' This was another ambition that would prove unfulfilled.

As he entered what turned out to be the final year of his life, O'Toole began to plan for what he knew was the inevitable. He certainly knew he was dying as he began to put his life in some kind of order. For some time Johnnie Planco had got the sense that O'Toole was beginning to distance himself. 'Just at the point when I was beginning to take it personally, I looked around at our mutual friends and I realized he was pulling back from everybody, first emotionally and then professionally.' Suddenly, and quite out of the blue, Planco was told by O'Toole's lawyer that his services were no longer required. 'Peter doesn't feel the need for representation in America any more.' Planco was understandably upset, more by the fact that it wasn't O'Toole himself on the phone but his lawyer. 'Can I talk to Peter, because we've been together for thirty years,' said Planco. 'No,' said the lawyer. 'He really wants me to do it.' In the end Planco respected O'Toole's wishes. 'I think I sent him an email and that was it.'

Billy Foyle was at home in Clifden when he got a call that O'Toole was in town and wanted to see him. The two men had grown apart somewhat over the last few years. 'We'd sort of gone our separate ways. I wasn't socializing any more and he liked a bit of peace and quiet. So we'd met up every now and then but never went out boozing like we did in the old days.' When O'Toole saw Foyle he threw his arms around him and hugged him tightly. Foyle was shocked, O'Toole had never been the most robust of men but there was hardly anything left of him but skin and bone. 'He didn't say anything to me but I had a feeling something was wrong because he looked terrible.'

As the two men walked slowly along the beach they talked. It was O'Toole who brought up all the old memories. 'By this stage with me it was a bore – the drinks we drank, the songs we sang and the fights we had. I was tired of it all but we sat and remembered the old times. We talked about that first night he arrived in the town and how I'd helped him and how grateful he was. And when we parted that day with a hug I could see the tears in his eyes. Now, Peter wasn't that emotional, he didn't show his emotions, but I saw the tears that day when we parted. I think he knew then he wasn't coming back. I think that's why he wanted to see me.'

In the last few months of his life O'Toole was a virtual recluse, seeing people only in the company of Lorcan. The faithful Lucy was still around and his daughters were never far from his side. As he became frailer and too difficult to care for at home, he was moved to the Wellington Hospital in St John's Wood where on 14 December 2013 he passed away; his body had finally given up on him. As arrangements were made for his funeral he lay in the same morgue as Ronnie Biggs, the great train robber, who died a few days later.

The wake was anything but a sombre occasion, remembers Martin Bell, who gate-crashed the event. 'It was celebratory.' And a proper old Irish wake with people playing the fiddle and having a few jars and sharing stories and memories. At one point O'Toole's devoted cat Sydney jumped into the open coffin and sat on his master's chest for the whole evening as people passed by paying their last respects.

By contrast the funeral service at Golders Green crematorium was low key, with just family and close friends in attendance, including Siân Phillips, to the surprise of many. In rehearsals for a play when the news of O'Toole's death was announced, Siân felt she had no alternative but to go. 'It was a big shock when he died,' she told the press. 'I somehow thought he would be there for ever.'

Lorcan and his mother Karen Somerville also attended, as did Kate and Patricia. Addressing the congregation with a eulogy, Kate said: 'The world has lost a great actor, but I'm not concerned with that. I simply have lost a great dad and the best friend I ever had. Daddy made me laugh more than anyone else I have ever met in my life. He was always there for me in times of crisis and frequently danced with me in times of joy and celebration.' When Noël Coward's 'Someday I'll Find You' was played at the end of the service, Kate and Patricia waltzed down the aisle together to the delight of the other mourners, in much the same way O'Toole himself had celebrated the life of his mother by waltzing in the chapel at her funeral.

In accordance with his last wish, O'Toole's ashes were scattered on Eyrephort Beach near the home in Clifden where he spent some of the happiest times of his life.

O'Toole was once asked what he might like written on his headstone. He didn't have to think long. It arrived early in his life, in the sixties when he owned an old leather jacket of which he was inordinately fond. It was covered in Guinness, blood, you name it. One day Siân had had enough and sent it to the cleaners. It came back and pinned on it was a large notice: 'Sycamore Cleaners. It distresses us to return work which is not perfect.' O'Toole thought that was ideal for his final message. While in the end he never had a headstone, you can't deny it stands as a fitting epitaph.

BIBLIOGRAPHY

Peter O'Toole: A Biography by Michael Freedland (W. H. Allen, 1983)

Peter O'Toole by Nicholas Wapshott (New English Library, 1983)

A Divided Life by Bryan Forbes (William Heinemann, 1992)

What's It All About? by Michael Caine (Random House, 1992)

Loitering with Intent by Peter O'Toole (Pan Macmillan, 1993)

The Making of David Lean's Lawrence of Arabia by Adrian Turner (Dragon's World, 1994)

Power Play: The Life and Times of Peter Hall by Stephan Fay (Hodder & Stoughton, 1995)

Denholm Elliott: Quest For Love by Susan Elliott with Barry Turner (Headline, 1995)

Loitering with Intent: The Apprentice by Peter O'Toole (Pan Macmillan, 1996)

Making an Exhibition of Myself: The Autobiography of Peter Hall (Oberon Books, 2000)

Public Places: The Autobiography by Siân Phillips (Hodder and Stoughton, 2001)

Alec Guinness: The Authorised Biography by Piers Paul Read (Simon and Schuster, 2003)

Dirk Bogarde: The Authorised Biography by John Coldstream (Orion, 2004)

Hal Wallis: Producer to the Stars by Bernard F. Dick (University Press of Kentucky, 2004)

And the Stars Spoke Back by Frawley Becker (Scarecrow Press, 2004)

Acting My Life by Ian Holm (Bantam Press, 2004)

Ned Sherrin: The Autobiography (Sphere, 2006)

Beyond The Epic: The Life and Films of David Lean by Gene D. Phillips (University Press of Kentucky, 2006)

Huston, We Have a Problem: A Kaleidoscope of Filmmaking Memories by Oswald Morris (Rowman & Littlefield Education, 2006)

Otto Preminger: The Man Who Would be King by Foster Hirsch (Knopf, 2007)

David Lean: Interviews edited by Steven Organ (University Press of Mississippi, 2009)

Who's Going to Look at You?: My Journey from 'no Hope Street' to Coronation Street by Mark Eden (Matador, 2010)

As Much As I Can: Peter Glenville's Very British Life by Carol King (Peter Glenville Foundation, 2010)

Sir John Gielgud: A Life in Letters edited by Richard Mangan (Arcade Publishing, 2011)

The Richard Burton Diaries edited by Chris Williams (Yale University Press, 2012)

Down Under Milk Wood by Andrew Sinclair (Timon Films, 2014)

NOTES

PROLOGUE

xiii   **Can you believe it** author's interview with Steve Railsback.

xiii   **It's a bore** Artsbeat *New York Times* blog, 6 June 2011.

xiv   **So in the end** author's interview with Johnnie Planco.

xiv   **He had the whole of the Oscar people** author's interview with Planco.

ONE

2   **He used his Irishness** author's interview with Billy Foyle.

2   **a friend's memory** author's interview with Michael Craig.

2   **He insisted on being Irish** author's interview with Michael Craig.

2   **I thought as a boy** Marian Christy, *Arts&Entertainment*, September 1993.

3   **Jump, boy** Peter O'Toole's memoirs.

3   **which is probably now a housing estate** author's interview with Martin Bell.

3   **Everything they meant to me** email response by Steve Kenis to http://salutsunderland.com/.

4   **I'm not from the working class** Peter O'Toole's memoirs.

4   **joyful** Peter O'Toole's memoirs.

4   **My mother was my literary conscience** Peter O'Toole's memoirs.

5   **rabbit hutches** *Parkinson*, 1972.

5   **The sheenies hated the micks** Peter O'Toole's memoirs.

5   **My little mum** Peter O'Toole's memoirs.

6   **I remember looking up** Peter O'Toole's memoirs.

6   **Always where he shouldn't be** Peter O'Toole's memoirs.

7   **C'mon, son** Peter O'Toole's memoirs.

7   **When he'd come home** Peter O'Toole's memoirs.

7   **That cost me** *Parkinson*, 1972.

7   **with a mop of golden hair** Peter O'Toole's memoirs.

7   **You mention it** Peter O'Toole's memoirs.

7   **It is abusive behaviour** author's interview with Jane Merrow.

8   **flapping nuns** *Playboy* interview, 1965.

9   **I loved every second** Peter O'Toole's memoirs.

9   **Then along came Hitler** O'Toole and Roger Ebert, on-stage Q&A, Telluride film festival 2002.

9   **this profoundly strange** Peter O'Toole's memoirs.

10 **Finders keepers** Peter O'Toole's memoirs.

10 **Completely awed** Peter O'Toole's memoirs.

10 **It's one of the most incredible experiences** Peter O'Toole's memoirs.

12 **popularly elected** Peter O'Toole's memoirs.

12 **when I was a Little Lord Fauntleroy** *Rolling Stone*, 25 November 1982.

13 **a retired Christian** O'Toole described himself thus in numerous interviews, including in the *New York Times* in 2007 and a TV interview with Charlie Rose on PBS in 2008.

13 **It was abominable** TVGuide.com, 2008.

13 **They were shocked** *Playboy* interview 1965.

TWO

14 **His eye for photography** author's interview with Michael Redwood.

15 **It didn't always work** Peter O'Toole's memoirs.

15 **Peter always used to ask me out** author's interview with Barbara Taylor Bradford.

16 **He had lanky hair** author's interview with Barbara Taylor Bradford.

16 **I preferred the sea** *Parkinson*, 1972.

16 **How would you lift** Peter O'Toole's memoirs.

17 **I would stand alone** Peter O'Toole's memoirs.

17 **What was I doing** Peter O'Toole's memoirs.

18 **Well, I'm trying to be a journalist** Peter O'Toole's memoirs.

19 **a total waste** Peter O'Toole's memoirs.

19 **where it soon became clear** Peter O'Toole's memoirs.

19 **I wanted to be the event** Peter O'Toole's memoirs.

20 **But that had not been the case** Peter O'Toole's memoirs.

20 **of a delinquent fellow spirit** Peter O'Toole's memoirs.

20 **two yards and more** Peter O'Toole's memoirs.

21 **Why don't you give it a crack** Peter O'Toole's memoirs.

21 **I had been awkward** Peter O'Toole's memoirs.

21 **read aloud to myself** Peter O'Toole's memoirs.

22 **Blowing things up** British *GQ*, 2013.

22 **Did you ever find yourself** Peter O'Toole's memoirs.

23 **That's your shop** Peter O'Toole's memoirs.

23 **Indeed not** Peter O'Toole's memoirs.

24 **Peter decided upon a whim** author's interview with Richard Oliver.

24 **So there it was. My life had completely changed** Peter O'Toole's memoirs.

THREE

25 **buzzed with a confident energy** Peter O'Toole's memoirs.

25 **Though we weren't reckoned for much at the time** *New York Times*, 17 September 1972.

25 **It was because we all knew we had potential** in Robert Sellers, *Don't Let the Bastards Grind You Down* (Preface, 2011).

26 **RADA was a fairly conservative and traditional school** author's interview with Bryan Hands.

26 **That was the sort of theatre Kenneth Barnes represented** author's interview with Keith Baxter.

26 **But I think he knew talent when he saw it** author's interview with Sheila Allen.

27 **My god, what the hell does he know?** author's interview with Bryan Hands.

27 **He'd never take direction** Michael Freedland, *Peter O'Toole*.

27 **That's all right,' said the teacher** author's interview with Malcolm Rogers.

27 **Even then Peter did not suffer fools gladly** author's interview with Malcolm Rogers.

27 **I was from Wales** author's interview with Keith Baxter.

28 **When Richard Burton strutted his Bastard on to the stage** Peter O'Toole's memoirs.

28 **lift his pint with an ease** Peter O'Toole's memoirs.

28 **but though I can see and hear all this** Peter O'Toole's memoirs.

28 **as big as it was friendly** Peter O'Toole's memoirs.

29 **Not in public, my boy** Peter O'Toole's memoirs.

29 **We had to man the pump at the stern** Peter O'Toole's memoirs.

29 **Hello, Peter, which hedge did you sleep under last night** author's interview with Malcolm Rogers.

30 **O'Toole, there are no small *parts*** author's interview with Malcolm Rogers.

30 **He was the one who turned the key** Peter O'Toole's memoirs.

30 **Tristram Jellinek was in it** author's interview with Malcolm Rogers.

30 **It was a real knockabout part** author's interview with Keith Baxter.

30 **So we'd been pounding the pavement hard for two hours** author's interview with Keith Baxter.

31 **The main thing I remember about Peter** author's interview with Pauline Devaney.

31 **And a bloody bandage** author's interview with Elizabeth Harris.

31 **Really to impress Sir Kenneth** author's interview with Malcolm Rogers.

32 **And apparently O'Toole came on** author's interview with Lisa Harrow.

32 **He cut a dashing figure** author's interview with Delia Corrie.

32 **Peter was not into getting on with people** author's interview with Pauline Devaney.

32 **an embracer** author's interview with Elizabeth Harris.

33 **Richard recognized in Peter** author's interview with Elizabeth Harris.

33 **We've got to leave now, Peter, how much money have you got?** Richard Harris on *David Letterman*, 1994.

34 **When Peter or Albie were doing anything** author's interview with Elizabeth Harris.

34 **People already knew who they were** author's interview with William Gaskill.

35 **They were the two** author's interview with Malcolm Rogers.

35 **He was absolutely riveting** Michael Freedland, *Peter O'Toole*.

FOUR

36 **It always will be** Peter O'Toole's memoirs.

36 **There was so much energy pouring out from that stage** author's interview with John Cairney.

37 **We've got this young actor coming soon** author's interview with Edward Hardwicke.

37 **It said that he was related** author's interview with Edward Hardwicke.

37 **Peter said that when he first auditioned at RADA** author's interview with Edward Hardwicke.

38 **which I'm glad to say he never used on me** author's interview with John Cairney.

38 **smouldering with resentment for the aristocracy** *Washington Post*, 1978.

38 **He was so depressed** author's interview with Phyllida Law.

38 **She invited Peter and me out to lunch** author's interview with Edward Hardwicke.

38 **an extraordinary personality** author's interview with Edward Hardwicke.

39 **a whirling windmill of passion and enthusiasm** author's interview with John Cairney.

39 **long gangling legs** author's interview with John Cairney.

39 **and very much the father of the company** author's interview with Susan Engel.

40 **a real catalyst** *Los Angeles Times*, 2007.

40 **He couldn't cope with his own sexuality** author's interview with Susan Engel.

40 **What are you playing, old son** O'Toole on *The Tonight Show* in 2007.

41 **You don't mind ducking under it** O'Toole on *The Tonight Show* in 2007.

41 **That's because they were always worried** author's interview with Edward Hardwicke.

41 **He'd go to bed plastered** author's interview with Sheila Allen.

42 **We made gallons of it** Robert Sellers, *Hellraisers* (Preface, 2008).

42 **He cultivated the friendship** Michael Freedland, *Peter O'Toole*.

42 **All the other actors were little tiny mice** author's interview with Susan Engel.

43 **Nat was a big guru for Peter** author's interview with Susan Engel.

43 **I had to biff him one** author's interview with Phyllida Law.

43 **I would think that was the case** author's interview with Phyllida Law.

43 **Peter came** author's interview with Phyllida Law.

44 **I felt like singing** in Robert Sellers, *Hellraisers* (Preface, 2008).

44 **While the play itself got hammered** author's interview with Phyllida Law.

44 **What have these young actors in common?** *Encore* magazine.

44 **and somehow found wherever this bizarre place** *Independent*, 1995.

45 **I saw it for three weeks** author's interview with Susan Engel.

45 **And O'Toole has been my benchmark** *Independent*, 2009.

46 **I can't remember who wrote the script** author's interview with Susan Engel.

46 **It's all right, darling** author's interview with Susan Engel.

47 **And Peter couldn't stand this girl** author's interview with Susan Engel.

47 **He was so badly behaved at Bristol** author's interview with Phyllida Law.

48 **A young actor like he ought to be sacked** Michael Freedland, *Peter O'Toole*.

48 **This was when Peter was doing awfully well at Bristol** author's interview with Phyllida Law.

48 **Often you'd follow O'Toole** author's interview with Sheila Allen.

49 **I don't know that he really cared** author's interview with Sheila Allen.

49 **There was a quiet side to him** author's interview with Sheila Allen.

49 **Because Peter was always getting** author's interview with Patrick Dromgoole.

50 **You're just a drunken twit** author's interview with Patrick Dromgoole.

51 **He was a very striking actor** author's interview with Patrick Dromgoole.

51 **a humbling and humiliating** obituaries in the *Independent* and *New York Times*.

51 **I sat in the back of the stalls** author's interview with Sheila Allen.

52 **It was everything it was supposed to be** *Independent*, 1995.

52 **You can smell their breath** *Esquire*, 1963.

52 **Golden days** in Michael Feeney Callan, *Richard Harris: Sex, Death & the Movies: an Intimate Biography* (Robson, 2003).

52 **Nobody knew how to deal with them** author's interview with Elizabeth Harris.

FIVE

54 **'Griffith!' he yelled. 'It's got to end!** *Independent*, 1995.

54 **dazzled** Siân Phillips' autobiography.

55 **Siân once told me** author's interview with Michael Byrne.

55   **You look as though you're in mourning for your sex life** Siân Phillips' autobiography.

55   **Siân was doing her best to quieten him down** author's interview with Elizabeth Harris.

56   **Of course, Richard and Peter took great exception** author's interview with Elizabeth Harris.

56   **Peter and Richard were incredibly good looking** author's interview with Elizabeth Harris.

57   **We didn't want any of that** Robert Sellers, *Hellraisers* (Preface, 2008).

57   **Well, we were doing that in the fifties** *Night and Day*, April 2001.

58   **We'd get off at Sloane Square** *Night and Day*, April 2001.

58   **They were the two foremost actors** Oscar Lewenstein, *Kicking Against the Pricks* (Nick Hern Books, 1994).

58   **and please let it be me** Oscar Lewenstein, *Kicking Against the Pricks*.

59   **I'd been at a party** author's interview with David Andrews.

59   **After that first rehearsal** author's interview with David Andrews.

60   **the curse of middle class inhibitions** author's interview with David Andrews.

60   **too much of a star performer** author's interview with David Andrews.

60   **Lindsay's idea of the working class** author's interview with David Andrews.

60   **Peter hated Lindsay** author's interview with David Andrews.

60   **I'm furious** author's interview with David Andrews.

60   **who, in those days** author's interview with Bruce Montague.

61   **I hero-worshipped Peter** author's interview with David Andrews.

61   **My confidence growing** author's interview with David Andrews.

61   **I say, where can I find the boys** author's interview with David Andrews.

62   **They were so self-destructive** author's interview with David Tringham.

62   **We didn't want** in Robert Sellers, *Hellraisers*.

62 **We weren't pause and think** author's interview with Elizabeth Harris.

63 **When my father collected Dame Edith** author's interview with Oliver Senton.

64 **Michael began to get extremely agitated** author's interview with David Andrews.

64 **I'd have made a wonderful pimp** in Michael Caine, *What's It All About?*.

65 **This for a start was a surprise** in Michael Caine, *What's It All About?*.

66 **my first step towards becoming a star** in Michael Caine, *What's It All About?*

67 **Mr O'Toole, please, it's time** Robert Sellers, *Don't Let the Bastards Grind You Down* (Preface, 2011).

67 **Because an icy soberness** Robert Sellers, *Don't Let the Bastards Grind You Down*.

SIX

68 **I swallowed a fly** Peter O'Toole's memoirs.

69 **He also had the arrogance** in Michael Ciment, *Conversations with Losey* (Methuen, 1985).

69 **There's only one actor** in Nicholas Wapshott, *Peter O'Toole*.

69 **It never occurred to me I'd be mediocre** *New York Times*, 6 March 1966.

69 **It's how you handle those bastards** *Parkinson*.

69 **I told a lie** *Parkinson*.

70 **He and O'Toole were on the lash** *David Letterman*, 2007.

71 **As second assistant I was delegated to go** author's interview with David Tringham.

71 **O'Toole helpfully suggested** Nicholas Wapshott, *Peter O'Toole*.

72 **While Ray thought Olivier 'unbelievable'** Nicholas Ray, *I Was Interrupted: Nicholas Ray on Making Movies* (University of California Press, 1993).

72 **I don't want anything to do with it** Nicholas Wapshott, *Peter O'Toole*.

73 **Jules was very charming** author's interview with Michael Deeley.

73 **There was nothing for it** Nicholas Wapshott, *Peter O'Toole*.

73 **One friend who accepted a lift off O'Toole** Siân Phillips' autobiography.

74 **Do you just want to become** Michael Freedland, *Peter O'Toole*.

74 **It was a great nose, very sardonic** author's interview with Phyllida Law.

74 **I'm sure he wasn't** author's interview with Phyllida Law.

75 **Peter's nose was massive** author's interview with David Andrews.

75 **I was horrified and for days** Nicholas Wapshott, *Peter O'Toole*.

75 **If you don't like me** Siân Phillips' autobiography.

75 **Get your passport** Siân Phillips' autobiography.

76 **You cannot marry** Siân Phillips' autobiography.

76 **I was so deliriously in love** Siân Phillips' autobiography.

76 **Have my children** Siân Phillips' autobiography.

SEVEN

78 **Not in a grand way** author's interview with Donald Douglas.

78 **by a delicate** Peter Hall, *Making an Exhibition of Myself*.

78 **I'm going to be a film star** Peter Hall, *Making an Exhibition of Myself*.

78 **Not asleep** Michael Freedland, *Peter O'Toole*.

80 **He brought tremendous naturalism** author's interview with Donald Douglas.

80 **mesmeric** Peter Hall, *Making an Exhibition of Myself*.

80 **O'Toole's is still the best Shylock** author's interview with Derek Fowlds.

80 **On several occasions** author's interview with Stephen Thorne.

80 **He'd quickly drop the robe** author's interview with Donald Douglas.

81 **One of his best pranks** author's interview with Philip Bond.

81 **For the younger and impressionable** author's interview with Stephen Thorne.

82 **Take for example the party** author's interview with Stephen Thorne.

82 **That didn't go down very well with Peter** author's interview with Stephen Thorne.

83 **I get awfully nervous** Susan Elliott with Barry Turner, *Denholm Elliott: Quest for Love*.

83 **Probably because he was so melodramatically different** Ian Holm, *Acting My Life*.

84 **I remember one evening** author's interview with Stephen Thorne.

84 **Playing Shylock one night** Robert Sellers, *Hellraisers* (Preface, 2008).

84 **a bad side** Siân Phillips' autobiography.

84 **clever women never nagged** Siân Phillips' autobiography.

85 **They had this almighty row** author's interview with Gary Raymond.

85 **I think Peter Hall was a bit nonplussed** author's interview with Stephen Thorne.

85 **The BBC even sent an interviewer down to profile this rising star** Robert Sellers, *Hellraisers*.

86 **One great Peggy story** author's interview with Susan Engel.

86 **Peter became difficult** author's interview with Stephen Thorne.

86 **She was in love with him** author's interview with Susan Engel.

86 **Full of hell raiser energy** author's interview with Donald Douglas.

86 **He had this sort of force field** author's interview with Stephen Thorne.

87 **took forty quid off her in blackjack** Nicholas Wapshott, *Peter O'Toole*.

88 **I don't think he was particularly happy** author's interview with Donald Douglas.

88 **I couldn't make the words** Nicholas Wapshott, *Peter O'Toole*.

88 **In the old days** author's interview with Stephen Thorne.

EIGHT

91 **my bitterest disappointment** Adrian Turner, *The Making of David Lean's Lawrence of Arabia*.

91 **I started to spend all of my days** Steven Organ (ed.), *David Lean: interviews*.

93 **I've forgotten who they were** Steven Organ (ed.), *David Lean: interviews*.

93 **When Jules heard that Finney's people** author's interview with Michael Deeley.

93 **There is also a story of O'Toole being rushed over to New York** Robert Sellers, *Hellraisers* (Preface, 2008).

94 **walk and let them sue you** Adrian Turner, *Robert Bolt: scenes from two lives* (Hutchinson, 1998).

94 **So Peter nearly wrecked the start of the RSC** Adrian Turner, *Robert Bolt* (Hutchinson, 1998).

94 **Still friends?** author's interview with William Gaskill.

96 **Look, if you don't stay sober** in Gene D. Phillips, *Beyond The Epic: The Life and Films of David Lean*.

96 **Peter sniffed a battle** Nicholas Wapshott, *Peter O'Toole*.

96 **But within a month** *TIME*, 6 February 1989.

96 **All that you can do is to find a beast** O'Toole interview, TCM film festival.

96 **delicate Irish arse** *Esquire*, 1963.

97 **O'Toole walked in with a welcoming smile** author's interview with Zia Mohyeddin.

97 **Around mid-day I suggested** author's interview with Zia Mohyeddin.

97 **Peter was already claiming** author's interview with Zia Mohyeddin.

98 **Peter read out his lines** author's interview with Zia Mohyeddin.

98 **You could see plump ladies** author's interview with Zia Mohyeddin.

98 **I collapsed once simply** author's interview with Tony Rimmington.

99 **David Lean was a bit perturbed** author's interview with Zia Mohyeddin.

99 **Ask Zia, he has been conducting** author's interview with Zia Mohyeddin.

99 **All the Arab workers knew him** author's interview with David Tringham.

99 **Tringham stood and watched** author's interview with David Tringham.

100 **Your name must be Fred** author's interview with David Tringham.

100 **He was fond of holding forth** author's interview with Zia Mohyeddin.

100 **She was a remarkably self-possessed lady** author's interview with Zia Mohyeddin.

100 **Siân began to recite the famous Dylan Thomas poem** author's interview with Zia Mohyeddin.

100 **You do it, Peter** author's interview with Zia Mohyeddin.

101 **Pete, this is the beginning of a great adventure** Gene D. Phillips, *Beyond The Epic*.

101 **Peter takes a gulp from his canteen** author's interview with Zia Mohyeddin.

101 **I think you'll like your work** author's interview with Zia Mohyeddin.

102 **And you never questioned** author's interview with David Tringham.

102 **David was very intense with Peter** author's interview with David Tringham.

103 **Lean shot it several ways** author's interview with David Tringham.

103 **What do you think a young man would do** author's interview with David Tringham.

103 **There used to be much merriment** author's interview with Tony Rimmington.

104 **He has great wayward charm** Piers Paul Read, *Alec Guinness: The Authorised Biography*.

104 **O'Toole got drunk** Piers Paul Read, *Alec Guinness*.

104 **Here, you have to be a little mad** Siân Phillips' autobiography.

104 **It was like being** Robert Sellers, *Hellraisers*.

105 **His knuckles were in a terrible mess** author's interview with Tony Rimmington.

105 **We misbehaved ourselves appallingly** *Night & Day*, April 2001.

105 **We once did about nine months' wages** *Night & Day*, April 2001.

106 **I want to find out who that is** author's interview with Tony Rimmington.

106 **had to be dragged screaming from his caravan** Gene D. Phillips, *Beyond The Epic*.

106 **OK, Skip. Let's go to the station** Nicholas Wapshott, *Peter O'Toole*.

106 **You're not supposed** Nicholas Wapshott, *Peter O'Toole*.

NINE

107 **Pontefract with scorpions** *Daily Telegraph*, 16 December 2013.

107 **chaos** O'Toole interview, TCM film festival.

107 **What are you doing** O'Toole interview, TCM film festival.

108 **It was quite funny** author's interview with David Tringham.

108 **He had this fabulous looking Mexican girl** author's interview with David Tringham.

109 **I was fucked by some Turks** Gene D. Phillips, *Beyond The Epic: The Life and Films of David Lean*.

109 **The fact that we used to have some rousing sessions together** Gene D. Phillips, *Beyond The Epic*.

109 **I left feeling dreadful** *Chicago Sun-Times*, 2002.

110 **Anything he saw** Gene D. Phillips, *Beyond The Epic*.

110 **I'd love a Martini** author's interview with Johnnie Planco.

111 **It was some kind of pure alcohol** author's interview with Johnnie Planco.

111 **And David just shot it** *TIME*, 6 February 1989.

111 **The fucking picture's finished** author's interview with David Tringham.

113 **Daddy, Daddy! I broke my eyes** Michael Freedland, *Peter O'Toole*.

113 **I haven't got a penny** *Daily Express*, 1963.

113 **As in I keep what I earn** Michael Freedland, *Peter O'Toole*.

114 **Come on, mush** Siân Phillips' autobiography.

TEN

121 **He was a very dashing person** author's interview with William Gaskill.

121 **This show is cursed** author's interview with William Gaskill.

122 **It was an extraordinary production** author's interview with Gemma Jones.

122 **Guinevere Roberts was her name** author's interview with Gemma Jones.

122 **If you could keep awake** author's interview with David Andrews.

123 **I went with a mate of mine** *The David Letterman Show*.

123 **I went up to the north of England** *The David Letterman Show*.

123 **the greatest potential force** obituaries, *Daily Telegraph* and *Stage*.

123 **It was that wonderful moment** author's interview with William Gaskill.

124 **People were fired** Siân Phillips' autobiography.

125 **Fixing me** Carol King, *As Much As I Can: Peter Glenville's Very British Life*.

125 **Full of nervous energy** Carol King, *As Much As I Can*.

125 **He is not a young man** Carol King, *As Much As I Can*.

125 **intolerably demanding** Carol King, *As Much As I Can*.

126 **For this I do not blame him** Carol King, *As Much As I Can*.

126 **He looked like a beautiful, emaciated secretary bird** *LIFE*, 13 March 1964.

126 **Peter, me boy** Melvyn Bragg, *Rich: The Life of Richard Burton* (Hodder & Stoughton, 1988).

126 **It was rather like trying to thread a needle** Melvyn Bragg, *Rich*.

127 **Now is the winter of our discontent** Melvyn Bragg, *Rich*.

127 **It's an Irish birthday** *Down Under Milk Wood* (Timon Films, 2014) © Andrew Sinclair.

127 **Brian Trenchard-Smith remembers** author's interview with Brian Trenchard-Smith.

128 **We laboured like lunatics** Nicholas Wapshott, *Peter O'Toole*.

128 **sophisticated, well informed and hard working** Carol King, *As Much As I Can*.

129 **the disciplined old-fashioned way** Carol King, *As Much As I Can*.

129 **Practically everything the scriptwriter put in** *New York Times*, 6 March 1966.

129 **I wasn't sure if this was a pose** Siân Phillips' autobiography.

130 **but the noise and the destruction terrified me** Siân Phillips' autobiography.

130 **Do you really think** Siân Phillips' autobiography.

ELEVEN

131 **If you want to know what it's like** *Guardian*, March 2003.

131 **Let's be masochists** *New York Times*, 6 March 1966.

132 **the whole place was still littered with rubble** Robert Sellers, *Hellraisers* (Preface, 2008).

132 **Peter was like the young buck** author's interview with Rosemary Harris.

133 **Why should I be the only man** Nicholas Wapshott, *Peter O'Toole*.

133 **I mean, he's done it** *Playboy*, 1965.

133 **I know my way about the map** author's interview with William Gaskill.

133 **He tried to make O'Toole** author's interview with William Gaskill.

133 **Peter wasn't too keen** author's interview with Rosemary Harris.

133 **a tiny, strange** British *GQ*, 2013.

133 **So the actors came on** author's interview with William Gaskill.

134 **a God with bright blonde hair** *Guardian*, March 2003.

134 **People were very** author's interview with Terence Knapp.

134 **Olivier grabbed O'Toole** author's interview with William Gaskill.

134 **I don't understand why Peter was criticized** author's interview with Peter Cellier.

134 **O'Toole was a smashing Hamlet** *Arena*, BBC4, 2013.

134 **a pale shadow** Siân Phillips' autobiography.

135 **I think the critics felt** author's interview with William Gaskill.

135 **It was a very clever idea** author's interview with Rosemary Harris.

135 **I was on the ceiling** *Playboy*, 1965.

135 **an amusing lapse** author's interview with Rosemary Harris.

136 **We used to have lovely chats** author's interview with Rosemary Harris.

136 **I was fighting, literally** *Arena*, BBC4, 2013.

137 **It was very long and Peter wasn't very good** author's interview with Malcolm Rogers.

137 **Spun gold** author's interview with Malcolm Rogers.

137 **So we didn't have to discuss his performance** author's interview with Gary Raymond.

137 **This was the beginning of the National Theatre** author's interview with Peter Cellier.

137 **I must say I took to Peter enormously** author's interview with Terence Knapp.

138 **One night after the performance** author's interview with Terence Knapp.

138 **Another anecdote has the actor Tony Selby** author's interview with Stephen Thorne.

139 **Of course, I think it's the worst bloody play** Nicholas Wapshott, *Peter O'Toole*.

139 **I'd put them all to bed** author's interview with Rosemary Harris.

139 **I said afterwards** author's interview with Rosemary Harris.

140 **The next bloody day** *Life*, 22 January 1964.

140 **carrying a pint of bitter** *Life*, 22 January 1964.

140 **Manchester with slanted eyes** *Life*, 22 January 1964.

141 **He'd rush to the side of the ship** *Life*, 22 January 1964.

141 **That hotel** *Life*, 22 January 1964.

141 **They say no snake can travel faster** *Life*, 22 January 1964.

141 **It bites you** *Life*, 22 January 1964.

142 **a lunatic in the middle of the jungle** Douglass K. Daniel, *Tough as Nails: The Life and Films of Richard Brooks* (University of Wisconsin Press, 2011).

142 **He started yelling the usual anti-British crud** *Life*, 22 January 1964.

142 **Western imperialist invaders** *Life*, 22 January 1964.

142 **If I live to be a thousand** *Life*, 22 January 1964.

142 **I can't believe all that tonnage can float in the air** *Playboy*, 1965.

143 **I came home in a box** *Playboy*, 1965.

143 **We'd left Japan on Monday** *The Johnny Carson Show*, 1978.

143 **I was in danger of becoming known** Nicholas Wapshott, *Peter O'Toole*.

144 **I like having money** *New York Times*, 6 March 1966.

144 **A splendid throne was dragged out of the props room** author's interview with Richard Oliver.

144 **Now, my father was** author's interview with Richard Oliver.

TWELVE

146 **Pete, this is a day for getting drunk** *Chicago Sun-Times*, 2002.

146 **John in his green kimono** *Chicago Sun-Times*, 2002.

147 **he joked to Huston** Nicholas Wapshott, *Peter O'Toole*.

149 **I think he knows *Lear* in his bones** *Playboy*, 1965.

149 **but I would rather suppress his exhibitionism** Adrian Turner, *Robert Bolt: scenes from two lives* (Hutchinson, 1998).

150 **Warren and Woody thought** author's interview with Clive Donner.

150 **write something where we can all go to Paris and chase girls** author's interview with Clive Donner.

150 **Warren and Charlie were very good friends** author's interview with Clive Donner.

150 **How about O'Toole?** author's interview with Clive Donner.

150 **For what was farce** Nicholas Wapshott, *Peter O'Toole*.

151 **Let Sellers have what he wants** author's interview with Clive Donner.

151 **It was sometimes downright edgy** Ed Sikov, *Mr Strangelove: A Biography of Peter Sellers* (Sidgwick & Jackson, 2002).

152 **By the time I'd finished with him** Nicholas Wapshott, *Peter O'Toole*.

152 **There was a big chair** author's interview with Bruce Montague.

153 **O'Toole actually "fed" me** Siân Phillips' autobiography.

153 **From then on things** author's interview with Mark Eden.

153 **Peter was there waiting for me** author's interview with Mark Eden.

153 **I like being around men** Robert Sellers, *Hellraisers* (Preface, 2008).

156 **refused entry by the captain** *Sunday Telegraph* magazine, 1980.

156 **We were silly and young and drunken** *Entertainment Weekly*, 2001.

156 **Evenings with Peter** Adrian Turner, *Robert Bolt*.

156 **a deep philosophical attitude** author's interview with Sheila Allen.

157 **If you wanted to be a proper actor** *USA Today*, 2007.

157 **the common man** author's interview with Frawley Becker.

158 **a drunk** author's interview with Frawley Becker.

158 **But whatever he did in the evening** author's interview with Frawley Becker.

158 **I give Peter three more years** author's interview with Frawley Becker.

159 **This must be what death feels like** author's interview with Frawley Becker.

159 **Why don't we go back to the original** author's interview with Frawley Becker.

160 **Spiegel will die** Andrew Sinclair, *Spiegel: The Man Behind the Pictures* (Weidenfeld & Nicolson, 1987).

161 **If anyone goes** author's interview with Frawley Becker.

161 **He put his arm around me** author's interview with Frawley Becker.

161 **Everyone went still** author's interview with Frawley Becker.

THIRTEEN

164 **The thought of Peter O'Toole on his hands and knees** *Guardian*, 2013.

164 **One afternoon she raised the issue** Siân Phillips' autobiography.

165 **intermittently ecstatic or unbelievably dreadful** Siân Phillips' autobiography.

165 **My father decreed** politico.ie, 2007.

165 **I lock myself away for a month** *New York Times* blog, 2011.

167 **I didn't want to become** Michael Freedland, *Peter O'Toole*.

167 **If it's going to be wrong** Michael Freedland, *Peter O'Toole*.

168 **I might as well do it** O'Toole interview, TCM film festival.

168 **I don't quite know** author's interview with Anthony Harvey.

169 **Do you think** author's interview with Anthony Harvey.

170 **I don't believe a word** author's interview with Jane Merrow.

170 **There was something about being** author's interview with Anthony Harvey.

170 **was always rolling** author's interview with Anthony Harvey.

170 **I know I had a crush** author's interview with Jane Merrow.

171 **Harvey remembers** author's interview with Anthony Harvey.

171 **And Peter was no exception** author's interview with Jane Merrow.

171 **Hello, pig** author's interview with Anthony Harvey.

171 **When O'Toole kept her waiting** author's interview with Anthony Harvey.

172 **Jane explains what happened next** author's interview with Jane Merrow.

172 **Many of us were** Telluride Film Festival, 2002.

172 **I thought he was** author's interview with Anthony Harvey.

172 **About two in the morning** author's interview with Anthony Harvey.

173 **That was one of the conditions** author's interview with Jane Merrow.

173 **Jane herself can recall** author's interview with Jane Merrow.

173 **One night Nigel Stock** Quentin Falk, *Anthony Hopkins: The Biography* (Virgin, 2004).

173 **Bloody agony it was** Robert Sellers, *Hellraisers* (Preface, 2008).

174 **At first I tried to put the thing out** *Guardian*, 2013.

174 **The gloves are off** author's interview with Anthony Harvey.

174 **The problem was keeping a straight face** Nicholas Wapshott, *Peter O'Toole*.

174 **I never enjoyed** author's interview with Anthony Harvey.

174 **Bliss** author's interview with Jane Merrow.

174 disgraceful conduct Michael Freedland, *Peter O'Toole*.

175 It was an amazing performance author's interview with Roger Young.

176 It's always a little tricky author's interview with Petula Clark.

177 After dinner word must have got out author's interview with Petula Clark.

177 Although when I went out with Peter author's interview with Petula Clark.

177 I thought he pulled it off author's interview with Petula Clark.

177 Every morning I would see him drinking author's interview with Petula Clark.

178 As usual, the meal turned into a boisterous occasion author's interview with Petula Clark.

178 He was always trying to get his hands on author's interview with Petula Clark.

179 I had the feeling author's interview with Petula Clark.

179 That's how we felt about each other author's interview with Petula Clark.

179 That was the real Peter author's interview with Petula Clark.

179 I don't think he was in great health author's interview with Petula Clark.

FOURTEEN

181 And this big, tall, lanky author's interview with Billy Foyle.

183 You know we're not going to make Michael Freedland, *Peter O'Toole*.

184 We had to rejig the shooting author's interview with Michael Craig.

185 We were standing there Chris Williams (ed.), *The Richard Burton Diaries*.

185 To be quite honest author's interview with Phyllida Law.

185 The finest thing I've ever seen Michael Freedland, *Peter O'Toole*.

185 Siân remembers one extraordinary episode Siân Phillips' autobiography.

186 Because of one's fear author's interview with Michael Deeley.

187 **It was a dangerous location** author's interview with Michael Deeley.

187 **The fella who was driving the boat** author's interview with Michael Deeley.

187 **Peter was the absolute soul** author's interview with Michael Deeley.

188 **We had a few more drinks** *Tonight Show*, 2007.

189 **who clearly decided** *Tonight Show*, 2007.

189 **We drank every single drop** *Tonight Show*, 2007.

190 **Yates had this passion** author's interview with Michael Deeley.

191 **Finally, one night we came back** author's interview with Peter Medak.

191 **They wanted him to do** author's interview with Peter Medak.

191 **I remember the plane for some reason** author's interview with Peter Medak.

192 **We were having lunch** author's interview with Peter Medak.

192 **They all involved bars** author's interview with Carolyn Seymour.

192 **He gave me everything** author's interview with Carolyn Seymour.

192 **But in those days everybody was drinking** author's interview with Peter Medak.

193 **That is the measure of his talent** author's interview with Carolyn Seymour.

193 **Peter was incredibly intelligent and bright** author's interview with Peter Medak.

193 **O'Toole was one in a million** author's interview with Carolyn Seymour.

193 **All the Sloane ranger types** author's interview with Carolyn Seymour.

195 **O'Toole sang songs all night** *Down Under Milk Wood* (Timon Films, 2014) © Andrew Sinclair.

195 **And once he heard O'Toole was on board** author's interview with Andrew Sinclair.

195 **Andrew, you're a lucky bastard** *Down Under Milk Wood* (Timon Films, 2014) © Andrew Sinclair.

196 **I am not drinking on your film** *Down Under Milk Wood* (Timon Films, 2014) © Andrew Sinclair.

196 **If he had not been capable** *Down Under Milk Wood* (Timon Films, 2014) © Andrew Sinclair.

196 **In the middle of a line** *Down Under Milk Wood* (Timon Films, 2014) © Andrew Sinclair.

197 **That won't do** *Down Under Milk Wood* (Timon Films, 2014) © Andrew Sinclair.

197 **You've lost your filum, Andrew** *Down Under Milk Wood* (Timon Films, 2014) © Andrew Sinclair.

197 **So off they went** author's interview with Andrew Sinclair.

198 **And irrepressible** *Down Under Milk Wood* (Timon Films, 2014) © Andrew Sinclair.

198 **Why's that?** Robert Sellers, *Hellraisers* (Preface, 2008).

198 **And then we'd carry the other home** *Esquire*, 2007.

199 **'Elizabeth,' said Burton** *Esquire*, 2007.

199 **I was thrown out of the car** author's interview with Andrew Sinclair.

199 **I didn't do very much directing** author's interview with Arthur Hiller.

199 **About ten minutes into the first act** author's interview with Arthur Hiller.

200 **One afternoon, as the cameraman was setting up a shot** author's interview with Arthur Hiller.

201 **No, we don't need you** author's interview with Arthur Hiller.

202 **I couldn't work for eight months** author's interview with Arthur Hiller.

202 **he never even saw the film** author's interview with Arthur Hiller.

202 **The business is run by the cornflakes men** Nicholas Wapshott, *Peter O'Toole*.

203 **twenty years of it in one uninterrupted lump** Nicholas Wapshott, *Peter O'Toole*.

FIFTEEN

204 **Foyle will never forget one occasion** author's interview with Billy Foyle.

204 **And really he shouldn't have got planning permission** author's interview with Billy Foyle.

204 **Plants must be sturdy** *Playboy*, 1982.

205 **They had swimming pools** politico.ie, 2007.

205 **There was a coldness** author's interview with Billy Foyle.

205 **Peter rarely talked about his personal life** author's interview with Johnnie Planco.

206 **You could go in and out** author's interview with Billy Foyle.

206 **I don't attend either** *Playboy*, 1982.

206 **After a while** author's interview with Billy Foyle.

206 **We had some jolly old evenings** author's interview with Billy Foyle.

207 **Mummy, Daddy** author's interview with Billy Foyle.

207 **Pete Postlethwaite was called out from class** author's interview with Oliver Senton.

208 **I imagine that he might have been** author's interview with Sara Kestelman.

208 **In the rehearsal room** author's interview with Sara Kestelman.

209 **It was a completely brilliant** author's interview with Sara Kestelman.

209 **He would humiliate him** author's interview with Sara Kestelman.

209 **But I wasn't expecting O'Toole** author's interview with Sara Kestelman.

210 **Certainly there were little liaisons** author's interview with Sara Kestelman.

210 **He was maddening** author's interview with Sara Kestelman.

210 **He was a star** author's interview with Sara Kestelman.

210 **He saved our bacon** Michael Freedland, *Peter O'Toole*.

211 **Hell, that's like** Robert Sellers, *Hellraisers* (Preface, 2008).

211 **Looking totally dissipated** Foster Hirsch, *Otto Preminger: The Man Who Would Be King*.

212 **This was the height of the bombings** *Observer*, 2007.

212 **Or the script** author's interview with Erik Preminger.

213 **Otto loved British actors** author's interview with Erik Preminger.

213 **I remember though Peter rubbing the back of my neck** author's interview with Erik Preminger.

213 **Peter came with a fully realized portrait** author's interview with Jack Gold.

214 **We used to do some of his old routines** author's interview with Jack Gold.

214 **He was old and arthritic** author's interview with Jack Gold.

214 **It wasn't intelligent white man** author's interview with Jack Gold.

215 **It also had to have** author's interview with Jack Gold.

SIXTEEN

216 **Hey, don't do that** Michael Freedland, *Peter O'Toole*.

217 **I suggested they put in a zip** Nicholas Wapshott, *Peter O'Toole*.

217 **hovered between life and death** Siân Phillips' autobiography.

217 **He'll outlive us all** Siân Phillips' autobiography.

218 **It was a photo-finish** Nicholas Wapshott, *Peter O'Toole*.

218 **'You know,' he said, 'I've got to tell** author's interview with Barbara Carrera.

218 **The pirate ship has berthed** *Independent*, 13 February 1998.

218 **It was all becoming a bore** *People*, 1987.

219 **We both smoked Gauloises** author's interview with Michael Craig.

219 **He idolized O'Toole** author's interview with Billy Foyle.

220 **Poor McCann was very upset** author's interview with Billy Foyle.

SEVENTEEN

222 **It depends what sort of mood** Michael Freedland, *Peter O'Toole*.

222 **all right** Michael Freedland, *Peter O'Toole*.

223 **Peter found that** author's interview with Michael Byrne.

224 **Before a take** author's interview with Michael Byrne.

224 **I'm seeing a Mrs Jones** author's interview with Michael Byrne.

225 **about as popular** Nicholas Wapshott, *Peter O'Toole*.

225 **Hello, Johnny** Malcolm McDowell interview, *Guardian*, 2013.

225 **Peter was smoking** Malcolm McDowell interview, *Guardian*, 2013.

225 **Are they doing the Irish jig** Malcolm McDowell interview, *Guardian*, 2013.

225 **But by this time** Malcolm McDowell interview, *Guardian*, 2013.

226 **How you like to be** Nicholas Wapshott, *Peter O'Toole*.

226 **He doesn't drink any more** *Penthouse*, May 1980.

226 **As for being erotic** Robert Sellers, *Hellraisers* (Preface, 2008).

226 **gulf that had opened** Siân Phillips' autobiography.

227 **I never remember seeing them together** author's interview with Elizabeth Harris.

227 **O'Toole prided himself** Siân Phillips' autobiography.

227 **He respected people** author's interview with Jane Merrow.

227 **Ooh, I was a hopeless husband** *Night & Day*, April 2001.

228 **dangerous, disruptive** *Observer*, 2001.

228 **He did and does** *Irish Times*, 2001.

228 **I think probably my mother and father** *Rolling Stone*, 25 November 1982.

229 **Heartbreak House** Nicholas Wapshott, *Peter O'Toole*.

229 **They took him to hospital** Peter O'Toole's memoirs.

229 **He talked about Siân** author's interview with Martyn Burke.

230 **But the odd thing was** author's interview with Martyn Burke.

230 **He was despondent** author's interview with Martyn Burke.

230 **Darling, I hope you always get your man** author's interview with Martyn Burke.

230 **electrifying** author's interview with Martyn Burke.

230 **There was something in Peter** author's interview with Martyn Burke.

231 **We went into this room** author's interview with Martyn Burke.

232 **It threw him several times** author's interview with Nate Kohn.

232 **He was among the most intelligent actors** author's interview with Nate Kohn.

233 **Something about removing his spleen** author's interview with Nate Kohn.

233 **I thought, three months of this tour** author's interview with Nonnie Griffin.

234 **The prospect of staying** author's interview with Nonnie Griffin.

EIGHTEEN

235 **He defined the outer limits** author's interview with Richard Rush.

235 **At the beginning you recognize him** author's interview with Richard Rush.

235 **But I never brought up the screenplay** author's interview with Richard Rush.

236 **It was not easy casting Peter** author's interview with Richard Rush.

236 **You couldn't ask** author's interview with Richard Rush.

236 **When you work with somebody like a Peter O'Toole** author's interview with Steve Railsback.

236 **That night I went to my trailer** author's interview with Steve Railsback.

237 **And that man could tell a story** author's interview with Steve Railsback.

237 **And I would get up** author's interview with Steve Railsback.
We couldn't wait to get to work author's interview with Steve Railsback.

237 **One day Peter came to me and said** author's interview with Richard Rush.

237 **Mostly the magic** author's interview with Richard Rush.

237 **And the Americans were very health conscious** author's interview with Peter Strauss.

239 **Once he meandered off** author's interview with Peter Strauss.

239 **Peter was not an actor you got close to on the set** author's interview with Peter Strauss.

239 **And I was blown away** author's interview with Barbara Carrera.

240 **Did they get to you yesterday?** author's interview with Barbara Carrera.

240 **mentor** author's interview with Barbara Carrera.

241 **This scene is a close-up** author's interview with Barbara Carrera.

241 **And you know, Barbara** author's interview with Barbara Carrera.

241 **Mr O'Toole, Miss Carrera** author's interview with Barbara Carrera.

242 **At the end of perhaps their most pivotal scene together** author's interview with Peter Strauss.

NINETEEN

243 **Frawley Becker, the dialogue coach, remembers** author's interview with Frawley Becker.

244 **All working for buttons** *Sunday Telegraph* magazine, 1980.

245 **Peter was very much his own man** author's interview with Jack Gold.

245 **In the last analysis** Bryan Forbes, *A Divided Life*.

246 **To a great extent** Bryan Forbes, *A Divided Life*.

246 **It was like listening to a mature public schoolboy** author's interview with Kevin Quarmby.

246 **Peter did his soliloquies** author's interview with Christopher Fulford.

246 **I can still hear him** author's interview with Kevin Quarmby.

247 **Right, now Kevin** author's interview with Kevin Quarmby.

248 **Let's say he was sailing** author's interview with Kevin Quarmby.

248 **He was stoned out of his mind** author's interview with Susan Engel.

248 **Do you know how many times** Bryan Forbes, *A Divided Life*.

248 **What you need is some Kensington gore** Bryan Forbes, *A Divided Life*.

248 **This guy would have killed anyone for Peter** author's interview with Kevin Quarmby.

249 **He was very genial to me** author's interview with Christopher Fulford.

249 **You should be looking at me** author's interview with Kevin Quarmby.

249 **It was an inevitable car crash** author's interview with Kevin Quarmby.

249 **It was an imbalance** Bryan Forbes, *A Divided Life*.

250 **We had chilli con carne** author's interview with Christopher Fulford.

250 **would provoke an explosion** Bryan Forbes, *A Divided Life*.

250 **Peter, old son** Bryan Forbes, *A Divided Life*.

251 **In the wings** author's interview with Kevin Quarmby.

252 **In my view** author's interview with Kevin Dromgoole.

252 **What's it like to be laughed at** author's interview with Patrick Dromgoole.

252 **I view it almost like** author's interview with Kevin Quarmby.

253 **There was a real sense** author's interview with Kevin Quarmby.

253 **It was farcically** author's interview with Kevin Quarmby.

253 **In a cry for help** author's interview with Patrick Dromgoole.

254 **I've forgotten how to do it** author's interview with Patrick Dromgoole.

254 **If you're going to have a disaster** Robert Sellers, *Hellraisers* (Preface, 2008).

254 **I hear you've had a bit of stick** Melvyn Bragg, *Rich: The Life of Richard Burton* (Hodder & Stoughton, 1988).

254 **The word was that Nat** author's interview with Kevin Quarmby.

255 **When I had my moments on stage with him** author's interview with Christopher Fulford.

255 **Absolutely, no problem** author's interview with Christopher Fulford.

255 **all right** author's interview with Christopher Fulford.

256 **One really just felt so bloody relieved** author's interview with Patrick Quarmby.

256 **My nose starts bleeding** *Night & Day*, April 2001.

256 **For I admire nothing more** Bryan Forbes, *A Divided Life*.

TWENTY

257 **It didn't fit into the wrapper** author's interview with Richard Rush.

258 **I love company** *Rolling Stone*, 25 November 1982.

259 **Albert read it and said** author's interview with Michael Gruskoff.

259 **Peter, er, it's really good** avclub.com, 2012.

259 **Peter very kindly** author's interview with Mark Linn Baker.

260 **Michael, we simply can't do this** author's interview with Michael Gruskoff.

260 **He must be a real Method actor** author's interview with Michael Gruskoff.

260 **I'm going to his hotel** author's interview with Michael Gruskoff.

261 **Peter got immediately sick** author's interview with Mark Linn Baker.

261 **Dear boy, there's only two things to remember** author's interview with Mark Linn Baker.

261 **He made the movie what it is** author's interview with Michael Gruskoff.

262 **You need money to win an Oscar** author's interview with Michael Gruskoff.

262 **Planco was asked to drop by the set** author's interview with Johnnie Planco.

263 **And Peter was one of those** author's interview with Johnnie Planco.

263 **We were always being followed** author's interview with Anthony Harvey.

263 **He gave her enormous encouragement** author's interview with Anthony Harvey.

264 **It cured me of most of the insecurities** *Esquire*, 1982.

264 **This is Zulu-style living** *Playboy*, 1982.

264 **Jesus, Peter, they're mighty plants** author's interview with Paul D'Alton.

265 **He went absolutely mad** author's interview with Paul D'Alton.

266 **He was also a great lover of young people** author's interview with Paul D'Alton.

266 **He was a contradiction** author's interview with Amanda Plummer.

267 **I have to go!** author's interview with Paul D'Alton.

TWENTY-ONE

268 **We could have rows, not speak for years** author's interview with Patrick Dromgoole.

268 **Peter was not a man who was obedient** author's interview with Patrick Dromgoole.

269 **When you have a character** author's interview with Patrick Dromgoole.

269 **Sometimes I'd just look across the stage** author's interview with Lisa Harrow.

269 **He sometimes used to soar** author's interview with Lisa Harrow.

269 **He was technically brilliant** author's interview with Michael Byrne.

270 **I think a critic once said** author's interview with Patrick Dromgoole.

270 **When in a clinch with Lisa Harrow** author's interview with Michael Byrne.

270 **He was an actor** author's interview with Michael Byrne.

270 **I think he only had half a pancreas** author's interview with Michael Byrne.

270 **Something had gone wrong with Peter** author's interview with Lisa Harrow.

271 **I'll never forget it** author's interview with Lisa Harrow.

271 **As I began my lines** author's interview with Lisa Harrow.

272 **Delighted, he called his friend Hohn Standing** British *GQ*, 2013.

272 **The only thing I want more than life itself** *Irish Examiner*, February 2014.

272 **Karen was a lovely woman** author's interview with Paul D'Alton.

273 **It's strange that for such a gregarious** author's interview with Paul D'Alton.

273 **There was a slight** author's interview with Paul D'Alton.

274 **a little something** Christopher Fox, *The Cambridge Companion to Jonathan Swift* (Cambridge University Press, 2003).

275 **Ray would love to direct you in it** author's interview with Ray Cooney.

275 **The thing that really impressed me** author's interview with Ray Cooney.

275 **Over the following weekend** author's interview with Ray Cooney.

275 **He was very much like Donald Sinden** author's interview with Ray Cooney.

276 **Peter was terrific as Higgins** author's interview with Ray Cooney.

276 **Peter was amazing with her** author's interview with Ray Cooney.

276 **It was a breathtaking** author's interview with Steve Railsback.

277 **Richard lost touch** email to the author from Burton's widow Sally.

277 **Because if we did** Elizabeth Harris.

277 **And Richard told me afterwards** Elizabeth Harris.

278 **Peter loved Richard** author's interview with Johnnie Planco.

279 **Onstage, Peter lay back** *Daily Mail*, 1986.

279 **Peter was really the obvious choice** author's interview with Jeremy Thomas.

280 **Peter had been unwell** author's interview with Jeremy Thomas.

280 **Now, outside that hotel** author's interview with Jeremy Thomas.

280 **He knew everything that you did** author's interview with Jeremy Thomas.

280 **And they helped us** author's interview with Jeremy Thomas.

281 **We would talk culture** author's interview with Jeremy Thomas.

281 **He'd talk to people he was interested in** author's interview with Basil Pao.

282 **Peter stood in front of that grave** author's interview with Basil Pao.

TWENTY-TWO

284 **Mr O'Toole has lost his voice** author's interview with Ivar Brogger.

285 **I'll never forget this particular night** author's interview with Ivar Brogger.

285 **Ivar, do you know** author's interview with Ivar Brogger.

286 **Peter, I have to tell you** author's interview with Ivar Brogger.

286 **They never worked together** author's interview with Johnnie Planco.

286 **I calculated** author's interview with Amanda Plummer.

286 **I was in extreme awe of him** author's interview with Amanda Plummer.

287 **Playing with Peter** author's interview with Amanda Plummer.

287 **Oh Christ, she's acting again** author's interview with Ivar Brogger.

287 **Lorcan was the apple of his eye** author's interview with Ivar Brogger.

288 **There was the occasion** author's interview with Ivar Brogger.

288 **He loved her** author's interview with Ivar Brogger.

288 **I think a lot of people** author's interview with Ivar Brogger.

288 **Not knowing what a Tony was** *People Magazine*, 1987.

288 **When we were making** author's interview with Steve Railsback.

289 **Peter was funny** author's interview with Paul D'Alton.

289 **and was nearly decapitated** author's interview with Paul D'Alton.

290 **He told us lots and lots** author's interview with Mary Coughlan.

290 **He'd say, always do something different** author's interview with Steve Guttenberg.

290 **How do you avoid kicking the dog** author's interview with Steve Guttenberg.

290 **absolutely great craic to make** author's interview with Mary Coughlan.

291 **He was so theatrical in himself** author's interview with Steve Guttenberg.

291 **There were always tears** irishmirror.ie/news, 2007.

292 **fairly emotional** *Los Angeles Times*, 1988.

292 **brood mare** *Night & Day*, April 2001.

292 **It's a lifestyle question** *People Magazine*, 1987.

292 **What are you doing?** author's interview with Johnnie Planco.

293 **Peter went through the roof** author's interview with Johnnie Planco.

293 **Lorcan had a particular significance** author's interview with Johnnie Planco.

294 **To their surprise** *Ned Sherrin: The Autobiography*.

294 **Keith, you bastard** *Ned Sherrin: The Autobiography*.

294 **Just as well** *Ned Sherrin: The Autobiography*.

294 **No, you won** *Ned Sherrin: The Autobiography*.

295 **He did nothing** author's interview with Royce Mills.

295 **In this way** *Ned Sherrin: The Autobiography*.

295 **It was like music** author's interview with Royce Mills.

295 **We gave him twenty Benson and Hedges** author's interview with Royce Mills.

295 **Oh fucking hell** author's interview with Royce Mills.

296 **This one's a corpse** author's interview with Royce Mills.

296 **He didn't trust me at all** author's interview with Royce Mills.

296 **You know that three or four pages** author's interview with Royce Mills.

297 **It was the most marvellous** author's interview with Johnnie Planco.

297 **And he looked just like Peter** author's interview with Johnnie Planco.

298 **The film was meant to be** *Night & Day*, April 2001.

TWENTY-THREE

299 **I think Lorcan's birth** British *GQ*, 2013.

299 **There was a proper twenty-two-yard strip** author's interview with Michael Neilson.

300 **They all went to a hallway** author's interview with Johnnie Planco.

300 **It does absolutely nothing** Brian Johnston, *A Further Slice of Johnners* (Virgin, 2011).

300 **It took off very quickly** author's interview with Michael Neilson.

301 **You like a drink, don't you, mate** author's interview with Michael Neilson.

301 **He always looked extremely fragile** author's interview with Michael Neilson.

302 **He always used to say to me** author's interview with Michael Neilson.

302 **What happens in cricket teams is guys grow up** author's interview with Michael Neilson.

302 **I wanted Lorcs to know** British *GQ*, 2013.

303 **But then she'd forget** author's interview with Keith Hunt.

303 **He adored Lorcan** author's interview with Keith Hunt.

303 **He wafted into a room** author's interview with Keith Hunt.

304 **He had a room with a bar** author's interview with Keith Hunt.

304 **He paid for the use** author's interview with Keith Hunt.

304 **One of the guys got out** author's interview with Keith Hunt.

TWENTY-FOUR

306 **But then Australian Equity objected to me** author's interview with Royce Mills.

306 **It feels like old times** author's interview with Tony Palmer.

307 **Sing it, hum it, shout it** author's interview with Tony Palmer.

307 **As I understood it** author's interview with Tony Palmer.

307 **Well, no** author's interview with Tony Palmer.

308 **That's got no relevance to Jimmy Porter** author's interview with Tony Palmer.

308 **If he arrived on a movie set** author's interview with Johnnie Planco.

309 **He was frail, though** author's interview with Jack Gold.

309 **It was put together** author's interview with Lee Nelson.

309 **They literally stopped** author's interview with Lee Nelson.

310 **The trailer that he had** author's interview with Lee Nelson.

310 **So I open the door** author's interview with Lee Nelson.

310 **When I saw** author's interview with Lee Nelson.

310 **The common denominator** *Independent*, 13 February 1998.

311 **I lived a few houses away** author's interview with Bruce Montague.

311 **They were really close** author's interview with Johnnie Planco.

311 **Peter got very depressed** author's interview with Johnnie Planco.

312 **Ah, Jesus, I miss waking up** *Entertainment Weekly*, 2001.

312 **Chaps like us** Robert Sellers, *Hellraisers* (Preface, 2008).

312 **Now – disease** *Independent*, 13 February 1998.

312 **Over similar calls** author's interview with Joe Chappelle.

313 **Not surprisingly** author's interview with Joe Chappelle.

313 **And Peter nailed it** author's interview with Joe Chappelle.

313 **I thought he was quite spry** author's interview with Joe Chappelle.

314 **I just wish** author's interview with Joe Chappelle.

314 **Funny, brilliant** *Maxim*, 2001.

314 **It fitted him** author's interview with Royce Mills.

315 **He has managed to improve** 'This Is London', Associated Newspapers, 5 August 1999.

315 **Spacey! What have you got me into now** *Parkinson*, 2002.

315 **It's a wonderful play** Spacey on *David Letterman*, 2007.

315 **Absolutely appalling** Spacey on *David Letterman*, 2007.

316 **It was an ideal play** British *GQ*, 2013.

TWENTY-FIVE

317 **There is a saying** author's interview with Bernardo Stella.

317 **He smoked** author's interview with Martin Bell.

317 **When he talked about politics** author's interview with Johnnie Planco.

318 **If we were at the Players Club** author's interview with Johnnie Planco.

318 **Peter said** author's interview with Barry Cryer.

319 **until I got a call** author's interview with Johnnie Planco.

319 **When they took him away** author's interview with Peter Medak.

319 **Peter used to come in** author's interview with Elizabeth Harris.

319 **Peter was in tears** author's interview with Elizabeth Harris.

319 **He was very frail** author's interview with Andrew Sinclair.

319 **Both of them, Peter told me** *Down Under Milk Wood* (Timon Films, 2014) © Andrew Sinclair.

320 **Peter's coming on** author's interview with Andrew Sinclair.

320 **O'Toole, look at you** *Down Under Milk Wood* (Timon Films, 2014) © Andrew Sinclair.

320 **We'd planned to meet** author's interview with Jeremy Thomas.

321 **I could barely ask him** author's interview with Roger Young.

321 **We thought it was serious** author's interview with Roger Young.

321 **I don't want you** author's interview with Roger Young.

321 **It's an experience** author's interview with Roger Young.

322 **That evening we were supposed to have dinner** author's interview with Johnnie Planco.

322 **I want it up** author's interview with Johnnie Planco.

323 **and absolutely not** author's interview with Roger Michell.

324 **This is slightly bollocks** author's interview with Roger Michell.

325 **Well, I am very sorry** author's interview with Roger Michell.

325 **It's expanded a touch** author's interview with Roger Michell.

325 **He is clearly under the illusion** author's interview with Roger Michell.

326 **Maurice's spare, simple dialogue** author's interview with Roger Michell.

327 **Oh, well** author's interview with Roger Michell.

328 **Battsek told us that O'Toole** author's interview with Roger Michell.

328 **We feel him peering** author's interview with Roger Michell.

328 **When who did I see** author's interview with Roger Michell.

328 **Peter smiles and the room lights up** author's interview with Roger Michell.

328 **O'Toole getting more** author's interview with Roger Michell.

329 **when he is fractious** author's interview with Roger Michell.

329 **Darling, I can't understand** author's interview with Roger Michell.

329 **How unnerving for an actress** author's interview with Roger Michell.

330 **As the weeks went on** author's interview with Roger Michell.

330 **Richard Griffiths was a narcoleptic** author's interview with Roger Michell.

330 **knackered and panting** author's interview with Roger Michell.

331 **He collapsed** author's interview with Roger Michell.

331 **He is too fucking knackered** author's interview with Roger Michell.

332 **a competitive geriatric ballet** author's interview with Roger Michell.

332 **He's a cunt** author's interview with Roger Michell.

332 **He really is** author's interview with Roger Michell.

332 **God knows what reserves of strength** author's interview with Roger Michell.

333 **He was very ambivalent** author's interview with Roger Michell.

334 **a Roger Michell picture** author's interview with Roger Michell.

334 **The old cunt** author's interview with Roger Michell.

334 **O'Toole true to form** author's interview with Roger Michell.

334 **We were very lucky** author's interview with Roger Michell.

334 **And that's the reason** author's interview with Roger Michell.

TWENTY-SIX

335 **There's only one voice in my head** author's interview with Brad Lewis.

335 **He seemed to really enjoy the process** author's interview with Brad Lewis.

336 **Peter gave me the biggest** author's interview with Brad Lewis.

336 **Dad introduced us** *People*, 1981.

337 **And he was lionized there** author's interview with Martin Bell.

337 **At one** *Oldie* **lunch** author's interview with Barry Cryer.

337 **He loved wrong-footing people** author's interview with Barry Cryer.

337 **His legs had gone** author's interview with Barry Cryer.

337 **I can no longer walk** British *GQ*, 2013.

337 **I knew I was finished** *Guardian*, 2007.

338 **If he was ill** author's interview with Michael Redwood.

338 **His memory was like a computer** author's interview with Michael Redwood.

338 **I went to speak to him** author's interview with Gary Raymond.

338 **There were, of course, lapses** author's interview with Michael Redwood.

338 **How fucking dare you** author's interview with Michael Redwood.

339 **They were quite close** author's interview with Nicole Reinheart.

339 **And he worked till he dropped** author's interview with Michael Redwood.

TWENTY-SEVEN

340 **I'm not bloody Edith Piaf** British *GQ*, 2013.

341 **They live at the side of my bed** British *GQ*, 2013.

341 **Just at the point** author's interview with Johnnie Planco.

341 **Peter doesn't feel the need** author's interview with Johnnie Planco.

342 **We'd sort of gone** author's interview with Billy Foyle.

342 **By this stage with me** author's interview with Billy Foyle.

343 **It was celebratory** author's interview with Martin Bell.

343 **It was a big shock** *Telegraph*, 2014.

343 **The world has lost a great actor** *Independent*, 2013.

PETER O'TOOLE'S WORK IN FILM, TELEVISION AND THEATRE

FILMS

Kidnapped (1960)
Director: Robert Stevenson
Cast: Peter Finch, James MacArthur, Bernard Lee, John Laurie, Niall MacGinnis, Finlay Currie, Peter O'Toole (Robin Macgregor)

The Savage Innocents (1960)
Director: Nicholas Ray
Cast: Anthony Quinn, Yoko Tani, Carlo Giustini, Marie Yang, Andy Ho, Peter O'Toole (uncredited)

The Day They Robbed The Bank Of England (1960)
Director: John Guillermin
Cast: Aldo Ray, Elizabeth Sellars, Peter O'Toole (Capt. Monty Fitch), Kieron Moore, Albert Sharpe, Joseph Tomelty, John Le Mesurier, Andrew Keir, Hugh Griffith, Arthur Lowe

Lawrence of Arabia (1962)
Director: David Lean
Cast: Peter O'Toole (T. E. Lawrence), Alec Guinness, Anthony Quinn, Jack Hawkins, Omar Sharif, José Ferrer, Anthony Quayle, Claude Rains, Arthur Kennedy, Donald Wolfit

Becket (1964)
Director: Peter Glenville
Cast: Richard Burton, Peter O'Toole (King Henry II), John Gielgud,

Gino Cervi, Paolo Stoppa, Donald Wolfit, David Weston, Martita Hunt, Pamela Brown, Siân Phillips, Felix Aylmer

Lord Jim (1965)
Director: Richard Brooks
Cast: Peter O'Toole (Lord Jim), James Mason, Curt Jurgens, Eli Wallach, Jack Hawkins, Paul Lukas, Daliah Lavi, Akim Tamiroff

What's New Pussycat? (1965)
Director: Clive Donner
Cast: Peter Sellers, Peter O'Toole (Michael James), Romy Schneider, Capucine, Paula Prentiss, Woody Allen, Ursula Andress

How To Steal A Million (1966)
Director: William Wyler
Cast: Audrey Hepburn, Peter O'Toole (Simon Dermott), Eli Wallach, Hugh Griffith, Charles Boyer

The Bible: In The Beginning (1966)
Director: John Huston
Cast: Michael Parks, Richard Harris, John Huston, Stephen Boyd, George C. Scott, Ava Gardner, Peter O'Toole (The Three Angels), Franco Nero

The Night of the Generals (1967)
Director: Anatole Litvak
Cast: Peter O'Toole (General Tanz), Omar Sharif, Tom Courtenay, Donald Pleasence, Joanna Pettet, Philippe Noiret, Charles Gray, Coral Browne, John Gregson, Nigel Stock, Christopher Plummer

Casino Royale (1967)
Director: Val Guest, Ken Hughes, John Huston, Joseph McGrath, Robert Parrish and Richard Talmadge
Cast: Peter Sellers, Ursula Andress, David Niven, Orson Welles, Joanna Pettet, Daliah Lavi, Woody Allen, Deborah Kerr, William Holden, John Huston, Peter O'Toole (cameo – Scottish piper)

The Lion In Winter (1968)
Director: Anthony Harvey

Cast: Peter O'Toole (Henry II), Katharine Hepburn, Anthony Hopkins, John Castle, Nigel Terry, Timothy Dalton, Jane Merrow

Great Catherine (1968)
Director: Gordon Flemyng
Cast: Peter O'Toole (Captain Charles Edstaston), Zero Mostel, Jeanne Moreau, Jack Hawkins, Akim Tamiroff

Goodbye Mr Chips (1969)
Director: Herbert Ross
Cast: Peter O'Toole (Arthur Chipping), Petula Clark, Michael Redgrave, George Baker, Siân Phillips, Michael Bryant

Country Dance (1970)
Director: J. Lee Thompson
Cast: Peter O'Toole (Sir Charles Ferguson), Susannah York, Michael Craig, Harry Andrews, Cyril Cusack, Brian Blessed

Murphy's War (1971)
Director: Peter Yates
Cast: Peter O'Toole (Murphy), Siân Phillips, Philippe Noiret, Horst Janson

Under Milk Wood (1972)
Director: Andrew Sinclair
Cast: Richard Burton, Elizabeth Taylor, Peter O'Toole (Captain Cat), Glynis Johns, Vivien Merchant, Siân Phillips, Victor Spinetti, Ryan Davies, Angharad Rees, David Jason, Susan Penhaligon

The Ruling Class (1972)
Director: Peter Medak
Cast: Peter O'Toole (14th Earl of Gurney), Alastair Sim, Arthur Lowe, Harry Andrews, Coral Browne, William Mervyn, James Villiers, Michael Bryant, Carolyn Seymour, Nigel Green

Man of La Mancha (1972)
Director: Arthur Hiller
Cast: Peter O'Toole (Don Quixote), Sophia Loren, James Coco, Harry Andrews, John Castle, Brian Blessed, Ian Richardson

Rosebud (1975)

Director: Otto Preminger
Cast: Peter O'Toole (Larry Martin), Richard Attenborough, Cliff Gorman, Claude Dauphin, Peter Lawford, Raf Vallone, Isabelle Huppert

Man Friday (1975)

Director: Jack Gold
Cast: Peter O'Toole (Robinson Crusoe), Richard Roundtree, Peter Cellier

The Far Side of Paradise (aka Foxtrot) (1976)

Director: Arturo Ripstein
Cast: Peter O'Toole (Liviu), Charlotte Rampling, Max Von Sydow

Power Play (1978)

Director: Martyn Burke
Cast: Peter O'Toole (Colonel Zeller), David Hemmings, Donald Pleasence, Barry Morse

Zulu Dawn (1979)

Director: Douglas Hickox
Cast: Burt Lancaster, Peter O'Toole (Lord Chelmsford), Simon Ward, Denholm Elliott, John Mills, Michael Jayston, Bob Hoskins, Nigel Davenport, Christopher Cazenove

Caligula (1979)

Director: Tinto Brass
Cast: Malcolm McDowell, Helen Mirren, Peter O'Toole (Tiberius), John Gielgud

The Stunt Man (1980)

Director: Richard Rush
Cast: Peter O'Toole (Eli Cross), Steve Railsback, Barbara Hershey, Allen Garfield, Alex Rocco

My Favourite Year (1982)

Director: Richard Benjamin

Cast: Peter O'Toole (Alan Swann), Mark Linn-Baker, Jessica Harper, Joseph Bologna, Bill Macy

Supergirl (1984)
Director: Jeannot Szwarc
Cast: Faye Dunaway, Helen Slater, Peter O'Toole (Zaltar), Hart Bochner, Mia Farrow, Brenda Vaccaro, Peter Cook, Simon Ward, Marc McClure

Creator (1985)
Director: Ivan Passer
Cast: Peter O'Toole (Dr Harry Wolper), Mariel Hemingway, Vincent Spano, Virginia Madsen, David Ogden Stiers

Club Paradise (1986)
Director: Harold Ramis
Cast: Robin Williams, Peter O'Toole (Governor Anthony Cloyden Hayes), Rick Moranis, Jimmy Cliff, Twiggy, Eugene Levy, Joanna Cassidy

The Last Emperor (1987)
Director: Bernardo Bertolucci
Cast: John Lone, Joan Chen, Peter O'Toole (Reginald Johnston), Victor Wong, Ruyuichi Sakamoto, Vivian Wu

High Spirits (1988)
Director: Neil Jordan
Cast: Peter O'Toole (Peter Plunkett), Steve Guttenberg, Daryl Hannah, Beverly D'Angelo, Jennifer Tilly, Liam Neeson, Peter Gallagher, Ray McNally

On A Moonlit Night (1989)
Director: Lina Wertmüller
Cast: Rutger Hauer, Nastassja Kinski, Peter O'Toole (Prof. Yan McShoul), Faye Dunaway, Lorraine Bracco

Wings of Fame (1990)
Director: Otakar Votocek

Cast: Peter O'Toole (Cesar Valentin), Colin Firth, Marie Trintignant, Robert Stephens

The Rainbow Thief (1990)
Director: Alejandro Jodorowsky
Cast: Omar Sharif, Peter O'Toole (Prince Meleagre), Christopher Lee

King Ralph (1991)
Director: David S. Ward
Cast: John Goodman, Peter O'Toole (Sir Cedric Charles Willingham), John Hurt, Camille Coduri, Richard Griffiths, Leslie Phillips, James Villiers

Isabelle Eberhardt (1991)
Director: Ian Pringle
Cast: Mathilda May, Tchéky Karyo, Peter O'Toole (Maj. Lyautey)

Rebecca's Daughters (1992)
Director: Karl Francis
Cast: Peter O'Toole (Lord Sarn), Paul Rhys, Joely Richardson, Keith Allen

The Seventh Coin (1993)
Director: Dror Soref
Cast: Alexandra Powers, Navin Chowdhry, Peter O'Toole (Emil Saber), John Rhys-Davies

FairyTale: A True Story (1997)
Director: Charles Sturridge
Cast: Harvey Keitel, Paul McGann, Peter O'Toole (Sir Arthur Conan Doyle), Elizabeth Earl, Florence Hoath

Phantoms (1998)
Director: Joe Chappelle
Cast: Peter O'Toole (Dr Timothy Flyte), Rose McGowan, Joanna Going, Liev Schreiber, Ben Affleck

The Manor (1999)
Director: Ken Berris
Cast: Greta Scacchi, Gabrielle Anwar, Peter O'Toole (Mr Ravenscroft)

Molokai (1999)
Director: Paul Cox
Cast: Peter O'Toole (William Williamson), Kris Kristofferson, Sam Neill, David Wenham, Derek Jacobi, Tom Wilkinson

Rock My World (2002)
Director: Sidney J. Furie
Cast: Peter O'Toole (Lord Foxley), Joan Plowright, Alicia Silverstone, Martin Clunes

The Final Curtain (2002)
Director: Patrick Harkins
Cast: Aidan Gillen, Peter O'Toole (JJ Curtis), Adrian Lester, Julia Sawalha

Bright Young Things (2003)
Director: Stephen Fry
Cast: James McAvoy, Michael Sheen, Emily Mortimer, Stephen Campbell Moore, Stockard Channing, Jim Carter, Dan Aykroyd, Peter O'Toole (Colonel Blount), Jim Broadbent

Troy (2004)
Director: Wolfgang Petersen
Cast: Brad Pitt, Eric Bana, Orlando Bloom, Sean Bean, Peter O'Toole (Priam), Diane Kruger, Brian Cox, Brendan Gleeson, Julie Christie, Julian Glover, Trevor Eve

Lassie (2005)
Director: Charles Sturridge
Cast: Peter O'Toole (The Duke), Samantha Morton, John Lynch, Peter Dinklage, Edward Fox

Venus (2006)
Director: Roger Michell
Cast: Peter O'Toole (Maurice), Leslie Phillips, Jodie Whittaker, Richard Griffiths, Vanessa Redgrave

One Night with the King (2006)
Director: Michael O. Sajbel

Cast: Tiffany Dupont, Luke Goss, John Noble, John Rhys-Davies, Peter O'Toole (Samuel, the Prophet), Omar Sharif

Ratatouille (2007)
Director: Brad Bird and Jan Pinkava
Voice Cast: Patton Oswalt, Ian Holm, Lou Romano, Brian Dennehy, Peter O'Toole (Anton Ego)

Stardust (2007)
Director: Matthew Vaughn
Cast: Clare Danes, Michelle Pfeiffer, Robert De Niro, Sienna Miller, Ricky Gervais, Peter O'Toole (King)

My Talks with Dean Spanley (2008)
Director: Toa Fraser
Cast: Jeremy Northam, Sam Neill, Bryan Brown, Peter O'Toole (Fisk Senior), Art Malik

Thomas Kinkade's Christmas Cottage (2008)
Director: Michael Campus
Cast: Jared Padalecki, Marcia Gay Harden, Peter O'Toole (Glen), Aaron Ashmore, Geoffrey Lewis

Eager to Die (2010)
Director: Michael Mandell
Cast: Peter O'Toole (Lord Pelican), Michelle Rodriquez, Tony Devon, David Morse

For Greater Glory: The True Story of Cristiada (2012)
Director: Dean Wright
Cast: Andy Garcia, Oscar Isaac, Eva Longoria, Peter O'Toole (Father Christopher)

Decline of an Empire (2014)
Director: Michael Redwood
Cast: Nicole Keniheart, Peter O'Toole (Gallus), Joss Ackland, Steven Berkoff, Edward Fox, Dudley Sutton

The Whole World at Our Feet (2015)
Director: Salamat Mukhammed-Ali and Dauren Mussa

Cast: Armand Assante, Peter O'Toole (Tugboat), Michael Madsen, Tommy Lister, Cary-Hiroyuki Tagawa

TELEVISION

Siwan: The King's Daughter (TV drama, 1960)
Cast: Peter O'Toole (Gwilym De Breos), Siân Phillips, Clifford Evans

Rendezvous (TV series, 1959–1961)
O'Toole appeared in three episodes, as John.

Present Laughter (TV drama, 1967)
Director: Gordon Flemyng
Cast: Peter O'Toole (Gary Essendine), Honor Blackman, Isla Blair, Edward Hardwicke

Rogue Male (TV movie, 1976)
Director: Clive Donner
Cast: Peter O'Toole (Sir Robert Hunter), John Standing, Alastair Sim, Harold Pinter, Michael Byrne

Strumpet City (TV series, 1980)
Director: Tony Barry
Cast: David Kelly, Frank Grimes, Donal McCann, Bryan Murray, Peter O'Toole (Jim Larkin)

Masada (TV mini-series, 1981)
Director: Boris Sagal
Cast: Peter O'Toole (General Cornelius Flavius Silva), Peter Strauss, Barbara Carrera, Anthony Quayle, David Warner, Joseph Wiseman

Pygmalion (TV drama, 1983)
Director: Alan Cooke
Cast: Peter O'Toole (Professor Henry Higgins), Margot Kidder, John Standing

Svengali (TV movie, 1983)
Director: Anthony Harvey

Cast: Peter O'Toole (Anton Bosnyak), Jodie Foster, Elizabeth Ashley, Larry Joshua, Holly Hunter

Kim (TV movie, 1984)
Director: John Davies
Cast: Peter O'Toole (Lama), Bryan Brown, John Rhys-Davies, Ravi Sheth, Julian Glover

Uncle Silas (TV mini-series, 1987, aka The Dark Angel)
Director: Peter Hammond
Cast: Peter O'Toole (Uncle Silas Ruthyn), Jane Lapotaire, Beatie Edney, Guy Rolfe, Barbara Shelley

The Pied Piper (TV movie, 1990)
Director: Norman Stone
Cast: Peter O'Toole (John Sidney Howard), Mare Winningham, Michael Kitchen

Civvies (TV series, 1992)
Director: Karl Francis
Cast: Jason Issacs, Elizabeth Rider, Lennie James, Peter Howitt, Peter O'Toole (Barry Newman)

Heaven & Hell: North & South, Book III (TV mini-series, 1994)
Director: Larry Peerce
Cast: Philip Casnoff, Kyle Chandler, Cathy Lee Crosby, Lesley-Anne Down, Jonathan Frakes, Rip Torn, Robert Wagner, Billy Dee Williams, Peter O'Toole (Sam Trump)

Heavy Weather (TV movie, 1995)
Director: Jack Gold
Cast: Peter O'Toole (Clarence, Earl of Emsworth), Judy Parfitt, Richard Briers, Roy Hudd, David Bamber, Richard Johnson, Samuel West, Bryan Pringle

Gulliver's Travels (TV movie, 1996)
Director: Charles Sturridge
Cast: Ted Danson, Mary Steenburgen, James Fox, Ned Beatty,

Edward Fox, Robert Hardy, Nicholas Lyndhurst, Peter O'Toole (Emperor of Lilliput), Omar Sharif

Coming Home (TV movie, 1998)
Director: Giles Foster
Cast: Peter O'Toole (Colonel Carey-Lewis), Joanna Lumley, Emily Mortimer, David McCallum, Paul Bettany

Joan of Arc (TV movie, 1999)
Director: Christian Duguay
Cast: Leelee Sobieski, Chad Willett, Jacqueline Bisset, Powers Boothe, Olympia Dukakis, Neil Patrick Harris, Maximilian Schell, Shirley MacLaine, Peter O'Toole (Bishop Pierre Cauchon)

Hitler: The Rise of Evil (TV mini-series, 2003)
Director: Christian Duguay
Cast: Robert Carlyle, Stockard Channing, Matthew Modine, Liev Schreiber, Peter O'Toole (President Paul von Hindenburg)

Imperium: Augustus (TV movie, 2003)
Director: Roger Young
Cast: Peter O'Toole (Augustus Caesar), Charlotte Rampling

Casanova (TV series, 2005)
Director: Sheree Folkson
Cast: David Tennant, Rose Byrne, Peter O'Toole (Older Casanova), Rupert Penry-Jones

The Tudors (TV series, 2007–2010)
Creator: Michael Hirst
Cast: Jonathan Rhys Meyers, Henry Cavill, Anthony Brophy, James Frain, Simon Ward, Jeremy Northam, Sam Neill, Peter O'Toole (Pope Paul III)

Iron Road (TV mini-series, 2008)
Director: David Wu
Cast: Li Sun, Luke Macfarlane, Sam Neill, Tony Ka Fai Leung, Peter O'Toole (Lionel Relic)

THEATRE

1955–1958
The Bristol Old Vic Company
Numerous roles

1957
Oh! My Papa
Garrick Theatre, London

1958
The Holiday by John Hall. Directed by Frank Dunlop
Cambridge Arts Theatre and UK tour

1959
The Long and the Short and the Tall by Willis Hall. Directed by Lindsay Anderson
The Royal Court and The New Theatre, London

1960
The Merchant of Venice by William Shakespeare. Directed by Michael Langham
The Taming of the Shrew by William Shakespeare. Directed by John Barton
Troilus and Cressida by William Shakespeare. Directed by John Barton and Peter Hall
Shakespeare Memorial Theatre, Stratford-upon-Avon (Season)

1963
Baal by Bertolt Brecht. Directed by William Gaskill
Phoenix Theatre
Hamlet by William Shakespeare. Directed by Laurence Olivier
National Theatre, London

1965
Ride a Cock Horse by David Mercer. Directed by Gordon Flemyng
Piccadilly Theatre, London

1969

Man and Superman by George Bernard Shaw. Directed by Nat Brenner
Gaiety Theatre, Dublin
Waiting for Godot by Samuel Beckett. Directed by Sean Cotter
Abbey Theatre, Dublin

1971

Waiting for Godot by Samuel Beckett. Directed by Frederick Monnoyer
Nottingham Playhouse

1973

Uncle Vanya by Anton Chekhov. Directed by Val May
Plunder by Ben Travers. Directed by Nat Brenner
The Apple Cart by George Bernard Shaw. Directed by David Phethean
Bristol Old Vic (Season)

1976

Dead Eyed Dicks by Peter King. Directed by Lionel Harris
Theatre Royal, Brighton

1978

Uncle Vanya by Anton Chekov. Directed by Nat Brenner
Present Laughter by Noël Coward. Directed by Nat Brenner
Canada and US Tour

1980

Macbeth by William Shakespeare. Directed by Bryan Forbes
Old Vic, London

1982

Man and Superman by George Bernard Shaw. Directed by Patrick Dromgoole
Theatre Royal, Haymarket, London

1984

Pygmalion by George Bernard Shaw. Directed by Ray Cooney
Shaftesbury Theatre, London

1986
The Apple Cart by George Bernard Shaw. Directed by Val May
Theatre Royal, Haymarket, London

1987
Pygmalion by George Bernard Shaw. Directed by Val May
The Plymouth Theatre, Broadway

1989
Jeffrey Bernard is Unwell by Keith Waterhouse. Directed by Ned
Sherrin
Apollo Theatre, London

1991
Jeffrey Bernard is Unwell by Keith Waterhouse. Directed by Ned
Sherrin
Shaftesbury Theatre, London

1992
Our Song by Keith Waterhouse. Directed by Ned Sherrin
Apollo Theatre, London

1999
Jeffrey Bernard is Unwell by Keith Waterhouse. Directed by Ned
Sherrin
Old Vic, London

INDEX

401

PICTURE ACKNOWLEDGEMENTS

SECTION ONE
Page
1 top: © Crown Copyright
  bottom: © Evening News / REX
2 top: Douglas Hess / Associated Newspapers / REX
  bottom: John Twine / Associated Newspapers / REX
3 main: Everett Collection / REX
  inset: Ullstein Bild / Getty Images
4 top: Everett Collection / REX
  bottom: Leopald Joseph / Associated Newspapers / REX
5 top: Corbis
  bottom: Ullstein Bild / Getty Images
6 top: AFP / Getty Images
  bottom: Corbis
7 top: Silver Screen Collection / Getty Images
  bottom: Manchester Daily Express / SSPL / Getty Images
8 top: Everett Collection / REX
  bottom: Corbis

SECTION TWO
Page
9 top: Everett Collection / REX
  bottom: Associated Newspapers / REX
10 top: Alan Davidson / Camera Press
   bottom: Everett Collection / REX
11 top: Michael Ochs Archives / Getty Images
   bottom: The LIFE Picture Collection / Getty Images
12 top: James Meehan / Camera Press
   bottom: Donald Cooper / REX
13 top: Corbis
   bottom Mark Richards / Associated Newspapers / REX
14 top: Richard Corkery / NY Daily News Archive / Getty Images
   bottom: Alan Singer / CBS / Getty Images
15 top: Timothy A. Clary / AFP / Getty Images
   bottom: Kmazur / WireImag
16 top: Miramax / Everett / REX
   bottom: Corbis